LONG BARROWS
OF THE COTSWOLDS

LONG BARROWS
OF THE COTSWOLDS
AND SURROUNDING AREAS

TIMOTHY DARVILL

TEMPUS

To the pixie of Buckholt Wood

Front cover illustration Belas Knap (GLO 1), looking north

First published 2004

Tempus Publishing Ltd
The Mill, Brimscombe Port
Stroud, Gloucestershire GL5 2QG
www.tempus-publishing.com

© Timothy Darvill, 2004

The right of Timothy Darvill to be identified as the Author of this work has been asserted by him in accordance with the Copyrights, Designs and Patents Act 1988.

All rights reserved. No part of this book may be reprinted or reproduced or utilised in any form or by any electronic, mechanical or other means, now known or hereafter invented, including photocopying and recording, or in any information storage or retrieval system, without the permission in writing from the Publishers.

British Library Cataloguing in Publication Data.
A catalogue record for this book is available from the British Library.

ISBN 0 7524 2907 8

Typesetting and origination by Tempus Publishing.
Printed and bound in Great Britain.

CONTENTS

Preface and acknowledgements	6
1 Introduction	9
2 Long barrows and megalithic enquiries	17
3 Before the long barrows	46
4 Long barrows: a new tradition	67
5 The anatomy of Cotswold long barrows	89
6 People, ceremonies and objects	132
7 Blocking barrows and breaking traditions	173
8 Cotswold-Severn long barrows in context	187
9 After the long barrow tradition	214
Appendix A Long barrows in the Cotswold-Severn region	242
Appendix B Radiocarbon dates from long barrows	255
Sites to visit	260
Notes	281
Bibliography	293
Index	313

PREFACE AND ACKNOWLEDGEMENTS

The research embodied in this volume has taken place over many years and has benefited from the help and interest of numerous individuals and organizations. In particular I would like to thank: Arthur ApSimon, Paul Ashbee, Mick Aston, Gordon Barclay, Chris Barker, Don Benson, Richard Bradley, Bill Britnell, Jenny Britnell, Neil Brodie, Humphrey Case, Ros Cleal, Wilf Cox, Glyn Daniel, David Field, David Fraser, Julie Gardiner, Alex Gibson, Leslie Grinsell, Gill Hey, Ian Kinnes, Frances Lynch, Caroline Malone, Dai Morgan Evans, John Paddock, Mike Parker Pearson, Julien Parsons, Stuart Piggott, Colin Renfrew, Colin Richards, Paul Robinson, Colin Renfrew, Miles Russell, Alan Saville, Chris Scarre, Isobel Smith, Simon Stoddart, Julian Thomas, Nick Thorpe, Peter Ucko, David Viner, Geoff Wainwright and Alasdair Whittle for fruitful discussions about long barrows, and their comments and constructive criticism. Special thanks go to Yvette Staelens, without whose love this book would never have been finished. Anne Chippindale and Libby Peachy assisted with the source of illustration 1; Paul Robinson of Devizes Museum advised on Stuart Piggott's archive of work at the West Kennet long barrow (illustrations 58 and 72); R. Desmond of the Cambridge University Collection of Air Photographs advised on the use of pictures of Belas Knap; and Adrian James assisted with access to illustrations in publications held in the Library of the Society of Antiquaries of London. Rick Schulting of Belfast University kindly made available the radiocarbon dates resulting from collaborative work with others on the human remains from Belas Knap. Don Benson, Alasdair Whittle (Cardiff University), Dawn Galer (Natural History Museum), Lauren Gilmore (Oxfordshire County Museums Service), and Ian Dennis and Lesley McFadyen (Cardiff University) kindly facilitated the use of pictures of the excavations at Ascott-under-Wychwood in advance of the final publication. Richard Brooks of the Meteorological Office, Chris McDowell at Newsquest, and Mark Lawrence at the Centre for Oxfordshire Studies kindly tracked down various snippets of historical information relating to the Cotswolds.

For help in preparing the illustrations I would like to thank Jane Timby for the reconstruction drawing in illustration *24* and the artefacts in illustrations *68* and *69*; Neville Stokes for the reconstruction drawing in illustration *80*; and especially Vanessa Constant who single-handedly created all the remaining line drawings, diagrams and maps. Most of the photographs are drawn from my personal collection, and I would like to thank those excavators who kindly allowed me to take pictures of their excavations. The following kindly allowed the reproduction here of images, drawings and photographs: Antiquity Publications *(1* and *10)*; Mick Aston *(9)*; Cheltenham Museum and Art Gallery *(20)*; Clwyd-Powys Archaeological Trust *(49D* and *74)*; Corinium Museum and Cotswold District Council *(4)*; Defence Procurement Agency *(3)*; Oxford Archaeology *(29)*; Oxfordshire County Museums Service and Cardiff University *(41* and *70)*; Prehistoric Society *(5A, 44, 63* and *71)*; Alan Saville *(13, 56* and *59)*; and the Society of Antiquaries of London *(5B, 5C, 6A* and *6B)*.

Researching and preparing this volume was greatly assisted by research grants made available through the School of Conservation Sciences at Bournemouth University and by assistance through the University's Human Resources Strategy initiative funding. Publication of this volume could not have happened without the patience and calm endurance of Peter Kemmis Betty, Tim Clarke, Alex Cameron and Emma Parkin at Tempus Publishing; Frances Brown for copy-editing and proof correction; Vanessa Constant and Tim Darvill for the index; Louise Pearson for secretarial help; and Vanessa Constant for co-ordinating everything.

As discussed more fully in Chapter 1, much of the nomenclature used to refer to specific long barrows follows that established by Glyn Daniel in his study of *The prehistoric chamber tombs of England and Wales* (Daniel 1950a), elaborated and expanded by John Corcoran in the symposium volume *Megalithic enquiries in the west of Britain* (Corcoran 1969a). This system uses an alphabetic county code followed by a unique numerical identifier. One complicating factor with this system is that the physical extents of administrative counties, and in some cases their names, have changed several times over the last 50 years or so. The counties used here are thus historical administrative areas as they were in 1970. The map overleaf shows the alphabetic code used for each. Appendix A lists the known long barrows in the Cotswold-Severn region, identifying for special comment those excavated over the last 300 years or so, and providing a concordance between the names of individual sites and the unique alpha-numeric identifiers used in the main text. Long barrows and other sites outside this region are referred to in the text by their common name with the modern county/unitary authority in parenthesis. All the plans of long barrows and other sites reproduced in this book have been redrawn to a set of common conventions; these are shown on the key overleaf.

Timothy Darvill
Bournemouth
May Day, 2003

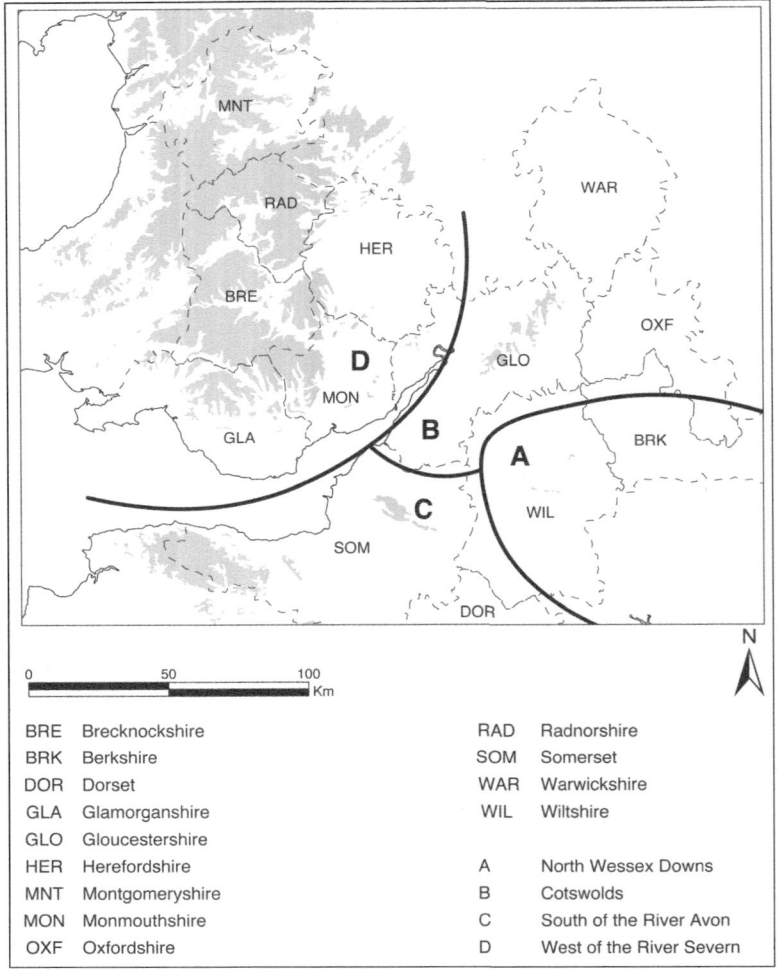

BRE	Brecknockshire	RAD	Radnorshire
BRK	Berkshire	SOM	Somerset
DOR	Dorset	WAR	Warwickshire
GLA	Glamorganshire	WIL	Wiltshire
GLO	Gloucestershire		
HER	Herefordshire	A	North Wessex Downs
MNT	Montgomeryshire	B	Cotswolds
MON	Monmouthshire	C	South of the River Avon
OXF	Oxfordshire	D	West of the River Severn

Map of the area covered by this book

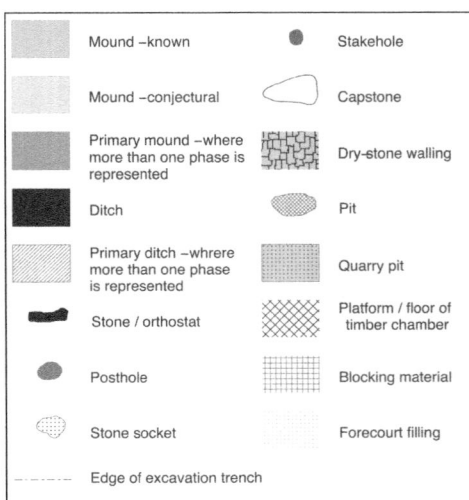

Table of signs and conventions used on the long barrow plans

1

INTRODUCTION

On the Cotswold Hills, 22 December 1920 was cold, damp and wintry, a day when most people were snuggled up at home starting their Yuletide festivities. Not so O.G.S. Crawford, a pioneer of British field archaeology *(1)*.[1] He was out in the wilds, visiting ancient monuments and diligently recording details of their condition and structure. Just two months earlier he had been appointed as the first Archaeological Officer with Britain's official map-makers, the Ordnance Survey, and one of the tasks he set himself was surveying all the long barrows in the Cotswolds and surrounding areas so that up-to-date information could be included on new maps being prepared elsewhere in the organization. Travelling between sites on foot, or using his trusty bicycle, he visited no fewer than six long barrows in the neighbourhood of Northleach in the central Cotswolds on that December day in 1920. Among them was a delightful and untouched mound in Lodge Park, Farmington, which he described as being 'the finest long barrow I have ever seen, it is certainly the most perfect specimen in Gloucestershire'.[2] And indeed it was and has remained so ever since. An elongated grassy mound, 55m on its long axis, 22m wide and 2.6m high at the southeast end, tapering to 10m wide and 1m high at the northwest *(2)*. Projecting from the south-eastern end of the mound were three large blocks of local limestone, tell-tale signs that within the tump lay a stone-built chamber. Two of the visible stones were upright, side by side with a gap of about 1m between, while the third was tilted, propped on the edge of the uprights with every appearance of once having been a roofing slab supported by the other two.

More than 140 similar sites, although not all in such good condition, are known scattered across the rolling Cotswold Hills from Broadway in the north to Bath in the south. Comparable barrows are also known in several adjacent areas: the north Wessex Downs of southern Oxfordshire and northwestern Wiltshire; on and around the Mendips south of the Bristol Avon; in the valley of the River Severn as far upstream as Welshpool; west of the Severn across the Herefordshire uplands, along the Wye valley and in the Black Mountains of Brecknock; and

1 Left O.G.S. Crawford (1886–1957), Ordnance Survey Archaeological Officer 1920–40 and pioneer of long barrow studies in the Cotswolds, walking the Wessex Downs in 1954. *Photograph by Irwin Scollar, reproduced courtesy of Antiquity Publications*

2 Below Lodge Park, Farmington (GLO 5). General view looking north: possibly the best-preserved long barrow in Gloucestershire. *Photograph by Timothy Darvill, August 1977*

along the coastlands flanking the Bristol Channel as far west as the Gower peninsula. All the long barrows in these areas share certain common characteristics of shape, size and internal structure which in 1937 led Glyn Daniel to dub them the 'Cotswold-Severn Group',[3] while later scholars have emphasized the geographical coherence of their distribution by speaking of a 'Cotswold-Severn region' as the more or less discrete territory within which such long barrows occur.[4]

Crawford's pioneering survey of these sites, eventually published in 1925 by John Bellows of Gloucester as *The long barrows of the Cotswolds*, marked a watershed in their study. It set out a rich corpus of systematically collected information from original fieldwork, and a synthesis of results from more than 200 years of antiquarian investigation and speculation. Crawford established the origin of the Cotswold long barrows amongst the early farming communities of the region, and argued that their use involved complicated rituals around the edge of the mound as well as within the chambers deep inside. Perhaps most important of all, he recognized that long barrows were probably the oldest substantial monuments remaining in the English countryside, asking 'are we to allow the graves of our earliest ancestors to be desecrated without taking effective measures to preserve them?' and then declaring that 'surely these far older monuments deserve preferential treatment!'[5]

More than three-quarters of a century on much has changed, in large measure prompted by the popularization of the subject through Crawford's magnificent and still much sought-after publication. Previously unrecognized examples have been recorded to swell the distribution mapped by Crawford. Excavations have been carried out at more than two dozen examples since Crawford's day. New methods of dating and scientific analysis have been brought to bear on the contents of the barrows and the materials used in their construction. Better conservation and novel management measures have been applied in order to help protect and preserve examples, and make them more easily accessible to the general public. And perhaps most significantly, the study of comparable monuments in other regions of northwestern Europe has caught up with Crawford's pioneering efforts, so that it is now possible to see the long barrows of the Cotswolds within the broader context of early farming communities along the Atlantic seaboard from northern France to southern Scandinavia.

The aim of this book is to review what is now known of the long barrows of the Cotswolds and surrounding areas in the light of recent work within the region and beyond. An overtly social perspective is developed, focusing on what these monuments were, how they were used and what they meant to people at the time. It is argued that these remarkable structures appeared fairly abruptly about 3700 BC, replacing and complementing a series of diverse but generally rather small-scale earth and stone monuments and burial places. In contrast to these simple early structures, the long barrows were large monumental constructions that shared common architectural themes and symbolic references over wide areas of Atlantic Europe, and in some cases provided a resting place for the ancestors of those who built and used them *(3)*. After a florescence of perhaps six centuries,

Long Barrows of the Cotswolds

3 Belas Knap (GLO 1). Aerial view of the long barrow looking southeastwards. The horns and forecourt at the north end of the mound are very clear. The enclosing dry-stone wall is modern. *Photograph from the Cambridge University Committee for Aerial Photography (GX-10); Crown copyright: MOD. Reproduced with the permission of the Controller of Her Majesty's Stationery Office*

however, no further examples seem to have been raised, and by about 2600 BC very few were still in use. Indeed, many were deliberately blocked up and made inaccessible to the descendants of the long barrow builders. But this is not the end of the story, for these great stone and earth structures continued to be perceived as sacred places down into medieval times when eventually their existence became enshrined in local folklore as the works of giants and fairies, or hazy reminders of mythical events.[6]

Inevitably, the choice of material to include in this synthesis has been highly selective, and the perspectives and arguments advanced naturally represent a personal discourse. But having grown up in the Cotswolds and retraced many of Crawford's steps through the landscape to visit the sites time and again, I feel able to glimpse a little of why these mounds and their contents have attracted interest, attention and curiosity over the centuries. Quite apart from being situated amid some of the most visually wonderful, comfortably rounded and spectacularly dramatic countryside in the British Isles, the massive mounds and projecting stones have an almost magnetic charm that belies their great age. The honey-coloured limestone and green vegetation of the structures themselves flow seamlessly into their multi-textured surroundings, subtly and gracefully welding together the short-term efforts of ancient communities with the long-term drift of natural processes. Yet a moment of reflection reminds us that they were not like this in the distant past. Over 5,000 years ago, when these sites were new, they were brutal and hard; bright white rocky mounds covering dark dank shadowy chambers *(4)*. What people at that time thought, and how they felt when they were building and using these barrows, we can only guess at. But there are patterns in the surviving remains, and it these that I want to explore here, gently teasing out some of the possible meanings and purposes behind these structures, albeit in a provisional and tentative way.

After more than a century of study, there is naturally a very considerable body of literature dealing with early farming peoples in Britain, conventionally referred to as Neolithic communities,[7] and the monumental architecture they created. A small sample of it is listed in the bibliography at the end of this book, with most of the works cited there having their own bibliographies that will lead still deeper into the literature. For anyone looking for short cuts, help is at hand. Alasdair Whittle comprehensively and thoughtfully summarized much of the wider European context of Britain's early farmers in his book *Europe in the Neolithic*. Stuart Piggott's *Neolithic cultures of the British Isles* published back in 1954 remains the most detailed overview of the evidence from these Islands, but is now hopelessly out of date in terms of the chronologies used and is heavily slanted towards the recognition of geographically distinct cultural groupings. More up to date are Julian Thomas's contemplative *Understanding the Neolithic* and Caroline Malone's wide-ranging *Neolithic Britain and Ireland*. Joshua Pollard's *Neolithic Britain*, published in the Shire Archaeology series, provides a highly readable summary of the archaeology of the fourth and third millennia BC. Also in that series is a useful

4 Hazleton North (GLO 54). A reconstruction drawing by John Sibbick showing the long barrow as it might have looked when in use around 3500 BC. *Reproduced by permission of the Corinium Museum, Cirencester. Copyright: Cotswold District Council*

overview of *Megalithic tombs and long barrows in Britain* by Frances Lynch. Since Crawford's seminal volume a goodly number of gazetteers have been published listing certain, probable and possible long barrows and related monuments. Sadly, however, there has never been a full survey of the long barrows and related monuments of England and Wales to set alongside the standard works on Scotland, Ireland and France.[8] Together, however, Glyn Daniel's *The prehistoric chamber tombs of England and Wales* and Paul Ashbee's *The earthen long barrow in Britain* cover much of the ground.

County-based surveys painstakingly compiled by Leslie Grinsell, sometimes with assistance from others, are the most detailed inventories available for England, usually arranged by civil parish and referring to the administrative boundaries of shire counties prior to local government reorganization in 1974. Relevant to the Cotswolds and surrounding areas are his published surveys for Berkshire between 1935 and 1939; Wiltshire in 1957; Gloucestershire in 1960 (with Helen O'Neil) and 1989 (with Timothy Darvill); and north Somerset in 1971. Full details can be found in the bibliography. When Glyn Daniel published his account of *The prehistoric chamber tombs of England and Wales* already referred to, he set out an inventory of sites organized by county, with each barrow individually numbered. This system has been followed by later authors, the listings and accompanying overview of the long barrows of the Cotswold-Severn region published by John Corcoran in 1969 being the most comprehensive hitherto. As noted in the preface, this system is used throughout the present volume in expanded form to identify specific sites and obviate the need for repetitive locational and source referencing in the text. The county numbers given in the text (e.g. GLO 1) can be checked against the listing in Appendix A to find the position of the site and a note of any recorded excavations. In addition to the works already mentioned there are numerous regional surveys relating to long barrows in the Cotswold-Severn region, including: W.F. Grimes for the Black Mountains area and also Wales as a whole, published in 1936; Glyn Daniel for Glamorgan in 1957 and the Gloucestershire Cotswolds in 1964; Lisa Brown's listing of Oxfordshire barrows in 1978; Chris Barker's very detailed account of the long mounds of the Avebury region, published in 1985; and surveys by the Royal Commission on the Ancient and Historical Monuments of Wales covering monuments in Glamorgan and Brecknock, published in 1976 and 1997 respectively.

As may already have become apparent, the vocabulary used to discuss the monuments of early farming communities in Britain is highly varied and idiosyncratic, changes through time and, above all, can be very confusing. Yet we need vocabulary to handle ideas. Something of the origins and thinking behind specific terms is touched upon in Chapter 2, but it is perhaps useful to consider here, very briefly, a few underpinning terms and concepts, and the way they are applied in this book. Two different but related approaches lie behind the most common terminology. First is the long-lived, but gradually evolving, concept of the long barrow as a widespread and fairly distinct class of monument comprising a long rectangular or trapezoidal mound that usually, but not always, contains human burials deposited within carefully constructed chambers set within the mound. In this line of thinking, the class as a whole is often sub-divided into stone-chambered long barrows, timber-chambered long barrows and chamberless long barrows. This simple and time-hallowed scheme forms the core of the terminology used in this book. However, in the wider archaeological literature the timber-chambered and chamberless kinds of long barrow are variously referred to as 'earthen long barrows' because of the nature of the construction materials used, or 'unchambered long barrows' where the negative 'un-' element usually refers to the lack of a stone chamber rather than the absence of any chamber at all. Over the last century or so there has been a lamentable tendency to study these earthen or unchambered long barrows independently of the stone-chambered variety, a point that will be discussed further in Chapter 2. However, as a further ingredient to the milieu of confusion, where the mound of a long barrow is mainly composed of stones the term 'long cairn' is used synonymously with 'long barrow'.

The second, broadly parallel, strand of thinking privileges through its terminology those monuments constructed using large stones – the so-called 'megalithic tombs', 'chamber tombs', or 'chambered tombs'. Although they were central to antiquarian thinking of the eighteenth and nineteenth centuries, it is now widely recognized that these terms embrace such a very wide variety of architecturally distinct structures constructed at different times in different places (some are introduced in Chapter 3) that their usefulness has been eroded. Nowadays these words remain handy only as general cover-terms, especially in cases where the original form of the monument is not clear. Terminology referring to distinctive arrangements for access to internal chambers (e.g. passage grave, gallery grave, etc.), chamber plans (e.g. transepted, polygonal, etc.) or the presence of a single large elevated stone (e.g. dolmen) is sometimes used in the literature in a descriptive sense, but can also form the nominative basis for defining distinct classes of monument, as will be seen in Chapter 3.

In order further to untangle this web of thinking about long barrows, Chapter 2 pursues an historical perspective on the way that enquiries about these and related sites have unfolded since the seventeenth century. Attention focuses on two interconnected themes: first, the pattern of investigation through survey, description, digging and, more recently, full-scale archaeological excavation; and, second, the way long barrows on the Cotswolds and in surrounding areas have been seen in relation to related structures within a wider geographical compass. A significant recent trend is the reintegration of various kinds of long barrow that have traditionally been studied separately, and the recognition that they represent a highly visible and widespread horizon within a series of regionally distinct but very long-lived sequences of monument construction and use. Chapter 3 takes up the sequence as it can be seen for the Cotswold-Severn region, illustrating the diversity of monument-building traditions prevalent before long barrows became fashionable. Chapters 4 to 7 focus on the long barrow tradition within and around the Cotswolds, looking first at their character, distribution, placement in the landscape, origins and wider contemporary relationships. It is suggested that although regional groupings of long barrows can be identified across the British Isles these are geographical clusters rather than robust expressions of cultural territories. Chapter 5 presents an examination of the construction and design of long barrows in the Cotswold-Severn region, Chapter 6 considers the evidence for their use and Chapter 7 looks at how they were finally blocked up and abandoned. All these chapters illustrate the variety of ways in which general ideas circulating in the fourth millennium BC seem to have been adapted and given expression by individual communities responsible for building and using particular barrows. Chapter 8 sets the long barrows within their wider setting by looking at what we know of contemporary settlements and other related sites. How these long barrow-using communities perceived their monuments, and what they may have meant to them, is also explored. Finally, Chapter 9 considers the end of the long barrow tradition and what happened to the sites through later millennia down to the present day.

In support of the main text, Appendix B provides a consolidated list of radiocarbon dates from long barrows and closely related monuments in the Cotswolds and surrounding areas. Appendix C provides a select list of long barrows that are easily accessible to visit and a few notes on how to find them and what to look for while at the site. The bibliography provides a fairly comprehensive account of published works pertaining to Cotswold-Severn long barrows and is linked to the main text by way of endnotes so that points of detail can be followed up.

2

LONG BARROWS AND MEGALITHIC ENQUIRIES

What we now call long barrows have been part of Britain's landscape for more than 5,000 years, even if at times they were not seen for what they were by contemporary eyes. We have no idea what these great mounds of earth and stone were called in prehistoric times, nor of the ways in which the vocabulary of their builders reflected any perceived differences in the form, construction, or use. As noted in Chapter 1, modern studies use modern words and terminology that is constantly changing to reflect new lines of enquiry, fresh interpretations and new understandings. Our word 'barrow' ultimately derives from the Anglo-Saxon word *beorh*, a term that Leslie Grinsell suggested was used from the mid-first millennium AD onwards to refer mainly to ancient burial places, including those to which contemporary Saxon burials had been added.[1] But there was already depth and texture to the language of barrows by late Anglo-Saxon times. The word *hlaew* was almost invariably used to refer to burial mounds constructed anew by Anglo-Saxon communities, while the term *cnaep* was variously and inexactly used for either burial mounds or small hills. Pole's Wood South (GLO 2) is named *Longam Beorge* in an Anglo-Saxon charter that in all lists no fewer than eleven barrows of various sorts.[2] This use of a name that would translate as 'long barrow' suggests considerable familiarity with the landscape as a whole, as well as the character of individual components within it. Another term widely used for barrows and hill-like mounds in the Cotswolds is the word *tump*. Its origins are obscure, but it was certainly in use by the late sixteenth century AD when Thomas Nashe (1567–1601) wrote, rather ominously, that 'they brought him unawares to a dunghill, taking it for a tumpe, since a tombe might not be had'.[3]

Seeing and naming long barrows is one thing, understanding them and explaining their existence and purpose quite another. For centuries now, scholars and field investigators have been enquiring into the origin, associations, context and meaning of long barrows, along the way amassing collections of finds, lists of measurements, page after page of descriptions and sheaves of plans, section drawings and photographs. But how has this all been interpreted? What theories and hypotheses have been advanced to explain the origins and spread of long barrows? How do examples in the Cotswolds fit into the bigger picture of emergent monument-building traditions across northwest Europe in prehistoric times? What are the sources of the evidence behind our understandings of these sites? How have they been investigated? And when and why did people first start trying to make sense of these enigmatic elongated mounds scattered across the countryside?

SCHOLARSHIP AND ROMANTICISM

It was the Enlightenment scholarship of seventeenth-century England that prompted an intellectual interest in barrows generally, and long barrows in particular, making them subjects considered worthy of study, investigation and comment. One scholar who did much to set this process in train was John Aubrey (1626–97). Born and raised at Lower Easton Piercy, between Castle Combe and Chippenham in the southern Cotswolds, he was able to experience at first hand the earthworks and barrows of the district.[4] In his *Monumenta Britannica*, compiled in the main between 1665 and 1693 but left languishing as a manuscript in the Bodleian Library, Oxford, until its eventual publication in 1982,[5] he distinguished between round barrows and long barrows, and was the first person to use the term 'long barrow' in its modern meaning as a sepulchral structure within an elongated mound of earth and stone. He described a string of long barrows in his neighbourhood, including many that would later become household names to barrow scholars: Lugbury (WIL 1), the Giant's Caves (WIL 2) which he visited in 1659, Lanhill (WIL 3), West Kennet (WIL 4), Millbarrow (WIL 11) and Leighterton (GLO 18) amongst others. He sketched many of the sites he visited, and these drawings now represent important records of monuments that have slowly changed over the intervening three centuries or so *(5A)*. Although wrongly ascribing long barrows to the Danes, his notes reveal a depth to his scholarship. There is, for example, a remarkable understanding of the nature of these structures and he made connections between the English long barrows and similar monuments in Denmark that are still relevant. Above all, Aubrey's observations and illustrations reflect his scientific approach, and even today provide the starting point for anyone exploring one of the long barrows he documented.

William Stukeley (1687–1765), one of the most colourful antiquarians of the early eighteenth century, also contributed much to the early understanding of long barrows, but from a quite different perspective.[6] Like Aubrey his early life was influenced by an essentially scientific philosophy, born no doubt of Enlightenment

5 Opposite Long barrows in the antiquarian gaze. *A top:* Lanhill (WIL 3) drawn by John Aubrey in the late seventeenth century. *B middle:* The 'Arch-Druids' Barrow' at West Kennet (WIL 4) by William Stukeley in the mid-eighteenth century. *C bottom:* Hetty Pegler's Tump (GLO 14) by John Thurnam and E.A. Freeman in the mid-nineteenth century. *Reproduced courtesy of the Prehistoric Society (A) and the Society of Antiquaries of London (B and C)*

On the left hand of the rode from Chippenham to Bristow, about halfe a mile short of Biteston, near a hill of ground called Lam hill in Chippenham parish, is a Barrow, or Tumulus, commonly known by the name of *Barrow-hill*, where they say one *Hubba* lies buried.

traditions and bolstered by his study of medicine at Bennet College, Cambridge (now Corpus Christi). From about 1710 he began a series of tours around the country, visiting the north Wessex Downs and eastern Cotswolds during several of these adventures and recording in his notebook some of the things he saw in a rather matter of fact if slightly flamboyant style *(5B)*. However, after moving to London in 1717, he became increasingly absorbed in the emergent Romanticist tradition, a reaction to the classical scholarship of the Enlightenment. It was a way of thinking that sought to establish the importance and unique identity of indigenous European peoples – the *Volksgeist*. Naturally, he applied this approach to his work on antiquities, most notably his fanciful Druidical interpretations of Stonehenge and Avebury. Underneath the whimsical interpretations, however, he perpetuated Aubrey's separation of barrows into long and round forms, and true to his early training subdivided them further on the basis of their external appearance and what he found in them during a short campaign of excavations around Stonehenge in 1723–4.[7] His observations were sometimes blinkered and his suggested terminology idiosyncratic, but his basic extensive classification of barrows based on their shape and profile remains in use today, even though the names he applied – for example 'King's Barrow', 'Druid's Barrow', 'Arch Druid's Barrow' and the 'Druid and his Wife's Barrow' – have long since been abandoned.[8]

Surprisingly, travellers and diarists of the later seventeenth and eighteenth centuries rarely visited the Cotswolds and their long barrows. Although Daniel Defoe (1659–1731), Celia Fiennes of Broughton (1662–1741) and Thomas Hearne (1678–1735) all toured Oxfordshire and parts of the Cotswolds they make only slight mention of the Rollright Stones and say almost nothing on other notable sites.[9] Map-makers such as Isaac Taylor (1730–87) and Thomas Leman (1751–1826), and the early county historians including Sir Robert Atkyns (1647–1711), Samuel Rudder (1726–1801), Thomas Rudge (1754–1825) and Thomas Fosbroke (1770–1842), included some long barrows in their works, but the coverage is also less than comprehensive.

Early antiquarian interest in the long barrows west of the Severn was equally poor. Edward Lhwyd (1660–1709), a 'Cambro-Briton' who studied at Oxford and became keeper of archaeology in the Ashmolean Museum in Oxford from 1691 until his death, made major contributions relating to Wales for the 1695 and later editions of Camden's *Britannia*.[10] Lhwyd achieved his contributions by building up a network of correspondents throughout the Principality. He travelled extensively, preferring this to his museum duties, and made descriptions and drawings of several long barrows and megalithic monuments in southeast Wales and the Black Mountains, including Ty Illtyd (BRE 6) and Arthur's Stone (GLA 3).[11] But Lhwyd's work was exceptional. As in England, later travellers such as Thomas Pennant (1726–96) and Richard Fenton (1747–1821) make useful passing references to long barrows but provide little detail. As Stephen Briggs summed it up: 'eighteenth century tourist literature, both manuscript and printed, furnishes little information on megaliths. Most travellers tended to carry extracts from Gibson's *Britannia* and to rely upon the maps and commentaries of Speed, Saxton, Ogilby and Bowen for information about sites.'[12]

So if it was not people looking at ruins from horseback that enhanced seventeenth- and eighteenth-century understandings of long barrows, what was it that moved studies forward? Ironically, it was investigations carried out with the aim of finding buried treasure, winning raw materials for mending roads and occasionally exploring inexplicable mounds or stones sticking out of the ground where they should not be, that together played a formative role. It was hardly scientific work in the modern sense, but at times empirical all the same. Some of the first sites to be examined were those listed by Aubrey and Stukeley. In about 1700, for example, Matthew Huntley dug into one of the sites Aubrey described, West Barrow at Leighterton (GLO 18). Here he found 'three vaults arched over like ovens, and at the entrance of each was found an earthen urn containing ashes and burnt human bones, but the skulls and thighbones were found unburnt'.[13] Over the following century perhaps half a dozen diggings gradually extended the little pool of knowledge about Cotswold long barrows. Tidcombe Hill (WIL 9) was dug into by local people about 1750 at considerable cost in time and effort. As R. Willis records in the style of his day: 'the peasants, being perfuaded that great riches were hid in this barrow . . . beftowed almost a fummer's labour to dig into it'.[14] Stoney Littleton (SOM 1) was first opened in about 1760 when the farmer-occupier forced an entry into the chamber to obtain stone for road mending. For some time afterwards the site remained accessible to local people, who entered it and removed human bones and anything else that took their fancy.[15] A trench was dug into Crippets Barrow, Coberley (GLO 7) sometime before 1779, revealing a large burial chamber containing a single skeleton and 'several articles'. Burn Ground (GLO 60) may also have been explored as early as 1781,[16] and in the last decade of the eighteenth century the Revd Thomas Bere, rector of nearby Butcombe, twice investigated the Fairy's Toot (SOM 2), first in 1789 and again in 1792.[17]

In retrospect, most of these eighteenth-century investigations were hasty, small-scale, badly recorded and, as time went by, increasingly grounded in the Romanticist curiosity that had so distracted Stukeley and many others beside. The results rarely reached a wide audience and for the most part remain poorly published in early antiquarian journals. In some cases archaeological evidence itself is now the only surviving record of these endeavours. But all that changed at the end of the eighteenth century when some of Britain's most notorious barrow-diggers got to work in the region, bringing with them ideas as well as prejudices from their researches elsewhere. Their endeavours marked a drift back towards more scientifically based approaches.[18]

BARROW KNIGHTS AND THE BARROW–DIGGERS

Sir Richard Colt Hoare (1758–1838) was one of the most influential contributors to the advancement of knowledge about long barrows in southern England. He is best known for his monumental study entitled *Ancient Wiltshire* published in five parts between 1810 and 1821, which remains a triumph of problem-

6 The Hoar Stone (GLO 9), one of the earliest investigations at a Cotswold long barrow recorded using drawings. *A top:* View from the southeast before it was opened. *B middle:* Chamber on the south side after it was opened by Anthony Freston in 1806. *C bottom:* The site in 2003 with the capstone of the chamber in the foreground and the massive Hoar Stone (probably the central element of a false-portal) behind. *A and B: reproduced courtesy of the Society of Antiquaries of London; C: photograph by Timothy Darvill*

focused archaeological investigation. In the introduction he famously declared that 'we speak from facts, not theory',[19] a dictum that was supported by his fieldwork and careful observations during excavations. Yet it was in south Wales rather than the Cotswolds that he made his first, unwitting, contribution to the study of long barrows. He began visiting Wales regularly from about 1793, building friendships and making new contacts amongst the antiquarian community there.[20] On Saturday 26 May 1803, together with Theophilus Jones, Richard Fenton, Admiral Gell, Sir William Ouseley, a Mr Everest and the Revd H.T. Payne, Colt Hoare supervised a brief examination of the south chamber at Gwernvale (BRE 7).[21] They found relatively little and in retrospect it is clear that they did not even realize that it was a long barrow that was being investigated. But the operation served to implant the idea of scientific excavation among Welsh antiquarians and set the scene for nearly two centuries of megalithic enquiries in the region.

Meanwhile, on the Gloucestershire Cotswolds, the stirrings of inquisitive minds and the sound of picks and shovels reverberated around the hills. The Revd Anthony Freston dug into the Hoar Stone barrow at Duntisbourne Abbots (GLO 9) in 1806, raising a flat slab near the middle of the mound to expose the remains of a chamber, divided into two segments, in which were the remains of eight or nine skeletons *(6)*. His findings were promptly reported at a meeting of the Society of Antiquaries of London on 20 November 1806 and later noted in the *Archaeologia*.[22] Today the barrow survives more or less as Freston left it, a small tree beside the Hoar Stone itself being the most visible addition *(6C)*. Also in 1806, the Revd W.H. Thornbury, rector of Avening parish, excavated a nearby long barrow (probably GLO 17), removing the three stone chambers that he found there and later re-erecting them beside the drive leading to his house.[23] The Symond's Hall Farm barrow at Wotton-under-Edge (GLO 85) was examined before 1807, but by whom is not known. Apart from human remains, early long barrow excavations did not reveal much in the way of interesting finds or exotic items that would grace the curiosity cabinets of collectors or antiquaries. But these early pieces of work were the first splashes of interest that in due course became a steady trickle, and still later a torrent, of investigations whose collective outcome revealed progressively more of the internal structure, content, age and use of long barrows.

Over the five decades between 1801 and 1850 about 18 long barrows in the Cotswold-Severn region were investigated, over half of them within the Cotswolds *(7A)*. Some 13 years after opening Gwernvale, Colt Hoare was drawn into the investigation of another stone-chambered tomb by a near neighbour of his, the Revd John Skinner, rector of Camerton. Skinner was a quarrelsome individual who sought refuge in the study of local antiquities, and in May 1816 he turned his attention to the long barrow at Stoney Littleton near Wellow (SOM 1). Together with his brother Russell Skinner, Sir Richard Colt Hoare, Philip Crocker and a labourer named Zebedee Weston, they gained entry to the chambers through a hole made during the earlier excavations in 1760. They then proceeded to clear 'rubbish' from the interior. Amongst this rubbish there were

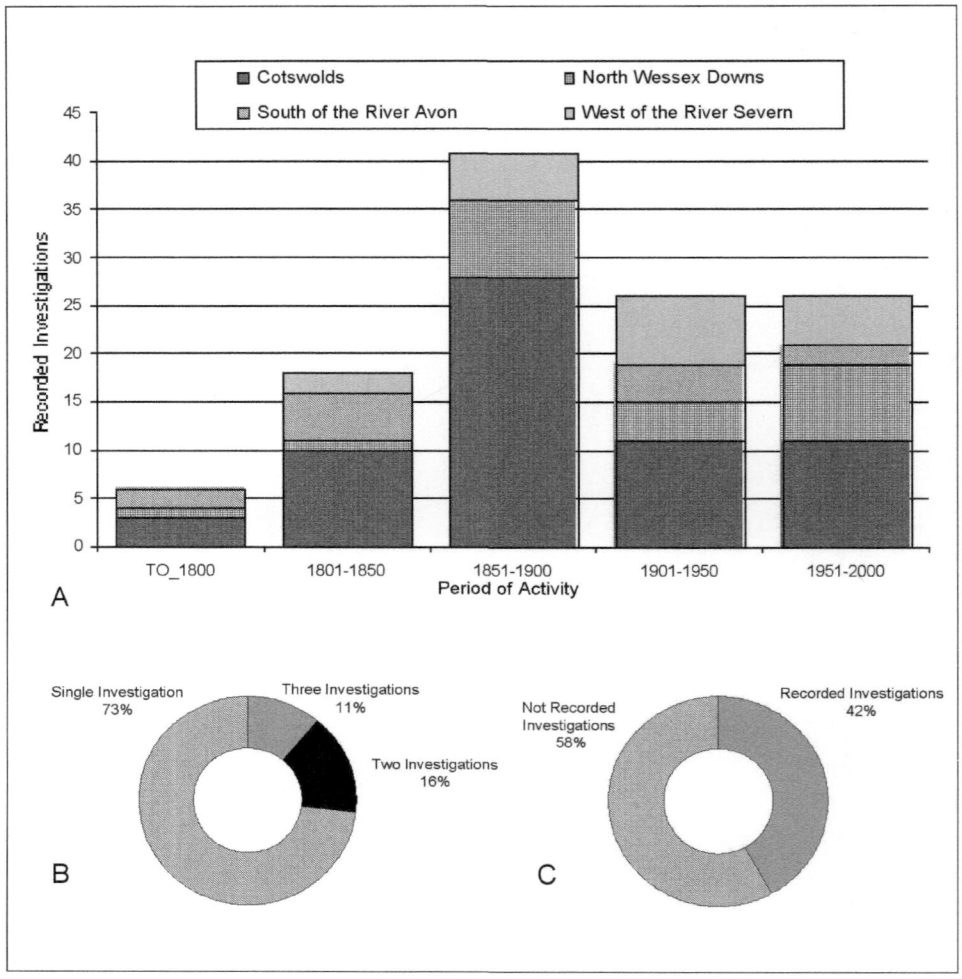

7 Excavating long barrows in the Cotswold-Severn region. *A:* Changing patterns of investigation c.AD 1750–2000. *B:* Percentage of long barrows investigated. *C:* Pattern of multiple investigations

human remains from perhaps ten individuals. Colt Hoare read an account of the work to a meeting of the Society of Antiquaries of London on 22 May 1817, enthusing that:

> A new species of tumulus now excites my attention, which I shall denominate the stone barrow, varying from the long barrow not in its external, but in its internal mode of construction. None of this kind occurred to me during my researches in South Wiltshire; for the material of stone with which they were partly formed was wanting. [24]

It is hard now to imagine the thrill of anticipation and discovery that must have accompanied these early investigations, and still more the surprise at the identification of previously unrecorded but well-preserved examples. In 1820, during the clearance of woodland and stone quarrying on the Cotswold escarpment north of Uley, a previously unrecorded long barrow was revealed. It was promptly investigated on 22 and 23 February 1821 by Dr Fry of Dursley and T.J. Lloyd Baker of Hardwick Court, who found the remains of at least 15 individuals scattered through the chambers, passage and entrance. This was the long barrow now affectionately known as Hetty Pegler's Tump (GLO 14); the hollows from the quarrying and the investigations are still visible on the top of the mound. Later the same year Sir Richard Colt Hoare continued his interest in the 'new species' of tumulus with work at Lugbury (WIL 1), uncovering four side chambers along the south side of the mound and the stones of a massive false entrance at the east end. Colt Hoare's friend the Revd John Skinner was active in north Somerset in the early 1800s, digging into Gray's Down long barrow (SOM 21) in 1815, the Priddy long barrow (SOM 16) in August 1816 and the Fairy's Toot (SOM 2) in 1822. Work at this last site provided what is now the only reliable record of an important long barrow; the site was largely destroyed by quarrying very soon afterwards. Skinner went on to work at the Giant's Grave (SOM 4) in 1826, but little of consequence seems to have been found.

Of course, not everyone was as meticulous in recording and reporting their work as Colt Hoare and Skinner; poorly documented investigations took place between 1819 and 1820 at Fromefield (SOM 6), possibly in connection with landscaping works, and at many other sites besides. Nor was it only curiosity and quarrying that revealed new sites and prompted their investigation. Calamity and misfortune were sometimes to blame. In May 1844, for example, farm labourers ploughing land at Grickstone Farm were surprised when 'the ground gave way under one of the horses' and the roof of a chamber in a previously unknown long barrow fell in (GLO 19).[25]

The pace of enquiry increased still further in the second half of the nineteenth century as more antiquaries turned their attention to examples of what was by this time recognized as an extremely widespread and very ancient class of monument. More than twice as many barrows were excavated between 1851 and 1900 as had been examined in the previous half-century, the majority again being on the Cotswolds (7A). There were improvements to excavation methodology in the form of larger and more carefully positioned trenches, while stimulating new scientific ideas were circulating ever more widely, gradually trickling down into antiquarian thinking. Amongst these were Carl Linnaeus's binomial system of classification and nomenclature applied in the biological sciences, Charles Lyell's propositions about stratigraphy published in 1833 and Charles Darwin's theory of evolution and natural selection from 1859. From 1865 there was John Lubbock's book entitled *Prehistoric times* in which he defined the 'Palaeolithic' and the 'Neolithic' as major subdivisions of the Stone Age, the latter being characterized by polished stone implements and monuments such as long barrows.[26]

In the field, Professor J. Buckman and C.H. Newmarch dug into the Querns Barrow in Cirencester (GLO 79) in about 1850; Dean John Merewether was at Monkton Down (WIL 22) and Longstones long barrow (WIL 34) about the same time; while in 1854 G.P. Scrope was investigating Lugbury (WIL 1) by expanding the work previously done by Colt Hoare. In the same year the physician John Thurnam and the historian Professor E.A. Freeman undertook a second investigation of Hetty Pegler's Tump (GLO 14) and Revd Samuel Lysons was working at Lamborough Banks (GLO 25). J.Y. Akerman examined Pinkwell, Chedworth (GLO 65) in 1856 and Crawley (OXF 9) in 1858. John Thurnam worked at Beckhampton Road (WIL 27) and Easton Down (WIL 19) in the late 1850s, West Kennet (WIL 4) in 1859 and Adam's Grave (WIL 6) in 1860. Thurnam's excavations in particular reflected new currents in scientific thinking, as one of his aims was to recover ancient human crania for biometrical studies of the physical anthropology of these early populations and the determination of their racial affinities and relationships. However, recording generally remained poor, with a focus on general views of what was discovered rather than detailed plans and sections *(5C)*.

The 20 years between 1860 and 1880 represent one of the most prolific periods ever for long barrow investigations. More than a score of excavations took place at long barrows in the Cotswold-Severn region, and these were just a small fraction of the work taking place across the British Isles as a whole. Continuing an early tradition, many campaigns were led by churchmen seeking to understand something of the parishes they looked after.[27] But academics and interested amateurs were involved as well. E. James and M. Moggridge uncovered part of the long barrow on Pen-maen Burrows (GLA 5) in 1860, the same year that an unknown investigator was digging into Camp Barrow North (GLO 11). W.C. Lukis and A.C. Smith examined Temple Bottom (WIL 10) in June 1861 while the following summer E. Martin Atkins investigated the long barrow on White Horse Hill (BRK 5), perhaps the mound on which Thomas Hughes, author of *Tom Brown's Schooldays*, had sat a few years before to observe the last ceremony for the scouring of the Uffington White Horse in 1857. Work took place at the Bisley Barrow (GLO 74) in 1863, when a rather unusual trephined skull was found (see Chapter 6). In the same year John Thurnam was excavating Millbarrow (WIL 11) and Horton Down (WIL 20) on the north Wessex Downs. The Revd Samuel Lysons, rector of Rodmarton, was at Windmill Tump (GLO 16) in his own parish in 1863 and at Gatcombe Lodge (GLO 15) in adjacent Minchinhampton in 1870. Professor J. Buckman of Oxford University excavated at Nympsfield (GLO 13) in 1862. And so the list rolls on, with an ever-expanding roster of investigators. W.H. Paine and E. Witchell were excavating Bown Hill (GLO 20) in 1863; W. Lawrence and L. Winterbotham were at Belas Knap (GLO 1) in 1863–5; William Cunnington was at Oldbury Hill (WIL 17) in 1864; A.E.W. Paine excavated the Avenis Barrow (GLO 75) between 1865 and 1875; the Revd David Royce, rector of Nether Swell, was at Cow Common Long (GLO 22) in 1867–8; Sir John Lubbock opened Parc le Breos Cwm (GLA 4) in 1869; Canon William Greenwell of Durham and George Rolleston, Linacre Professor of Anatomy and Physiology at Oxford University, examined more of Cow Common Long and Pole's Wood South (GLO 2) in 1874; Royce, Rolleston and Greenwell opened Eyford Hill (GLO 3) together in 1874; Royce and Rolleston worked together again at Pole's Wood East (GLO 24) in 1875–6; and an unknown investigator was working at Jack Barrow (GLO 27) in 1875, the same year that J.W. Lukis investigated Maesyfelin (GLA 10).

The early 1880s were dominated by the efforts of George Witts of Leckhampton, whose enthusiasm for long barrows was fired up when he discovered West Tump in Cranham Woods (GLO 8) in 1880. He promptly excavated this very large and previously untouched mound before moving on to examine Notgrove (GLO 4) in April 1881, College Plantation I (GLO 72) in 1882 and, in partnership with C.A. Witchell, Randwick (GLO 10) in 1883. It was with the results of most of this work to hand that Witts was able to devote a whole chapter to long barrows in his *Archaeological handbook of the County of Gloucestershire*, listing and describing no fewer than 40 examples. The significance of this can perhaps be judged from the fact that only 26 Roman villas were included, despite the wealth of such sites in the area.[28] But not all excavations of the period were down to Witts. In July 1880 a Mr Leigh cleared the chambers at Nympsfield (GLO 13), in 1881 a Miss Bostock was working at Pen-maen Burrows (GLA 5), and at about the same time Sir Henry Meux cut into the centre of the West Woods long barrow (WIL 15). It was all very energetic stuff, but in reality rather little was actually found.

The closing decades of the nineteenth century saw a slight slackening in the pace of work and the number of new investigations started. Moreover, there was a notable shift from the essentially private enterprise of antiquarians through the middle and late nineteenth century to the more public and communal endeavours of archaeological and antiquarian societies from the 1870s onwards. Local societies, which often included interests in natural history as well as archaeology, were very popular and several in the Cotswolds and surrounding areas flourished, with an expanding membership base, through the last quarter of the nineteenth century and beyond. Visiting sites in the company of experts and seeing monuments opened up for inspection was an important part of the attraction. Thus, for example, G.B. Witts opened the Willersey long barrow (GLO 34) inside Willersey hillfort especially for a field meeting of the Bristol and Gloucestershire Archaeological Society in 1884, while M.E. Bagnall-Oakeley and the Monmouth and Caerleon Antiquarian Association dug into Heston Brake (MON 3) in 1888.

The first half of the twentieth century saw a renewed interest in the examination of long barrows, perhaps spurred by increasing public interest. More than 25 were investigated *(7A)*, a good number considering the turbulent political and economic climate. Trenches tended to be small, but the value of investigating parts of the mound as well as the chamber areas gradually began to be realized *(8A)*. On the whole the standards of reporting improved, and some work was carried out in order to help conserve sites and open them for public viewing, as well as to find out more about them. C.R. Peers and R.A. Smith, for example, excavated at Wayland's Smithy (BRK 1) in 1919–20 in an effort to help protect the site, while

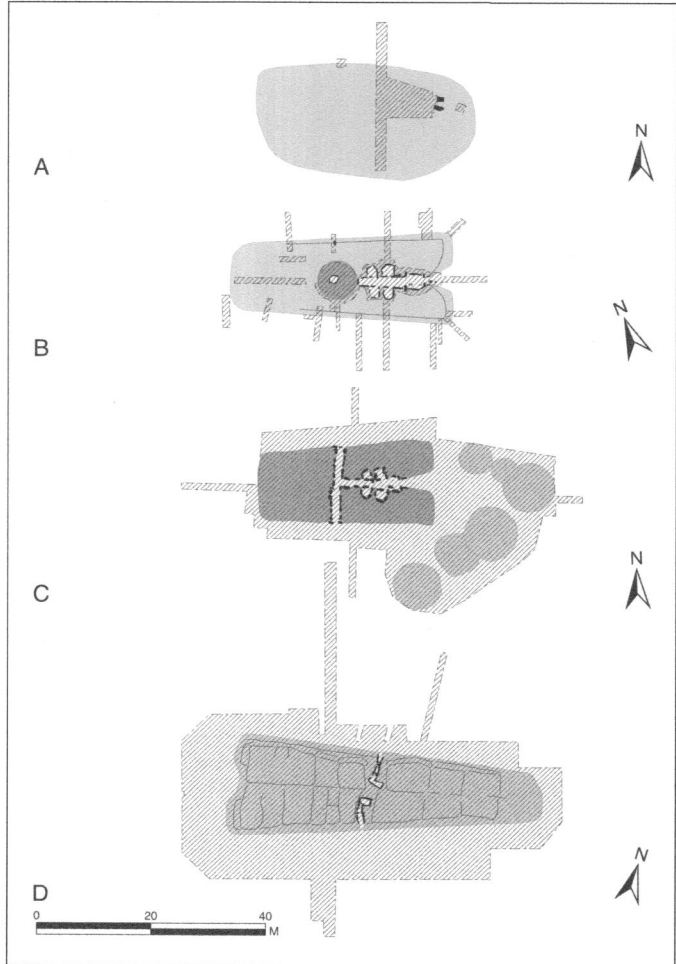

8 Twentieth-century excavation strategies. *A:* Murtry Hill (SOM 8), 1915–20. *B:* Notgrove (GLO 4), 1935–6. *C:* Burn Ground (GLO 60), 1940–1. *D:* Hazleton North (GLO 54), 1979–83

A.D. Passmore excavated at the Devil's Den (WIL 8) in 1921 prior to reconstruction works. West of the Severn, John Ward, Keeper of Archaeology in the National Museum of Wales, excavated at Tinkinswood (GLA 9) in 1914 prior to its restoration and the creation of public access. In the early 1920s there was a vigorous campaign of investigations amongst the long barrows of the Black Mountains in eastern Wales. C.E. Vulliamy examined Ffostyll South (BRE 4) in 1921–2 and Ffostyll North (BRE 3) in 1922; while the Revd W.E.T. Morgan and George Marshall excavated at Pen-y-wyrlod (BRE 1) in 1920–1. This last excavation was actually taking place when O.G.S. Crawford visited the site on 12 August 1921, towards the end of the fieldwork for his survey of long barrows, *The long barrows of the Cotswolds*, already touched upon in Chapter 1. The publication of Crawford's work, the *LBC* as it is fondly known to numerous subsequent authors and editors, was truly seminal and marked a turning point in long barrow studies not just in the Cotswolds but also in Britain as a whole.

CRAWFORD AND THE *LBC*

The initial impetus for a survey of Cotswold barrows came from the fact that when Crawford joined the Ordnance Survey as its Archaeological Officer in October 1920 revision of the small-scale mapping for Gloucestershire was already half completed. Crawford himself takes up the story:

> My first field-work was carried out in that county [Gloucestershire] during the last three months of 1920. The area included the Cotswolds, about whose stone-chambered Long Barrows I had read in the works of Rice-Holmes and Thurnam. They were amongst the most famous of our prehistoric monuments, and it was a great surprise to me to find that some of them were not even marked upon the map. That was as much to the discredit of archaeologists as of the Ordnance Survey; one would have expected some learned society to have noticed the defect and done something to remedy it.[29]

From this necessity to deal with the small-scale mapping sprang the idea of producing a series of synoptic large-scale maps with associated commentaries. Crawford's study of Cotswold long barrows suddenly mushroomed into something much more than the title suggests; it actually covers the long barrows and megalithic structures on Sheet 8 (Midlands S) in the series of Quarter-Inch (1:253,440 scale) Ordnance Survey maps published in the 1920s that covered the whole of England, Wales, Scotland and the Isle of Man. Sheet 8 embraces a large area – 20,475 square kilometres – and within its bounds just over 150 separate monuments were eventually listed. Initially unable to publish a full account of the survey, Crawford contented himself with a volume in the series of Professional Papers produced by the Ordnance Survey. Published in 1922, this slim volume comprised a printed map at 1:253,440 scale, a short accompanying commentary, a listing of 70 long barrows and seven stone circles, and two plates containing a selection of plans. It was only after meeting Max and William Bellows from a family of Gloucester printers with a long interest in archaeology that the possibility of a more substantial publication on Cotswold long barrows came about. Meanwhile, Crawford had conceived the idea that the whole of Britain should be covered by regional surveys of long barrows and megalithic monuments. In time, three more appeared: Wessex by Crawford himself in 1932;[30] South Wales by W.F. Grimes in 1936;[31] and the Trent Basin by C.W. Phillips in 1933.[32] Further progress was slowed by the outbreak of World War II, and finally came to an abrupt halt with the loss of many papers and records during enemy action in 1940.[33]

Crawford took up the study of megalithic monuments more or less accidentally, but brought to the subject something that had hitherto been missing – a strong sense of geography. Thus the *LBC* begins with a study of distribution, focusing on two case studies: the Swell region and the Avening region, both in Gloucestershire. In later sections, full attention is given to position, purpose, age, structure, fauna and flora, folklore and the present and future state of the sites. There is also some consideration of the results and finds from the excavations that had taken place up until the early 1920s. The great strength of the volume and one of the things that give it lasting value is the way that sites are described from first-hand knowledge and careful fieldwork.

FIELDWORK 1925 TO 1960

Excavation and survey developed fast as archaeological fieldcraft during the inter-war years, pushed along by the establishment of more formal excavation methods and recording systems. The scale of work moved up a gear too, and with a still-growing public interest in archaeology the restoration of sites for display gained further importance. At Belas Knap (GLO 1) emergency repairs and scrub clearance were carried out in 1928 under the supervision of W.J. Hemp when the monument was transferred into State Guardianship.[34] There followed excavations by Sir James Berry in 1929 and 1930 that uncovered much of the mound and cleared all four chambers.[35] The Bristol and Gloucestershire Archaeological Society met the labourers' wages for both seasons. Alongside these investigations there were further restoration works, supervised by Ralegh Radford, which culminated in a sustained programme of reconstruction between September 1930 and March 1931. The labour for this work was provided through the then Government's 'Increased Employment Programme', an early example of numerous initiatives during the twentieth century to combat unemployment, which thereby indirectly benefited archaeology.[36]

Elsewhere in the north Cotswolds a new recruit to long barrow studies, Mrs Elsie Clifford, undertook a thorough examination of the Notgrove long barrow (GLO 4) between October and November 1934, with further work between August and October 1935. This followed the discovery of stonework and walls when attempts were made by the Ministry of Works to fence the barrow.[37] By this time excavation methods had developed significantly beyond what they had been at the turn of the century, and she used a series of 14 carefully positioned trenches around the edge of the barrow, with a more open-area investigation through the forecourt, chambers and central area of the mound *(8B)*. The approach paid off because she showed, for the first time in the Cotswold-Severn region, that the monument was of at least two phases, with an early circular structure superseded by the trapezoidal long barrow.

Notgrove was the start of an abiding interest in long barrows on the Cotswolds, not only for Elsie Clifford but also for Glyn Daniel, who at this time was a young student of archaeology studying at Cambridge and whom we shall meet again shortly. On the Cotswolds Clifford excavated a series of trenches at Jack Barrow (GLO 27) in 1936 in the hope of finding the position and extent of the levelled mound, a task that was moderately successful.[38] The following year she excavated the long barrow at Nympsfield (GLO 13), a site perched right on the edge of the Cotswold escarpment overlooking the Vale of Berkeley and the River Severn beyond. The technique she used here again involved a rather irregular trench over the chambers and forecourt with linear trenches to define the edges of the mound.[39] Continuing the pace, in 1939 Elsie Clifford carried out limited investigations at Windmill Tump, Rodmarton (GLO 16), in order to re-examine the curious porthole entrances to the chambers originally discovered by the Revd Samuel Lysons in 1863. Again Glyn Daniel assisted her in the work, and she reported the Rodmarton excavations in 1940 as part of a more wide-ranging paper written jointly with Daniel, who by this time had been elected a Fellow of St John's College, Cambridge.[40]

Another formidable, and in a sense rival, force in Cotswold archaeology was Helen Donovan; Helen O'Neil after she married Bryan O'Neil in 1939.[41] Donovan was committed to archaeological work and her first excursion into the early prehistoric monuments of the Cotswolds came in 1935-8 with the difficult excavation of the barrow on Adlestrop Hill (GLO 44), now best interpreted as a portal dolmen.[42]

West of the Severn, C.E. Vulliamy continued the programme of earlier work at sites in the Black Mountains with relatively small-scale excavations at Little Lodge (BRE 2) in 1929. Nearby, members of the Brecknockshire Society undertook the excavation of Ty Isaf (BRE 5) in 1938 under the direction of W.F. Grimes. This involved a series of interconnecting linear trenches in total covering about 60 per cent of the barrow, probably one of the largest-scale excavations until that time. Like Clifford at Notgrove, Grimes revealed a monument with a complicated history in which the possibility is discussed that a trapezoidal long barrow was added to a small oval structure.[43] The discovery of a previously unrecorded long barrow at Nicholaston on the Gower (GLA 11) prompted an excavation in May 1939, directed by Audrey Williams, wife of W.F. Grimes. It revealed a substantial oval mound, in the centre of which was a roughly square chamber quite unlike the structures found in other long barrows known at that time in Britain (see Chapter 3).

In north Wiltshire, A.D Passmore excavated at the Giant's Caves (WIL 2) in 1932, while Alexander Keiller and Stuart Piggott undertook further excavations at Lanhill (WIL 3). On this occasion they explored an undisturbed chamber originally discovered by Passmore in 1937. Work was confined to the inside of the chamber and approach passage, entry being gained through a small opening in the roof of the chamber at the north end.

As a result of all these excavations there began to emerge an understanding of the nature, extent, construction, complexity and design of these barrows. The excavation strategies adopted are as revealing in terms of the evolving methodology as they are about the sites themselves. These trends reached their culmination between October 1939 and March 1940 with perhaps the most extraordinary excavations undertaken in Britain to that time: the total excavation of the Saltway Barn long barrow, Bibury (GLO 92) between October 1940 and March 1941, followed by the total excavation of the Burn Ground long barrow, Hampnett (GLO 60), in the ensuing months. Through this work more was achieved in the space of 18 months than had built up over the previous century. The excavations at both sites were directed by W.F. Grimes, who was employed by the Ministry of Defence to record archaeological remains faced with destruction in the course of

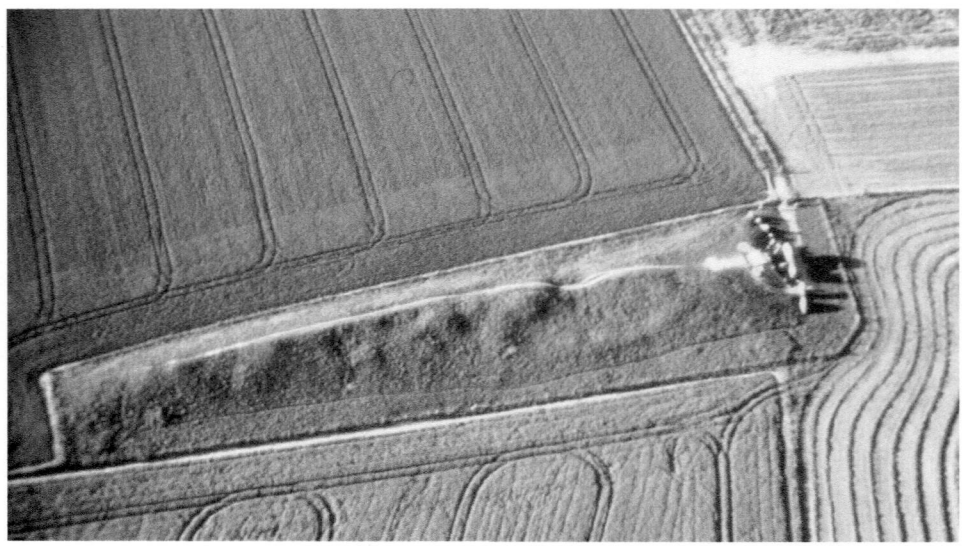

9 West Kennet long barrow, Avebury (WIL 4). Aerial view with the east end of the barrow to the right-hand side of the picture. *Photograph by Mick Aston. Copyright reserved*

engineering and military works connected with the war effort. Both Saltway Barn and Burn Ground lay in the way of proposed airfields deep in the heart of the Cotswolds. The work is all the more remarkable because it was carried out in difficult circumstances with a 'labour force that often consisted of one old man'.[44] At Saltway Barn a trench of about 900 square metres was set out over the mound and excavated to reveal a simple passage grave that was later elaborated through the addition of extra stonework to form a rather oddly shaped long barrow. At Burn Ground a single large trench covering more than 1400 square metres was cleared to reveal three main phases in the use of the spot as a burial place: a long barrow, succeeded in due course by six overlapping round barrows, followed perhaps two millennia later by a dispersed Anglo-Saxon cemetery comprising both inhumations and cremations *(8C)*. Grimes presented a commentary on his methodology for barrow excavation that not only advocated total excavation, but also introduced the idea of open-plan excavation in which all the exposed stonework was recorded in plan as each successive layer was removed. It was a time-consuming strategy, a variation of the plano-stratigraphic method that had found increasing popularity in Germany and a few other parts of Europe during the inter-war years. The rigid application of such a methodology was all the more remarkable in this case, however, given the grave national emergency that was unfolding all around as Britain joined the war against Germany. The only lamentable aspect of the programme was that the report, and Grimes's exposition on the approach used, were not published until 1960 – too late to contribute to the development of methodologies for a series of excavations through the 1940s, 1950s and early 1960s: Stoney Littleton (SOM 1) by Arthur Bulleid in 1941; Pipton (BRE 8) by H.N. Savory in 1955; West Kennet (WIL 4) by Stuart Piggott and Richard

Atkinson in 1955-6 *(9* and *10)*; the Horslip barrow (WIL 30) by Paul Ashbee in 1959; the Giant's Caves (WIL 2) by John Corcoran in 1960–2; and Parc le Breos Cwm (GLA 4) by Richard Atkinson in 1960–1. These investigations all adopted fairly conventional methodologies, but the results contributed handsomely to a series of wider debates about the origins, nature and relationships of long barrows within the Cotswold-Severn region and beyond. Of all of them, it was probably the rapidly published work in 1955–6 at West Kennet that had the greatest impact.

MAPPING THE BIGGER PICTURE

It was not only excavations and surveys that occupied scholars of Cotswold long barrows in the decades following the publication of the *LBC*. The place of these monuments within the emerging picture of European megaliths was the subject of a wide, diverse and sometimes contradictory literature that fiercely debated the origins, relationships and evolution of long barrows and related structures. Central to the debate were attacks on a number of influential ways of thinking about long barrows that began back in the nineteenth century or earlier and which had coloured a great deal of subsequent discussion. One important issue was, quite simply, what was a long barrow? To get a handle on the arguments about this, however, we need to recap some of the ideas circulating well before 1925.

10 Stuart Piggott's isometric view of the chamber area at West Kennet (WIL 4) following excavations in 1955–6. *Reproduced courtesy of Antiquity Publications*

For John Aubrey and William Stukeley all ancient roughly rectangular barrows were seen as one broad group and considered to be sepulchral monuments. This was also the way that Sir Richard Colt Hoare seems to have viewed them, even though his excavations led him to suspect that within the broad class there were probably several regional types, as his words about Stoney Littleton quoted above seem to suggest. But John Thurnam changed this holistic way of thinking in 1868. In an important and influential paper in the *Archaeologia* he proposed that the long barrows of Wessex, most of which were constructed from earth, rubble and timber, should be seen as 'simple or unchambered long barrows', and these should be differentiated from the stone-built 'chambered long barrows' found in the north and west of the British Isles.[45] Moreover, he proposed that a crucial way of sub-dividing the stone-chambered long barrows was by reference to the way the chambers were entered relative to the shape of the mound – from the sides (lateral chambers) or from the end (terminal chambers). Both these themes remained steady influences on the study of long barrows for over a century, the former being especially significant despite its superficial focus on building materials which were, after all, largely conditioned by the natural resources available within the environment of a given district.

On a wider front, the recognition of prehistoric stone-built tombs and long barrows of various sorts over much of northwest Europe led to various attempts at identifying broad patterns. The foremost Swedish prehistorian of his day, Oscar Montelius (1843–1921), proposed several schemes for classifying Scandinavian megalithic graves between 1876 and 1905,[46] all of which focused on recognizing three main broad categories which can be summarized as:

Dolmens: rectangular, polygonal or almost circular tombs, walled with orthostats and roofed with one capstone. In plan they are entirely closed or have one side open, and in some of this latter type two low stones form a small passage outside the entrance. They stand quite free or in the centre of a low rectangular or round mound, which never reaches up to the level of the capstone.

Passage graves: circular, polygonal or rectangular covered chambers in the centre of round mounds, accessible from the outside of the mound via a narrow passage. The chamber is usually differentiated from the passage in being wider, bigger and demarcated from the passage by protecting stone slabs.

Gallery graves: burial chambers, often rectangular or sub-rectangular in form, the whole of which is normally used for burial, and in which there is no formal approaching element between the entrance and the chamber proper. Such chambers are typically set in a rectangular or trapezoidal mound.

As Glyn Daniel remarked when reviewing this scheme in 1939, its influence has been tremendous, but it has unfortunately led prehistorians to classify monuments not on the basis of their objective morphology, but in so far as they fit in with the Montelian classification.[47] Indeed, in the same year that Crawford published his

LBC, Gordon Childe published the first edition of his wide-ranging work *The dawn of European civilization*. Here he accepted that 'the tombs in question do not belong to a single culture and were not therefore erected and used by a single people. But architectural details recur with such regularity at so many distinct places.'[48] For him the distribution of chambered tombs was accounted for by the spread of a religious idea expressed in architecture and funerary ritual, and for most regions he accepted the translation of Montelius's classificatory system into a simple developmental sequence: dolmens, followed by passage graves, followed in turn by gallery graves or long stone cists as he preferred to call them. Following the principles of soft diffusionism, for which he was well known, Childe suggested that the origins of these structures lay in the Middle East and that the 'culture grows in every aspect poorer as we pass westward and northward from the East Mediterranean to Scotland and Denmark'.[49]

Childe was working on a wide canvas; applying broad principles that work at a European scale to local situations is far more difficult. Thus archaeologists working in eastern England were content to retain the idea of long barrows as a fairly unitary phenomenon; those working in northern and western regions saw what they variously called megalithic tombs or chamber tombs as an extremely diverse phenomenon calling for ever more complicated models and schemes to explain them. For some the stone-built megalithic tombs provided the inspiration for the earthen long barrows and thus pre-dated them,[50] but Stuart Piggott made a strong case for reversing this sequence.[51] Sorting out the long barrows of the Cotswolds, which geographically sit between the earthen mounds of eastern Britain and the stark stone structures of western parts, was widely recognized as critical to resolving issues of chronology, sequence and cultural relationships. It was a task taken up by Glyn Daniel. As we have already seen, in 1937 he proposed that the 100 or so examples known at the time should be considered together as a group – the Cotswold-Severn Group. Following the Montelian view he saw them as gallery graves and, picking up on the earlier studies by Thurnam and Crawford, characterized them as chambered long barrows divisible into two groups: those with terminal chambers and those with lateral chambers. There was little doubt in Daniel's mind that terminal-chambered long barrows were earlier, and that within the Cotswold-Severn region the typological sequence revolved around the degeneration of the terminal-chambered form to the lateral-chambered form, and eventually to those with chambers fully contained within the body of the mound. As gallery graves, these Cotswold-Severn tombs were late in the overall sequence of megalithic tombs in the British Isles and, so far as origins were concerned, parallels were drawn with a small group of tombs in southern Brittany (Keriaval-Herbignac type tombs) which were morphologically very similar to the transepted variety of the terminal-chambered sub-group and therefore stood at the head of the sequence discussed by Daniel in 1937 and 1939,[52] later elaborated in a more diagrammatic form by Grimes *(11)*.[53]

Daryll Forde heavily criticized Daniel's propositions in a paper published in 1940, based largely on his studies of megaliths in northern France and the Atlantic coastlands.[54] Forde found wholly unacceptable the idea of gallery graves

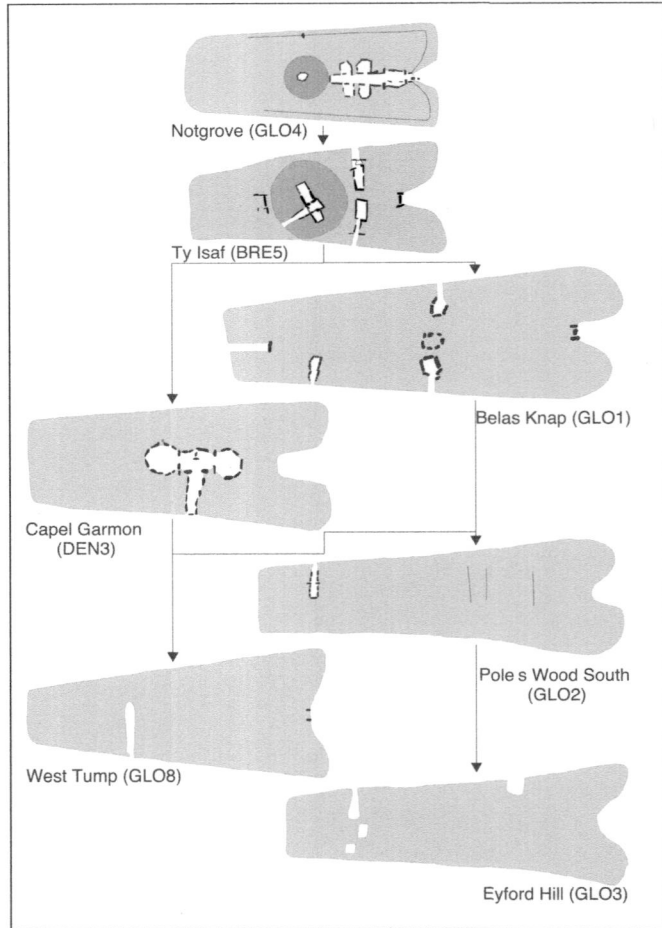

11 Mid-twentieth-century diffusionist scheme for ordering the main recognized kinds of long barrow found in the Cotswold-Severn region. Compare this scheme with illustration 33 in Chapter 4. *After Grimes 1939, fig. 8*

applied to any sites but those of the Seine-Oise-Marne Culture of the Paris Basin and the Swedish long cists. All other tombs he preferred to see as passage graves or collateral descendants of passage graves. Daniel responded the following year with a paper in the *Proceedings of the Prehistoric Society* in which he elaborated his original scheme and consolidated an idea already hinted at by Gordon Childe, Christopher Hawkes, Estyn Evans, Terrance Powell and others, that the megalithic colonization of Europe was the result of two separate movements. One diffused passage graves from their perceived origins among Cretan tholos tombs *(12A)*; the other diffused gallery graves from putative origins amongst the megalithic tombs of Sardinia *(12B)*.[55] This 'Dual Colonization Model' with intrusive monument styles standing at the head of local degenerative sequences remained largely intact for the next 20 years or so. Quite naturally it underlies Daniel's account of the origins of different groups of tombs set out in his book *The prehistoric chamber tombs of England and Wales*, published in 1950, but mainly based on his PhD thesis submitted to Cambridge University in 1940. Rather later it also appears in the discussions set out in his book *The megalithic builders of western Europe*, a volume he generously dedicated to Elsie Clifford and the memories of excavating at Notgrove (GLO 4), Nympsfield (GLO 13) and Rodmarton (GLO 16) in the Cotswolds.[56]

In 1954 Stuart Piggott discussed what he calls the 'Severn-Cotswold long cairns' as if they represented a distinct cultural grouping.[57] In this Piggott perpetuated a view popularized a few years earlier by Gordon Childe who referred to a 'Severn Culture' in his discussion of megalithic religion in his highly influential book entitled *Prehistoric communities of the British Isles*.[58] Both scholars therefore chose to emphasize the place of the River Severn as articulating the distribution of long barrows. It was a preference followed by other writers too, much to the consternation of John Corcoran and the disapproval of Glyn Daniel.[59] Both Childe and Piggott endorsed the degenerative model of tomb evolution and by the time that Grimes came to write up his wartime excavations at Burn Ground the original scheme had been elaborated to no fewer than eight stages leading from the 'classic' transepted gallery graves exemplified by such sites at Notgrove and Wayland's Smithy (BRK 1) through to the putatively very late tomb of Nicholaston (GLA 11) with its central chamber.[60]

As so often happens, of course, when theoretical schemes reach a precariously high level of elaboration they quickly come crashing down as the principles on which they were built get stripped away and replaced. So it was with understanding the megalithic tombs of northern Europe. Through the later 1960s, 1970s and 1980s a number of things changed to alter fundamentally many seemingly unshakable views, four of which deserve special attention.

The radiocarbon revolution
First and foremost was the effect of radiocarbon dating. The initial impact of this was the severing of links that underpinned diffusionist thinking, a story well told by Colin Renfrew in his book *Before civilization*.[61] Some of the megalithic sites in northern Europe were found to be more than 2,000 years older than their supposed progenitors in the central Mediterranean, and what may be described as a 'chronological fault-line' opened up in the network of connections possible between communities living in different parts of Europe *(12C)*. Such a view opened up all sorts of possibilities for regional developments and local sequences — Renfrew suggested five such areas — and led scholars away from the idea that all megaliths must somehow be related.[62] As more radiocarbon dates became available it also became clear that within northern Europe as a whole the construction and use of megalithic tombs and long barrows spanned at least three millennia, but that not all types of monument were contemporary and not all areas used such structures at the same time. The first radiocarbon determination for a sample from a long barrow in the Cotswold-Severn region was published in *Antiquity* for 1965 and related to the site of Wayland's Smithy.[63] The calibrated age for the determination is 3950–3100 BC, confirming a fourth-millennium BC date for the construction of the primary phase of the monument and suggesting that the overlying long barrow was built around the middle of the fourth millennium BC.

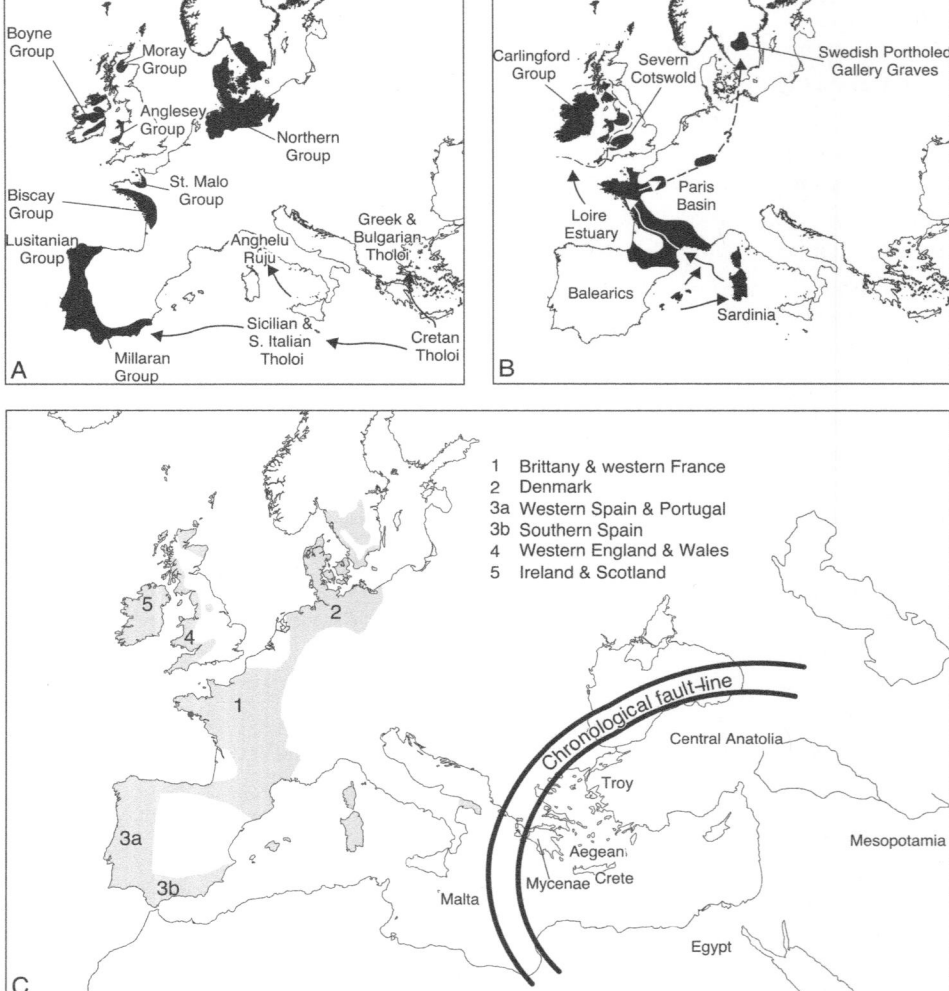

12 Mapping the development of long barrows and chambered tombs in time and space. Glyn Daniel's model of dual colonization for passage graves (A) and gallery graves (B); Colin Renfrew's model of multi-regional independent development separated from east Mediterranean influences (C). A and B: after Daniel 1941, figs 2 and 16; C: after Renfrew 1973a, fig. 21

Multi-period monuments

A second fundamental change was the recognition that while some long barrows and megalithic tombs seemed to have been built as single-phase structures, others clearly developed through several phases on the same spot. Atkinson's excavation at Wayland's Smithy was again pivotal here because he revealed a classic Cotswold-Severn long barrow covering a much smaller and earlier oval barrow. Similar patterns were being revealed elsewhere, not only amongst Cotswold-Severn tombs, leading Terrance Powell and John Corcoran to introduce the idea of multi-phase megaliths in a series of papers published between 1969 and 1973.[64] Together with radiocarbon dating, these stratigraphic relationships began to add real weight to emergent regional sequences, and further challenged the simple degenerative schemes of the diffusionist school. Closely related was the realization that when developing models and schemes in order to explain spatial and chronological variations between monuments it was unwise to rely on results from antiquarian excavations, excavations of heavily damaged sites, or visible features at unexcavated sites. High-quality data from fresh excavations were needed in order to build credible and robust models.

Fluid typologies

The third area of changed thinking concerns breaking out of the straitjacket imposed by rigid and overly elaborate classifications. Ian Kinnes and others showed that a tremendous range of burial monuments, mounds and enclosures of various sorts were constructed in Britain during the fourth and third millennia BC, and that many shared constructional features and perhaps had overlapping functions.[65] Conventional typologies that focused almost exclusively on construction materials were found to be inadequate to deal with the evident diversity.[66] Some structurally comparable monuments were found to have been made of stone, wood and earth in whatever combinations suited the builders. In place of the sub-divisions of earlier schemes, two very broad groupings of monuments became recognized: round structures and long structures. These provide the basis for many recent analyses which have tended to focus on the way people built and used barrows, the way in which space inside and out was structured and organized, and the possible meanings that might have been attached to different parts of the structure. As a result, stone-chambered long barrows and earthen long barrows with timber chambers have been reunified in a way anticipated by some scholars for decades but neatly summed up by Paul Ashbee in the introduction to the second edition of his masterful survey of *The earthen long barrow in Britain*:

> A decade ago the term 'earthen long barrows' was used to denote long mounds which covered rectangular wooden chambers, often paved, usually with a gabled or pitched roof supported by wooden uprights, at the proximal end of a rectangular or trapezoidal, timber-built, enclosure which has retained chalk rubble, its collapse resulting in the characteristic long mound . . . Although broadly similar to their stone compeers, these seemed distinct enough to justify the sub-division set down, more than a century ago, by Thurnam. Separation will undoubtedly continue but now it can be seen that the boundary is blurred and that *earthen* long barrows are only one constituent of a series of long monuments, widespread in Britain and Ireland.[67]

Local sequences and regional traditions

Finally, as local sequences for different parts of the British Isles began to be worked out, and absolute dates determined for the wide range of structures now recognized, it has become increasingly clear that long barrows were rarely the first kind of monument to be built in an area. In most cases they were preceded by a diverse range of generally smaller structures. Moreover, most true long barrows seem to have been built and used over a relatively short period from about 3800 BC down to about 3200 BC. The idea of a 'long barrow horizon' was first mooted back in the 1970s, but its utility has strengthened as more radiocarbon determinations on samples of charcoal and bone from an ever-wider range of sites have become available. John Corcoran recognized something of this diversity in his magisterial synthesis of the Cotswold-Severn Group presented to a symposium published as *Megalithic enquiries in the west of Britain* in 1969.[68] He argued that 'it was too complex to discuss one type in isolation, and that it was necessary to examine all relevant evidence from the region'.[69] Glyn Daniel disputed this position, insisting that

> my original definition of this group was morphological and cultural: to include portal chambers like the two Sweyne's Howes in Gower, or Arthur's Stone in that same delightful Glamorgan peninsula, is, intentionally or unintentionally, to confuse a carefully defined archaeological group with the limits of an arbitrarily defined geographical region. It is to make nonsense of what has been written before.[70]

Nonsense or not, the complexity of long barrow development, and the relationships that can be seen among a range of monuments in time and space, mean that not to follow Corcoran's lead would risk missing several critical scenes in the unfolding drama of monument construction and use by early farming communities in the west of England and southeast Wales.

LATE TWENTIETH-CENTURY INVESTIGATIONS

Between the early 1960s and the turn of the millennium nearly a dozen long barrows within the Cotswold-Severn region were excavated on a substantial scale, and a handful of others were subject to small-scale investigations.[71] In north Wiltshire, the long barrows at Beckhampton Road (WIL 27) and South Street (WIL 36) were excavated between 1964 and 1967 by Isobel Smith and John Evans respectively. Like the Horslip barrow (WIL 30) excavated earlier by Paul Ashbee, both these mounds appeared not to have covered any burial deposits or chamber structures, although their poor condition (South Street in particular had been heavily ploughed) may have militated against finding ephemeral structures. However, in 1989 a team led by Alasdair Whittle did find traces of a destroyed stone chamber in the equally badly damaged Millbarrow (WIL 11).

To the east, on the Berkshire Downs, excavations at Wayland's Smithy by Richard Atkinson and Stuart Piggott in 1962–3 also revealed unexpected results in the form of a two-period monument discussed in the previous section. The following year, 1964, John Wymer made nine cuttings into the Lambourn long barrow (BRK 2) to show that it probably had a simple timber chamber at its eastern end.

On the Cotswolds, Helen O'Neil undertook a large-scale excavation at Sale's Lot (GLO 94) in 1965 in the expectation that the site would be bulldozed as part of an agricultural improvement scheme. At the same time, Don Benson began work at Ascott-under-Wychwood (OXF 6), a project that lasted five years and involved the total excavation of the site. The structure revealed here included a closed chamber comprising a line of seven separate cells arranged transversely across the barrow towards its distal end. In 1974 the well-known site at Nympsfield (GLO 13) was excavated for the third time, on this occasion by Alan Saville, prior to being restored for public display in a small country park managed by Gloucestershire County Council *(13)*. This work and the problems faced a decade earlier at Sale's Lot helped draw attention to the increasing impact of arable cultivation on Cotswold long barrows. Following a series of surveys,[72] the pair of barrows at Hazleton in the central Cotswolds was selected for study. Hazleton North (GLO 54) was completely excavated between 1979 and 1983 and is now the most comprehensively studied and fully reported example in the region *(8D)*. Hazleton South (GLO 33) was sampled in 1980, work that was reported alongside that of its partner in the same field.[73]

To the west, among the Black Mountain tombs, a previously unknown long barrow came to light in 1972 at Penywyrlod (BRE 14) when groundworks for the construction of an agricultural building broke into a large unrecorded mound. This proved to be the biggest long barrow ever recorded in Wales, 60m long, 25m wide and at the time still standing 3m high. Its discovery highlighted just how partial and inadequate our knowledge of the distribution of these sites probably

13 Nympsfield, Frocester (GLO 13). View of the forecourt and chambers under excavation in 1974. Looking west. Scales each total 2m. *Photograph by Alan Saville. Copyright reserved*

was. Subsequent excavations in 1972–3 by Hubert Savory revealed at least three well-preserved lateral chambers along the east side of the mound. Later, in 1977–9, Bill Britnell substantially excavated another tomb with later chambers, Gwernvale (BRE 7) in the Usk valley, the site where the scientific examination of Cotswold-Severn long barrows began nearly two centuries earlier.

In addition to new results from excavation, the contribution to long barrow studies from aerial photography and field survey has increased too. Several previously unrecognized long barrows were identified on the Cotswolds between 1960 and 1990,[74] and mention has already been made of the discovery in June 1972 of the Penywyrlod long barrow near Talgarth.[75] Simple field observation accounts for the recognition of a long barrow beside the Ridgeway southwest of the Uffington White Horse (BRK 5) that had been partly investigated by E. Martin Atkins in 1862 but then 'lost' in the archaeological literature.[76] In lowland landscapes, especially the apparently barrowless river valleys of the upper Thames and Severn, aerial photography has an important role to play and the ongoing National Mapping Programme will undoubtedly provide evidence of previously unrecognized long barrows in England.[77] One such site at Drayton (OXF 21) was recognized in 1978 following the inspection of photographs taken by J.K. St Joseph of the Cambridge Committee for Aerial Photography.[78] The dry summer of 1995 provided the surprise find of a previously unrecognized long barrow at Lockeridge (WIL 39) right in the heart of the well-studied Avebury area of the north Wessex Downs.[79] Aerial photographs were also responsible for the recognition of a long barrow at Lower Luggy, Berriew, in Montgomeryshire (MNT 3) on the floodplain of the River Severn near Welshpool. Subsequent trial excavations and surveys by Alex Gibson and others confirmed the site as a long barrow some 60m long and 20m wide, with a timber façade.[80] Not only does this example significantly extend the distribution of the long barrows in the region, but it also serves to underline the apparent diversity of construction techniques used. Geophysical surveys played an important role in defining the Lower Luggy long barrow, and high-resolution geophysical surveys have also made useful contributions to the definition of quarries and other features around long barrows on the Cotswolds.[81] It is a technique that deserves to be applied to as many examples as possible.

By the year 2000, excavations of one sort or another had taken place at 42 per cent of the long barrows known in the Cotswold-Severn region; nearly a quarter of those investigated had been examined more than once, and 11 per cent had been examined three times or more *(7B and 7C)*. All of these excavations, and the surveys too, highlight the complexity of the long barrows both in terms of their construction and use, and in terms of the long history of activity represented at many sites. In one sense many of these recent studies served to confirm, elaborate and document through intensive excavation and careful sampling some of the things that had already been glimpsed in earlier operations. But, more importantly, these recent studies emphasize how any understanding of long barrows in the region needs to be set against a wider background of changing customs and traditions, and how unwise it is to see long barrows in isolation from earlier, later and contemporary structures elsewhere in the landscape.

DIVERSITY AND THE QUEST FOR ORIGINS

As a result of changing perspectives and the steady accumulation of high-quality data about specific sites and overall distributions, the question of origins and the relationships between monuments at different times and in different areas has become incredibly complicated. So far as northwest Europe is concerned, the breaking of putative links with the Mediterranean world meant that essentially local origins had to be sought. But while the processualist thinking of the 1970s brand of 'New Archaeology' accepted the idea of multiple origins creating diversity in the structures that communities produced, there was an almost pathological fanaticism for finding a single model that could explain how and why various kinds of monument developed where they did. The core idea that emerged focused on the idea of parallel developments in relation to parallel pressures. As Colin Renfrew suggested, 'it requires simply that a particular set of conditions existed in the Atlantic region at this time, conditions which were not seen elsewhere in Europe, and that these favoured the construction of stone monuments by the small-scale societies of the time'.[82] In reviewing the various proposals that have been put forward to help solve this problem Chris Scarre has usefully condensed thinking down into two broad models:[83]

The Bandkeramic Hypothesis, advocated especially by Ian Hodder,[84] Serge Cassen,[85] Christine Boujot,[86] Richard Bradley,[87] Mark Patton[88] and others, sees all long barrows and other kinds of megalithic tomb ultimately deriving from Bandkeramic influences and the spread of early farmers northward and westward from the Paris Basin.

The Atlantic Hypothesis, advocated especially by Colin Renfrew,[89] Chris Scarre[90] and others, proposes that during the fifth millennium BC a number of local monument-building traditions became established amongst indigenous populations, and that these provided the inspiration for the construction of larger structures, the impetus for this being social tensions between essentially hunter-gatherer and farmer communities along the Atlantic seaboard.

Both models have utility, the Bandkeramic Hypothesis providing a comfortable fit with evidence for the distribution of long mounds, while the Atlantic Hypothesis seems to provide a better explanation for the appearance of the internal chambers and structures within both long and round mounds. Indeed, Ian Kinnes attempted to integrate these seemingly conflicting positions by emphasizing the varied geography of Europe's Atlantic coast and the need to recognize that social distance between communities, and physical distances over diverse terrain, mean that people living in different areas are naturally exposed to different influences *(14)*.[91] Similarly, Andrew Sherratt spoke of 'a meeting of the indigenous and the exotic'[92] in the creation of many kinds of structure. But all these approaches still suffer from the processualist malaise of trying to collapse long periods of time, traditions spread over wide geographical areas, and varied social conditions, into a single

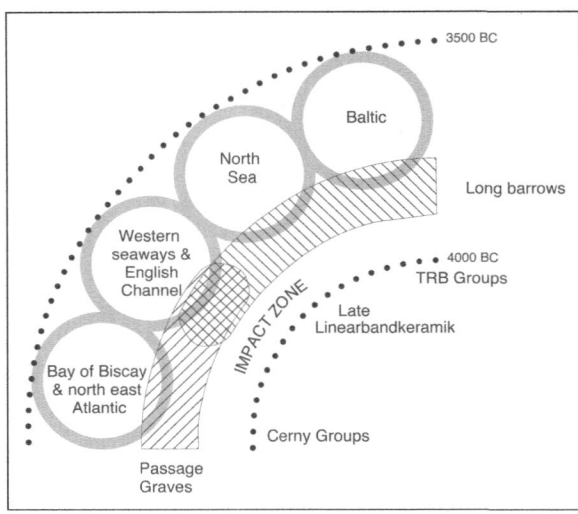

14 Ian Kinnes's model showing the effects of east–west and north–south influences on the development and distribution of long barrows and passage graves along the Atlantic margin of Europe. After Kinnes 1982, fig. 3, with amendments

explanation. Attention tended to focus on the homogeneity of the phenomenon that has come to be known as megalithic architecture, yet even a superficial scan of the available corpora of sites reveals very considerable heterogeneity. The problem can perhaps be turned on its head and examined from another perspective.

Instead of emphasizing similarities, focus on diversity. To do this it is important to develop understandings of local distributions, to establish patterns in the local and regional co-existence of monuments, and to sort out sequences or construction cycles which illustrate the changing preferences in monument structure among particular communities. With such information to hand it is possible to develop a more nuanced and socially specific perspective in which recurrent preferences and consistent patterns of change within and between adjacent areas come to be seen as elements of a network. Connections and links between communities in different areas, or across the centuries in the same area, come in and out of focus to provide a dynamic force behind the accumulation and selection of ideas, beliefs, understandings and referencing that underpins the creation by each individual community of a distinctive monumental structure.

One area that has long been recognized as potentially significant for the development of monument building in and around the Cotswolds is Brittany and northwest France. Set at the other end of a network of communications based on travel across the Celtic Sea and through the Western Approaches rather than overland, the potential for contact between communities in these two regions is considerable. Investigations over the last 50 years or so in France allow the main trends in monument construction to be identified and debated.[93] Christine Boujot and Serge Cassen, on the basis mainly of the fruits of their investigations in the Morbihan, have proposed one highly plausible scheme.[94] As originally set out, their sequence starts with small cists and standing stones (*menhirs*) in the early fifth millennium BC, followed by a series of long rectangular and trapezoidal structures with closed central cists (*tertres*), followed in the late fifth and early fourth millennium BC by the familiar passage graves with round or polygonal chambers in round or long mounds and later still the transepted, angled and T-shaped passage graves in long mounds. Finally, there are elongated gallery graves (*alleés couvertes*) of the later third millennium BC that link the area with the Paris Basin. However, Chris Scarre sees some elements of the cycle rather differently, suggesting that the long mounds always seem to be secondary to small round and oval structures whose ancestry is to be found amongst the earlier Mesolithic traditions of the area.[95] Revised in this way, a series of rather small and diverse monuments would characterize the mid-fifth millennium BC, with *tertres* appearing towards the end of the fifth millennium at the head of a growing interest in long mounds within which were a variety of chamber structures whose origins are both local and ancient.

Brittany and Normandy are just two amongst many areas where local sequences have become clear in recent years. Taking a broader view, the beginnings and ends of all the many local sequences around northwest Europe are as spread in time as they are in space, but they all include horizons during which traditions in one particular area connect with others elsewhere around the Atlantic coastlands and islands. Equally, they all show a degree of innovation and adaptation in the way that general architectural styles as well as specific features are combined and configured. In some cases these may be indigenous developments; in other cases ideas were brought in from adjacent contact zones perhaps through such mechanisms as alliance structures and exchange systems. As Scarre has emphasized, the early stages in the sequences seem to relate to recognizable transitions between hunter-gatherer lifestyles and the integration of agricultural elements within local subsistence economies. But whether these monuments were instruments of conversion,[96] or the consequences of changed relationships between communities and the worlds they created for themselves, is more problematic. Finding the early stages of a local sequence for the Cotswold-Severn region, and exploring the networks behind the patterns, are therefore crucial to any consideration of long barrows proper and provide the focus of the next chapter.

3

BEFORE THE LONG BARROWS

In the beginning, before the appearance of long barrows, there were, scattered across the British Isles, many different kinds of relatively small stone, earth and timber structures. These represent the first adventures into monumental architecture by communities of the later fifth and early fourth millennia BC. Traditionally, these monuments are viewed as an essential 'invention' of early farming groups, physically representing new views of the landscape. Now it seems increasingly possible that some at least were built by hunter-gatherer communities. Inherently difficult to date, and tricky to recognize except when well preserved, these putatively early structures were often open to the elements and continued to attract attention through the fourth millennium and beyond. What nails down their early date is that some became incorporated into later structures in such a way that stratigraphic sequence rather than associated finds provides evidence of order and age. Overall, many long barrows in the Cotswolds and surrounding areas seal earlier structures that can be matched with freestanding counterparts that never became modified in this way. We should not, however, rule out the possibility that some conservative groups continued building and using these early types of monument well beyond the time when other nearby communities were motivated to build long barrows.

At least five main kinds of early structure can be identified scattered across the Cotswold-Severn region *(15)*, each of which is discussed in the following sections. Some have much wider distributions than the geographical region being considered here, and in a few cases the greatest density of such monuments lies elsewhere entirely. Within the Cotswolds and surrounding areas it is notable that the distribution of early monuments is highly clustered within distinct topographic units, and it may be suggested that monument building first broke out in a few discrete areas. But did the communities in each area all build the same kind of structure or were they geographically mixed? What influences, if any, did communities draw on as inspiration for the design of their monuments? Do these early structures relate to wider networks of contact and exchange? And how do they compare with recognized monuments elsewhere in northwest Europe?

Before the Long Barrows

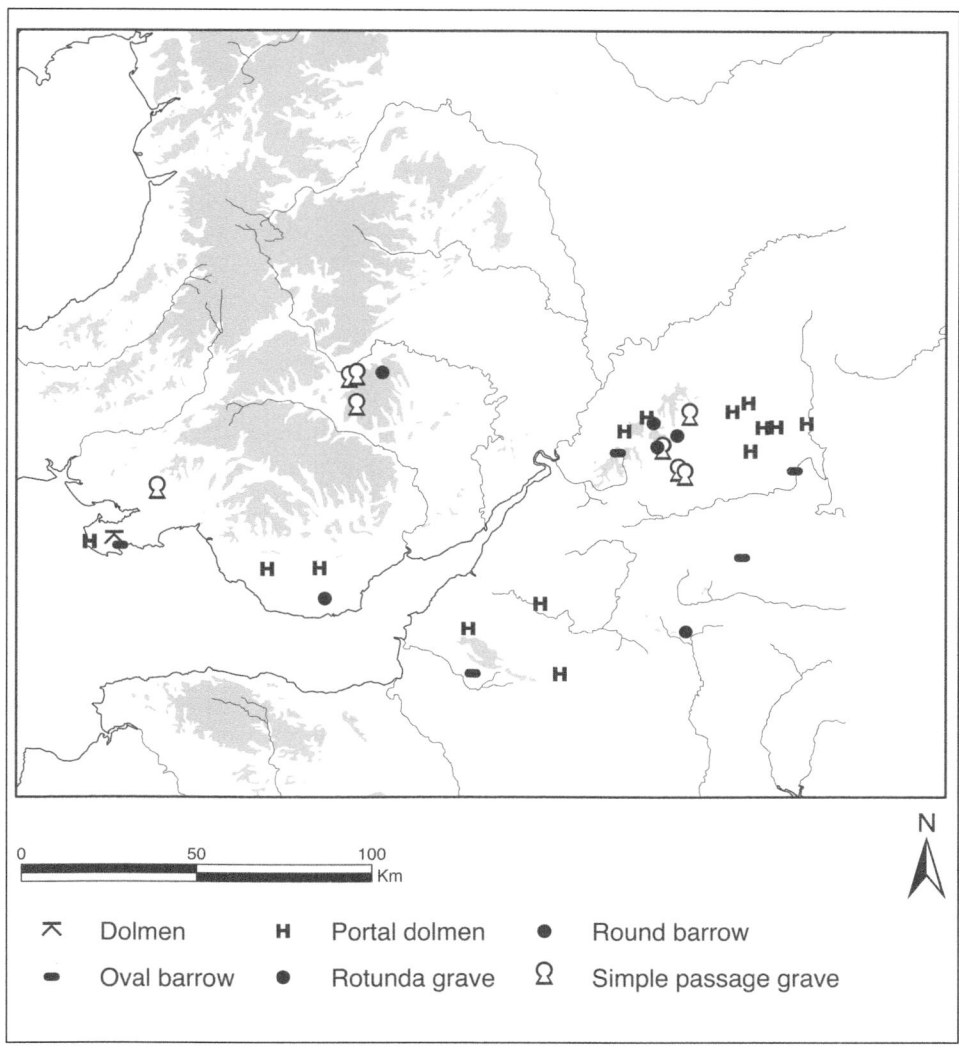

15 Distribution of pre-long barrow and early style monuments within the Cotswold-Severn region. Land over 244m OD is shaded

DOLMENS

The origin of the word 'dolmen' is much disputed, but here it is applied following the usage of Oscar Montelius to refer to a large block of stone that has been raised up above the ground, supported on smaller upright pillar-stones or chocks, forming the capstone or cover over a small more-or-less closed space or chamber below.[1] Traditionally, it is the chamber element of these structures that has been emphasized, but more recently attention has focused on the raised stone and its possible significance. Chris Tilley, for example, has argued that on Bodmin Moor natural topographic features of the landscape were emphasized and sometimes reproduced in order to create symbolic links between people and the world in which they lived.[2] Similarities between the form of constructed monuments and nearby natural landforms have also been noted in several other parts of Atlantic Europe,[3] with commensurate emphasis on the appropriation of natural places. The symbolic meanings and mythologies that attached to such places, and the inherent ambiguities thus created between the 'cultural' and the 'natural',[4] are matters that deserve further study. By implication, however, the range of recorded archaeology that can be considered under the general heading of dolmens has expanded well beyond the 'sub-megalithic tombs' and 'demi-dolmens' of conventional typologies to include 'propped stones' and a whole raft of structures for which no suitable terminology currently exists but which are essentially raised boulders and rearranged slabs of various kinds.

The majority of recorded dolmens lie along the coastlands of the Irish Sea and the Atlantic fringe of the British Isles, with some of the finest clustered in southwest Wales and in County Sligo on the west coast of Ireland. The Welsh material has been discussed by Frances Lynch,[5] and more recently by Vicki Cummings, who suggests that these sites were built in places with views to particular mountains.[6] A large group around Carrowmore, Sligo, was the subject of extensive excavations by Göran Burenhult and the Swedish Archaeological Expedition between 1977 and 1982, part of a quest to identify the origins of megalithic tombs in Europe. Although some are certainly simple passage graves (see below), many of the monuments at Carrowmore are dolmens in the sense defined here. When excavated it is clear that each dolmen sits at the centre of a low round mound or platform with a well-defined edge. It is especially interesting to note the range of early dates and an essentially hunter-gatherer context for them.[7]

The only certain dolmen in the Cotswold-Severn region lies in the far west of the area at Maen Ceti (GLA 3), popularly known as Arthur's Stone, on the Gower peninsula *(16)*. Here, on the brow of the northern slope of Cefn Bryn, a massive boulder of local conglomerate, estimated to weigh 30–35 tonnes, is supported on ten small blocks of similar stone *(17)*. The raised boulder is 4m long by 3m wide

16 Arthur's Stone (GLA 3). General view of the dolmen looking east. *Photograph by Timothy Darvill, April 1988*

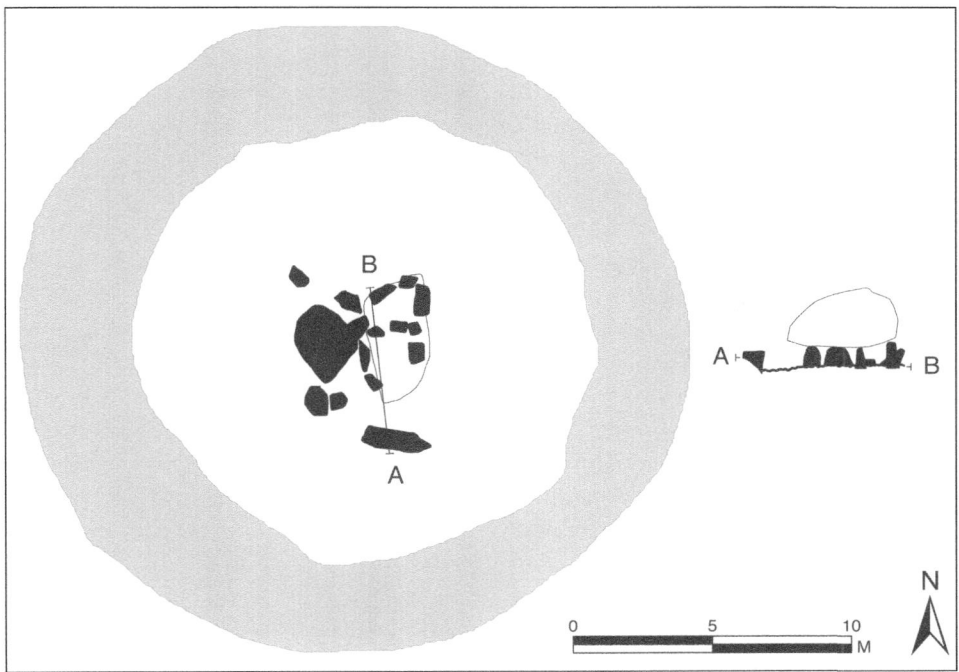

17 Arthur's Stone (GLA 3), a dolmen on the Gower Peninsula of south Wales. After RCAHMW 1976, fig. 6

by 2.2m high; about a quarter of the original stone has broken off and now lies shattered in three pieces on the ground to the west.[8] The method of construction is not clear, but presumably the boulder was either lifted slightly so the props could be inserted, or, more likely, the ground underneath and around about was dug away and the props inserted as the soil and rock were removed. Whichever, the stone stands proud of the ground surface within a shallow hollow about 19m across. Around the edge of the hollow is a low stony bank, 23m in external diameter and about 4m wide, perhaps formed from rubble removed from below and around the elevated boulder. No excavations have taken place at the site and no finds have been reported. There is no certain evidence that Arthur's Stone, or indeed any other dolmen, was built primarily as a burial monument; they may be constructions that simply emphasize some special significance attaching to the place or the elevated stone.

PORTAL DOLMENS

An elaboration of the basic dolmen is the 'portal dolmen', also widely recognized in western parts of the British Isles for many years, especially in the lands around the Irish Sea. Described by Frances Lynch as 'confident structures of surprisingly uniform appearance',[9] portal dolmens essentially comprise a large block of stone (typically a boulder or slab) set atop four or more orthostats, three of which are usually set in an H-shaped or 'portal' formation. Traditionally, this portal setting is seen as the focus or front of the monument, a stone doorway to another world. In this, the capstone formed the lintel, the side-stones of the H formed the jambs and the transversely set cross-slab (often missing on poorly preserved examples) was the door itself.[10] The idea that the portal was the focus of the monument is enhanced by its being the tallest element, with the capstone sloping backwards and downwards from it. The stone structure is typically surrounded by a low circular stone platform, sometimes recessed to form what might be termed a 'forecourt' immediately in front of the portal setting. Portal dolmens sometimes form the primary element of multi-phase monuments, as for example at Dyffryn Ardudwy, Merioneth,[11] and Pentre Ifan, Pembrokeshire.[12] They are widely recognized as being amongst the earliest styles of megalithic architecture in the British Isles, even though none has been adequately dated. Several authors have sought the origins of portal dolmens in timber structures in the lands bordering the Irish Sea, but no very convincing prototypes have been found and the origin of these curious structures remains obscure.[13]

Portal dolmens are represented in three clusters within the Cotswolds and surrounding areas, most notably in the north Cotswolds *(15)*.[14] Here the classic example is the Whispering Knights (OXF 1) within the group of monuments focused on the Rollright Stones on a narrow limestone ridge overlooking the headwaters of the River Evenlode *(18)*. The massive portal setting stands 2.4m high, with the broad closing slab facing to the south-southeast. The capstone, which measures approximately 2.5m long by 1.75m wide by 0.7m thick, has fallen and now lies behind the portal setting; the fourth orthostat, originally supporting the capstone at the northwest end, has also collapsed *(19A)*. Excavations in 1983 revealed slight traces of a surrounding mound which accords with antiquarian accounts suggesting a low round mound or platform about 20m across.[15]

Five other portal dolmens can be recognized in the northeast Cotswolds with a fair degree of certainty, all with rather similar names: the Hoare Stone at Enstone (OXF 2), the Hoar Stone at Langley (OXF 5), the Hawkestone at Spelbury (OXF 7) and the Hoar Stone at Steeple Barton (OXF 4). Excavations at a mound on Adlestrop Hill (GLO 44) in 1935-6 revealed another probable portal dolmen,[16] although the chamber appears to have been heavily disturbed in Roman times and some of the orthostats and the capstone had been removed *(19B)*. As at the Whispering Knights, a low oval mound or platform surrounded the portal dolmen itself. At Adlestrop, however, some of the fill of the chamber was preserved and this proved to contain the disarticulated remains of at least eight people including an adult male, two other adults, an adolescent and four children.

It is tempting to interpret the H-shaped portal setting (the so-called false-entrance or false-portal) in the forecourt of Belas Knap (GLO 1) as the remains of a portal dolmen that was later incorporated into a long barrow. The lintel stone seen today is a nineteenth-century replacement, but when the original lintel was lifted during excavations in 1863 the skeletons of a young man of less than 20 years

18 Above The Whispering Knights, Rollright (OXF 1). View of the portal dolmen looking northwestwards at the H-shaped portal setting. Don Benson provides a scale. *Photograph by Timothy Darvill, September 1979*

19 Right Portal dolmens in the Cotswold-Severn region.
A: Whispering Knights (OXF 1); B: Adlestrop Hill (GLO 44); C: Sweyne's Howe South (GLA 2); D: Sweyne's Howe North (GLA 1); E: Cae'rarfau (GLA 8); F: Murtry Hill (SOM 8)

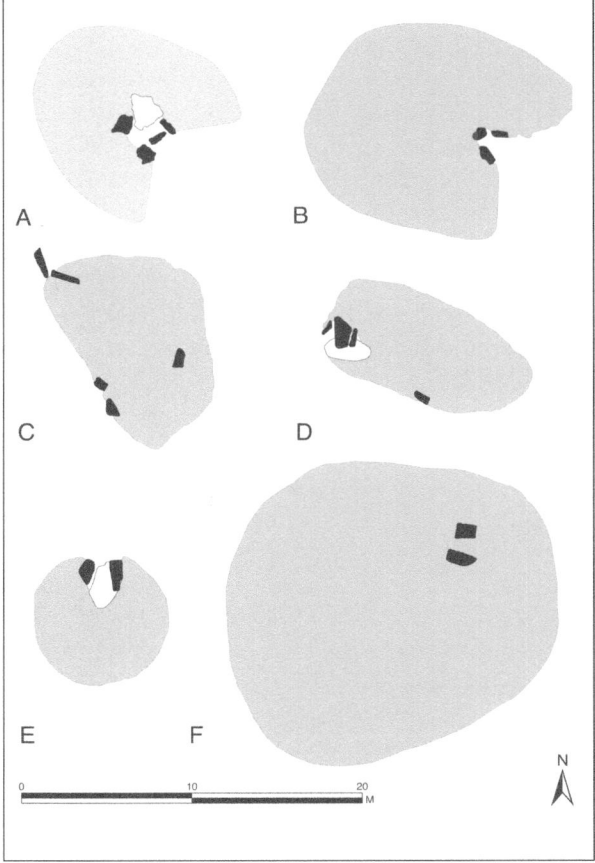

of age and five children variously aged between six months and eight years were found within the rubble behind the portal. Also present were bones of horse and pig, several flint flakes, including a serrated blade, and fragments of coarse pottery.[17] Curiously, the biometric characteristics of the adult skull were quite unlike those of the skulls from the other (putatively later) chambers in the long barrow at Belas Knap,[18] perhaps endorsing the view that the portal dolmen was an independent structure and just possibly contained the remains of a population different from that later responsible for the long barrow. Another possible portal dolmen is at the Knap in Cheltenham, known only through the distinctive placename and an early nineteenth-century depiction on a painting by T. Westall that now hangs in Cheltenham Art Gallery and Museum *(20)*.[19]

Southwards, there are two possible portal dolmens in Somerset. At the Waterstone (SOM 5), overlooking the valley of the River Yeo, there are three fallen orthostats and a capstone. Two of the orthostats would have made sizable portal jambs. The name of the monument derives from the fact that the capstone has a hollow in the upper surface in which rain collects, but whether this effect was appreciated by the builders and users of the site is unknown. At Murtry Hill (SOM 8) the remaining complete portal stone stands 3m high while a second broken example is leaning against it *(19F)*. The site was excavated in 1803-4 and again in 1920. As a result of these later excavations H. St George Gray suggested that some of the stones had been re-erected in 1804, but this is not widely accepted.[20] Both excavations recovered quantities of human skeletal remains, the finds in 1920 being just west of the portal setting. It is a site that deserves a thorough re-examination as it is probably a multi-period barrow.

West of the Severn four probable portal dolmens have been recognized, two on the Gower peninsula, one above the Ely valley and one in the valley of the River Ogmore. At Sweyne's Howe on the Gower a pair of portal dolmens (GLA 1 and GLA 2) stand less than 100m apart on the east side of Rhossili Common. Both are ruinous and much disturbed *(19C and D)*. However, the portals can be recognized, and closing slabs and capstones are present, albeit displaced. Slightly oval mounds form low platforms around the stones. Even less well preserved are Cae'rarfau (GLA 8; *19E*) and Coedparcgarw (GLA 7) where a fallen stone now supports the dislodged capstone.

OVAL BARROWS

Originally one of the categories of barrow defined by Stukeley in the mid-eighteenth century, the class was revised by John Thurnam following excavations at Winterbourne Stoke Down near Stonehenge in 1869.[21] Since that time the idea of oval barrows has had a chequered history, with examples sometimes being confused with short long barrows. Peter Drewett reaffirmed the integrity and validity of the class as a result of excavations in Sussex,[22] with excavations by Richard Bradley at Barrow Hills, Abingdon, in 1983–4 adding further dimensions.[23] It is now apparent that building oval barrows was a very long-lived

20 The Knap, St James's Square, Cheltenham (GLO 98), a possible portal dolmen depicted in a painting of about 1830 by T. Westall. Reproduced courtesy of Cheltenham Art Gallery and Museum. Copyright reserved

tradition spanning the early fourth millennium through into the later third millennium BC. Within the Cotswolds and surrounding areas there are five recorded examples, all discovered through excavation *(15)*. Others no doubt await discovery in due course.

At Wayland's Smithy (BRK 1), an oval barrow (known as Wayland's Smithy I) was found to be the primary monument on the site during excavations in 1962–3 by Richard Atkinson and Stuart Piggott. It was sealed beneath the much larger long barrow and dated to before 3950–3100 BC. The oval barrow was 14m long and 7m wide, its limits marked by a kerb of stones *(21A)*. The mound was constructed of earth and rubble taken from a pair of flanking ditches. In the southern half of the mound was a timber chamber, believed by Atkinson to have been tent-like in appearance, represented archaeologically as two large D-shaped postholes 4.6m apart with a pavement of sarsen slabs between. Linear banks of sarsen boulders either side of the pavement suggest the position of the walls of the chamber structure; the upright timber posts at each end would have supported the ridge and may well have extended upwards through the mound as ornamental markers. Two slightly splayed rows of postholes southwest of the chamber seem to be the remains of an entrance porch. On the sarsen pavement within the chamber was what Atkinson described as 'a dense and confused mass of human bones'.[24] After careful study it was revealed that a minimum of 14 people in various states of completeness were represented. The most disturbed and incomplete skeletons

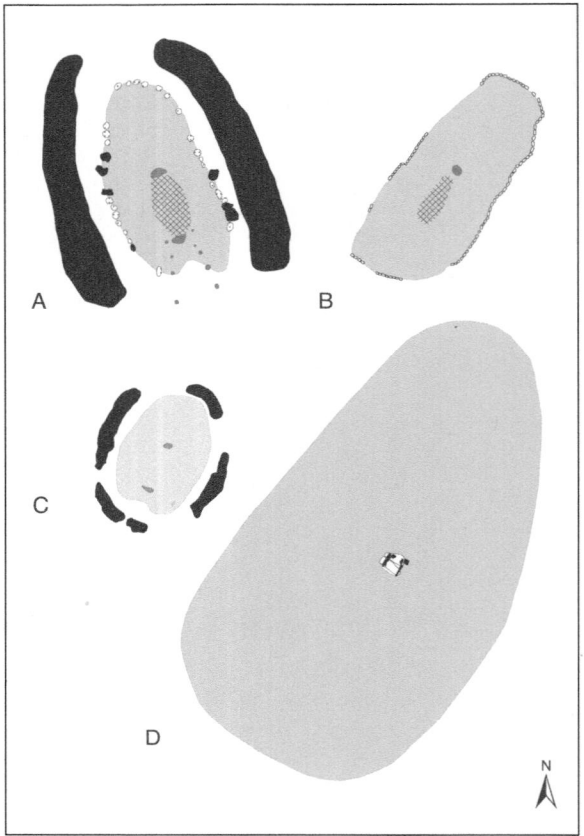

21 Oval barrows in the Cotswold-Severn region. A: Wayland's Smithy I (BRK 1); B: Priddy (SOM 16); C: New Wintles Farm; D: Nicholaston (GLA 11)

lay at the bottom of the deposit while in the upper layers more or less complete sets of remains existed in fair articulation, suggesting the deposition within the chamber of complete corpses. It is likely that, over time, decomposing corpses were moved about to make space for new additions, while some bones were removed altogether. Of the 14 burials, nine seem to have been males, three or four were females and one was a child aged about ten. The adults were mainly aged between 20 and 40. Three leaf-shaped arrowheads in the deposit, each found in contact with a pelvis, may have been lodged in corpses at the time of burial; they may indeed have been the cause of death of the poor individuals.

The sequence of events and the nature of the monument at Wayland's Smithy I have been the subject of much discussion and speculation since the original excavation. Alasdair Whittle has plausibly proposed that initially the site was a small shrine or exposure site, marked by a platform between two large posts. Whether burials were deposited there is not known, although any that were would presumably have been exposed to the elements and attacked by wild animals. It is more likely that the timber chamber was built fairly soon after the posts were set up, although its original form remains problematic. Derek Simpson questioned the proposed ridge-tent structure and prompted a debate that served to open up a number of interesting possibilities.[25] Ian Kinnes subsequently published a highly attractive alternative comprising an embanked area, roofed with planks and framed at either end by the D-shaped posts.[26] A more box-like structure, perhaps partly projecting above the mound and possibly accessible from above by way of a removable roof, is now the favoured interpretation. Whittle prefers to see this as free standing for a period, before the addition of the oval mound.[27] However, given the materials used and the poverty of evidence for longevity represented by silting, collapse and rebuilding, a short chronology involving the construction of the whole thing over a few weeks or months followed by perhaps a century or so of use for burial seems preferable. What is especially interesting about Wayland's Smithy I is the symbolism inherent to its form and construction. The two large upright posts flanking the burial area were halves of a split tree trunk, the flat inner split faces set opposite each other across the stone platform. In this respect the dead lay within a tree, in the same way that, elsewhere, big slabs of stone physically and perhaps metaphorically embraced the corpse.[28]

Rather similar to Wayland's Smithy I is the barrow at New Wintles Farm excavated in advance of gravel extraction in the summer of 1968 *(21C)*. It was poorly preserved following years of ploughing and erosion, and the excavations revealed a circuit of irregular quarry ditches that defined an area about 12m long by 10m wide. Within was a pair of pits/postholes 3.5m apart flanked on either side by a shallow gully that perhaps held the walls of a wooden chamber. Fragments of burnt bone were found in and around the features forming the central setting.[29]

A third possible oval barrow with a timber chamber is known high on the Mendips near Priddy (SOM 16). Excavated first in 1816 by the Revd Skinner and again in 1928 by the Bristol University Spelaeological Society, very little of the rather confusing discoveries was published until the 1970s.[30] More recently, a reworking of some of the original records by Jodie Lewis suggests a certain amount of pre-barrow activity involving hearths and a pit, followed by the construction of a roughly oval mound 22m by 10m, bounded by closely set stones forming a sort of kerb, at the southwest end of which was what appears to have been a rectangular chamber *(21B)*.[31] One probable posthole was found at the northeast end, but the array of trenches would have missed anything similar at the southwest. The floor of the chamber was at least partly paved; the remains of at least two individuals were discovered, one cremated, the other not.

The timber chambers found in these three oval barrows find parallels in the timber chambers of many putatively later long barrows in southern and eastern England and eastern Scotland. Similar chambers also occur in round barrows of the early third millennium BC in northern Britain, as at Pitnacree, Perthshire.[32] On a wider front, comparable timber chambers, known as Konens Høj type graves, have been recorded in Denmark, for example at Brøndum, Søgård and Konens Høj, all in Jutland.[33] At Søgård the timber chambers lay within a multi-period barrow in which the earliest phase comprised small oval mounds covering timber chambers. These were later covered by a mound 45m long by 13m wide and later still by an even longer mound.[34] The oval mounds and timber chambers at these Danish sites belong to the middle TRB period, broadly the early fourth millennium BC,[35] and thus seem to be part of a widespread tradition that is broadly contemporary on both sides of the North Sea. Exchanges between the two areas are demonstrated by the presence in Britain of a few Scandinavian four-faced flint axes.

In the Cotswolds and westward there are other oval barrows, but these contain rather different kinds of internal features. In Gloucestershire, excavations at Crickley Hill revealed what Philip Dixon described as a 'banana-barrow', sealed beneath the inner bank of the causewayed enclosure on the site.[36] This monument comprised an enclosure about 8m long, bounded by a series of quarry pits each up to 2m across, and, as the name suggests, was banana-shaped in plan. Spoil from the pits had seemingly been piled up in the central area, but was removed when the causewayed enclosure was built. The purpose of the structure is unclear, although it may have been a burial monument and certainly seems to fall within the wider tradition of early oval barrows. Finally, mention may be made of the extraordinary site of Nicholaston (GLA 11) on Cefn Bryn, the hilly backbone of the Gower peninsula in southeast Wales. Discovered during gravel quarrying in 1938, it was partly excavated by Audrey Williams under less than ideal conditions in May 1939. The mound was made of local conglomerate and soil. It is slightly pear-shaped in plan, 37m long by 20m wide at the broadest point and about 1m high *(21D)*. Roughly in the centre was a stone-built chamber about 1m square and 1m high, open to the northeast, with a square orthostat to the east. Carefully built, the floor was level and paved, but apart from a small amount of oak and hazel charcoal nothing was found inside.[37] In plan, the nearest parallels for the site lie with the closed chambers within late fifth-millennium BC structures in western France, for example Mane-er-Hroeck and St Michel in southern Brittany.[38] While the proximity of the Welsh example to the necessary maritime connections is highly appropriate to such a link, independent dating is desperately needed in order to give the Nicholaston monument a secure context.

SIMPLE PASSAGE GRAVES

Passage graves are one of the most widely recognized classes of tomb in north-western Europe. They typically comprise a round mound covering a centrally placed chamber that is accessible from the edge of the mound via a narrow passage. Larger rectangular, oval and round mounds containing more than one chamber are well known in Brittany and Normandy, although some of these developed through several phases. The earliest examples are generally small and may conveniently be referred to as 'simple passage graves' to distinguish them from the very large elaborate structures of the third millennium BC such as Knowth or Newgrange in Ireland.[39] The origins of passage graves have been widely discussed, but in Britain their derivation from communities in northwestern France via the Celtic Sea and the Western Approaches is widely accepted. When they first appeared in Brittany and Normandy at around 4100 BC they typically had circular or oval chambers with long passages; only later did the rectangular, polygonal and

T-shaped forms develop.[40] Especially notable is the use of corbelled roofing in the early examples at Fonteney-le-Marmion, Normandy, and Barnenez, Brittany, the combination of orthostats and dry-stone walling for the construction of the chambers and passages, and the general poverty of burial deposits within the chambers.[41]

At least nine certain and probable simple passage graves are known in the Cotswold-Severn region, although few have been investigated under ideal conditions *(15)*. In Gloucestershire the Swell 2 round barrow at the west end of Cow Common (GLO 23) was investigated in about 1874 by Canon William Greenwell.[42] During that work he examined a round mound 11m in diameter but only about 0.5m high; the upper part of the mound had been lost through quarrying for stone during the construction of a neighbouring wall. In the centre of the mound was a circular chamber 1.75m in diameter, built of fine dry-stone walling *(22A)*. The whole chamber had been sunk nearly 0.8m into the ground in order to maximize its internal height in relation to the size of the mound. Originally it had a corbelled stone roof, the corbelling beginning to grade inwards at a height of 1.2m above the floor. A passage just 0.8m wide that opened to the northwest allowed access to the chamber, the floor of the passage gradually sloping downwards from ground level at the edge of the mound to the floor level of the sunken chamber in the centre. Greenwell found charcoal on the floor of the chamber as well as a few pieces of 'coarse pottery' and some evidence of burning on the walls of the passage. There were also abundant modern objects and debris from the time when the site had been used as a quarry.

More recently, a large circular structure was discovered at the southeastern end of the Sale's Lot long barrow (GLO 94) during excavations by Helen O'Neil in 1965; this may well be a simple passage grave later incorporated into a long barrow. The round mound was 12m across, with what appears to be an inner concentric revetment wall perhaps suggestive of a stepped profile *(22B)*. Although heavily disturbed by later robbing, the irregular oval chamber appears to have been slightly northwest of centre, with its passage opening to the southeast. The sides of the chamber were made of dry-stone walling, except on the southwest side where a single orthostat had been used. The roof had probably been a corbelled beehive structure, but few traces survived. A sherd of plain bowl-style pottery typical of the earlier fourth millennium BC was found on the floor of the chamber. No human remains were present in the chamber, but in the rubble-stone packing of the south wall were two fragments of bone pins and the jawbones of a fox and a cat. The passage grave seems to have been built over the top of an earlier structure, perhaps a house, and this may account for the distribution of some of the finds.[43] About 15m northwest of the simple passage grave was a rotunda grave, presumably contemporary as it too was later encapsulated within the long barrow (see below).

Just 8km east of Sale's Lot is the site of Saltway Barn (GLO 92), excavated by W.F. Grimes between October 1939 and March 1940. Prior to excavation this site appeared to be a 'low, unpromising looking mound, broader and higher at the west end, tapering off in plan and falling away in height to the east'.[44] Removal of the

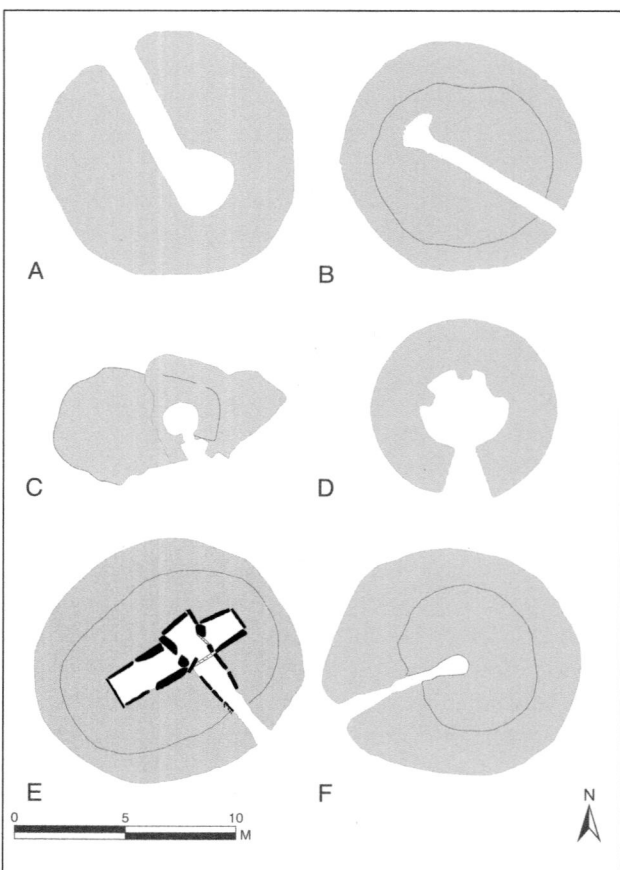

22 Simple passage graves in the Cotswold-Severn region. *A:* Cow Common Round (GLO 23); *B:* Sale's Lot (GLO 94); *C:* Saltway Barn (GLO 92); *D:* Ablington (GLO 26); *E:* Ty Isaf (BRE 5); *F:* Cefn Drum, Glamorgan

topsoil and the application of Grimes's careful attention to the plano-stratigraphy of the stonework quickly revealed that this site was an incredibly complicated structure with several phases of remodelling *(22C)*. At the centre was a shallow and rather irregular rock-cut pit 5.6m by 2.6m that had been excavated through the original topsoil and down into the living limestone to a depth of between 0.3 and 0.8m. A small central island of rock was left standing, and against this a circular chamber 1.6m in diameter had been built. The floor of the chamber was the bottom of the pit. The walls were of high-quality dry-stone construction; the roof was originally corbelled but this had collapsed in the eighteenth century AD when the chamber seems to have been entered and used as a shelter. The original height of the chamber was estimated at 1.7m. There were two niches in the chamber wall, one to the northeast at eye level and the other to the northwest at floor level. The entrance opened to the southeast and there was a short passage forming an approach to the chamber. The whole was enclosed within a rather irregular mound of pitched stone rubble. It was formed of two lobes: the eastern part physically covering the chamber was built first, followed by the western lobe which, according to the excavator, gave every impression of covering a second chamber but was in fact entirely rubble. Part of this irregular and amorphous heap was contained within a revetment, but most of it was poorly edged and it must have looked rather untidy set in the middle of an eroding depression. There were no human remains in the chamber, only some worked flints trodden into the floor and scraps of pottery outside.

These two sites, both excavated in modern times, help cast light on other structures known as 'bee-hive chambers' and said by Canon Samuel Lysons in the mid-nineteenth century to be shepherds' cots.[45] These share many characteristics with Sale's Lot and Saltway Barn, but because they were not incorporated into later long barrows they remain in their original condition with round covering mounds. The Ablington (GLO 26) chamber was noted by Lysons in relation to the large long barrow of Lamborough Banks (GLO 25) which lies less than 100m to the north. Subsequently, E.C. Daubeny and A.D. Passmore examined it in September 1925.[46] The mound here was small, just 4.2m in diameter, with a central chamber 1.7m in diameter at floor level *(22D)*. The walls were of dry-stone construction, being more or less vertical to a height of about 0.6m at which point there were some projecting slabs around parts of the west, east and north sides. Above these the walls began to curve inwards to form a corbelled dome. The top of the dome was sealed by a single large slab about 2m above the level of the floor. Two small recesses had been made in the walls of the chamber, one to the northeast, the other to the northwest. The entrance opened to the south with a short tapering passage providing access through the mound. Unfortunately, no finds were made within the structure that give any indication of its original date of construction, but its similarity to the Saltway Barn example allows it to be included within the emerging class of simple passage graves in the Cotswold-Severn region.

There are undoubtedly more simple passage graves around the Cotswolds yet to be found and others already excavated yet to be fully recognized. Sir James Berry suggested that each of the chambers at Belas Knap (GLO 1) was originally provided with a separate mound,[47] but he was probably looking at construction features intended to support the orthostats while the main mound was being built. A more probable example is within the eastern end of the Cow Common long barrow (GLO 22), where Canon Greenwell records the existence of an oval chamber with 'a strong resemblance to one found in an adjoining round barrow (GLO 23 described above). It contained human bones from at least two adults and of an infant, molars of an ox, one molar of a goat or a sheep, a single bone probably of a weasel and two flint flakes.'[48]

West of the Severn the most important simple passage grave is at Ty Isaf (BRE 5) in the Black Mountains *(22E)*. Here the excavation of a long barrow by W.F. Grimes and members of the Breconshire Society in 1937 revealed a roughly circular structure about 11m across within the core of the long barrow. Like Sale's Lot, the mound was bounded by two concentric walls which again suggest a stepped profile. The centrally placed chamber was of orthostatic construction, T-shaped in plan, with a pair of cells some 7m across opening from the 4m-long passage which led into the mound from the southeast. When entering the tomb the left-hand cell is about twice the size of the right-hand cell. Grimes discussed the sequence of construction and use of the site in his final report, concluding that the long barrow, including the passage grave element, was built as a single entity 'following one set of ideas'.[49] This view is not well supported by the photographs that accompany the report, where the walls of the inner structure seem quite distinct from the walls forming part of the long barrow. Unfortunately, the critical sections through the mound were not published, but John Corcoran summed up what can be seen in the report when he said that 'it would seem impossible to escape the conclusion that this had been a tomb of multi-period construction'.[50] Moreover, the form of the chamber within the simple passage grave is an example of a type occasionally found in northwest France, for example at Poulguen, Finistère, albeit here at a larger scale and originally within a mound 40m in diameter and 8m high.[51] At Ty Isaf the construction of the chamber embodies some interesting architecture that perhaps reflects binary oppositions in the selective placement of stones with distinctive shapes that carried special meanings. Grimes noted, for example, that the entrances to the east and west transepts were both 'flanked on one side by a flat slab, on the other by a pillar-like conglomerate boulder of half round section. But the pillars did not exactly balance, being to the north on the east and to the south on the west.'[52] Inside the chamber were the disarticulated remains of at least nine individuals as well as bones of sheep/goat and ox. Finds included two stone discs and sherds from at least five pots.

Other simple passage graves pre-dating long barrows west of the Severn can be glimpsed, but not confirmed without further excavation. At Pipton (BRE 8), there is an internal chamber associated with a curving wall (the so-called inner rotunda wall) that seems out of keeping with the straight lines of the long barrow structure, but the 1950 excavation was limited to selective trenching which revealed little of the internal structure of the barrow.[53] Something similar may be present at Little Lodge (BRE 2) to judge from the disposition of chamber elements.[54]

In south Wales, fieldwork during the summer of 2000 around Cefn Drum on the northern upland of the Gower peninsula brought to light another possible simple passage grave. Initially set in a round mound about 6m across, it was perhaps later enlarged *(22F)*. The central chamber is slightly pear-shaped about 1m wide and 1.4m long; the passage is about 2m long and opens to the southwest. Within the chamber were three white quartz pebbles. Initial radiocarbon dates on bone from a pit just outside the entrance proved to be medieval, but subsequent determinations relating to charcoal from outside the passage take the use of the site back to at least the late third millennium BC.[55]

ROUND BARROWS AND ROTUNDA GRAVES

The final group of monuments to consider here includes what are essentially round barrows: circular mounds built over a more or less centrally placed burial of some description *(15)*. Several variations on the basic form have been noted by Ian Kinnes in his study of early round barrows in Britain,[56] one variant distinctive to the Cotswold-Severn region having a stone-lined central cist. These are here called 'rotunda graves' in recognition of the term applied by Elsie Clifford to the example she uncovered within the Notgrove long barrow (GLO 4) in 1935.

The Notgrove rotunda grave was about 7m in diameter and stood 0.8m high. It was neatly built of local stone with a slightly sloping external wall and a domed top *(23A and 24)*. At its centre was a polygonal cist, constructed from thin slabs of local limestone. Within the cist were the remains of an adult male aged about 50, together with two pieces of unworked flint. A large stone to the north of the rotunda, later incorporated into the outer wall of the overlying long barrow, may have been an outlying standing stone.[57] A similar structure is known at Sale's Lot (GLO 94), where excavations by Helen O'Neil revealed traces of a circular monument about 5m across *(23B)*. Much of this example was destroyed before the excavation began, but traces of a burial in the form of a few human teeth and a flint leaf-shaped arrowhead remained in the centrally placed cist.[58] Yet another example may be at Belas Knap (GLO 1), where excavations in 1865 revealed a 'broken circle of stones' about 2.2m in diameter beneath the later tomb. Around this circle was a deposit of ashy soil, but no other finds.[59] It is very likely that some of the numerous round barrows scattered widely across the Cotswolds also belong to this group, but their form is not chronologically specific enough to permit positive identification and the results of early excavations are often inconclusive. Amongst those that merit further attention (but which are not mapped on illustration *15*) are Northfield Barrow (Charlton Kings 1) and the Hungerfield Barrow (Cranham 3).[60]

On the north Wessex Downs a possible round barrow of the early fourth millennium BC is known on a steep slope 40m to the southwest of the Knap Hill causewayed enclosure.[61] Excavated in 1937 by C.W. Phillips, the work has never been adequately published. However, from the few details available it seems that the barrow was small, about 5m in diameter, with a central crouched inhumation burial surrounded by flint-working waste and broken plain bowl-style pottery.

To the west of the Severn, rotunda graves can be seen at two sites. The Tinkinswood long barrow (GLA 9) excavated in 1914 has a curious structure embedded in the north side of the mound *(23C)*. John Ward thought that this was a secondary structure dug into the mound of the long barrow,[62] but his plan of the stonework of the mound shows slight evidence for a circular structure within the mound and Ward himself notes the presence of unusual kinds of stone in the same area. It is therefore possible that this represents an early structure later incorporated into the mound of a long barrow in the manner now recognized at other sites. Unfortunately, Ward's excavations revealed rather little about this stone-lined structure, although the fill contained bones of ox and sheep. Human bones were found in the stonework immediately around the cist, along with more animal remains. This, it seems, was the only place in the mound where such remains were found, further strengthening the idea that here was a primary structure. At Pen-y-wyrlod (BRE 1) a large slab-lined chamber lies more or less in the centre of a circular mound about 10m in diameter that Corcoran proposed as the primary element within what later became a substantial long barrow *(23D)*.[63] The cist measures about 2.1m square and was excavated by the Revd W.E.T. Morgan and

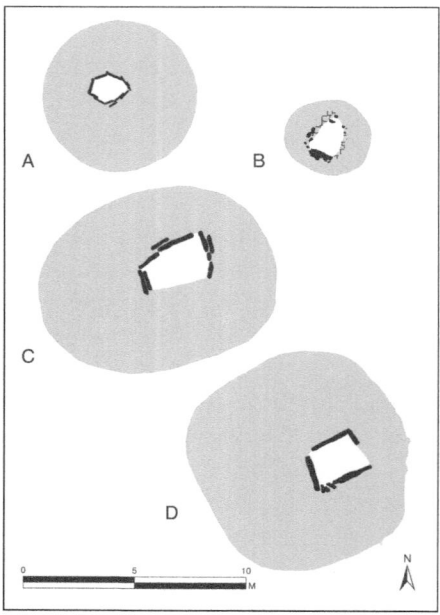

23 Round barrows and rotunda graves in the Cotswold-Severn region. *A:* Notgrove (GLO 4); *B:* Sale's Lot (GLO 94); *C:* Tinkinswood (GL 9); *D:* Pen-y-wyrlod (BRE 1)

others in 1920 and 1921. It contained disarticulated human remains representing perhaps as many as a dozen people – men, women and children – as well as bones from various domesticated animals. There was also some pottery and struck flint flakes.[64]

These round barrows and rotunda graves form part of a more widespread tradition found in several parts of the British Isles and beyond. One focus is in eastern England, especially the East Riding of Yorkshire, where round barrows account for more than half of the burial monuments of the fourth millennium BC.[65] In Ireland, the Linkardstown cists of eastern counties show certain similarities with the slab-lined rotunda graves of the Cotswold-Severn region, especially the polygonal chamber form and round covering mound.[66] Following Sheridan's phasing of the decorated ceramics from Ireland, these Linkardstown cists should be dated to the middle of the fourth millennium BC.[67] Rather earlier in date are the closed cists within round mounds at Kerlescan and Mané Lud in the Morbihan, Brittany,[68] where local indigenous origins have been suggested amongst the slab-lined graves at Téviec and elsewhere.[69]

MIXING MONUMENTS

Recognizing the existence of these early structures and their contribution to the development of long barrows in the area provides a new insight on the dynamics of monument design and use. All five early traditions find their roots in monumental architecture current in northwest Europe in the period from about 4250 BC through to 3600 BC, but not all can be traced back to the same geographical

Before the Long Barrows

area. This makes simple dual-origin models, whether as Glyn Daniel's northmen and southmen[70] or Stuart Piggott's eastern and western components,[71] of limited value. The dolmens and portal dolmens connect with comparable monuments westwards and northwestwards, especially around the Irish Sea and Atlantic fringes. There are no directly comparable monuments southwards on the Continental mainland. By contrast, the simple passage graves, rotunda graves and some variants of the oval barrow tradition find roots southwards from the Cotswolds, in the southwest peninsula of Britain, the Channel Islands and northwestern France. Of them all, the simple passage graves are the most widespread and perhaps indicate something of the extent of contacts at this time. Grahame Clark has argued that it was fishing, especially herring fishing, that united the coastal communities of Atlantic Europe from northern Spain through to Scandinavia and promoted the early and rapid spread of ideas leading to the construction of passage graves.[72] Paul Ashbee developed the idea for western Cornwall and the Isles of Scilly, suggesting very plausibly that the simple passage graves of that area could be associated with hunter-gatherer-fisher communities rather than their more conventional grounding in early agricultural groups. Finally, round barrows and the main elements of the oval barrow tradition can be traced northwards and northeastwards across northern Britain and into southern Scandinavia.

The rather special geographical characteristics of the Cotswold-Severn region make it wide open to these links with scattered and sometimes distant surrounding areas by land, river and sea. Overland routes either on a northeast to southwest axis or on a broadly east to west axis are well attested in medieval and later times as long-distance droveways, the so-called 'ridgeways', which were traditional routes for moving livestock.[73] These are certainly ancient and can arguably be

24 Reconstruction drawing by Jane Timby of the rotunda grave at Notgrove (GLO 4)

back-projected into a very remote past. River-based transport is perhaps one of the most neglected aspects of communications between communities of the fourth millennium BC, although Andrew Sherratt has usefully drawn attention to the existence of a potentially very significant link between the central south coast of England and the estuary of the River Dee on the Irish Sea that makes extensive use of rivers now known as the *Avon*, the 'Celtic' word for river still preserved in the Welsh *afon*.[74] Seaborne contact through the Bristol Channel into the Celtic Sea and thence northwards through St George's Channel into the Irish Sea, or southwards into the Western Approaches, English Channel and the Bay of Biscay, is well documented through later prehistoric and early Christian times, and can again be projected back into early prehistory with a reasonable degree of certainty as Barry Cunliffe has shown in his masterful study entitled *Facing the Ocean*.[75]

Culturally, the mix of monuments represented around the Cotswolds and surrounding areas exemplifies a number of traditions, and here it is especially interesting that at some sites there is more than one tradition represented in close proximity. At Sale's Lot (GLO 94), for example, a rotunda grave and a simple passage grave lie just a few metres apart, while at Belas Knap (GLO 1), if the readings of early excavations are correct, a portal dolmen and a rotunda grave occur together. Something similar happens at a slightly wider scale, with concentrations of different kinds of monuments around the headwaters of the Evenlode and the Glyme in the northeast Cotswolds. On the Gower peninsula there is one of the most diverse clusters of monuments anywhere in the area under consideration here, exactly as one might expect given its location on the Bristol Channel coast right at the mouth of the Severn estuary.

As noted at the beginning of this chapter, dating these early monuments is extremely difficult. There are very few associated finds that can be regarded as chronologically distinctive and as yet no satisfactory radiocarbon determinations. Most of the few finds from nineteenth-century excavations at these sites have been lost or become so jumbled that it is uncertain what comes from where. From more recent work, 84 small sherds of pottery come from the old ground surface below the oval barrow underneath Wayland's Smithy (BRK 1), but few are distinctive *(25A–D)*:[76] a body sherd from a carinated vessel and three rimsherds, all with expanded tops, from vessels of unknown form. One has a little decoration on the rim-top. The 30 or so pieces of pottery from excavations adjacent to the Whispering Knights (OXF 1) include a range of fourth-, third- and second-millennium BC wares, and none could be securely linked to either the construction or the use of the portal dolmen.[77] The same problem applies to the small assemblage of pottery from Sale's Lot, which includes one or two pieces that might be associated with the simple passage grave there, but the exact provenance of particular sherds is hard to establish.[78] Also of uncertain stratigraphic security is the small collection of sherds from the simple passage grave at Ty Isaf (BRE 5). This most probably derives from the use of the chamber rather than its construction, but it is the best group of ceramics currently available from a putatively early site. It is notable that the four rims present *(25E–H)* are all simple or slightly expanded in cross-section and in two cases may derive from carinated bowls *(F and G)*. They

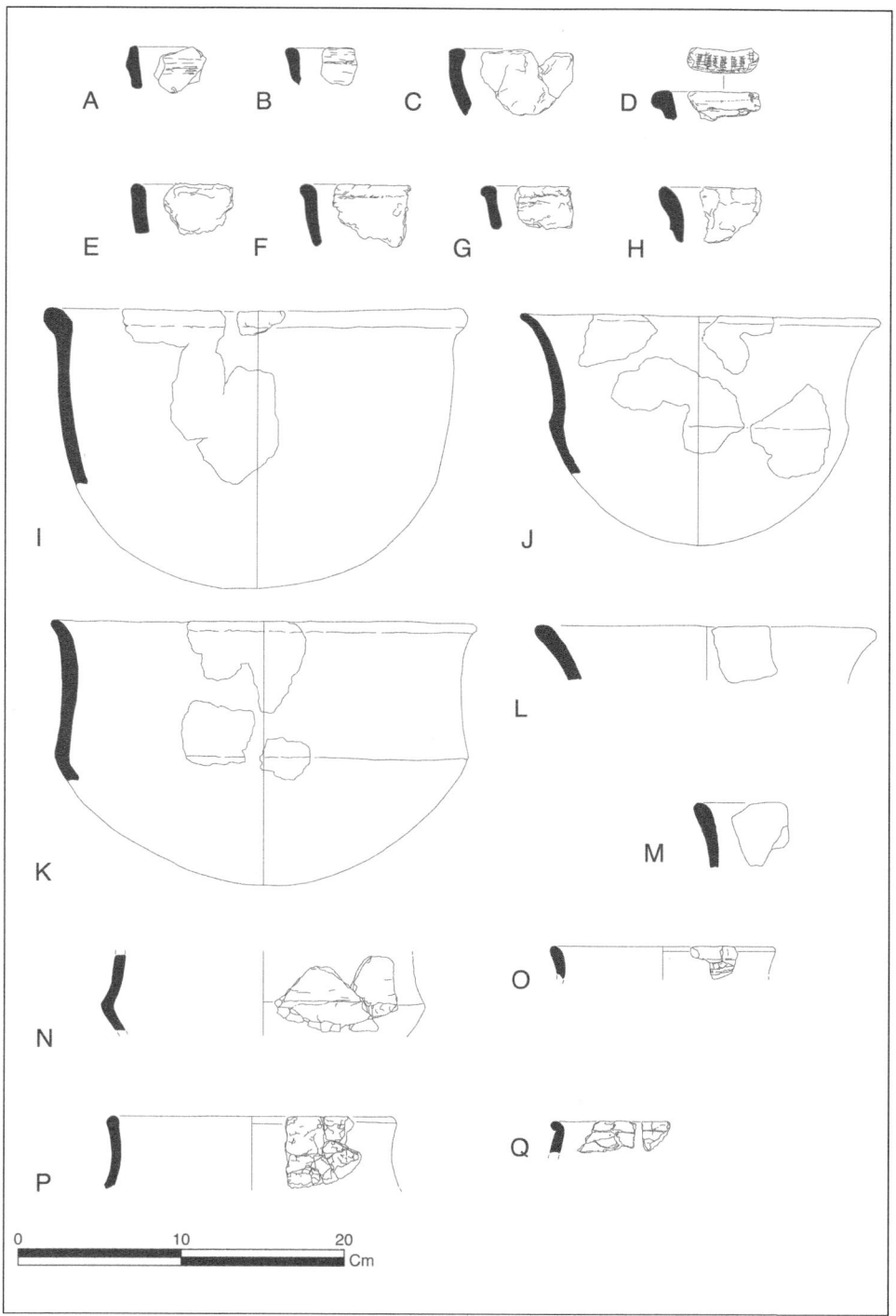

25 Fourth-millennium BC pottery from early monuments and below long barrows.
A–D: Wayland's Smithy (BRK 1); *E–H:* Ty Isaf (BRE 5); *I–K:* Gwernvale (BRE 7); *L–M:* Cow Common Long (GLO 22); *N–Q:* Hazleton North (GLO 54)

contrast with the much heavier rims on pottery from elsewhere on the site.[79] One notable feature of the pottery from both Ty Isaf and Wayland's Smithy is that it is broadly similar to the wares found underneath other long barrows *(25I–Q)*. These pre-long barrow assemblages tend to be better preserved and more substantial because they are associated with settlements of various kinds (see Chapter 5), but they are dominated by relatively thin-walled vessels with simple mainly out-turned rims and a high proportion of carinated bowls. Taken together, these assemblages can be considered as representative of the ceramic repertoire of pre-long barrow-using communities in the region.

How long the various early monuments lasted, and what their builders thought of them, is not known. Certainly they represented a considerable investment of time and labour, and although modest in scale must have been significant and important places within a hostile environment that communities struggled to tame. By about 3800 BC new and more widespread traditions began to have an impact on people then living in the Cotswolds and surrounding areas. The result was that some groups converted, enlarged, or replaced their existing monuments with the new-fangled structures we know as long barrows, while others built these new distinctive kinds of elongated structures from scratch.

4

LONG BARROWS: A NEW TRADITION

Long barrows began to be built in the British Isles around 3800 BC, although extravagant claims for much earlier beginnings have been made from time to time and then dismissed.[1] The start of the tradition is vague because obtaining secure samples for determining absolute dates for long barrows is far from easy. Material within, or on top of, the old ground surface underneath a barrow may have arrived there any time before the mound was built. Deciding what is contemporary with the monument's construction and what is residual from earlier activities is extremely difficult, more so since few if any barrows seem to have been built upon virgin ground. Equally, material taken from the chamber theoretically dates to any time after the construction of the barrow. As Stuart Piggott discussed some years ago, the way in which these monuments were used means that the chambers may have been cleared out periodically, and it is also possible that bones from elsewhere were introduced.[2] Ideally, the construction of a long barrow should be dated on short-lived material such as cereal grains taken from critical constructional horizons within the mound, but such carefully selected material is not widely available. As a second best, tools or short-lived material from peripheral construction contexts such as the primary fills of quarry ditches provide a good guide, but even here caution is needed as barrows were sometimes extended and remodelled. Linking a particular area of quarrying to a specific phase of construction is rarely certain.

Absolute dating is, however, only part of the picture. Sequences of monument building at individual sites show that throughout the British Isles long barrows replaced or elaborated earlier structures representing all the different sorts discussed in the last chapter. Some early monuments no doubt continued in use, while others were replaced or modified. A few early forms continued to be used through into the later third millennium BC, long after long barrows themselves fell out of use (Chapter 9). So where and when did long barrows first appear in the Cotswold-Severn region? How many are there and where are they typically found? What common features do they show? How similar are they? What are their origins? What general meanings did they carry? How do they relate to other long barrows in the British Isles? And what does the evidence from multi-period monuments in the region tell us about the onset of the new long barrow tradition?

LONG BARROWS ON OLD SITES

Inspired by the results from excavations in various parts of the British Isles, it was John Corcoran and Terrance Powell who first really recognized the significance of multi-period construction at long barrow sites.[3] They demonstrated that right across northwest Europe early structures had been extended and modified to form new kinds of monument, the later phases often involving the superimposition or creation of long mounds. In some cases the early monuments were simply built over, so that they were enveloped at the core of the new structure, inaccessible to those using the later long barrow. Within the Cotswold-Severn region there is good evidence that multi-phase construction was widely practised *(26)*. In every case recorded so far, the overall size of the monument increased considerably as a result of being modified.

At Notgrove (GLO 4) the rotunda grave and the possible standing stone to the north were both covered by the mound of a substantial long barrow measuring 40m by 14.5m, although the standing stone may have been visible in the outer revetment wall on the northern side of the long barrow *(26A)*. During the construction of the long barrow the fragmentary disarticulated remains of a young person, probably female, aged between 16 and 20, were placed on the domed top of the rotunda grave.[4] There was also evidence of burning on the stones here, but since the human remains showed no evidence of having been burnt they must have been added afterwards, perhaps a final act before the long barrow enveloped the earlier structure.

West of the Severn the round barrow or rotunda grave at the eastern end of Pen-y-wyrlod (BRE 1) seems to have been converted into a long barrow by the simple addition of a 'tail' on the west side, possibly with a new lateral chamber opening from the north side of the mound. The modified monument here would have been about 20m long.[5] Something similar seems to have happened at Sale's Lot (GLO 94) on the Cotswolds where the pre-existing simple passage grave and rotunda grave were linked together by sections of walling to delimit an elongated enlarged mound; small horns were added to the eastern end. The new monument here was 35m long and 10m wide, but compared with many long barrows must have looked rather irregular in outline *(26B)*.[6] The same applies at Saltway Barn (GLO 92) where the simple passage grave in its irregular double-domed mound was expanded by the addition of stonework to form a rather squat-shaped structure a little over 20m long.[7] Here it seems likely that the chamber remained accessible after the mound was enlarged, as no additional chambers were added to the monument.[8]

The simple passage grave at Ty Isaf (BRE 5) was incorporated into the central part of a classic long barrow 30m long by 17m wide *(21C)*. The alignment of the western long side of the long barrow shows slight evidence for an outward kink

Long Barrows: A New Tradition

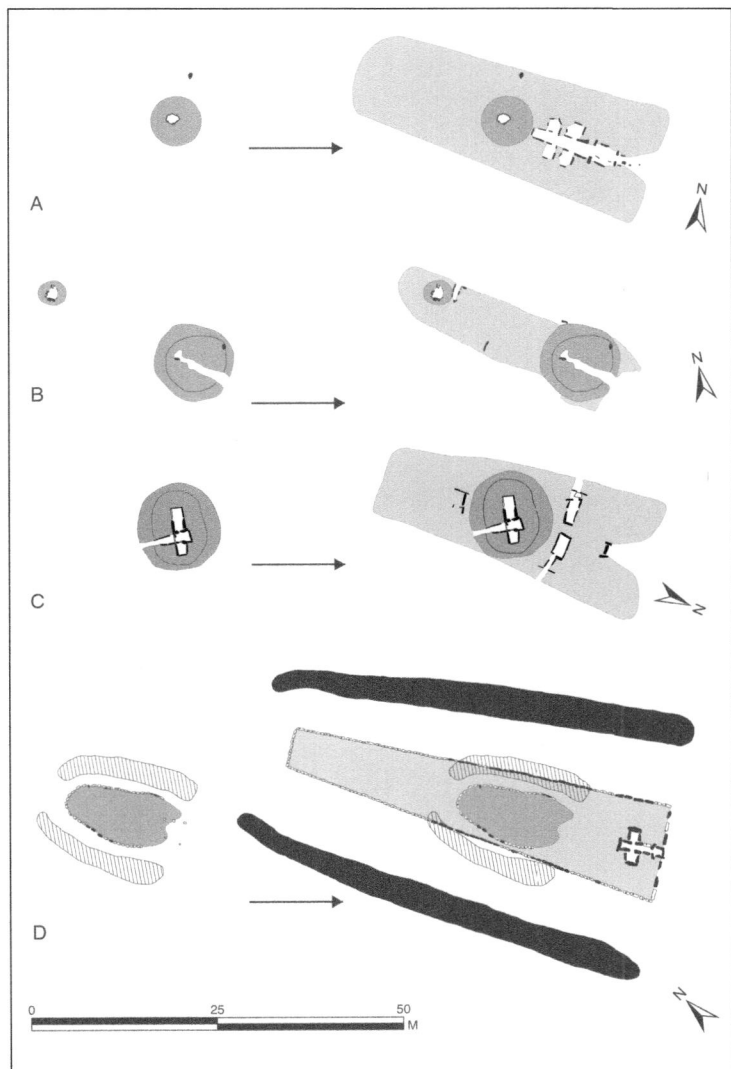

26 Multi-period monuments in the Cotswold-Severn region. A: Notgrove (GLO 4); B: Sale's Lot (GLO 94); C: Ty Isaf (BRE 5); D: Wayland's Smithy (BRK 1)

to accommodate the existing structure, while the eastern part of the mound of the simple passage grave seems to have been demolished so that the early monument here could be neatly spliced into the stonework forming the mound of the long barrow.[9] As at Saltway Barn, it seems likely that the central chamber of the simple passage grave here remained accessible after the construction of the long barrow.

Perhaps the most celebrated multi-period monument in the region is Wayland's Smithy (BRK 1). Here a very neatly constructed long barrow with a trapezoidal outline covered the small oval barrow, 67m long by 14m wide at the broader south end *(21D)*, a site that has become a real textbook example of its kind. Only small parts of the side ditches of the early structure would have poked out of the side of the later barrow, and these were probably fully silted up and more or less invisible.

Charcoal from the old ground surface between the two phases of this monument has been dated to the period 3950-3100 BC; although very broad, this is currently the only fairly secure date for a multi-period monument in the region.

Other multi-period monuments can be suspected from the glimpses provided by excavations, and in some cases would merit re-examination in order to clarify the sequences represented: Belas Knap (GLO 1) where a portal dolmen has been postulated under the mound at the north end; Pipton (BRE 8) where walling around chamber II near the centre of the mound strongly suggests an earlier oval construction incorporated into the mound of the long barrow; Tinkinswood (GLA 9) where a rotunda grave is postulated within the north side of the later mound; Murtry Hill (SOM 8) where it is suspected that a portal dolmen in a round mound was turned into a long barrow by the construction of a westward extension to the mound.

Multi-period construction has been recognized in many other parts of northwest Europe, very often involving the transformation of localized early-style monuments into far larger rectangular or trapezoidal structures. Chris Scarre has discussed four such monuments from the Morbihan area of Brittany – Kerlescan, Mané Lud, Le Manio II and the Tumulus de Saint-Michel – where small early round mounds with central closed cists were replaced by long mounds of various sorts.[10] From further north, in Denmark, Torsten Madsen discusses several sites with three or four stages of construction. Sjørup Plantage, for example, had three 'earth graves' in separate mounds, two of which were subsequently incorporated into a modest rectangular barrow. Later, a still larger long barrow measuring 45m by 13m engulfed this structure plus the remaining 'earth grave'.[11] At Lønt in southern Jutland a long barrow 38m long and 9m wide showed four successive phases of development: a small round barrow with a central closed cist, followed by the addition of a simple passage grave in a round mound, followed again by the addition of two further simple passage graves and finally the construction of a rectangular mound that covered and consolidated all the earlier structures.[12]

Right across northwest Europe there seems to be a series of parallel developments in which small simple structures were converted into or incorporated within large rectangular or trapezoidal mounds. Some of those simple monuments cover the burials of single individuals, while others cover multiple burials. What they are replaced with, however, almost always provided, or allowed access to, internal structures able to accommodate multiple burials.

As already noted, a few long barrows cover more than one earlier structure, and they are always bigger and in a sense more 'monumental' than their predecessors. In Britain long barrows represent a step-change in the scale of construction and, by implication, the labour invested in their production. Although long barrows are sometimes seen as the earliest monumental structures in the British landscape, this is not supported by the evidence now available. Rather, they fit more comfortably within a pattern of change usefully summarized by Humphrey Case as a transition from early scattered pioneer communities to what he termed 'mature' farming communities.[13] Updated and adapted, this scheme provides a useful model with which to start exploring long barrow construction: pioneer monument builders drawing on a diverse range of contacts, underpinned by a variety of subsistence economies, developed into larger communities that used far bigger monuments of a more uniform and widely recognized form. Thus when communities in the Cotswold-Severn region started building long barrows they locked themselves into a much wider set of traditions. In so doing they presumably aligned themselves with much more widely held beliefs and views of the world and these must be explored in the wider context of long barrows in the British Isles as a whole.

LONG BARROWS IN THE BRITISH ISLES

More than 500 long barrows are currently known across Britain (England, Wales and Scotland), Ireland and most of the main islands in between and around about as well *(27)*. Only the Isles of Scilly, some of the Inner Hebrides, a few of the Western Isles and Shetland amongst the larger islands in the archipelago seem to lack long barrows. In the case of Scilly this may be artificial, as much of the land area available for occupation in the fourth and third millennia BC is now submerged.[14]

Despite its extent, though, the distribution is far from even. Two substantial concentrations can be seen. The first lies within a broad block extending from the English Channel coast between Weymouth and Portsmouth northwards to the natural boundaries set by the River Severn and the upper Thames. Perhaps because of the density and diversity of examples in this area, long barrows elsewhere in Britain are often compared to them, and during the 1940s and 1950s, when archaeological interpretation was grounded in cultural-historical approaches, this spread was seen by Stuart Piggott and Gordon Childe as the territory of the Windmill Hill Culture and the Severn-Cotswold Culture.[15] The second concentration occurs in the northern part of Ireland, across into western Scotland around the mouth of the River Clyde and on the islands of the Irish Sea and North Channel, including the Isle of Man and Arran. Traditionally, this was the Clyde-Carlingford Cultural province, although Ruaidhrí de Valera, Jack Scott, John Corcoran, A.E.P. Collins and others have identified a number of regional groupings within the larger pattern,[16] as indeed John Corcoran and Paul Ashbee did for the Windmill Hill and Cotswold-Severn spreads at about the same time.[17] Between and around these major groupings there are about a dozen smaller, but no less significant, clusters: in the far southwest of England; on the South Downs of Sussex; around the Medway estuary in Kent; along the Chilterns and through into East Anglia; around the coastal fringes of Pembrokeshire and southwest Wales; in the Black Mountains; around Snowdonia and across into Anglesey; along the east coast either side of the Humber estuary; through the central Pennines; in the borderlands of England and Scotland; in Aberdeenshire; and in Caithness and across the Pentland Firth to Orkney.

Describing distributions is one thing; understanding what they mean is altogether different. As regional sequences of monument construction and formal variations in monument form are worked out, so an almost kaleidoscopic pattern

27 Distribution of long barrows in the British Isles. Land over 244m OD stippled

of constantly changing arrangements emerges with, at any point in time, complementary distributions of different types of long barrow across the country. At the time long barrows were built, broadly the later fourth millennium BC, communities living in the southern Peak District seemingly preferred to build monuments firmly grounded in the simple passage grave tradition.[18] By contrast, in the East Riding of Yorkshire it was round barrows that seem to have been favoured by many communities.[19] One of the issues here is that of scale. Taking the British Isles as a whole, general patterns can be seen. But as one zooms in to scrutinize particular areas it transpires that new and ever more local patterns appear. As discussed in the last chapter, topography, river systems and coasts played important roles in the development of these local patterns – what might be called the influence of the physical landscape. In parallel, some communities chose to build long barrows and some did not – what might be called the influence of the social landscape represented by group identity, kinship structures and perhaps alliance networks.

Those communities that chose to build long barrows constructed monuments that, superficially at least, show remarkable homogeneity over wide areas *(28)*. The mounds represent the most conspicuous element and are mainly rectangular or slightly trapezoidal. The longest example so far recognized is in central Scotland, at Auchenlaich, Stirling. It measures no less than 342m from end to end and varies between 15m and 11m wide, but a detailed study by Sally Foster and Jack Stevenson suggests that it may in fact be of two phases: a trapezoidal long barrow 48m in length which was later extended northeastwards by the addition of a substantial 'tail'.[20] Other substantial examples include Long Low, Derbyshire, at 210m long and 30m wide;[21] West Kennet (WIL 4) at 100m long by 20m wide;[22] and the unexcavated Colnpen (GLO 69) at 91m long by 21m wide.[23] Again, however, caution needs to be exercised here, as these are all rather exceptional and may be standard long barrows that were grossly elongated to form part of a monumental tradition that includes so-called 'bank barrows' and cursuses (see Chapters 5 and 8). More typically, long barrows are 30–50m long and 15–20m wide, but some are actually rather small: Nympsfield (GLO 13), for example, is just 27m long by 14m at its widest point;[24] the small but perfectly formed Mid Gleniron I, Wigtownshire, southwestern Scotland is just 18m long by 8m across the façade;[25] and Aillemore in Co Mayo, Ireland is less than 20m long.[26] The wider end tends also to be the higher end to judge from well-preserved examples, and it is the higher/wider ends that tend to be elaborated with some sort of façade or forecourt arrangement. Occasionally, there are double-ended examples with a forecourt at each end, a design tradition that is most common in Ireland.[27]

These details vary a little from one region to the next, and it very much depends upon the scale of view as to whether it is the similarities or the differences that are emphasized. To foreshadow the conclusions of some later discussion, the detailed design of specific long barrows in most areas draws heavily on traditions of monument construction that were already established in that same area in the early fourth millennium BC. Why though do communities across the British Isles adopt the idea of the long barrow? Where does the inspiration come from? And what, if anything, does the shape of the mound and the design of the internal structures mean?

ORIGINS, CONNECTIONS AND MEANINGS

The use of long mounds to cover burials is an extremely widespread tradition in northern Europe and has attracted a great deal of attention. From Ireland in the west to Poland in the east and from Brittany in the south to Orkney in the north, long mounds of various kinds are commonplace, although it would be wrong to assume that they all necessarily derive from a single source, or indeed represent a unitary phenomenon. In 1949, however, Gordon Childe sparked a line of thinking that strongly coloured the way such mounds were viewed during the second half of the twentieth century, and promoted searches for common origins and cross-cultural links. In what he describes as a 'topical appendix' he noted as a 'curious circumstance' that:

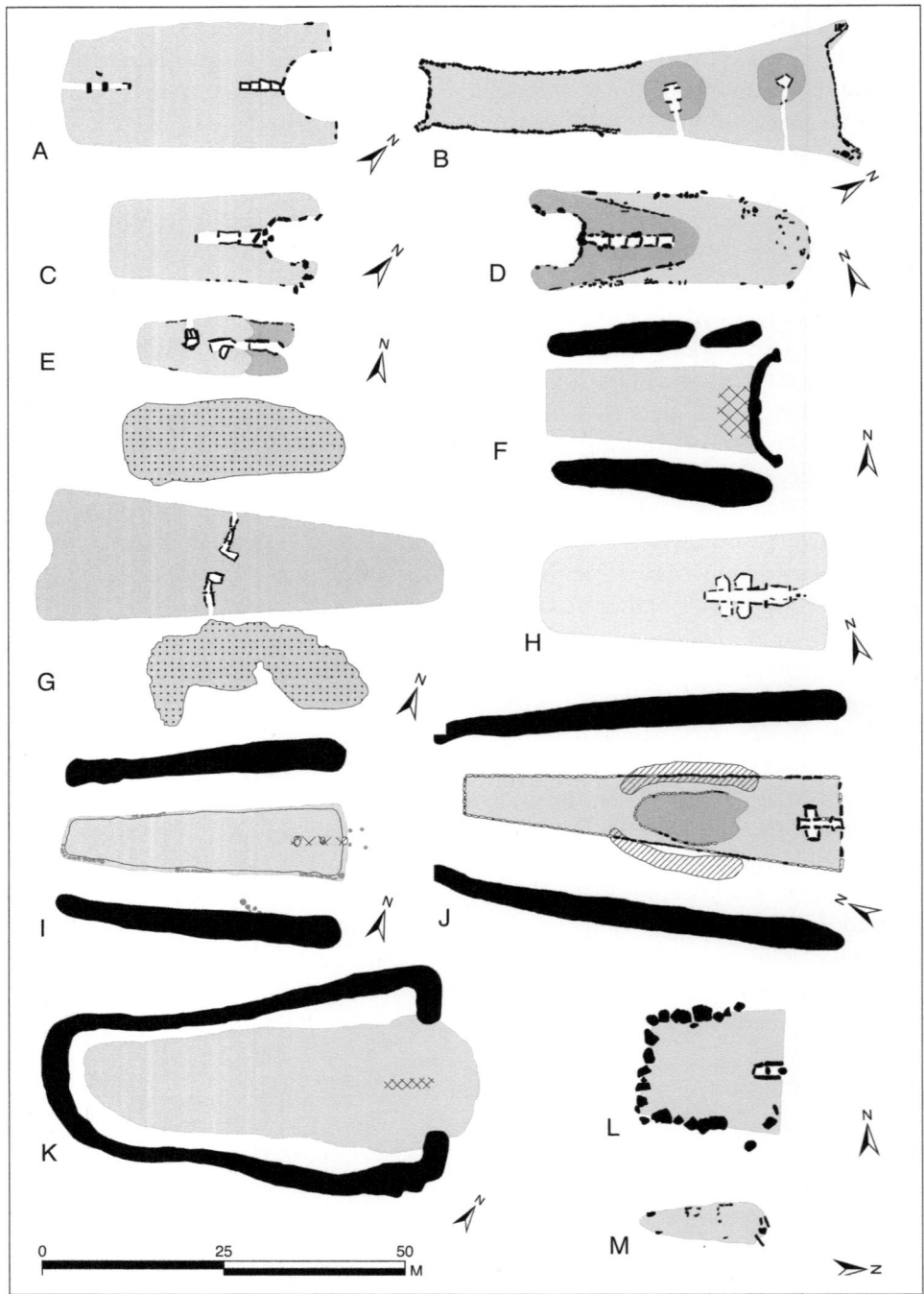

28 Specimen ground plans of long barrows in the British Isles. *A:* Carn Ban, Arran; *B:* Camster Long, Caithness; *C:* Carn, Co Monaghan, Ireland; *D:* Cashtal yn Ard, Isle of Man; *E:* Trefignath, Anglesey; *F:* Raisthorpe, East Riding; *G:* Hazleton North, Gloucestershire (GLO 54); *H:* Notgrove, Gloucestershire (GLO 4); *I:* Fussell's Lodge, Wiltshire; *J:* Wayland's Smithy, Berkshire (BRK 1); *K:* Haddenham, Cambridgeshire; *L:* Coldrum, Kent; *M:* Catshole, Cornwall

The Danubian peasants lived in very long houses, some rectangular others trapezoid in plan. Some at Brzesc Kujawski were as much as 32m long, 10m wide at the south end but only 5m wide at the inner extremity. Now some First Northern farmers in the East and South groups laid out the long barrows over their graves on a very similar plan . . . Sprockhoff indeed has pointed out that in its original form a North German long barrow (*Langdolmen*) would look very like a house with the wall timbers represented by stones and the thatched-gabled roof by turf. Can similar ideas have influenced the builders of our long barrows? [28]

So far as the long barrows of the British Isles were concerned, this throwaway suggestion stuck fast and prompted an interest in interpreting long barrows as houses for the dead, initiating a search for progenitors amongst the houses of living communities in mainland Europe. Much of this thinking was coherently brought together in 1966 when Paul Ashbee reported his excavations at Fussell's Lodge, Wiltshire. Here, following Childe, he drew attention to 'close resemblances' between long barrows and European rectangular and trapezoidal long houses of *Linearbandkeramik* (LBK) and later communities. Similarities were identified both at a general level (shape, size, etc.) and in the detail (use of internal divisions, construction techniques, etc.).[29] However, LBK-style long houses were built in central Europe and through to the coastlands of northern France and the Low Countries between about 5500 BC and 4500 BC, ending nearly a thousand years before long barrows in the British Isles began to be built. Such a gap is clearly a problem if it is argued that the design of LBK long houses had any direct impact on the form of long barrows. Alasdair Whittle noted in the conclusions to his study of the Continental background to early farming in southern Britain published in 1977 that the long barrows 'of Britain and Atlantic Europe may also be connected in some way with the decline of the timber long houses or the social conditions for its flourishing, but the practice of monument building cannot be related directly to the Linear Pottery culture tradition'.[30] In the ensuing two decades, however, the gap between the timber long houses of continental Europe and the long barrows of the British Isles has closed considerably and a more consistent pattern can now be glimpsed.

Critical to this is the recognition that many post-LBK cultures across the north European Plain, including the Rössen, Michelsberg, Chasseen and *Trichterrandbecher* (TRB) groups, spanning the period between 4500 BC and 3500 BC, built rectangular and trapezoidal houses whose origins can be traced back to the LBK. Many of these are highly relevant to discussions about the relationships between houses and barrows because, within a series of distinctive regional developments, a bigger picture of parallel change can be seen. It is perhaps most clear in Kujavia, Poland. The presence here of trapezoidal long houses and associated long barrows has often been noted, and examples of each were heavily used by Paul Ashbee in his discussion of the Fussell's Lodge excavations.[31] Detailed studies of the houses and barrows by Magdelana Midgley led her to conclude that these sites offer 'the strongest evidence yet for accepting the derivation of the earthen long barrow from the long house. Not only are the Kujavian long barrow cemeteries built contemporaneously with, and in close proximity to, long house villages, but the structures also resemble one another in dimensions, ground plan and spatial arrangements within the groups.'[32] Secure dating remains less than ideal, but the trapezoidal houses and trapezoidal long mounds occur within the Eastern TRB (Sarnowo, Pitkutlowo and Wiórek phases) in the period 4500–3500 BC. This is the only part of the TRB that overlaps chronologically with the late LBK in adjoining areas and thus the derivation of its long house architecture is certainly possible.[33]

Further west, a chain of connections linking late LBK long houses in central Europe with the long mounds of burial monuments along the Atlantic façade has been forged by Chris Scarre. He notes the discovery at Balloy in northern Burgundy of an extraordinary series of long houses that was followed by a group of long funerary structures. Trapezoidal houses have also been found at Villeneuve-Saint-Germain, Marolles and Le Haut Mée which can be paralleled in plan by the long funerary monuments at Le Manio 2, Mané Ty Ec and other sites besides. Also highly relevant are the long, narrow enclosures of Passy type dating to the mid-fifth millennium BC which have been found widely scattered across the gravel-lands of the Yoone, Armançon and Seine valleys of northwestern France. Both the houses and the enclosures may reflect, and in turn contribute to, the development of long, narrow funerary monuments.[34]

More important still for the British Isles is the increasing recognition that long houses from the period before 3500 BC are represented here too. Despite the widely rehearsed sceptical reservations about the interpretation of these structures,[35] the weight of evidence is now overbearingly in favour of long house settlements in many parts of the British Isles, comparable to late fifth-millennium BC structures represented at Berry-au-Bac, Aisne in France and Witterwater at Uelzen in Denmark, relating to late Rössen and TRB communities respectively.[36] More than 40 timber halls or long houses have come to light across Britain and Ireland. Some, like the examples at Gwernvale (BRE 7),[37] and Ballyglass, Co. Mayo, in the far west of Ireland,[38] actually underlie long barrows. What stronger evidence could there be for close ties between long houses and long mounds? Recent discoveries of post-built long houses as a result of development-prompted excavations include one at Yarnton in Oxfordshire *(29)*,[39] and another at the White Horse Stone near Maidstone in Kent.[40] Both are very substantial structures at 20m by 10m and 18m by 8m respectively, and lie within the overall size distribution of known long barrows. In Ireland, 14 long houses were recognized up until 1996, since when several further examples have come to light,[41] while in Scotland the unusually large long house at Balbridie[42] can now be matched by several others in southeastern Scotland.[43] All of these structures date to very much the same horizon as the long barrows. As with long barrows, they are generally found as isolated structures, although a few pairs and small groups are known. Likewise, long houses in the British Isles seem on the whole to be slightly smaller than the long barrows, but the size ranges do overlap quite considerably.

In summary then, a continuous thread of interest in, and the construction of, long houses can be traced across northern Europe from the end of the LBK

29 Yarnton, Oxfordshire. View of the fourth-millennium BC longhouse under excavation. The main postholes forming the walls of the structure are marked with wooden pegs. *Photograph courtesy of Oxford Archaeology. Copyright reserved*

through into the mid-fourth millennium BC. This provides the essential platform from which numerous local trajectories of monument could have developed, each reflecting specific representations of more widely understood traditions. But it is not just about demonstrating linkage, networks and common types of archaeological evidence across time and space. The matter of context and meaning is important too. Why should houses be relevant to long barrows?

Critical to this question is the notion of memory, the facility for individuals and the community at large to recall or keep in mind a store of recollections, whether real or imagined. By placing the dead in structures that looked like houses they perhaps encouraged the spirits of the deceased to return to their house of birth or the houses of their ancestors. Axiomatic to this is the idea that fundamental beliefs about the nature of the world were repeatedly embedded in the form and architecture of both houses and long barrows. As Alasdair Whittle has remarked, the 'longhouse for the living of past generations was transformed into a shrine for the ancestors of a timeless past. The long process of convergence was consolidated by the adoption of a form foreign to daily existence. That form could have been designed literally to house the spirits of imagined ancestors.'[44] And certainly this possibility may be allowed and evidence advanced in its favour. Richard Bradley, for example, has reconsidered the evidence from a number of LBK settlements to show that, following their abandonment as dwellings, many long houses were allowed to rot and collapse in such a way that they naturally formed long low mounds. Sight of these would perhaps stick in the minds of anyone visiting ancestral villages for centuries after the inhabitants themselves died off or moved elsewhere.[45] Moreover, he has convincingly shown how the alignment of the buildings in these villages was orientated towards the origin of the communities that lived in them, buildings which therefore 'mapped out the lives of the living and recalled the importance of the dead'.[46]

Ian Hodder has taken a still wider view and suggested that across central and northern Europe long barrows represent a transformation of the house structure, explicitly reflecting the productive base and social organization of those societies that built and used them. He discussed eight points of similarity between houses and long barrows:[47]

- The construction of houses and long barrows involves the use of continuous bedding trenches, lines of posts, stone walls, or a combination of these.
- Both houses and long barrows have trapezoidal and rectangular shapes with similar length to maximum breath ratios for trapezoidal forms.
- The entrances to the chambers in trapezoidal long barrows and houses are generally at the broader end.
- The entrances of the rectangular and trapezoidal houses and long barrows frequently face to the southeast.
- The entrances are elaborated, specifically with façades, antechambers, 'horns', forecourts, or activity concentrations.
- There is a tripartite division of the long house or mound, although frequently only one division is found one-third of the way along the length from the entrance.
- Tombs and houses frequently have internal decoration.
- Ditches or quarries flank the long sides of houses and barrows.

Given these similarities, he goes on to suggest that the social use of space within the long houses of early farming groups was also translated into the structure of the long barrows and the ways they were used. In this, he suggests, there would be a linear progression through the house from public open space via enclosed male-dominated areas to inner female-dominated space in which food was prepared and things were stored. This, he argues, can be seen in the way that the chambers within long barrows are set out and used, especially the presence of querns and perhaps also food preparation or eating equipment. Such symbols, he suggests, draw on both contemporary and historical references to link each society with its ancestry. Most significantly, Hodder sees the elaboration of long barrow structures as being related to pressure on natural resources. He suggests that labour rather than land was the limiting factor in the success and growth of early farming communities, and that productive success would have depended on women as reproducers, with descent groups competing for the labour power of offspring. Thus long barrows as monuments and the organization of space within them become highly gender structured and meaningful, although whether exactly the same structures were followed by every long barrow building community across northwest Europe is a matter that deserves careful investigation.

The symbolic significance of long barrows and related contemporary structures may also have other dimensions. Andrew Fleming, for example, noted the disproportionate relationship between the large size of most long barrow mounds and the small size of the chambers they contained, the chambers typically occupying less than 10 per cent of the area of the monument as a whole.[48] This he attributes to the fact that barrows had a role among the living population in symbolizing the identity of the community and its power: a kind of attention-focusing device. Colin Renfrew took this further by suggesting that the tombs were, in a very real sense, central places for a community, each engraving their identity on the landscape to create what was effectively a solid, robust and long-lived territorial marker legitimated by the presence of ancestral remains.[49] Like Hodder, Renfrew argued that the emergence of the long barrows in particular can be linked to pressure on resources, but he preferred to see land rather than labour as the critical resource. Again, this did not come to full expression with the initial development of monuments, but rather may be connected with the competition born of the successes achieved by groups of communities in filling up the landscape.

If these various observations are right, then the appearance of long barrows in the landscape of many parts of the British Isles during the fourth millennium BC can be linked to their symbolic meanings in two dimensions. First, the need for them resulted from the culmination of pressures connected with identity and ownership that required bold statements to be affixed to the landscape. Second, the choice of a long barrow as the symbol to be used for this purpose happened in a similar way in several different places around northwest Europe, and at slightly different times, but in each case drew on three main influences: the indigenous monument-building traditions already established in each area; contemporary and historic ideas about how long houses of trapezoidal or rectangular form could be translated into a house of the dead; and the symbolic representation of gender structure and power in the design and use of the monument. Different combinations of these three elements can be used to account for the local variability but regional homogeneity of long barrows as we now see them clustered along the Atlantic seaboard and scattered among northwest Europe's off-shore islands.

Powerful forces must have been at work to produce such a pattern over such a wide area, but what were they? One possibility involves the impact of social, economic and perceptual changes associated with the adoption of the kinds of agricultural economies ultimately emanating from the Near East and transmitted via central Europe and the Mediterranean coast to the Atlantic fringes. Colin Renfrew has hypothesized that this change may have been accompanied by the dispersal of a proto-Indo-European language, and this itself would have played a part in transforming the way indigenous communities thought about their world.[50] Developing the theme, Marek and Kamil Zvelebil have gone further by modifying Renfrew's model to make it more appropriate for the situation in northern and northwest Europe. In this they usefully separate out an initial early phase when agricultural practices were first intermittently adopted by indigenous populations, followed by a period of extensive and rapid take-up of these ideas as part of what has become known as the 'secondary products revolution'.[51] In this second phase, livestock and the products they provide (for example milk, blood, wool and traction power), assumed far greater importance than in earlier centuries, and it was at this time that new languages might be more fully assimilated too. In a way this second phase of change marks the transition already referred to earlier in this chapter between small-scale pioneer farmers and Case's 'mature farming communities'.

Although complicated, the relationship between language and the way people classify and understand the world around them is fundamental to the development of the meanings attributed to places and things, and the ideas and beliefs that people hold dear. Many such ideas and beliefs must have been brought together in order to construct a long barrow, the fundamental similarities in design between regions perhaps hinting that these were widely held ideas, communicated by a common language and regularly combined according to a series of structuring principles.

STRUCTURING PRINCIPLES

Despite what appears to be a degree of variety in the shape and form of long barrows, a few relatively simple principles underlie the main differences and provide a satisfactory scheme through which to explore other aspects of architecture, design and symbolism. In 1975 Ian Kinnes published a rather elegant modular system for the chamber elements of stone-chambered tombs, although in fact also applicable to many timber-chambered monuments as well *(30)*.[52] Much cited since then, this scheme makes use of two key structuring principles. First is the recognition of three patterns to the arrangement of the cells forming the chambers – linear, aggregated and dispersed. Second is the recognition that the number of cells within a given monument is variable, but that the majority have between one and seven cells/modules. For long barrows the basic idea can be modified slightly to reflect a third structuring principle: the position of the chambers relative to the long axis of the mound – lateral or terminal – and to account for examples with no chambers at all *(31)*.

In some respects this scheme perpetuates notions of pattern and order that can be traced back to the observations of John Thurnam and Richard Colt Hoare in the nineteenth century. Differences in the layout of long barrows have been apparent to antiquarians and archaeologists for centuries, but the extent to which any of these was important or significant to the builders and users of these sites cannot easily be determined. What is perhaps relevant is that most, but not all, of the modular patterns that flow from developing these very simple structuring principles can be found amongst the long barrows of the Cotswold-Severn region, and it is to the sites in this area that we can now return.

LONG BARROWS OF THE COTSWOLD-SEVERN REGION IN TIME

As discussed at the opening of this chapter, dating the construction of long barrows generally is extremely difficult. Examples from the Cotswold-Severn region are no exception. More than 80 radiocarbon determinations have been made on samples of charcoal, animal bone, antler and human bone from long barrows and related

Long Barrows: A New Tradition

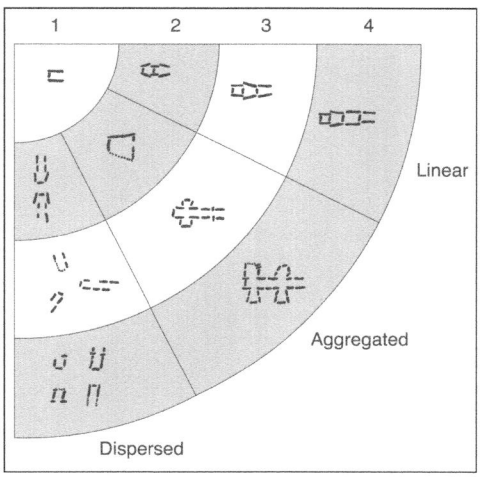

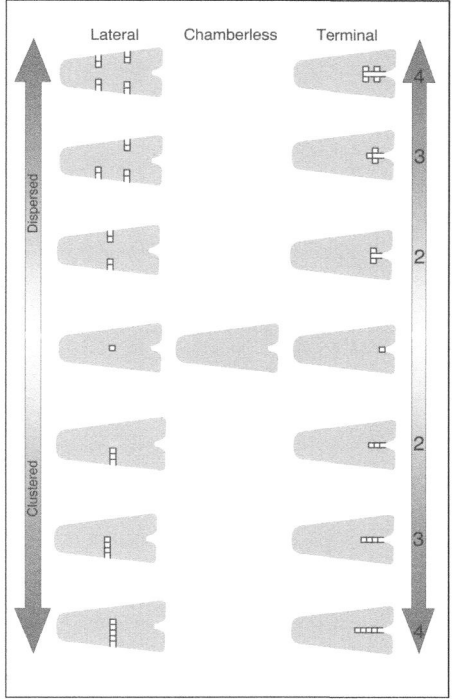

30 Above Modular system of chamber arrangements in long barrows and related monuments. *After Kinnes 1975, fig. 7A*

31 Right Schematic representation of the structuring principles applied to the form and lay-out of long barrows

monuments (Appendix B), but few provide reliable dates for the construction of the monument from which they derive. Two kinds of date are, however, useful in providing an overall chronology for the long barrow tradition.

First are dates on material from the old ground surface below monuments. These do not necessarily date the construction works, but they do provide an indication of the date after which the monument must have been built, whether that is weeks, years, decades, or centuries. There are 17 acceptable dates from pre-long barrow contexts at nine different long barrows in the Cotswold-Severn region *(32A)*. A few of these dates clearly relate to material that was already old by the time the long barrow was built, and there are perhaps one or two dates at the more recent end of the sequence whose exact origin and stratigraphic security deserve to be checked. The remainder are remarkably consistent and suggest a building phase for long barrows starting about 3800 BC, with only slight evidence for new construction or the expansion of mounds on to new ground after about 3400 BC.

The second group of dates relate to human burials in the chambers. These illustrate the age of the human remains connected with the use of the monument, and here we have to accept the possibility that some original material was cleared out of the chambers and that some intrusive, perhaps already ancient, material was sometimes added. There are 36 acceptable dates on human bone from the chambers of six long barrows *(32B)*. All are remarkably consistent, with most of the age spans falling within the period 3800 to 3000 BC, and most within the rather smaller range of 3600 to 3300 BC. The outliers are either clear secondary

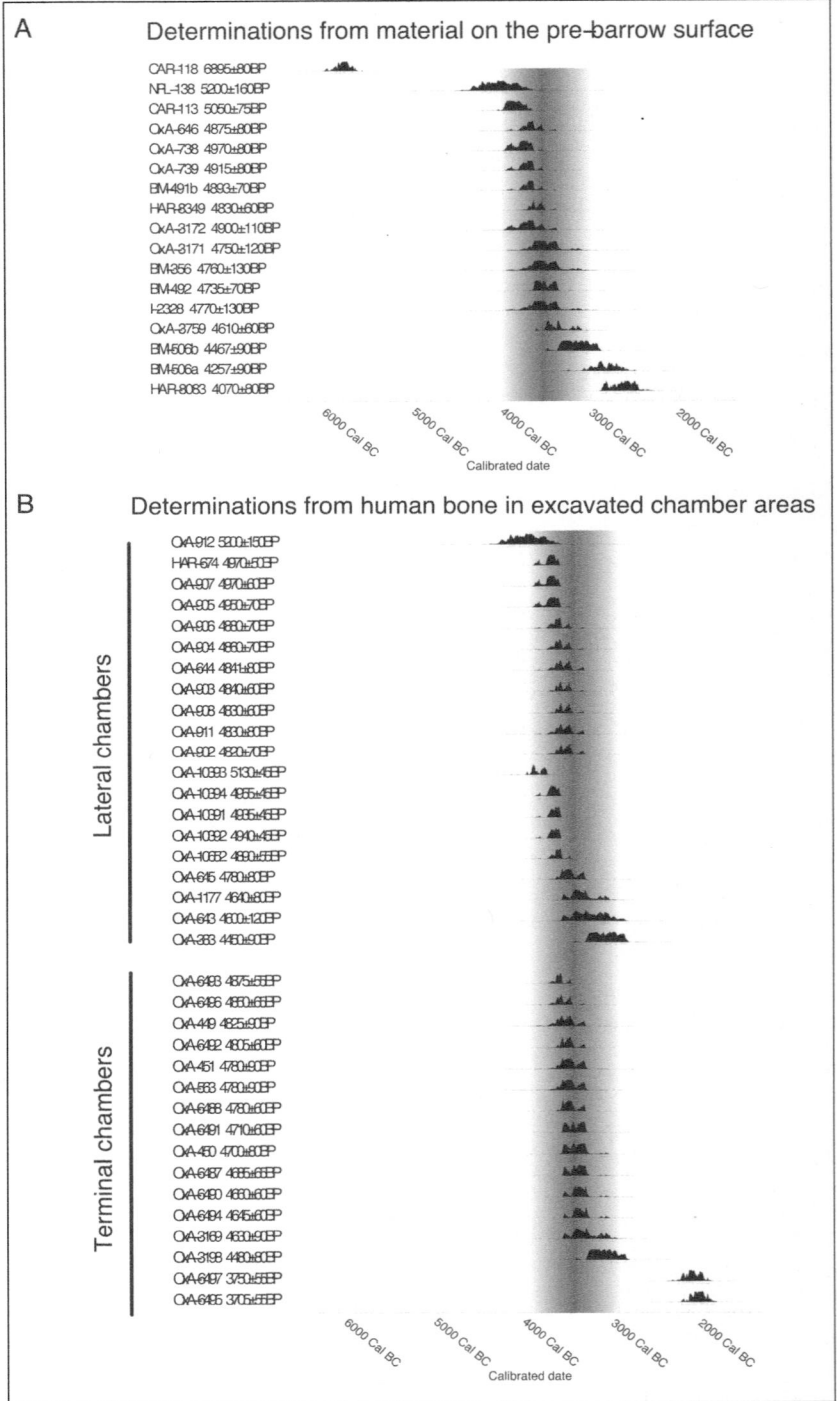

32 Radiocarbon dates for the use of long barrows in the Cotswold-Severn region.
A: Samples from pre-barrow surface; *B:* Deposits of human and animal bone within excavated chamber areas. For details of the dates see Appendix B

additions around 2100 BC, or determinations with large standard deviations. As expected, the dates for the burials are mainly later than the dates for the pre-barrow contexts, although the difference is slight.

The available dates on tools believed to have been used in the construction of long barrows, mainly from ditch fills and contexts within the mounds, are entirely consistent with these two key groups of dates. The same applies to dated samples from forecourts and peripheral locations.

Further radiocarbon dates from burial deposits in other long barrows would be highly desirable in order to test whether there are any differences in the age of populations found within the main styles of long barrow. At present, evidence for any sequence in the kinds of long barrows built in the Cotswold-Severn region is rather shaky, although the balance of evidence currently suggests that those with terminal chambers are perhaps slightly later than those with lateral chambers. Elsewhere I have used the evidence of associated pottery finds to argue that long barrows with lateral chambers may be slightly earlier than those with terminal chambers,[53] and this model still holds. With a short chronology for the long barrow tradition as a whole, however, radiocarbon dating may still be too crude to sort out the exact order of monuments that were effectively built and used over just a few centuries. More dates from multi-period long barrows may help to understand the time period over which monuments developed, and the speed of take-up, but the problem of improving resolution will not easily be solved.

Looked at over the whole span of the fourth millennium BC, a broad sequence of development and change can be suggested on the basis of pottery, available radiocarbon dates, and a few assumptions about architectural succession. This can be summarized in schematic form *(33)*, and provides a provisional model from which to develop further research. What it fails to show, of course, is any differences that might exist in the trajectory of change within different parts of the Cotswold-Severn region.

LONG BARROWS OF THE COTSWOLD-SEVERN REGION IN SPACE

About 200 long barrows have been recorded to date within the broad geographical area identified in Chapter 2 as the Cotswold-Severn region *(34)*. An unknown number of examples were destroyed before ever coming to the attention of antiquarians and archaeologists, while at least ten recorded examples have been lost since first coming to attention. Against this must be set the fact that previously unrecorded examples come to light from time to time either to fill out existing groups or to extend the distribution into apparently blank areas (see Chapter 2).

The spread of long barrows in the Cotswold-Severn region forms the northern part of the much larger group identified above which occupies much of central southern England. The southern edge of the Marlborough Downs marked by the deeply incised Vale of Pewsey may be taken as the southern limit of the Cotswold-Severn region, and seems to form a natural break in the spread of long barrows. Within the region, a number of clusters can be identified, between which are

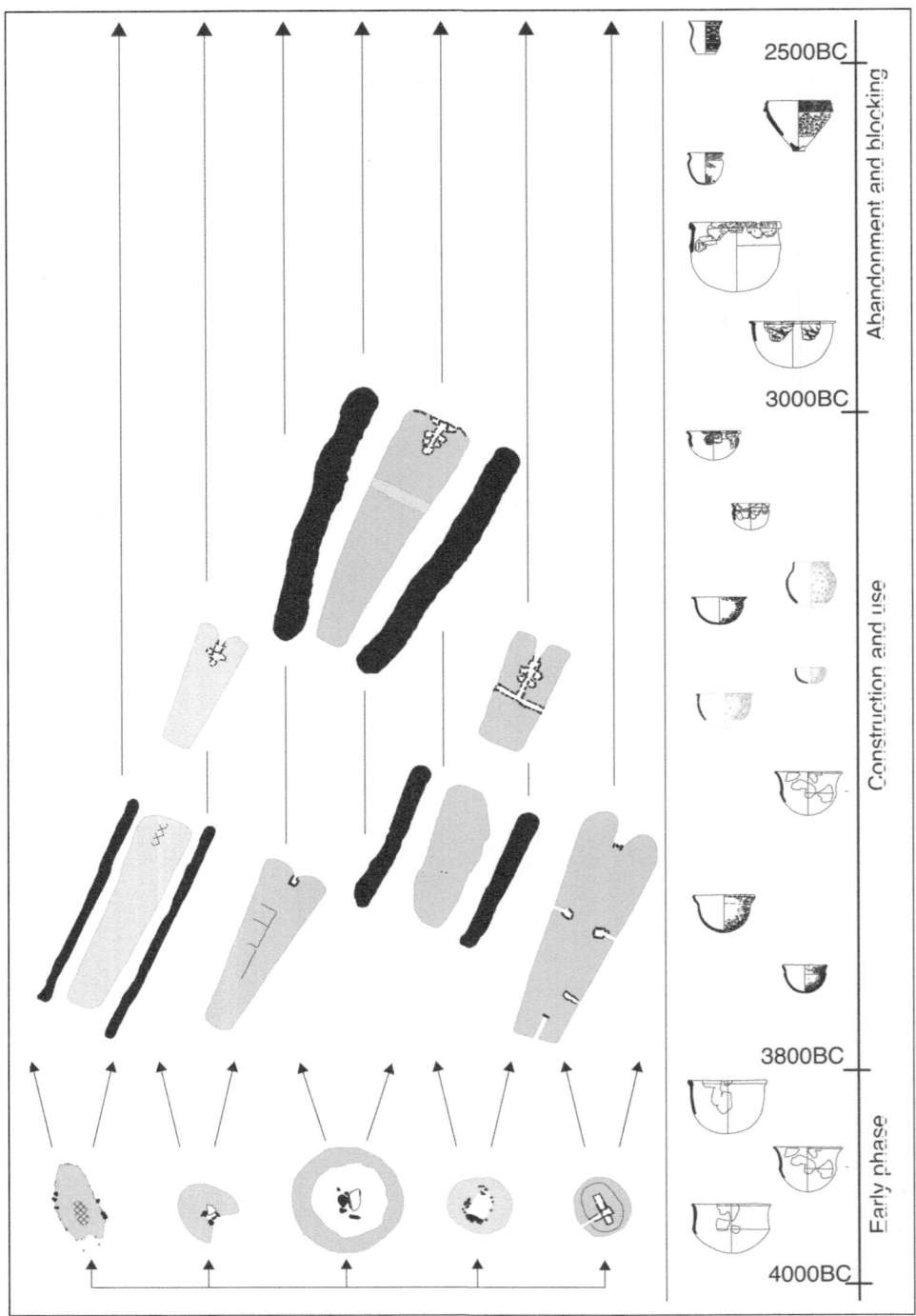

33 Provisional scheme of monument development in the Cotswold-Severn region linked to known pottery styles, absolute chronology and a general phasing of the long barrow tradition

rather lighter scatters of barrows. Most of these clusters seem to form around the headwaters of river catchments or along escarpment edges.

In general, long barrows in the Cotswold-Severn region occur singly and in relative isolation, even within the more marked clusters already referred to. Occasionally, however, there are pairs of long barrows perhaps 150m to 200m apart, as for example at Ffostyll (BRE 3 and 4), Eyford Hill (GLO 3 and 49), Camp (GLO 11 and 67), Hazleton (GLO 33 and 54), Leygore Manor (GLO 57 and 58), College Plantation (GLO 72 and 73), Ascott-under-Wychwood (OXF 6 and 15) and Pen Hill (SOM 17 and 18). Why two barrows should be set close together in this way is far from clear, and, strangely, no pair has had both barrows thoroughly investigated. At Hazleton, however, a detailed survey of and small cutting into the south barrow (GLO 33) showed that it was of similar size and type to the well-known Hazleton North.[54]

Starting in the southeast, there are about a dozen long barrows around the headwaters of the River Kennet and about the same number again around the edge of the Marlborough Downs, from the massive Adam's Grave (WIL 6) near Knap Hill through to Wayland's Smithy (BRK 1) on the Berkshire Ridgeway. To the west, between the Rivers Avon and Yeo, there are about ten sites on and around the Mendips and on the higher ground west of Chew Magna. The most westerly example on the south side of the Bristol Channel is at Battlegore (SOM 11), between Exmoor and the Quantock Hills near Watchet.

On the Cotswolds there are about 100 long barrows along the escarpment and across the dip slope from near Bath in the south to Shipston on Stour in the north. Within this area there are several clusters, especially around the headwaters of the River Frome, an east bank tributary of the Severn. Here there are also monuments set on impressive escarpment edges, as with Hetty Pegler's Tump (GLO 14), Nympsfield (GLO 13) and The Toots (GLO 76). In the far south, the Druid Stoke long barrow (GLO 28) in what is now a suburb of Bristol shows the potential for the discovery of examples along the Avon valley. Strangely perhaps, the head of the Thames, the largest river in southeastern Britain, is not a marked focus for sites, although Windmill Tump, Rodmarton (GLO 16) is very close to the modern recognized source at Thameshead. In the central Cotswolds the main spread of long barrows falls within the relatively flat upland plateau. The most marked cluster, more than a dozen barrows, lies around Swell in the north Cotswolds. Here, around the headwaters of the Rivers Dikler and Eye, the barrows overlook the shallow valleys. Both rivers feed into the Windrush, a north bank tributary of the Thames, which is arguably as much the source of this river as the currently identified principal rising near Kemble.

West of the River Severn the long barrows tend to lie on low ground, in river valleys rather than on the hills. The western limit of the region is marked by the exceptionally fine long barrow at Parc le Breos Cwm (GLA 4) set in the very bottom of a narrow valley that was occupied from at least 12,000 BC onwards. A small stream that is now largely underground originally crossed the valley floor, shifting its course over time and eroding the southwest corner of the barrow. Another seemingly rather similar tomb lies within sand dunes along the Gower coast at Pen-maen Burrows (GLA 5), illustrating yet another kind of environment in which these long barrows can be found. Heston Brake (MON 3) also lies near the coast, with views over the mouth of the Severn, part of a small scatter of terminal-chambered long barrows in the area.[55] Finally, the Black Mountain group contains about 15 examples, three in the valley of the River Usk, three in the valley of the River Wye and the remainder on higher ground around the edges of the central upland block, mainly overlooking the valley of the Wye. Three examples overlook the Golden Valley between the Bage and Pontrilas; traditionally the most northerly well-preserved long barrow within the Cotswold-Severn region was Arthur's Stone (HRF 1) perched high on a ridge-top near Dorstone.

In December 1994, however, the investigation of cropmarks recorded a few years before on the floodplain of the River Severn at Lower Luggy near Welshpool revealed a previously unrecognized long barrow 60m long and 20m wide, probably of the kind with a timber chamber.[56] No other such barrows are currently known in the middle and upper Severn valley, but more may well exist to be found in the area, thereby extending the overall distribution of long barrows into the central Marches.

At present, the distribution of long barrows within the Cotswold-Severn region can be separated into four broad groups on the basis of the topographic zones in which they lie *(34)*:

A. North Wessex Downs: comprising rolling chalk hills reaching a maximum altitude of 270m OD at Hackpen Hill, separated by wide, shallow river valleys in which the watercourses flow mainly to the southeast. A steep escarpment on the north side overlooks the upper Thames valley; the steep-sided Vale of Pewsey forms the south side.

B. Cotswold Hills: linear limestone upland running broadly southwest to northeast with a steep escarpment overlooking the Severn valley on the west side and a gentle dip slope to the upper Thames valley on the east. The southern Cotswolds are heavily dissected by steep-sided river valleys while the northern Cotswolds are more plateau-like with shallow valleys and high exposed upland reaching a maximum of 317m at Cleeve Cloud.

C. Mendip Hills and Chew valley south of the Bristol Avon: upland ridge rising to 325m northwest of Charterhouse, flanked by the Somerset Levels to the south, with the lowlands of the Severn estuary floodplain to the northwest and the Chew valley and low hills of the Bristol coalfield to the northeast.

D. Hill and vale country west of the Severn in southeast Wales: dramatic variable scenery with a narrow coastal fringe backed by high hills and mountains with deeply cut, sometimes winding, valleys caused by a varied natural geology dominated by carboniferous limestone and Old Red Sandstone. Marked contrasts exist between the valley floors and the adjacent mountain-tops, the maximum

Long Barrows: A New Tradition

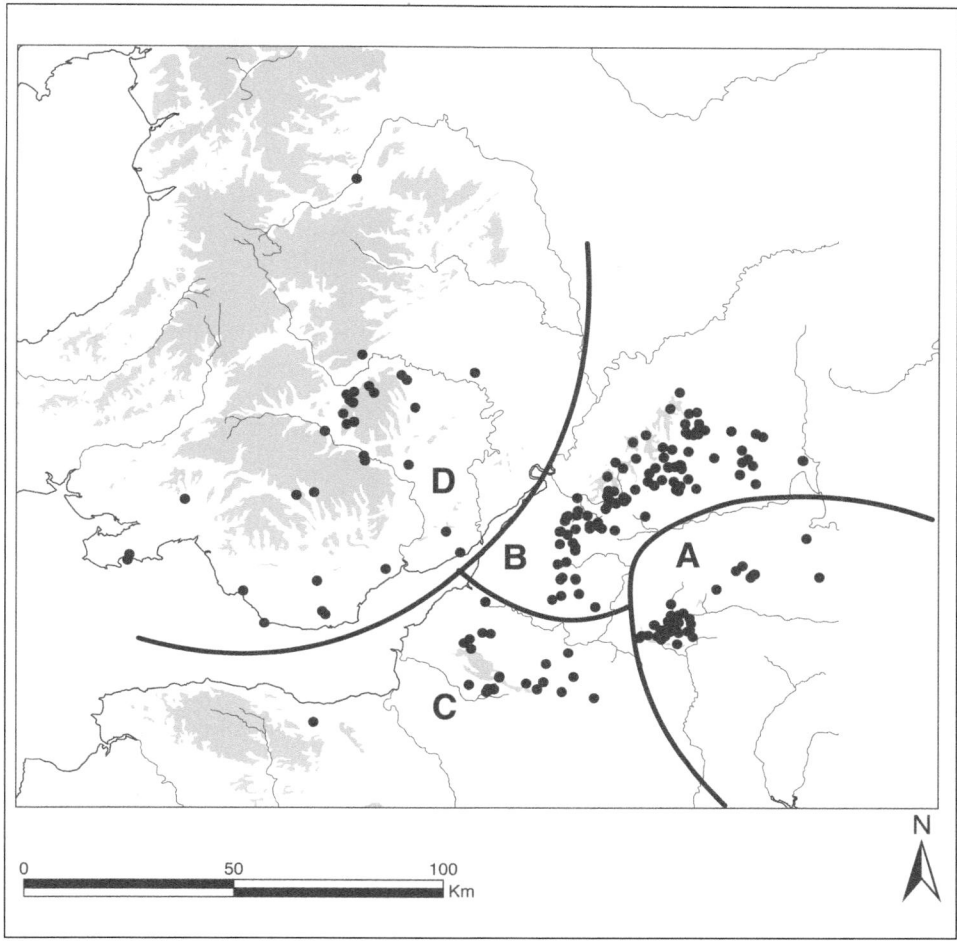

34 Distribution of recorded long barrows within the Cotswold-Severn region. The main topographic zones are marked: A: North Wessex Downs; B: Cotswold Hills; C: Mendips and south of the River Avon; D: Hill and vale country west of the River Severn. Land over 244m OD is stippled

elevations being in the Black Mountains, which reach 810m OD at Waun Fâch. The river valleys and coastal plain provide the main means of communications within and through the region.

The placement of a long barrow in its contemporary landscape is unlikely to have been random. Facets of the site itself were no doubt important and these are considered in the next chapter, but topography, setting, views and position represent wider considerations that might also have been important. Mark Edmunds has emphasized the role of pathways and tracks in leading people to long barrows, noting how many examples are visible from a distance while close-to they are revealed only after the final climb or by rounding a local topographic eminence.[57]

87

A number of recent studies have approached these matters through the use of phenomenology. In archaeology this means trying to understand the way in which people in the past experienced the world by re-inhabiting some of the places they used. Christopher Tilley's work provided a model that others have followed and which provides some potentially useful insights. One of his early case studies involved the long barrows of the Black Mountains. Three categories of site were identified: (1) those situated in a lowland location along the river valleys, on or near to river terraces above the floodplain; (2) intermediate situations above the river valleys, commanding extensive views but at a relatively low height; and (3) sites situated high up on ridges and saddles and on undulating terrain below the Black Mountains. About 50 per cent of sites fall into this third category, the remainder being distributed fairly evenly between the other two kinds of situation. He argued that long barrows in the first two groups tended to have their long axis running parallel with the major rivers or their tributaries, while the upland barrows in the third group tended to be orientated towards prominent spurs on the Black Mountains between 1km and 6km away. At least three sites (Ffostyll South (BRE 4), Ty Isaf (BRE 5) and Penywyrlod (BRE 14)) seemed to be orientated towards Mynydd Troed, a dome-topped mountain on the south side of which stands the Mynydd Troed long barrow (BRE 10). Tilley suggested that within the Black Mountains the 'monuments draw out and emphasize important features of the landscape: the axes of the river valleys and prominent spurs, paths of movement and prominent landmarks whose ancestral significance had already been established . . . and whose meanings were now being reworked through the process of monument construction'.[58]

Andrew Fleming later criticized Tilley's work because some of the fields of view did not quite seem to be as originally claimed, and a very useful theoretical approach seems to have been let down by some poor field observations.[59] This view is supported by detailed studies of the landscape setting of long barrows in the Black Mountains carried out by Vicki Cummings, Andrew Jones and Aaron Watson. For this they sketched the 360-degree view from a set point in the centre of a selection of long barrows. What they found was that the axis of each monument tended to divide the view between, say, hills to one side and valley land to the other, or between a restricted view in one direction and an open view the other way. Thus, 'rather than emphasizing impressive landscape features, the long axis of each monument seems to emphasize points of transition between contrasting parts of the landscape, and often where the nature of the view changed from open to restricted'.[60] They also took up the well-established point that many of the long barrows themselves seem to be asymmetrical in plan, in the layout of their chambers, in the plan of the chambers themselves, and in the way that stones had been selectively used in the construction of the chambers. By extension, they suggest possible relationships between the essential asymmetry of the landscape, the construction of the monuments and the symbolic expression of deeper understandings and beliefs. However, these things take us into the detail of site selection and long barrow construction, the subject of the next chapter.

5

THE ANATOMY OF COTSWOLD LONG BARROWS

Once rather quaintly described as looking like stranded whales across the Cotswold Hills,[1] even the rounded weathered appearance of well-preserved long barrows is but a pale reflection of what these monuments must have been. Some of the reconstructed examples, such as Belas Knap (GLO 1), Wayland's Smithy (BRK 1) and Parc le Breos Cwm (GLA 4) give good impressions of the original form and bulk of these monuments, but today's visitors still need to close their eyes and dream in order to image the brash surfaces of the mound and the dark corpse-strewn interior of the chambers.

Below the surface, the basic anatomy of Cotswold-Severn long barrows is fairly straightforward, although no two examples are quite the same. Inevitably, there are numerous permutations and variations to the disposition of elements and the range of components used at particular sites, just as might be expected amongst constructions put together by small-scale autonomous groups. The differences extend well beyond the basic arrangement of the chambers in relation to the mound discussed in the last chapter, but over the last two centuries or so an extensive terminology has developed in order to describe and refer to the various parts of a long barrow in a standardized fashion *(35)*. Ultimately, of course, we have to ask how these long barrows would have looked when new and what symbolism the architecture embodied. But before this it is important to consider what tools and equipment were used to build a long barrow. Where did the raw materials come from? How were the main elements constructed? What was the construction sequence? How was the site for a barrow chosen? And how much labour was needed to complete a long barrow?

LABOUR NEEDS AND THE SCALE OF THE TASK

Designing and building a long barrow would have been a major undertaking for a community whose tool-kit we know comprised antler and bone picks, levers,

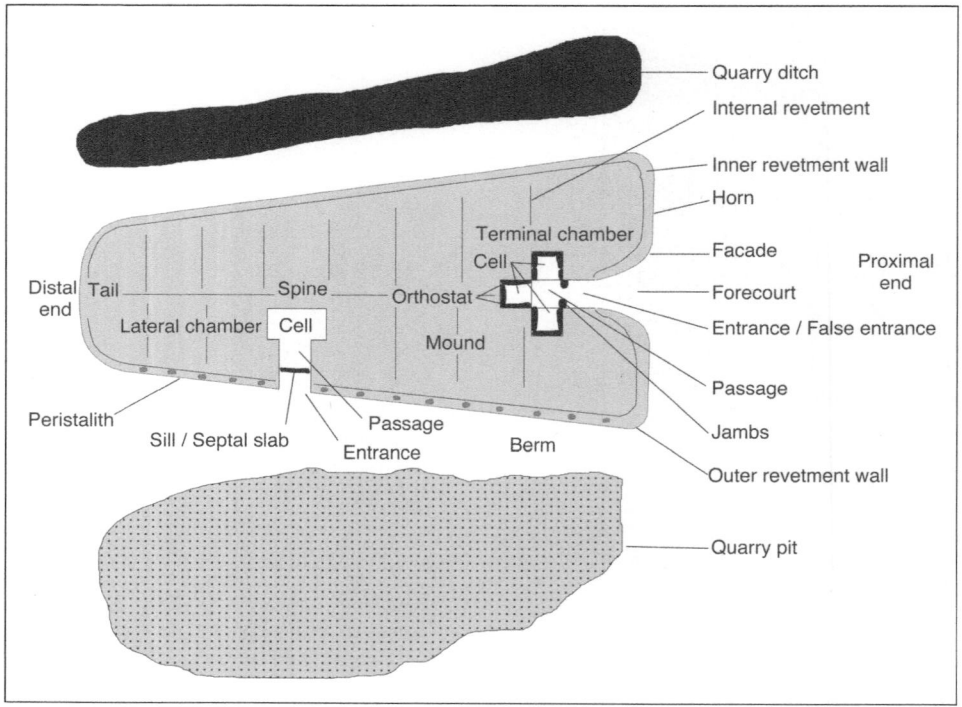

35 Terminology for the main structural components of a long barrow

wedges, rakes and shovels, and which we can strongly suspect also included baskets, leather bags, fibre or leather ropes and wooden rollers and levers. They had access to timber from managed woodland and natural wildwood forests, the stone tools to cut and fashion timber and some technical knowledge of making planks and jointing. Wickerwork of young withies was made in the form of hurdles. Experiments have been carried out to determine the speed of quarrying bedrock and shifting soil and rubble using this kind of technology, and once the basic skills have been acquired a surprising amount can be achieved in a relatively short time. Bill Startin and Richard Bradley estimated that a modest long barrow would require about 6,900 person-hours to build, a large one perhaps 15,700 person-hours;[2] Alan Saville suggested that Hazleton North (GLO 54) needed between 8,000 and 14,500 person-hours to construct.[3] Whether such effort was expended in a single session, say 40 people working more or less continuously eight hours a day for between 22 and 49 days (depending on the size of the monument), or whether their labour was spread over months, years, or even decades, is impossible to say.

One determining factor in assessing labour requirements is the effort needed to achieve the largest single task. So far as Hazleton North goes, the biggest single task is reckoned to have been moving orthostat 19 that weighs about half a tonne. This stone would have needed about six people to move and manhandle into position. This is essentially the minimum reasonable workforce, and such a group could have built the whole barrow in less than a year on their own. A community of 20–30 individuals should be able to raise a team of six able-bodied people to build a barrow, and even if they could not be spared for a whole year then 2–3 months a year for five years is still a very modest and achievable commitment.

Bigger monuments needed more effort, especially where very large stones had to be moved and positioned. In this respect, the capstones of the single-celled chambers at Tinkinswood (GLA 9) and Maesyfelin (GLA 10) are amongst the largest undertakings at any long barrow in the Cotswold-Severn region. Both weigh more than 20 tonnes apiece and would probably have needed a workforce of more than 100 strong people to move. Quite a crowd to organize. How exactly they lifted these giant stones into position is not known.

Any construction work of the scale and complexity of a long barrow inevitably means that there is a natural sequence or order in which tasks are undertaken. Sometimes this can be determined through the careful examination of the resultant structures and the application of common sense to the interpretation of excavated remains. In doing so it is necessary, of course, to set aside many of the constraints and process-driven management considerations that would determine the way a modern engineering project might unfold. Six thousand years ago such things simply did not count; getting a construction job done depended on the energy, enthusiasm, strength and devotion of the workforce, coupled no doubt with a big slice of luck, the imagined support of hermetic forces and perhaps even a little sorcery to help things run as smoothly as possible.

When it comes to working out the detail of how long barrows were made, the archaeological world splits into two camps. Some scholars see the construction process spread out over a moderately long period, with people using the various elements as freestanding structures along the way. Others take the opposite view and see long barrows as monuments created over a relatively short period with a certain unity and coherence to their design and construction. Without firm archaeological evidence to the contrary and excluding the clearly sequential multi-period structures that by definition must have developed gradually through a series of discrete stages, the short construction chronology is preferred here. However, it is fully accepted that, once built, long barrows, like many other classes of prehistoric monuments, were messed about with and modified by their users and perhaps by other communities as well.

As we have already seen, there is great variety in the kinds of long barrow built, so much so that each can be conceived of as the work of a single community, connected with, but autonomous of, others. There is no evidence that these groups were united by the kind of overarching authority that would demand close conformity in the design and construction of sacred monuments. Clearly there were structuring principles, as discussed in Chapter 4, but no common blueprint. The repertoire of elements drawn upon to build a long barrow owed much to the various forms of existing monuments such as dolmens, portal dolmens, simple passage graves, oval barrows and rotunda graves, as well as to novel exotic elements such as the long mound itself. Elsewhere I have discussed the way that elements used in the construction of a long barrow were selected out of a wider pool of ideas through a decision-making process faced by each barrow-building community. I concluded that such decisions were probably taken within small-scale social groups drawing on an extensive underpinning knowledge and sets of received and contested traditions.[4] In a similar vein, Richard Bradley has argued that choices underlying the construction of a particular type of monument are largely grounded in the routines that people followed and the conventions that they accepted as second nature; in other words the history and traditions of the builder and user community.[5] Overall, building a long barrow was probably the single biggest investment that an early farming community in Britain could make, but its success or otherwise must ultimately have hinged on finding the right place to build.

CHOOSING A SITE

Exactly why communities chose to build their long barrow where they did is far from clear, but one might guess that the three most important factors were: location, location and location. It is almost universal amongst traditional societies for sacred structures to be situated in special places, sites that for the builders at least had particular poignancy and meaning because of their position (hilltop, riverside, near a spring, etc.) or associations (with a particular person, animal, tree, etc.), or because the interpretation of divine guidance showed where it should be (lightning strike, sacred animal took people there, divination, necromancy, geomancy, etc.). As we have already seen, some long barrows were built on places that had previously been singled out for attention through the construction of earlier monuments, sometimes the aggregation of several separate structures that were later united in a single long barrow, as at Sale's Lot (GLO 94) where a simple passage grave and a rotunda grave stood side by side.

As briefly discussed in Chapter 4, it is hard to pick out at a broad scale any unifying locational characteristics, although a few common trends can be detected. Where long barrows were placed on hills, they rarely if ever seem to occur on a hilltop but rather on a slope or false-crest just below the hilltop. This has been recognized since the days of Crawford,[6] but strangely no one has ever excavated a large enough area around a long barrow to see whether there are associated features that might have a bearing on the specific position and orientation of the monument. Escarpment edge positions are common and many such long barrows command truly extraordinary views. These, and false-crest-situated barrows, share a third characteristic of location, which is that they can only be seen from certain directions, perhaps the homelands or residential zones of the user community. But by no means all long barrows lie on high ground. West of the Severn especially, valley floor locations and views towards rivers or the sea are common. Was there a single broad unifying factor for location? Probably not, or at least no one has recognized it yet.

Local factors may have been more important than general circumstances. At South Street long barrow (WIL 36) and Gwernvale (BRE 7), large earthfast boulders would have been visible at ground level, projecting up through the earth.

Perhaps these were in some way special and attracted attention for some reason. Equally, the nature of the land on which long barrows were built and their immediate environment were potentially important. Such things can be understood only where excavation has taken place on a considerable scale and where sampling for environmental indicators such as snail-shell sequences and pollen spectra has taken place. Where detailed studies of the pre-barrow surface have been carried out, there is almost always evidence for considerable activity over fairly long periods of time before the barrow was built; long barrows were very rarely, if ever, built on virgin ground.

At Nympsfield (GLO 13) at least one post, and perhaps two, pre-dated the mound towards its western end.[7] Standing stones may also have been present at several sites. At Pipton (BRE 8) two large slabs referred to as 'buttress' stones were found projecting through the mound,[8] while at Notgrove (GLO 4) a large stone incorporated into the outer revetment wall on the north side may have been an outlier to the earlier rotunda grave.[9] The presence of large standing stones embedded within, or perhaps even projecting through, the mounds at Tinglestone (GLO 31) and Lyneham (OXF 8) may also be noted but require further investigation.[10]

One of the best-studied pre-barrow ground surfaces is below Hazleton North (GLO 54) in the central Cotswolds. Here the old ground level was well preserved and proved to be an argillic brown soil up to 0.4m thick. It had probably developed in the early post-glacial period, under forest conditions. The sequence of events at the site is hard to reconstruct in exact detail because the soil had been cultivated and mixed before the long barrow was built, but four main phases of human settlement can be identified. The first is represented by a scatter of flintwork that accumulated during the early fifth millennium BC *(36A)*. Alan Saville suggested that this could be the remains of a temporary camp for the retooling of hunting equipment. No features such as pits or postholes seem to have been dug, and once these people left it is unlikely that later communities would have known of their visit. It is possible, however, that they played a role in the next phase, which saw tree clearance across the area. Following this clearance the soil was cultivated, probably for the production of cereals in small garden-like plots. Putatively domestic debris was scattered across the whole of the area later covered by the long barrow, but a particularly intensive spread may be the ploughed-out remains of a midden, southwest of which were the remains of a structure, perhaps a small gable-roofed house *(36B)*.[11] A line of shallow postholes running roughly north–south to the northwest of the midden and house may be the remains of a fence or land boundary. Three small groups of human skull fragments and two teeth were found near the top of the buried soil, suggesting the nearby presence of disturbed burials pre-dating the barrow. Finally, further cultivation seems to have taken place after the abandonment and decay of this small settlement, and by the time the long barrow began to be built the land had become hazel-dominated scrub with areas of cereal cultivation nearby.[12] Looked at one way, the long barrow could simply have been placed in an existing clearing that was no longer used for cultivation. Alternatively, the presence of the settlement, and in particular the site of its former midden, may have been symbolically special in some way, giving

Long Barrows of the Cotswolds

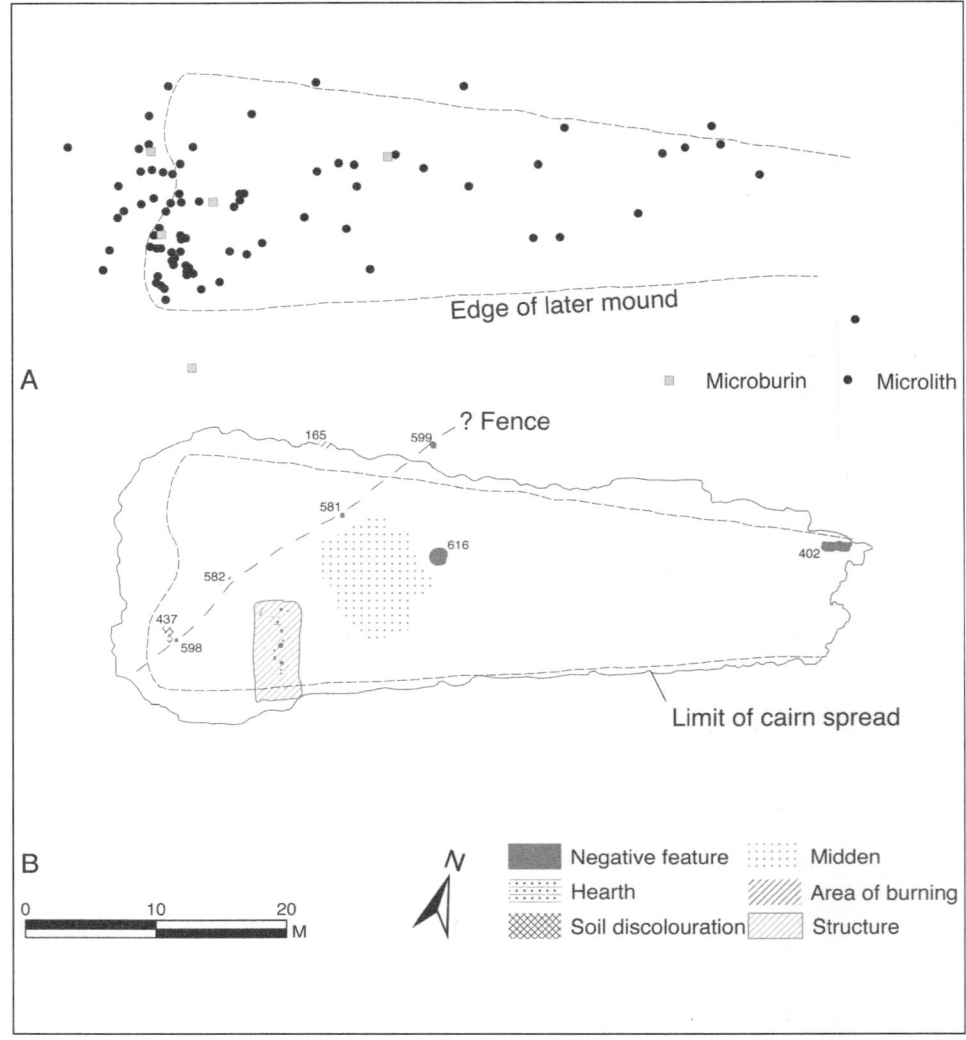

36 Pre-barrow features at Hazleton North (GLO 54). *A:* Distribution of fifth-millennium BC flintwork; *B:* Early fourth-millennium BC midden and structures. *After Saville 1990, figs 13 and 163*

meaning through association to the position of the subsequent long barrow. Radiocarbon dates suggest that very little time elapsed between the use of the settlement and the construction of the long barrow at about 3760–3640 BC.[13]

Hazleton North is typical of many other sites in the Cotswolds and the north Wessex Downs. At Ascott-under-Wychwood (OXF 6), there was again an extensive scatter of later fifth-millennium BC flintwork prior to, or perhaps connected with, localized forest clearance which made way for a small settlement that included several structures. Following their decay the area became open scrubby grassland, an environment that prevailed when the long barrow was built.[14] Grassland and scrub were also present at Wayland's Smithy (BRK 1) following the construction of the oval barrow and before the construction of the long barrow known as Wayland's Smithy II. Here too there were traces of earlier cultivation. Settlement occurred in the general vicinity, to judge from the scatter of flintwork, broken pottery, quernstone fragments, a smashed flint axe and animal bone in the buried soil below the long barrow.[15] At the Horslip barrow (WIL 30), open grassland conditions obtained when the barrow was built, and there were cereal crops on the site or in the vicinity. Seven intersecting pits pre-dated the construction of the barrow, although their purpose is not known.[16] Nearby, the Beckhampton Road long barrow (WIL 27) had been built in an area of long-term grassland with areas of cultivation and woodland nearby. A scatter of flintwork and animal bone occurred in the buried soil, together with charcoal-rich earth suggesting the former presence of hearths and a few scattered stakeholes. Some of the stakeholes clustered around one of three ox-skulls found on the old ground surface. It seems probable that before the mound was raised the ox-hide, replete with its head and hoofs, had been draped over a cluster of small timber posts and left for a while.[17] In the same area, the setting of the South Street long barrow was open grassland at the time the barrow was constructed, but prior to this there had been a phase of cultivation which left traces of cross-ploughing in the underlying chalk bedrock. This episode had been followed by the accumulation of flint-knapping debris. Spreads of charcoal, perhaps resulting from the incorporation into the topsoil of surface hearths, were found and there were a number of stake-holes suggestive of temporary structures and perhaps one or more fences. All of this had disappeared by the time the barrow was built, as the alignment of the fences had no impact on the orientation of the long barrow.[18] Finally, in the same area is Millbarrow (WIL 11). Here, open grassland conditions prevailed at the time the barrow was built, but again there was evidence of a small pre-barrow settlement represented by postholes and pits. The pit fills included the fragmentary remains of three or four individuals, including pieces from the skeleton of a child.[19] As elsewhere, human bones were in evidence at the sites later occupied by long barrows long before the barrows themselves were built.

West of the Severn broadly similar evidence is represented, although the sample of sites examined in detail through excavation is small. At Gwernvale (BRE 7), the earliest activity on the site could be traced back to the end of the last Ice Age, when flint tools and weapons were dropped on the old ground surface. Occupation dating to about 5700 BC, including a pit and a substantial spread of flintwork, extended across most of the area later covered by the long barrow. Around 3800 BC there was further fairly intensive occupation, with pits, postholes and bedding trenches for timber walls. Bill Britnell, excavator of the site, interpreted these as parts of at least two separate structures. But an alternative explanation is that they all relate to a single substantial long house that perhaps extended beyond the edge of the area protected by the later mound.[20] West of this house was the large natural stone already referred to that stood at least 0.7m above the old ground surface and perhaps provided a focus for the pre-barrow activity.

Overall, the evidence for pre-barrow activity at almost all of the thoroughly examined sites where there were no earlier monumental structures shows a remarkably coherent picture: small-scale visitations during the sixth and fifth millennia BC, woodland clearance, settlement on or near the site, cultivation and then finally a period of relatively low-intensity usage when open conditions, typically vegetated with grassland or scrub, developed immediately prior to the construction of the barrow in the early fourth millennium BC.[21] Human remains are represented among the finds from several sites, but the overall range of material represented is strongly suggestive of fairly substantial occupation by farming communities or, more likely, those with a mixed farming-hunting-gathering economy. That long barrow construction took place some centuries after these economies were first practised in the area conforms to the idea discussed in Chapter 4 that these were the monuments of mature communities rather than pioneer groups. Julian Thomas remarked that within the Cotswold-Severn area 'there are strong indications that these tombs were built in locations which had already gained some significance'[22] and this would seem to be confirmed. The presence of material of the sixth and fifth millennia BC on several sites suggests, however, that we should not only be looking to the farming communities for the initial ascription of such significance; if the place was, for example, somehow seen as being symbolically linked to ancestral communities, then the ancestors concerned may well have been hunter-gatherers rather than farmers.

What greeted the builders of each long barrow when they came to construct their new monument varied only in detail. Previously occupied open ground would probably have been rather uneven, and in the case of Gwernvale there were several earthfast boulders projecting out of the ground. Where detailed studies have taken place, the land-use prior to barrow construction was mainly grassland and scrub, in some cases systematically grazed, but at the very least periodically browsed by the wild herbivores of the time: red deer, wild pig and aurochs.

CONSTRUCTION SEQUENCE AND SETTING OUT

Detailed extensive excavations provide vivid insights into the way that long barrows were constructed. The basic sequence is fairly straightforward; the only difficulty, as explored above, is the time-period over which the operation should be stretched and the possibility that it was episodic, with some use of completed components along the way. The following broad stages can be identified:

- Define the site, set out the axis of the mound on the preferred orientation, carry out any necessary foundation ceremonies.

- Dig sockets, postholes, or bedding trenches to receive the orthostats and posts of the chambers, façade and any features in the forecourt.

- Obtain suitable stone or timber for the construction of the chambers and associated features.

- Construct the chambers and associated stone and timber settings.

- Set out the edges of the mound with a bedding trench or foundation slot, lay out internal divisions or bays and if appropriate erect hurdling or fencing to contain the matrix of the mound.

- Obtain turf, soil, rubble and rock for the construction of the mound, either from quarry pits or from surface collection and deposit it within the various defined elements of the mound.

- During the formation of the mound, construct the inner and outer revetment walls, peristalith, or post-edging around the outer limits.

Some of these stages could be carried out side by side – for example raising the mound could be started while the chambers were being built – but as a linear sequence it provides a useful framework around which to structure the examination of available archaeological evidence.

Since one essential feature of a long barrow is its linear form, each will naturally have an orientation. Whether the orientations selected were symbolically meaningful or allowed parts of the monument to be aligned on some significant landscape feature or celestial event is more difficult to gauge. There is, however, evidence for the deliberate creation of a central axis and it is easy to imagine that considerable trouble was taken to get it exactly as the builders felt it should be. A certain amount of ritual and ceremony might well have accompanied the act of laying down the axis of a barrow; in classical times setting the orientation of a sacred structure was known euphemistically as 'stretching the cord' and would normally involve divination and geomancy. At Hazleton North (GLO 54), the archaeological evidence shows that construction began by laying out an east-northeast to west-southwest axial alignment and then placing dumps of soil and stone to either side of it.[23] At Beckhampton Road (WIL 27) the main axis of the barrow, also east-north-east to west-south-west, was marked by a line of stakeholes, while nearby at South Street (WIL 36) the main east-southeast to west-northwest axis was marked by a hurdle fence. In all three cases the axis of the long barrow disregarded the orientation of earlier features on the site, presumably either because they were invisible to the builders or because the orientation of the barrow was more important and took precedence. Where pre-existing monuments were to be included within the mound of a long barrow different constraints may of course have applied, and a tension between the orientation of the desired long barrow and the edges of the earlier structures can sometimes be seen in the overall plan of these sites.

Taking all the long barrows within the Cotswold-Severn region together, the preferred orientation is between northeast to southwest and southeast to northwest, with more than 75 per cent of examples falling within this sector, the only other marked preference being almost exactly north to south (37A). Both of the two main kinds of long barrow defined in terms of chamber position have

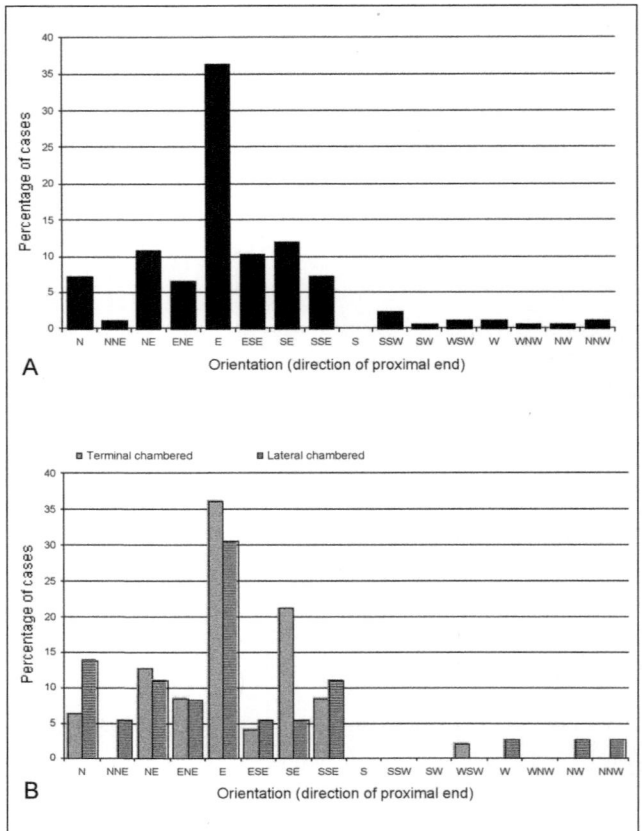

37 The orientation of long barrows in the Cotswold-Severn region. *A:* All examples; *B:* Separately by chamber position

similar orientations *(37B)*, but terminal-chambered barrows show a slightly stronger preference for having the proximal end opening between northeast and southeast, 83 per cent of examples as against 61 per cent of lateral-chambered barrows. Broken down into the four topographic zones within the region there are slight variations. More than 75 per cent of long barrows in the Cotswolds and north Wessex Downs have their proximal ends orientated between northeast and southeast, whereas in the area south of the River Avon, and on the west side of the Severn, the percentages are 73 per cent and 64 per cent respectively. Amongst the misfits that depart from this general pattern is Hazleton North, which has its proximal end towards the west. As one of a pair, however, it is possible that both barrows are arranged so that their forecourts overlook some kind of special place or significant feature that has yet to be identified.

The overwhelming interest in the eastern quarter of the compass accords well with what Paul Ashbee found for long barrows across southern and eastern Britain,[24] and strongly suggests that some significance attached to it. Superficially attractive is the idea that the orientation of these long barrows is aligned on the midsummer sunrise and the midwinter sunset, and there may be merit in this. However, Aubrey Burl has suggested that amongst these fourth-millennium BC

The Anatomy of Cotswold Long Barrows

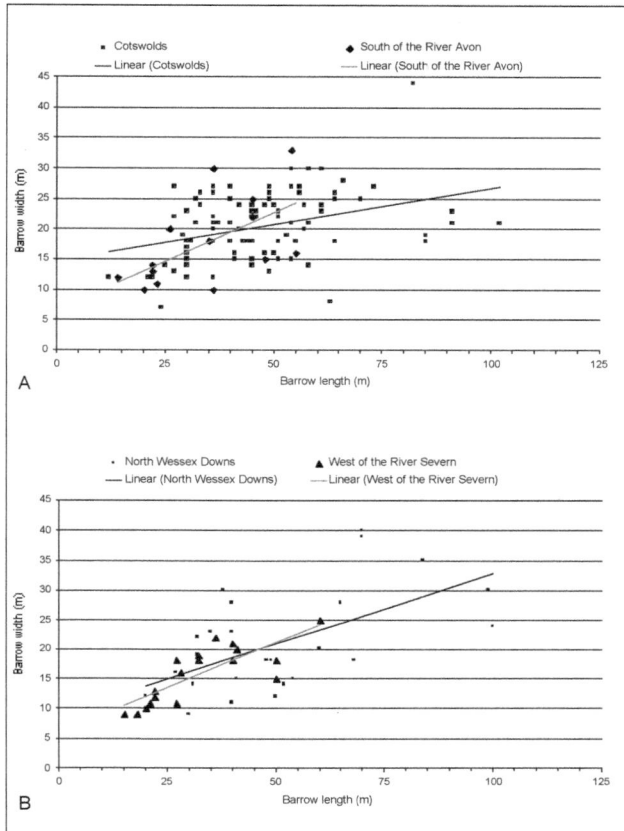

38 The size of long barrows in the Cotswold-Severn region. A: Cotswolds and the area south of the River Avon; B: North Wessex Downs and the area west of the River Severn

structures it was movements of the moon that were perhaps more relevant in determining the timing of ceremonies and perhaps also the movements and power of the ancestors represented by the skeletal remains in the chambers.[25]

The overall size of the long barrow to be raised must also have been in the minds of their builders at an early stage. As noted in Chapter 4, long barrows within the Cotswold-Severn region range from the rather diminutive Nympsfield (GLO 13) at just 27m long by 14m wide, through to West Kennet (WIL 4) at 100m long by 20m wide,[26] the unexcavated Colnpen (GLO 69) at 91m by 21m,[27] and Honeycombe Farm (GLO 68) at about 102m by 21m. The largest example in the region is at Pen Hill (SOM 18) on the southeastern part of the Mendip upland. Leslie Grinsell recorded its dimensions as 228m long by 8m,[28] suggesting that it might best be regarded as an example of what are sometimes called 'bank barrows'.[29] It is possible that some of the rather extravagantly elongated long barrows are in fact two barrows set end to end. This is certainly a strong possibility at West Kennet, where a linear hollow running across the mound 20m or so westwards of the chambers at the proximal end may mark the join *(9)*.[30]

There are slight variations in the size-range of the barrows constructed in the four topographic zones within the Cotswold-Severn region *(38)*. The greatest diversity is present amongst the long barrows on the Cotswolds and the north Wessex Downs, where the length:breadth ratio suggests that barrows in the former tend to be long and thin while the latter are shorter and fatter. With the exception of Pen Hill, which is not shown on the graph, the barrows south of the Bristol Avon lie mainly towards the lower end of the size spectrum and are markedly shorter and fatter than those on the Cotswolds. The barrows west of the Severn are also notably shorter than those on the Cotswolds and north Wessex Downs, but their overall length:breadth ratios are very similar. In a very general sense, the scale of the mound may reflect the size and capability of the community that built it; at the very least it must reflect something of their aspirations.

There are hints that at some sites the ground on which the mound was built underwent some kind of special preparation. At Nympsfield (GLO 13), for example, Mrs Clifford suggested that part of the topsoil had been stripped, perhaps by turf cutting, prior to the construction of the mound.[31] The turf may also have been stripped and the ground levelled up with spreads of clay at Notgrove (GLO 4).[32] Whether these practices were simply pragmatic solutions to local ground conditions or part of elaborate ceremonies concerned with establishing a new barrow is not clear, although some kind of foundation ceremonies might reasonably be expected. The ground below the South Street long barrow showed incontrovertible evidence of pre-barrow cultivation in the form of ard-marks cutting into the underlying chalk bedrock. These are sometimes interpreted as the result of special ceremonies to prepare the ground ahead of building the barrow,[33] but studies of the soil profile revealed that grassland developed after the ground had been cultivated, and this was still present when the barrow was built. Peter Fowler has suggested that, rather than being evidence of ritual ploughing, these marks cut so deep that they should be seen as the 'equivalent of a "prairie-busting" operation carried out with a tough traction implement fitted with a large stone or flint share'.[34]

In laying out long barrows some attention seems to have been given to planning, marking the limits of the site on the ground, and defining the position of the main structural elements. At a few sites there is some evidence for a 'setting-out trench' along the line of what would eventually become the outer revetment wall, although it is possible that on occasions what has been seen here is in fact marks left by stones forming the base of the wall pressing down into a soft topsoil and leaving their impression. At Burn Ground (GLO 60), Grimes recorded that the area selected to be the mound was defined by means of a trench, V-shaped in cross-section, the ground outside the trench being artificially lowered by a few centimetres by paring it away to a diminishing amount for some metres outwards, the effect being to set the body of the mound on a more or less level and slightly raised platform.[35] Something similar may have happened at Notgrove, Nympsfield and Ty Isaf (BRE 5), while at Tinkinswood (GLA 9) there is some evidence for a formal foundation trench to support the outer revetment wall.[36] In a few cases, for example at Penywyrlod (BRE 14), large stones seem to have been placed on the line that would become the edge of the mound to act as marker blocks.[37]

Stuart Piggott noted that at West Kennet the whole chamber area was contained within an isosceles triangle with a base of 9.75m on the cord of the forecourt area, bisected by the axis of the passage, and with its vertical height twice the length of the base. He points out that if such a triangle is drawn, it is found that its sides run through the stones forming the rear walls of all four side chambers, and that three of the stones involved are coincident in angle with the triangle's sides. Moreover, the west chamber at the far end of the central passage falls symmetrically within the converging sides, its rear wall being 6m from the apex.[38] Such regularity within the terms of a modern descriptive geometry does not mean that the builders of West Kennet, or any other long barrow for that matter, shared that knowledge. What it does suggest, however, is a pragmatic interest in form, balance, design and layout which allowed the physical realization of ideas and structures thought out in someone's mind.

In overall plan, long barrows within the Cotswold-Severn region are usually trapezoidal in outline, although a few are rectangular (e.g. Tinkinswood). Most appear superficially symmetrical either side of their long axis, but examined in detail they are somewhat less regular in both the design of the chambers and the layout of the mound. One explanation for this may be the use of simple measuring devices such as poles or ropes to create off-sets from a central base-line that could then be joined up to form the outline plan of the main elements. Another important consideration is the constraints imposed by existing pre-long barrow structures on the design and layout of the long barrow. Beyond these rather practical issues, Vicki Cummings and colleagues have suggested that perhaps the asymmetry seen in the long barrows of the Black Mountains reflected deep-seated views of the world which emphasized a 'sidedness' in relation to the human body,[39] and by extension into ways of thinking that involved binary oppositions: for example, left :: right in relation to male :: female, wild :: domesticated, or perhaps mountain :: valley. As discussed in Chapter 4, there is some evidence for large-scale relationships between the design and position of long barrows in relationship to the wider physical landscape, and as we look deeper into the structure of the monuments themselves there are regularities in small-scale relationships that might carry similar meanings. What is almost certainly the case is that in designing, laying out and building long barrows, the user communities were providing a structure for remembering in which the mound, entrances, passages, chambers, forecourts and so on were used to fix the memory of specific ideas so that anyone journeying through this mnemonic space could 'recollect' the memories that had been purposely stored within the physical structure of the long barrow.[40]

CHAMBER AREAS

At the heart of most long barrows is at least one chamber area comprising the chamber itself, an approach passage and an entrance space. These generally contain human skeletal material (see Chapter 6) and, since the times of Colt Hoare, have supported the idea that long barrows are essentially funerary monuments even though the rituals and ceremonies and the beliefs that lie behind them, are quite different from our own. As noted in Chapter 4, there are two main patterns to the arrangement of the chamber areas: those set laterally within the mound *(39)*; and those set in the end of the mound *(40)*. In both cases, the chamber area comprises one or more cells; the maximum number of cells recorded so far at a long barrow in the Cotswold-Severn region is seven.[41]

In plan, chambers exhibit considerable diversity in the way that general traditions are interpreted (see Chapter 4). Many are simple box-like structures opening directly off the front or side of the mound. Others involve a short passage leading directly to a single round, square or polygonal chamber. In yet other cases the passage leads to a chamber set more or less at right angles to it, either in the form of a sock leading off to left or right, or in the form of a T. More elaborate still are the cruciform arrangements with a single cell either side of a central passage and a cell beyond the crossing, and those with transepted chambers with two or more cells opening on either side of an axial passage. Whether in dispersed or aggregated form (see *31*), the individual chamber designs show clear relationships with the chambers of early style tombs such as might be found in simple passage graves and oval barrows, as well as with contemporary chambers in the lands around the western seaways, especially Ireland, Brittany and Normandy.[42]

Occasionally there are terminal chambers and lateral chambers in the same mound. Some of these result from multi-period construction (for example at Sale's Lot (GLO 94)), but others are of unitary design. At Burn Ground (GLO 60), for example, the inner end of a transepted chamber area with four cells links to a pair of back-to-back lateral chambers that effectively form a cross-passage through the mound.[43]

Not all chambers necessarily opened from the side or front of the mound; some may only have been accessible from above. At Ascott-under-Wychwood (OXF 6), excavations between 1965 and 1970 showed that although the position and overall form of the chambers were similar to arrangements at many lateral-chambered long barrows, there was no direct access from the edge of the mound into what were essentially cists that could only be entered from above *(41)*. Using results from antiquarian excavations, the list of chambers only accessible from the top of the mound can be extended to include Pole's Wood South (GLO 2), Pole's Wood East (GLO 24) and perhaps Lyneham (OXF 8). At Belas Knap (GLO 1) the outer revetment wall ran across the entrance to the southeastern chamber to a height of at least three courses of stonework, suggesting that access from above may have been necessary here too. Some timber chambers may also have been accessed from above. But caution needs to be exercised when considering these sites and especially the results of antiquarian excavations. A.D. Passmore thought that the northwest chamber at the Giant's Caves (WIL 2) lacked a passage through to the outer edge of the mound, but excavations in 1960-2 showed that this was not so.[44]

Timber chambers are rare in the Cotswold-Severn region, being confined to perhaps eight or nine sites on the north Wessex Downs, only two of which, Lambourn (BRK 2) and Kings Play Down (WIL 31), have been excavated since 1900. Timber chambers are of course much more common southwards through central southern England, such that in southern Wiltshire, Dorset and Hampshire the balance between stone and timber chambers seen in the Cotswold-Severn region is reversed. Timber chambers are also common in eastern England and southeastern Scotland,[45] and the recently discovered long barrow at Lower Luggy (MNT 3) in the Severn valley near Welshpool may also have had a timber chamber.[46] As a general rule, timber chambers tend to be of simple box-like construction, less elaborate than some of their stone counterparts but well within the range of single- and twin-celled chambers with short passages and entrance areas. In 1966 Stuart Piggott suggested that timber chambers should be regarded as temporary free-standing structures which were only covered by a mound when access was no longer needed, whereas stone chambers were built into the mound and so were freely accessed for as long as necessary.[47] Such a view is no long tenable as it is clear that timber chambers could easily have lasted for a century or more and that access to them was relatively easy, either from ground level at the front or side of the mound according to their position, or from above by lifting a section of roof.

The size of the chambers, and of individual cells within multi-cell chambers, is remarkably consistent at about 1.5m by 1m. It is notable that long barrows with multi-celled chambers are widely scattered through the region, especially where there is little evidence of bunching or clustering. By contrast, long barrows within the more dense clusters, for example around Minchinhampton and around Swell, appear to be mostly single-cell examples. However, it would be unwise to place too much emphasis on these apparent patterns, because the picture may be biased by the small number of well-excavated examples.

Chamber and passage walls

Throughout the Cotswold-Severn region the chamber and passageway walls of long barrows were constructed of large stone slabs known as orthostats. The only exceptions are those where timber planks and half-section tree-trunks were used in place of stones.

Orthostats were usually set edge to edge, each stone being fixed into the ground by being set in a shallow pit or socket dug down into the ground perhaps 0.2-0.5m. Chock stones, soil and rubble rammed into the gap between the orthostat and the wall of the socket held them in place. These contexts provide useful material for dating the construction work, although residual material from the disturbance of the old ground surface can sometimes become mixed with contemporary deposits. Although most chambers utilize orthostats of fairly modest size, typically 1m by 0.6m by perhaps 0.3m thick and weighing less than half a tonne, much larger stones were sometimes used. At Maesyfelin (GLA 10), for example, three huge slabs of local Triassic mudstone over 2m tall, 3m long and 0.8m thick were used to form the walls of a simple box-like chamber 2.7m long by 1.8m wide *(42)*.

Occasionally, the builders departed from the usual edge-to-edge arrangement for the orthostats, preferring instead to overlap the edges in a pattern known as 'imbrication'. This is most easily achieved where the orthostats are essentially slabs of tabular rock, as for example with the terminal chamber built of old red sandstone at Ffostyll South (BRE 4) and in oolitic limestone at the northeast chamber at the Giant's Caves.[48]

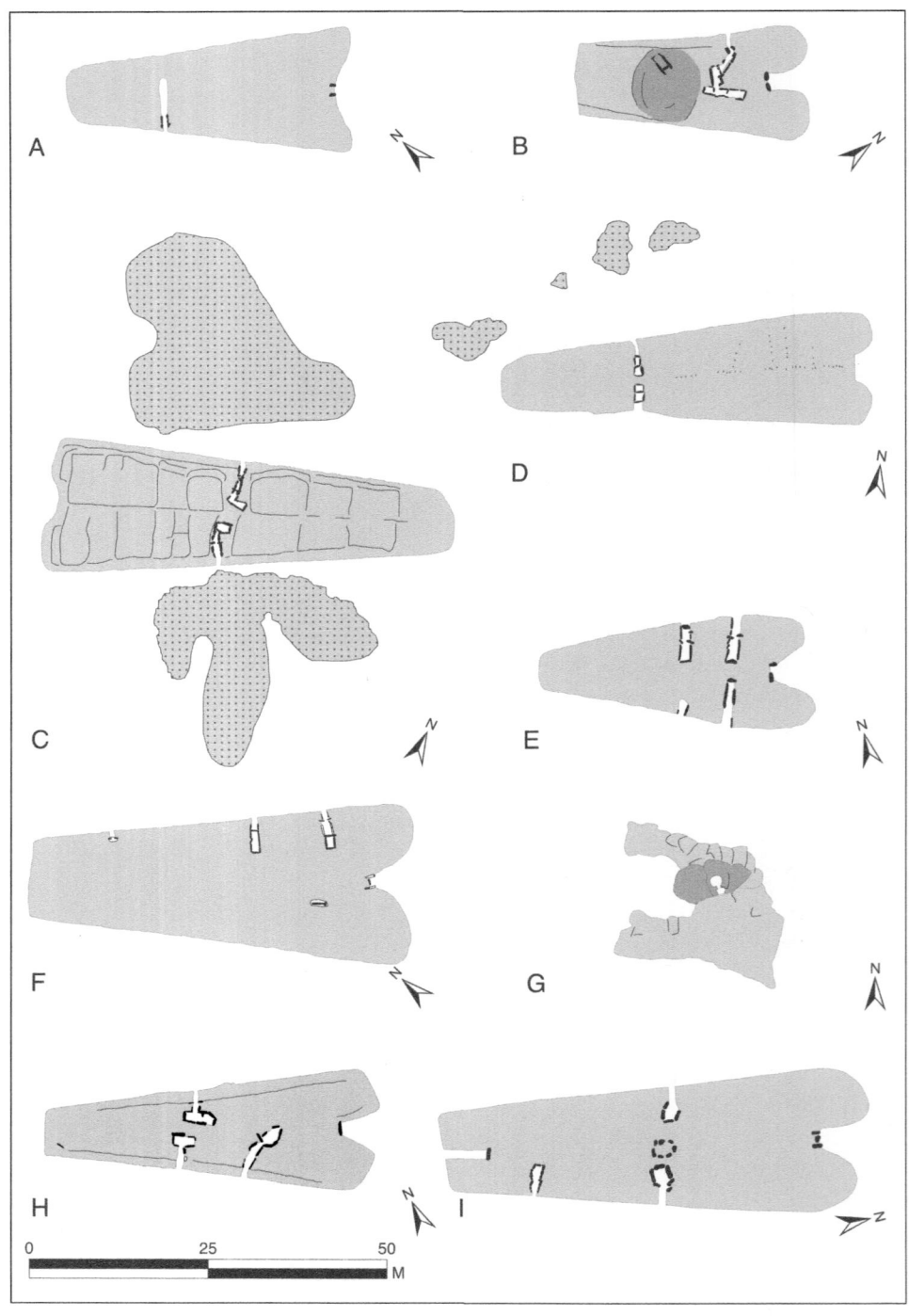

39 Ground plans of long barrows within the Cotswold-Severn region with lateral chambers. *A:* West Tump (GLO 8); *B:* Ty Isaf (BRE 5); *C:* Hazleton North (GLO 54); *D:* Ascott-under-Wychwood (OXF 6); *E:* Giant's Caves, Luckington (WIL 2); *F:* Penywyrlod (BRE 14); *G:* Saltway Barn (GLO 92); *H:* Gwernvale (BRE 7); *I:* Belas Knap (GLO 1)

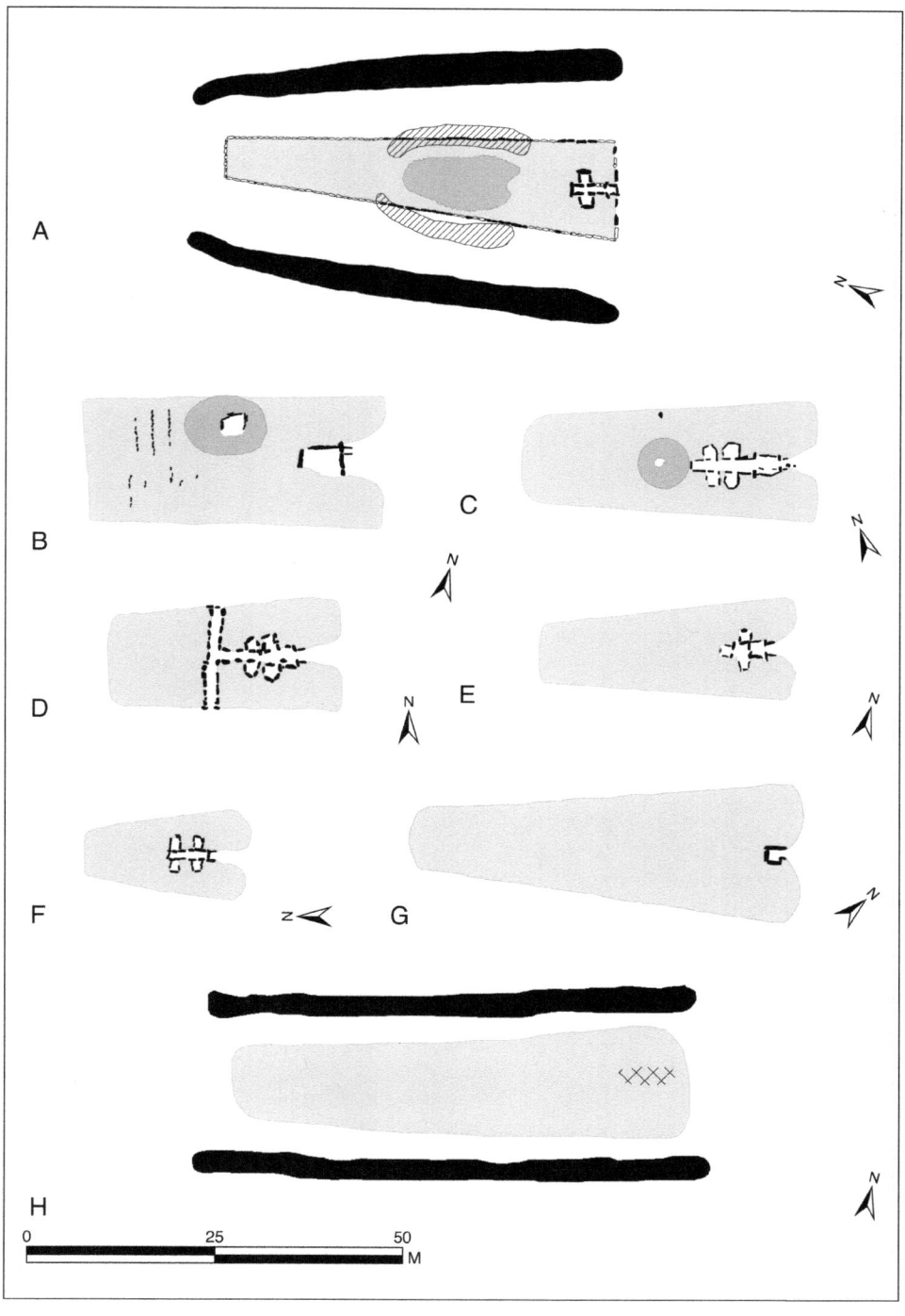

40 Ground plans of long barrows within the Cotswold-Severn region with terminal chambers.
A: Wayland's Smithy (BRK 1); B: Tinkinswood (GLA 9); C: Notgrove (GLO 4);
D: Burn Ground (GLO 60); E: Nympsfield (GLO 13); F: Parc le Breos Cwm (GLA 4);
G: Randwick (GLO 10); H: Lambourn (BRK 2)

Long Barrows of the Cotswolds

41 Ascott-under-Wychwood (OXF 6). View of the cist-chambers under excavation in 1965-70. Looking northwards with the revetment wall along the southern edge of the barrow in the foreground and cells 1, 2 and 3 of the chamber beyond. Horizontal scale totals 2m.
Photograph courtesy of Don Benson, the Oxfordshire County Museum Service and Cardiff University. Copyright reserved

Actually constructing the chambers in terms of manoeuvring the stones, setting them into position and supporting those already set up while others were added would have been a demanding task, even to those familiar with the tools and systems they had available. Upon excavation, a number of long barrows show evidence for rapidly constructed supporting stonework around the chambers and passages, typically large slabs pitched against the orthostats. Timber struts were no doubt also used, just as they are on building sites and archaeological excavations today. At Nympsfield (GLO 13) a roughly oval construction mound was recognized around the cruciform chamber, while at Belas Knap Sir James Berry noted something very similar and suggested that at an early stage in the building of the monument each chamber lay within its own separate mound.

Once the main orthostats were in place, the gaps between were usually filled with small panels of dry-stone walling. Much of this was of extremely high quality and had the effect of creating a fairly smooth face to the wall surface. Even though much of the dry-stone walling visible in long barrows today is the work of modern craftsmen, the combination of large orthostats and panels of walling at, for example, West Kennet, Hetty Pegler's Tump and Stoney Littleton nonetheless provides a good impression of the original appearance. Similar walling was also used to level up the tops of the orthostats in preparation for adding the roof.

The Anatomy of Cotswold Long Barrows

There is some evidence for the specific placement of objects during the construction of the chambers. At West Kennet (WIL 4), single Windmill Hill style pottery vessels were incorporated into the backfill of two stone sockets: one was the outermost stone on the north side of the passage, the other the southernmost stone of the massively constructed entrance façade (see below and *51B* and *C*). At Wayland's Smithy (BRK 1) a sarsen quernstone had been placed in the socket of the outermost orthostat of the passage on the west (left hand as you enter) side, perhaps as a packing stone but more likely as a placed deposit.

Where chambers were made of timber the ends are usually represented archaeologically by substantial postholes that would originally have held half-section split tree-trunks up to a metre in diameter. The sides and top would usually have been made of planks and longitudinally split trunks, but generally there is very little trace of these beyond the arrangement of rubble and stones that would have abutted the walls.[49] At Kings Play Down excavations in 1907 by Benjamin and Maud Cunnington revealed two large postholes, each 0.6m across and about 0.6m deep, which would have held the end-posts of a chamber 4.5m long and perhaps a little over 1m wide.[50] Turf had been packed around the sides of the box-like chamber to help support the walls. Whether the end-posts originally projected through the top of the mound cannot be determined, but it is certainly possible and would have created a most striking ornament.

Roofing

Three kinds of roofing structure were used for the chamber areas of long barrows. The most basic simply involved spanning the chambers and passages with stone slabs: so-called capstones. At West Kennet, Hetty Pegler's Tump (GLO 14) and Stony Littleton (SOM 1) this kind of roofing can still be seen in place, albeit partly

42 Maesyfelin, St Lythans (GLA 10). View of the massive chamber looking southwest. *Photograph by Timothy Darvill*

restored, with the walling and levelling blocks forming simple corbelling around the edge *(43)*. In some cases very substantial slabs and boulders were used. At Maesyfelin, for example, the huge uprights of this simple box-like chamber supported a still more massive capstone estimated to weigh about 30 tonnes *(42)*. Nearby, at Tinkinswood (GLA 9) a capstone estimated to weigh more than 40 tonnes provided the roof to a terminal chamber with a single cell. Lifting these on to the top of the orthostats must have been an enormous undertaking, requiring a labour force of more than 100 fit people. An experiment carried out in 1994 to move a 40-tonne concrete replica of part of a trilithon from Stonehenge showed that about 130 people could drag such a weight using a simple wooden sledge on timber rails.[51] Because of the size of the capstones at Tinkinswood and Maesyfelin it is possible that originally they projected out of the top of the mound rather like the raised blocks of the earlier dolmens and portal dolmens.

The second kind of roofing was more complicated and involved corbelling right across the chamber: layer upon layer of horizontally set slabs, each overlapping the one below by a few centimetres until finally the void was spanned. Corbelled roofs have been noted amongst the simple passage graves of the region, and amongst passage graves of all kinds along the Atlantic fringe of northwest Europe. Corbelling produces more headroom within the passages and chambers than roofing with capstones, but in the long term is less robust and is prone to collapse once a few of the component slabs are dislodged. It was used at Hazleton North (GLO 54) and Belas Knap amongst many other sites, although restoration works at the latter replaced the fine prehistoric structure with the concrete slabs visible today.

Finally, timber chambers were roofed with planks and beams, but, as with the walls of such chambers, very little evidence survives. Unless there was a hole in the proximal end-post of the chamber to allow access to the space within, the roofing of timber chambers must have been detachable so that part or all of it could be lifted when access was required.

Internal space and its structural subdivision

The chambers and passages within long barrows were generally cramped and most had rather low roofs. West Kennet is an exception, with its roofing set between 1.7m and 2.2m above the floor. It makes access relatively easy and it is possible for most people to stand upright while inside the barrow. More typical are Belas Knap and Hetty Pegler's Tump, where the maximum floor to ceiling height was less than a metre. There is some evidence that the roof level of some chamber areas increased towards the centre of the mound, in part at least creating the illusion of expanding space as one moved further into the structure. Similar architectural trickery is common in passage graves throughout northwest Europe and has been observed in the long barrows at Lanhill (WIL 3), Hazleton North and West Kennet among others. Rather unusually, at Rodmarton (GLO 16), entry into the passages of both the north and south chambers seems to have been at a relatively high level, about 1m above ground level on the outside of the mound, so that each has several steps in the floor of the passage (two in the south

The Anatomy of Cotswold Long Barrows

43 West Kennet, Avebury (WIL 4). Northern wall of the east chamber showing details of the chamber construction with orthostats to left and right, dry-stone walling between the orthostats and roofing slabs in corbelled formation above. Vertical scale totals 1m. Photograph by Timothy Darvill, May 2003

and three in the north) leading down to the chamber which was built on the original ground surface *(44)*.

During the construction of the stone-built chambers for sure, and possibly also the wooden ones, careful attention was paid to the physical subdivision of space through the use of jambs projecting from the walls, and sill and septal slabs set in the floor. These had the effect of further constricting access, concealing internal elements by restricting views into the chambers and demarcating boundaries between, for example, the passage and its associated chamber. Typically, three zones were created in the subdivision of space within chamber areas: the entrance zone, the passage zone and the chamber zone. This basic arrangement is very well represented amongst long barrows with lateral chambers and those with multi-cell terminal chambers *(45)*. Only the single-cell terminal chambers, and perhaps some timber chambers, seem to deviate from the rule, but few have been excavated to a standard that would allow a detailed examination of the use of space within. As will be discussed in Chapter 6, these three zones relate to patterning in the deposition of human remains within chamber areas.

At Hazleton North both chamber areas were divided into the usual three parts. Projecting jambs marked the division between the entrance zone and the passage zone, while low sills marked the junction between the passage zone and the chamber zone. It may be suggested, however, that many of these constricting features go beyond the simple function of partitioning space. At Wayland's Smithy, for example, the two jambs projecting into the central passage to separate the entrance zone from the passage zone also severely limit visibility into the tomb from the outside. This makes the interior even more private and hidden from view

Long Barrows of the Cotswolds

44 Windmill Tump, Rodmarton (GLO 16). Passage to the north chamber showing the steps, dry stone walling and orthostats. *From Clifford and Daniel 1940, plate X (upper), reproduced courtesy of the Prehistoric Society*

than it would be without these architectural elaborations. In timber-built chambers the large post at the proximal end of the chamber, which may well have been forked or perforated in some way, could have served the same purpose as the projecting side slabs in stone chambers; certainly it would have restricted direct movement into the chamber area from outside the barrow.

Projecting jambs, sills and portal stones of various kinds were no doubt carefully selected and positioned. Many pairs comprise slabs with contrasting shapes, usually an example with a pointed top set in juxtaposition to one with a flat top. At Lanhill the stones between the passage zone and the chamber zone of the southeast chamber area include a pointed-top stone to the left and a flat-topped stone to the right as you walk in.[52] At Hazleton North the division between the passage and the chamber in the south chamber area was marked by a pair of stones in which the left-hand one as you walked in had a pointed projection on top while the right-hand stone had a flat top. The comparable arrangement in the north chamber area was less well preserved, but also seems to include the same basic symbolism.[53] One site where a similar arrangement can still be seen is Nympsfield (GLO 13). Here the projecting jambs between the entrance zone and the passage zone have a thin pointed pillar-like stone on the right as you walk in and a broad slightly squat stone with a flat sloping top to the left. Sexual dimorphism may be represented in the opposition of these slabs, male stones being pointed and female ones lozenge-shaped or flat-topped. Similar patterns have been noted in the selection and positioning of façade slabs flanking the entrances to terminal chambers (see below).

The Anatomy of Cotswold Long Barrows

Occasionally, extremely elaborate arrangements are made to mark the innermost division of space, that between the passage zone and the chamber zone, in the form of so-called 'porthole' entrances. The best examples are at Rodmarton (GLO 14), first discovered by the Revd Samuel Lysons in 1863.[54] They comprise pairs of projecting jambs each with a semi-circular hollow worked into one edge so that when set side by side there is a round hole through the slabs. Others are known in lateral-chambered barrows at Avening (GLO 17; 46), and perhaps also Belas Knap chamber C, Gatcombe Lodge (GLO 15) and Lanhill. Possible examples have been reported in terminal chambers at the Fairy's Toot (SOM 2) and Tinkinswood (GLA 9), but details are obscure or the identification is tentative. The whole group was extensively discussed by Glyn Daniel and Elsie Clifford,[55] who noted superficially similar portholes in broadly contemporary monuments in three other parts of Europe: southern Iberia; northern France and adjoining parts of Belgium and Germany; and southern Sweden. Communities in all of these areas could have developed the idea of a porthole in parallel within their respective local and regional traditions. Whether portholes as such were also features represented in the architecture of timber chambers remains to be proven. It may be noted, however, that making a porthole would be infinitely easier in wood than stone and one cannot help wondering whether in fact the end-posts of timber chambers were not perforated by portholes to allow access into the chamber and that the stone examples are therefore simply copies of devices more commonly made in wood.

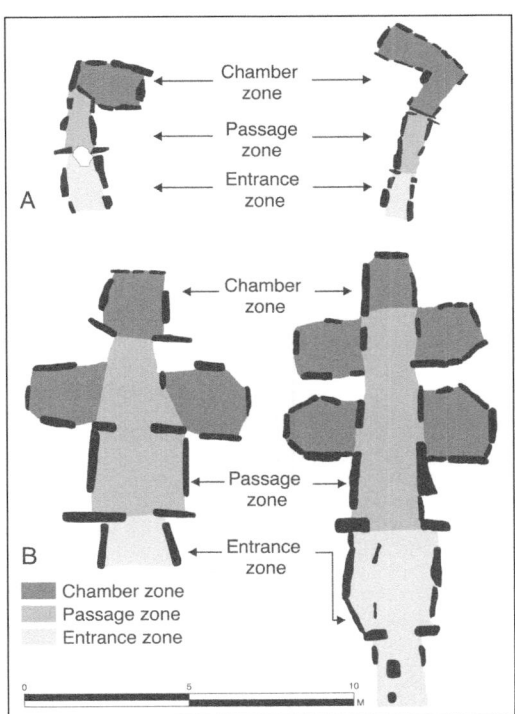

45 Chamber area partitioning into three zones. *A:* Hazleton North (GLO 54); *B:* Nympsfield (GLO 13); *C:* Notgrove (GLO 4). *A: after Saville 1990, figs 74 and 79; B: after Clifford 1937a, fig. 5; C: after Clifford 1936, general plan*

111

Long Barrows of the Cotswolds

Portholes, projecting jambs and septal slabs, whether between the entrance and the passage or between the passage and the chamber, were often used to support some kind of temporary blocking that would have prevented unwanted movement within the chamber area. In most cases these temporary blockings were stone slabs propped in place, and they are often found in place or dislodged slightly during excavations. At Rodmarton, for example, Lysons records that the porthole opening at the entrance to the north chamber 'was itself protected and closed up by another upright stone placed in front of it, which had to be removed before the chamber could be entered'.[56] Similar closing slabs have been noted in the entrance zone at Tinkinswood, between the entrance zone and the passage zone in the south chamber at Hazleton North and at the junction between the passage zone and the chamber zone in the northeast II chamber area at Penywyrlod (BRE 14).

Outer entrances

The outer edge of the entrance zone, where it meets the edge of the mound, is usually marked in some way, but not always very elaborately. In many lateral-chambered long barrows the outer revetment wall (see below) ran across the entrance gap and provided a foundation for the insertion of temporary walling as a blocking device (see Chapter 7). At barrows with terminal chambers there is

46 Left Porthole entrance probably from Avening Court long barrow (GLO 17), now beside the drive to the Old Rectory in Avening. *Photograph by Timothy Darvill*

47 Right Stoney Littleton, Wellow (SOM 1). Cast of a fossil ammonite on the southwestern entrance jamb. *Photograph by Timothy Darvill*

often a septal slab across the entrance, still visible for example at Parc le Breos Cwm (GLA 4), but little elaboration of the portal settings. An exception is Stoney Littleton (SOM 1), where a special slab containing the cast of a fossil ammonite seems to have been selected to mark the entrance *(47)*.

Flooring

In general, the chamber areas of long barrows were constructed on the contemporary ground surface, with only the stone sockets actually cut into the ground. The floor surfaces within the chambers and passages were usually either compacted soil, or, more commonly, covered by what today would be called 'crazy paving' — irregular stone slabs variously abutting or with small gaps between, forming a slightly uneven surface. Both techniques were used at some sites, perhaps to assist in the architectural definition of special spaces within the chamber area.

Rock art and decoration

No certain evidence for decoration or rock art has been noted on the walls of the chambers or passages of long barrows in the Cotswold-Severn region, although various claims have been made and the matter deserves a systematic re-examination. A photograph of the 1936 excavations of the antechamber at Notgrove seems to show a cup-mark low down on the outer face of stone N4 and Clifford suggests that some if not all of the orthostats used for the walls of the chamber area had been 'shaped before erection'.[57] Passmore has suggested the presence of two cup-marks low down on the inward-looking face of the southern (left-hand) stone at the entrance to the chamber at Wayland's Smithy,[58] but these indentations could well be natural. Crawford suggested that there were cup-marks on one of the stones detached from the chamber, perhaps forming part of a false-portal, at Arthur's Stone (HRF 1),[59] but again these are probably natural hollows in the surface of the stone. Leslie Grinsell has shown that crosses and lozenges cut into the Ty Illtyd (BRE 6) tomb are connected with its use as a hermit's cell during the medieval period (see Chapter 9).

Natural qualities inherent to the stone used in constructing long barrows do seem to have been noticed by the original builders. There is, as noted above, the cast of a fossil ammonite (identified as *Arietites* sp.) 0.31m in diameter on the western (left-hand side going in) portal slab at the entrance to Stoney Littleton *(47)*. It is probably the most striking example of an interest in fossils and other geological phenomena by these early farming communities. Elsewhere, natural holes have been noted in orthostats at Hetty Pegler's Tump (GLO 14), West Kennet and Heston Brake (MON 3) among others. Whether some of these were deliberately selected and positioned to make these features visible in a way that drew attention to them is impossible to say. At Sale's Lot (GLO 94), however, a slab of limestone used in the matrix of the mound has what appears to be a man-made hole through it, suggesting perhaps that such things did matter and, like portholes, were somehow significant.[60]

Whether the walls of the passages and chambers were ever decorated in any way is not known. However, the discovery of small blocks of haematite at Nympsfield and Rodmarton suggests that natural pigments were being used to colour something,[61] and it may just as well have been to highlight parts of the structure as to paint the human remains as so often assumed.

Sources of raw materials for chamber construction

Major structural components such as chambers often include exotic stone brought to the site from a considerable distance away, a task costly in time and labour. In some cases such work may have been necessary because local stone was unsuitable for building. In other cases it may have been the symbolic significance of the stone, its colour, or its source that somehow made it special and therefore worth acquiring and transporting. At West Kennet, the main orthostats are sarsen slabs of a kind that could have been obtained from the surrounding downland, but a considerable quantity of oolitic limestone from the Frome area 30km to the southwest had been imported to the site and used in the dry-stone walling between the orthostats. Pieces of similar limestone have also been found at the Easton Down long barrow (WIL 19), Shepherd's Shore long barrow (WIL 18) and Kitchen barrow (WIL 21). Thurnam recorded the presence of limestone walling in the façade of Adam's Grave (WIL 6), suggesting that here too imported material was used, perhaps in connection with the construction of a timber chamber. Pieces of tabular sandstone thought to originate in the Drybrook Series in the Forest of Dean were found in cut features during the examination of the much-disturbed Millbarrow (WIL 11) in 1989.[62] These must have travelled in excess of 60km. At Wayland's Smithy, coral ragstone from a source in the Vale of the White Horse probably not less than 6km to the north was used for dry-stone walling between the orthostats on the east side of the passage.

Further west, a study of the stones in the Stoney Littleton long barrow revealed that most of the orthostats used in the chamber, including those rich in fossils, derived from the Blue Lias rocks of the Jurassic system, the nearest outcrops of which are near Newton St Loe about 8km to the northwest. In contrast, the stone used for the dry-stone walling was Forest Marble, which would have been readily available within 1km of the site.[63] On the Cotswolds, the chambers of Hazleton North included two kinds of limestone: a fine-grained variety that could be obtained at the site itself and a coarse-grained variety that must have been imported from elsewhere, perhaps from several kilometres away.[64] Similarly, at the Giant's Caves many of the orthostats are of fossiliferous limestone available at an outcrop about 2km away to the northwest.[65] At Gwernvale stone for the orthostats of the chambers and for use in facing the outer revetment wall was brought to the site from quarries or outcrops some distance away.[66]

CHAMBERLESS LONG BARROWS

A small proportion of long barrows do not appear to have any chambers within them, although in every other respect they were constructed in much the same way as, and must have looked like, all other long barrows *(48)*. Three examples have so far been recognized within the Cotswold-Severn region – South Street (WIL 36), Beckhampton Road (WIL 27) and Horslip (WIL 30) – all of them around Avebury on the north Wessex Downs. Others may await discovery, as full excavation is needed for certain identification. Such long barrows have sometimes been seen as 'cenotaphs',[67] monuments of remembrance to people whose mortal remains lie elsewhere, and certainly this provides one possible explanation for this apparently rather isolated cluster of examples. Alternatively, the chamberless long barrows may have been 'fakes' in the sense that local communities in the Avebury area created long barrows in order to benefit from the symbolism that they represented without charging them up with human remains as neighbouring communities did. Yet another approach has been proposed by Miles Russell who notes that chamberless long barrows may be more widespread than commonly thought. Rather than emphasizing the role and content of the chambers, he argues that all long barrows should instead be viewed as 'structured mounds'. These, he suggests, represent a kind of cultural archive, or community statement, imposed on the landscape by communities who sometimes chose to include human remains while others chose to deposit the remains of the dead elsewhere.[68]

FALSE-PORTALS

A notable feature of some lateral-chambered barrows is the false-portal set at the rear of the forecourt *(49)*. These often include the largest stones within the structure and in general must have been erected early in the construction sequence. There are three main kinds: H-shaped where a portal stone is set transversely between the two uprights; II-shaped where there is no central portal, only upright jambs with a gap between (sometimes filled with dry-stone walling); and –-shaped where there is only a transverse portal slab. The first two types are sometimes topped by a lintel or cover-slab. The formal, H-shaped settings no doubt owe their origins to the front of portal dolmens, and in some cases may actually represent portal dolmens that were later incorporated into long barrows, as suggested in Chapter 4 for the false-portal at Belas Knap (GLO 1; *49A*). Other H-shaped portal settings include Penywyrlod II (BRE 14) and Ty Isaf (BRE 5). Examples of II-shaped portals occur at Lugbury (WIL 1; *49B*), the Giant's Caves at Luckington (WIL 2), West Tump (GLO 8; *49C*), Rodmarton (GLO 16) and, west of the Severn, Pipton (BRE 8). The third kind, –-shaped and involving a single slab, is represented at Gwernvale (BRE 7; *49D*) and Arthur's Stone (HRF 1). At Rodmarton, the two great portal slabs each 2.6m high probably once supported a lintel slab that was found broken in two at the back of the forecourt by the Revd Samuel Lysons in 1863.[69]

Long Barrows of the Cotswolds

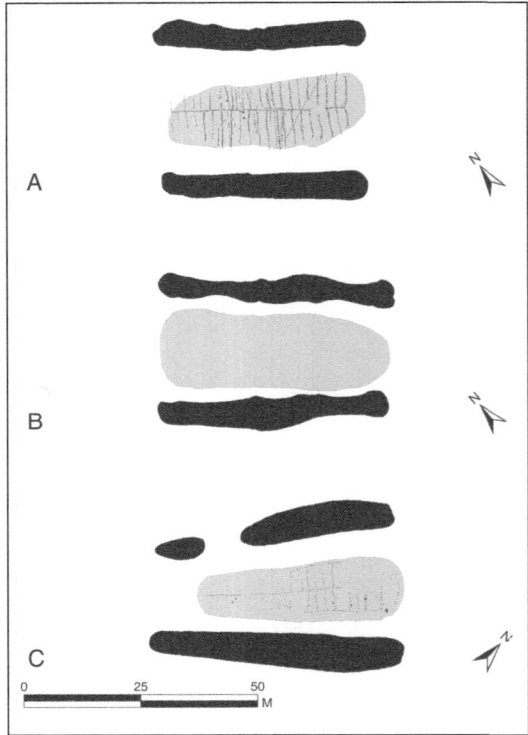

48 Left Ground plans of long barrows within the Cotswold-Severn region with no recorded chambers. *A:* South Street (WIL 36); *B:* Horslip long Barrow (WIL 30); *C:* Beckhampton Road (WIL 27). *After Ashbee et al. 1979, figs. 2, 11, 14, 23 and 25*

49 Opposite False-portals.
A top left: Belas Knap (GLO 1);
B top right: Lugbury (WIL 1);
C bottom left: West Tump (GLO 8);
D bottom right: Gwernvale (BRE 7). Scales in A and D each total 2m.
A and B: photographs by Timothy Darvill; C: after Crawford 1925, plate op. 70; D: photograph by Bill Britnell for Clwyd-Powys Archaeological Trust

The shape and form of the stones used in H-shaped and II-shaped portals may be significant. At Pipton the right-hand slab as you look into the forecourt is tall (2.4m) and narrow, while the left-hand slab is broader and perhaps originally not quite so tall although in its broken-off condition this is hard to tell. Similarly, Belas Knap has a thin pointed stone to the right and a broad flat-topped stone to the left *(49A)*.

It was once thought that these false-portals were built to deter tomb-robbers.[70] It is an idea that has been well and truly discredited by the early dating of north European long barrows in relation to supposed progenitor structures in the Mediterranean. Now it is the symbolic meaning of the portal settings as skeuomorphic doors into the houses of the dead, routeways into other worlds, or references back to portal dolmens that is emphasized.

MOUNDS

The mound is the most conspicuous element of any long barrow, universally built within the Cotswold-Severn region from a mixture of turf, soil, rubble and stone. These materials were not, however, simply piled up in a heap over the chambers. Excavators since at least the time of Colt Hoare have recognized the care taken in the construction of the mounds and the exceptional quality of what was achieved

The Anatomy of Cotswold Long Barrows

in making these elongated rectangular or trapezoid-shaped structures. As well as neat external walling defining the limits of the mound there are also internal walls and constructional devices suggesting that considerable time and trouble was taken to make the mound stable and durable. Architectural embellishments such as horns and forecourts add to the complexity and variety of the structures.

Mound construction

Where detailed studies of mound construction have taken place it is clear that they were built in modular fashion with a series of interlocking cells or sections. Grimes's work at Burn Ground (GLO 60) was one of the first excavations to reveal the detail of this, with the recognition of a regular series of cells defined by roughly built revetment walls.[71] At South Street (WIL 36) and Beckhampton Road (WIL 27) rather similar cells were initially defined with wooden fences and wattle hurdles, each then being filled with soil and rubble. A combination of wooden fences, hurdling and rough stone walls was used in defining and marking the cells at Ascott-under-Wychwood (OXF 6).[72] The best-studied site in terms of understanding the way the mound was built is Hazleton North (GLO 54).[73] Here the construction of the mound seems to have started at two places along the north side of the previously defined main axis, later spreading to the south side. The area around and between the two chambers was the last to be covered as the whole barrow was finished off with its outer revetment wall and façade *(50)*.

117

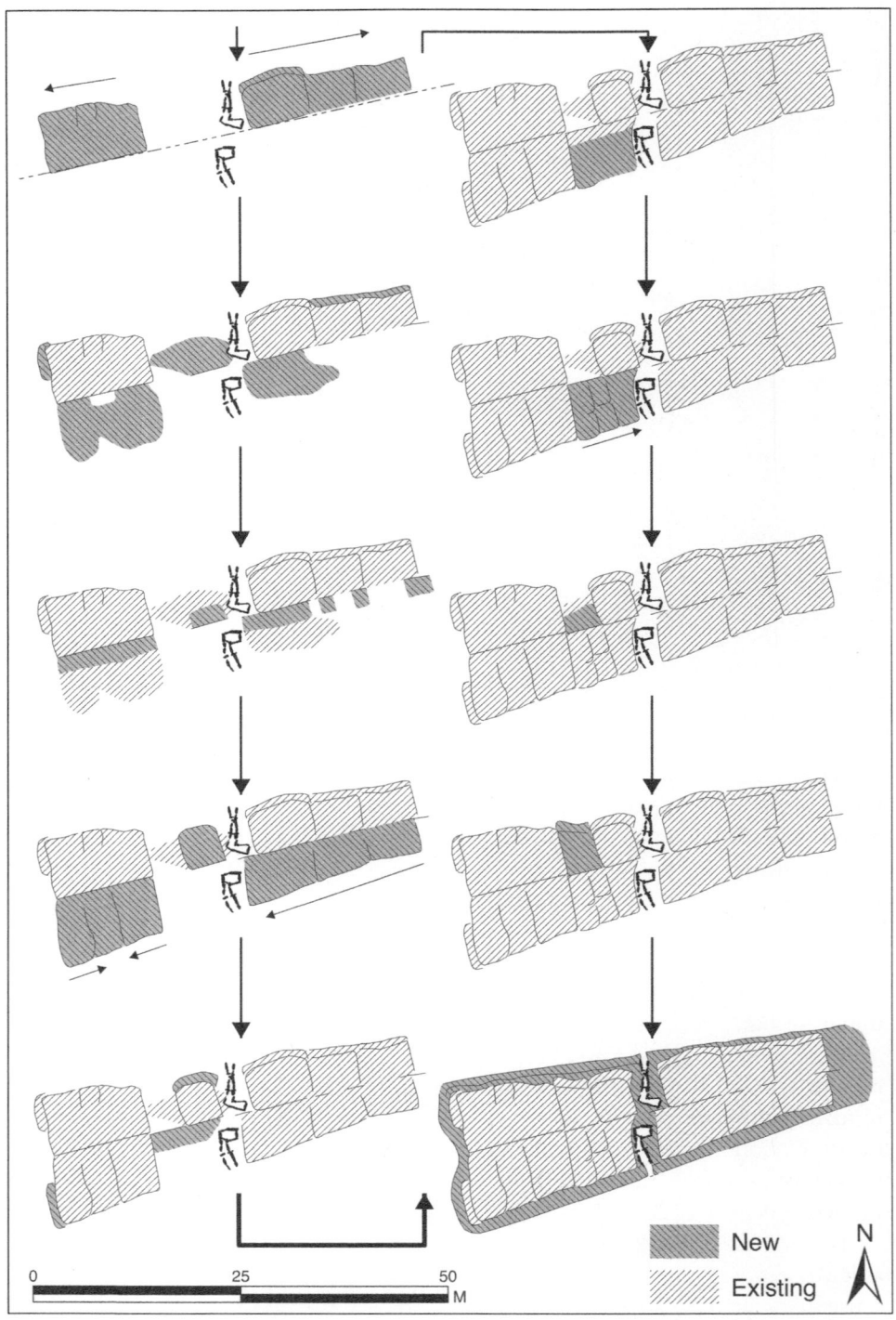

50 Mound construction sequence at Hazleton North (GLO 54), starting in the top-left corner and finishing with the final phase of construction bottom-right. *After Saville 1990, fig. 227*

In all, 21 structural components were recognized within the mound, each delimited by internal revetment walls and forming an integral part of the structure that in its final form was remarkably symmetrical and neatly delimited.

Several excavators have noted evidence for burning and the presence of burnt stones within the structure of the mound. Elsie Clifford listed eight areas of burning within the mound at Notgrove (GLO 4), while at Nympsfield (GLO 13) she recorded burnt material in every trench cutting into the mound.[74] Pottery, bone, worked flint, stone objects, animal bones and human remains were sometimes deposited or incorporated within the matrix of the mound, although generally they are rare and rather sparse compared with the overall volume of material used in a mound. At Hazleton North very few things seem to have been deposited during the building of the mound: half a dozen pieces of human bone, 14 animal bones, five small sherds of pottery and 25 pieces of struck flint. This led Alan Saville to conclude that the mound 'was not treated as a location for artefact deposition, ritual or otherwise'.[75] Bill Britnell shares this view on the basis of excavating Gwernvale (BRE 7) where the few finds present in the mound can mainly be attributed to the incorporation of soil from the pre-barrow occupation.[76] At South Street six fragments of red deer antler and four cattle scapulae were found within the matrix of the mound, probably the broken and discarded remains of tools used for quarrying the mound material (see below).[77]

There are, however, a few exceptional finds, but these should not colour the wider picture. Querns are the best represented and may suggest some special significance attached to them as things to be associated with the mound. One possibility is their role in transforming plants into foodstuff as a parallel for the progression from life to death. At Burn Ground, for example, a quernstone of arkosic sandstone lay within the mound to the north of the chamber area,[78] at Gwernvale parts of two querns were found in the body of the mound,[79] while at Lanhill (WIL 3) the lower stone of a sandstone saddle-quern was found towards the western end of the mound,[80] and at Wayland's Smithy (BRK 1) a saucer quern was found in the mound beside the chamber.[81]

Human bone is another kind of deposit that is widely represented. At Ascott-under-Wychwood, the space in the centre of the mound between chamber cells 3 on the south side and 5 on the north contained bones representing the fragmentary remains of three individuals, two male adults and a female adult. The remains had been covered by large stones and while haphazard in their distribution they were in good general condition.[82] Human remains within the mound have also been noted at the Giant's Caves (WIL 2), Rodmarton (GLO 16) and Hazleton North already mentioned.

Pottery is occasionally incorporated into the construction of the mound, just as it is occasionally present in orthostat sockets. In both cases it potentially provides a useful indicator of the date and cultural identity of the builders of individual barrows. At Nympsfield a substantial part of a bowl with an everted neck and nicked inturned rim *(51A)* was found within the construction of the mound south of the entrance to the chambers.[83]

Long Barrows of the Cotswolds

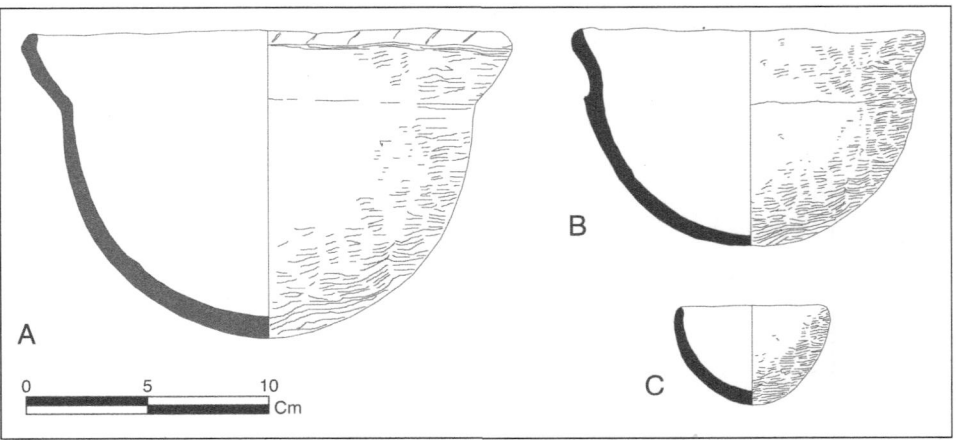

51 Pottery from construction contexts at long barrows in the Cotswold-Severn region. A: Nympsfield (GLO 13); *B* and *C:* West Kennet (WIL 4). *A: after Clifford 1938, fig. 3; B: after Piggott 1963, fig. 10*

The material used to fill each of the structural components of the mound at Hazleton North varied slightly according to what was available to the builders. Sometimes there was more soil than stone, at other times vice versa, with the result that adjacent components of the mound often look quite different in colour and texture. At Beckhampton Road (WIL 27) various components of the mound were filled with brickearth, chalk gravel, turf, marl and coombe rock so that the finished structure would have looked like a patchwork of yellow, brown and white. Similar contrasts have also been noted at other sites and this has formed the basis of various theories about the social implications of mound-building.

The strongly compartmentalized sub-divided structure to the mounds of long barrows has often been seen as reflecting the work of different gangs or discrete social groups coming together to build a communal work in a way that emphasized the social diversity of the individual contributors while at the same time expressing the solidarity of the overall community. Julian Thomas takes this argument further by proposing that the selective accumulation of naturally occurring materials may represent a deliberate attempt to mix the remains of the ancestors with material taken directly from the land in such as way as to strengthen ties between human communities and the natural world.[84] As well as these contemporary symbolic meanings that might be imposed on the evidence, it is also possible that the builders of these mounds viewed their work as the creation of permanent 'everlasting' structures, and for this reason they made them as robust as possible. If that was the intention, then the fact that many are still with us after more than 5,000 years means that their builders were remarkably successful!

Forecourts, horns and façades

The higher and wider ends of the mounds were often elaborated in various ways, usually through the construction of a recessed forecourt flanked by projecting horns. The size, shape and depth of the forecourts vary considerably *(39* and *40)*. At Belas Knap (GLO 1) the rather cuspate forecourt is about 9m wide and 6m deep, while at Tinkinswood (GLA 9) the forecourt is more funnel-shaped, some 8m wide and 5m deep. Hetty Pegler's Tump (GLO 14) has a particularly long but narrow forecourt, in marked contrast to Hazleton North where the forecourt is 7m wide but only 1.5m deep – little more than a slight recess. At Nympsfield early accounts suggested the possibility of a forecourt at both ends of the mound, but excavations in 1974 showed that the western forecourt was erroneous and that only the east end had projecting horns defining a forecourt.[85]

Terminal chambers open from the back of the forecourt, but at long barrows with lateral chambers the back wall of the forecourt is either left blank, as at Hazleton North, or connected to a false-portal or false-entrance as described above. Where no false-portal is present in the back of the forecourt at lateral-chambered barrows the forecourt wall is continuous with the outer revetment wall (see below) either on a shallow curve, as at Hazleton North, or as a flat face, as at Ascott-under-Wychwood.

The proximal ends of some long barrows in the Cotswold-Severn region are elaborated through the addition of an impressive façade. The best are those on the north Wessex Downs, especially the restored examples at Wayland's Smithy and West Kennet (WIL 4). Originally, Adam's Grave (WIL 6), Millbarrow (WIL 11) and probably also Manton Down (WIL 7) and Old Chapel (WIL 14) had equally good façades which have since become lost to view. At Wayland's Smithy six large sarsen slabs were set across the proximal end of the barrow, three either side of the entrance to the cruciform chamber *(52)*. The stone to the left (west) side of the chamber entrance looking in towards the mound has a distinctively pointed profile, while the one to the right (east) has a flat-topped outline. Much the same can be seen at West Kennet, where originally there were probably four stones to the right of the forecourt and at least two stones to the left, the latter being flat-topped and the former pointed. Similar patterns in the arrangement of distinctively shaped stones were noted in the construction of the chambers (see above). Elsewhere, I have shown that this pairing of flat-topped and pointed-top stones is common in long barrows and various other monuments of the third and second millennia BC in the British Isles, and that it may be linked to a sexual symbolism in which male pointed stones are juxtaposed with female flat-topped stones.[86]

Outer revetment walls and mound edges

Mound edges may be finished in any one of a number of ways, of which the most common involves an outer revetment wall *(53)*. Neatly coursed dry-stone walling is generally used, linked with or bonded to the ends of various inner walls and structural divisions, to form a continuous outer envelope broken only by the entrances to the chambers and the stones of false-portal settings. The preservation of these outer revetment walls is highly variable, but at Gwernvale (BRE 7) sections up to 0.6m high remained intact and give an impression of what presumably encircled the whole structure. Rather exceptionally, at Hazleton North the highest section of outer revetment wall stood 0.8m high in the back of the

52 Wayland's Smithy (BRK 1). South end of the barrow showing the monumental façade, linking dry-stone walling and centrally placed entrance. Photograph by Timothy Darvill

forecourt. Where preservation is good these walls seem to have been more or less vertical, although many lean outwards when excavated because of the way the mound has decayed over the intervening millennia. At Parc le Breos Cwm (GLA 4), the outer revetment walls forming the sides of the narrow forecourt include eye-catching oblique courses creating a sort of wave pattern in the stonework. Elsewhere, the quality of preserved original walling is extremely high, as for example in the lower parts of the forecourt walling at Belas Knap. Such fragments are testimony to the craftsmanship of the builders and of course stand at the head of the tradition that is still thriving today.

At long barrows on the north Wessex Downs other edging techniques are represented. At West Kennet and Wayland's Smithy, the mound is bounded by a kerb of widely spaced boulders linked with panels of dry-stone walling, known as a peristalith: a stone version of the 'post and panel' construction envisaged for the walls of houses. A similar effect was achieved using wooden posts with hurdles between; this might well have been the outward appearance of the Kings Play Down long barrow (WIL 31). Hurdles certainly seem to have formed the outer revetment of the mound at Beckhampton Road and perhaps also South Street (WIL 36) to judge from the position of stakeholes found around the edge of the mound.[87]

Outward appearance of the mound

Determining what the upper parts of long barrows looked like is made difficult by the fact that most have lost their upper layers because of natural decay and the effects of later cultivation. Some, but by no means all, have one and sometimes two inner revetment walls that are fairly substantial and extend down through the mound as internal structural devices. Similar elements are found on passage graves elsewhere along the Atlantic seaboard of northwest Europe and are often used to suggest that these mounds had stepped profiles. This could certainly apply also to some long barrows in the Cotswold-Severn region. The steps were perhaps used as shelves for the placement of pottery or offerings, much as P.-R. Giot suggested happened at Barnenez in Brittany,[88] and as has also been noted at Jordhøj, Denmark and elsewhere.[89]

There are also hints that the top of most if not all long barrows would have been finished off like the roof of a long house with a central ridge and sloping sides. The fact that mounds are usually built with a central axis carried up through the structure of the mound adds weight to this idea, while John Corcoran records seeing a central ridge in the preserved field evidence of several barrows including West Tump (GLO 8), Cow Common Long (GLO 22) and Lamborough Banks (GLO 25).[90]

In considering the evidence from Hazleton North, Alan Saville noted that the monument 'was designed to be seen with its outer revetment fully exposed'; he also provided a wide range of longitudinal and cross-sectional profiles that are possible given the available evidence, concluding that 'the final appearance of the monument remains entirely speculative'.[91] Whether it was round-topped, ridged, stepped, or elaborated in some other way, it is important to recognize that from a distance, and especially after the onset of even modest natural erosion, the detail about which it is possible only to speculate would have made little difference to overall appearance. More critical, perhaps, is how the top surface of the mound was finished: raw stone, gravel, soil, turf, or perhaps a combination of these. Again,

53 Hazleton North, Hazleton (GLO 54). View of the long barrow mound during excavation. The revetment wall is visible across lower left; the complicated pattern of stonework within the mound centre; and the orthostats of the northern chamber just visible in the stonework lower right. Looking southeast. *Photograph by Timothy Darvill, July 1981*

it is only possible to speculate as there is no direct evidence. Most excavators seem to prefer the idea that the top was simply exposed mound matrix with no special covering. If so, then most barrows would have been the colour of the available rock – mainly white, cream, yellow, or red – in some cases perhaps variegated by the contrasting fills of constructional sectors or bays.

Not all long barrows would have looked neat and tidy, as the foregoing discussion of examples that were mainly built from scratch would suggest. Where existing structures had to be incorporated into a long barrow less regular structures emerged. Indeed, irregularities in orientation and unusual positioning may be the result of working within established constraints rather than slavishly applying the new design principles. At Sale's Lot (GLO 94), for example, the short lengths of wall joining the simple passage grave and rotunda grave together do not align very well, and the horns and forecourt are irregular in outline even when a high level of later damage is taken into account.[92]

Collapse and 'extra-revetment'

Upon excavation, the edges of many long barrows are found to be shrouded in rubble and soil, some of it pitched up against the outer revetment wall, much of it seemingly structured and a lot of it spread across the ground surface immediately beyond the outer revetment wall for a distance of perhaps 4m or so. This material, often referred to as 'extra-revetment', has been the subject of much debate since it was first recognized as a potentially contentious issue in the later nineteenth century.[93] For many years there were essentially two schools of thought about its origins and purpose.[94] The first suggested that it resulted from the natural decay of the mound. In this view, stones and soil slid down the edge of the mound and built up outside the outer revetment walls, the walls themselves tumbling slightly and often leaning outwards because of lateral pressure from the weight of the mound.[95] The second, opposing view held that extra-revetment was deliberately constructed. As proof it was noted that the outer revetment walls generally showed little sign of having been exposed for very long; structure was present in the way that stones within the extra-revetment were placed; the angle of the stones of the extra-revetment against the outer revetment wall suggested deliberate placement; and arrangements around entrances suggested that the extra-revetment was earlier than formal blocking deposits.[96] In the light of recent evidence, neither of these rather simplistic and polarized views can be sustained. Instead, it has become apparent that the problem is more complicated than originally thought, and that what is generally referred to as 'extra-revetment' is not necessarily all the same in terms of its source or purpose.

Three main kinds of extra-mound material seem to be represented. The first is easiest to deal with for it is simply caused by the decay and collapse of the mound. As a result, the detached mound material eventually finds a natural angle of rest around the bottom of the outer revetment wall and beyond. This accounts for most of what was seen as extra-revetment in the traditional sense, and can still be seen in the field at sites such as Belas Knap (GLO 1). A second set of deposits that can be recognized is that of blocking materials introduced into and around the entrances to chambers and as filling in the forecourt. Large stones may sometimes be used in these works, the whole being quite deliberate and discussed in greater detail in Chapter 8. The third and final group of deposits is far less numerous and generally rather hard to identify. These deposits comprise material that was deliberately piled up against the side of a barrow, presumably either to strengthen the outer revetment wall or to create a slope for climbing up onto the mound for some reason. Such deposits have been recognized at Gwernvale and Penywyrlod,[97] where they have been the subject of much discussion. In his conclusions to the Gwernvale report Bill Britnell suggested that these additions to the primary mound might be attempts to make particular long barrows appear older than they really were – the 'antiquation' of the structures.[98] If correct, this may perhaps be somehow related to the construction of chamberless long barrows as attempts to give the appearance of being something they were not.

QUARRIES AND SOURCES OF MOUND MATERIAL

Turf, soil, rubble and stone, as raw materials for the construction of long barrow mounds, can usually be found in the immediate vicinity of the monument itself. It is often suggested that suitable material for the construction of the mound can be scraped up from the surrounding area, and certainly this may be true where turf can be taken from nearby grassland or rocks and boulders collected from clitter scatters. However, where excavations have specifically sought them, quarries of various kinds have usually been found adjacent to long barrows. Similar features are also occasionally visible as surface traces. Two main kinds of quarry or borrow pit have been recognized to date: regular quarry ditches and irregular quarry pits.

Regular quarry ditches flanking long barrows are common among examples in the north Wessex Downs and the Chew and Mendip areas south of the River Avon, just as they are elsewhere in central southern England. They can often be recognized as earthwork features at extant sites, or as cropmarks at plough-levelled sites. At West Kennet (WIL 4) excavation of a section through the north ditch revealed it to be a massive 7m wide and up to 3.6m deep. The bottom was irregular, deeper on the north side. An early example of the use of geophysical survey allowed the extent of the ditches on both sides of the mound to be plotted; both ditches were fairly straight, about 98m long, mirrored rather well the shape and orientation of the mound, and were separated from the mound by a berm about 10m wide. Wayland's Smithy (BRK 1) has broadly similar ditches although slightly less deep and very slightly curved in plan with a marked convergent kink at the distal ends. The berm between the barrow mound and the ditch edges is typically about 5m. In the same area the Lambourn long barrow (BRK 2) has fairly narrow but regular parallel ditches on either side of the mound, while all three of the apparently chamberless long barrows around Avebury were constructed from rubble taken from regular flanking side ditches. Rather different is Millbarrow (WIL 11), which seems to have two roughly parallel ditches on either side, perhaps suggestive of more than one phase of construction. Both were sampled by excavation in 1989. The inner ditches were about 5m wide and 2.7–2.8m deep, with steep sides and flat bottoms. The outer ditches were narrower at 3m wide and typically up to 2.5m deep. The inner ditches ran tight up against the edge of the mound as it could be determined from the samples excavated. At White Hill, Lockeridge (WIL 39) aerial photography has revealed a pair of tapering ditches that probably once flanked a trapezoidal mound.[99]

Regular quarry ditches are not confined to the north Wessex Downs. They have also been noted flanking the extremely long mound on Pen Hill, St Cuthbert Out (SOM 18), perhaps an indication of its inspiration from southern Wessex, as well as at the second long barrow on Pen Hill (SOM 17). The most northerly reported quarry ditch is at Lugbury (WIL 1), on the limestone of the south Cotswolds east of Bath.[100]

These generally regular quarry ditches contrast with the larger but more sprawling quarries associated with long barrows on the limestone of the Cotswold Hills. The differences may be cultural, but could equally be connected to the way in which stone is most effectively extracted. The most thoroughly investigated quarries are at Hazleton North (GLO 54), where quarry pits were identified and sampled on both sides of the mound. The south quarry was at least 29.8m west to east and 13.2m north to south with a maximum depth of 2.2m, while the north quarry was probably a little larger but about the same depth. Antler picks and levers had been used to prize off naturally shattered rock, the upper layers being fairly well broken up, but some of the lower strata consisted of more substantial blocks which may have provided some of the orthostats for building the chamber. It is estimated that between 950 and 1,425 cubic metres of soil, marl and stone could have been taken from the quarries, ample to build a trapezoidal mound roughly 55m long, up to 19m wide and tapering from 1.5m down to 0.5m high. What is perhaps curious is the fact that both quarries extend to within a metre or so of the entrances to both the chambers, so that anyone using the chambers first had to walk through the abandoned quarry.[101]

At least four relatively small discrete quarry pits have also been recorded at Ascott-under-Wychwood (OXF 6), on the north side of the mound. By chance, excavation of a round barrow south of Cow Common Long (GLO 22) revealed a major section of quarry pit at least 1m deep.[102] It has often been thought that some if not all the pits, hollows and protruding stones southeast of Tinkinswood (GLA 9) were the source of the stone used in constructing the mound,[103] and it is temping to think that some of the hollows around Randwick (GLO 10) and Belas Knap (GLO 1) may be original quarries rather than sources of stone for wall building in modern times.

Whether in the form of ditches or pits, the quarries were used for their intended purpose and then largely abandoned. Hearths were found in the south quarry at Hazleton North and in the lower fill of the example at Cow Common. At Lambourn, deposits in the lower fills of the ditches included part of a human cranium, animal bones, an antler pick and a spread of charcoal. Most of the material was found near the terminals.[104] Antler picks together with a small amount of flint-working debris were also found on the floor of the ditch at the Horslip long barrow (WIL 30),[105] a rather similar assemblage being recovered from the ditches at South Street (WIL 36).[106]

Not all the stone used in constructing the mounds of long barrows derived from formal quarries; some must have been taken from field clearance and scraping up locally available material. At Pipton (BRE 8) the mound contained water-rolled blocks and pebbles taken from the nearby River Wye or River Llynfi.[107] At Gwernvale (BRE 7), the material used in constructing the core of the mound was mainly weathered blocks of sandstone which probably derived from the river terrace on which the barrow stands. The outer revetment walls, however, were almost exclusively green micaceous sandstones that outcrop on the hillsides perhaps 100m above the site. This material was presumably chosen because of its superior splitting qualities that made it ideal for walling stone.[108]

CONSTRUCTION TOOLS AND EQUIPMENT

Building a long barrow needed not only skill and muscle-power, but also tools and equipment. Throughout the work there must have been a need for wooden levers, rollers, stays, struts, scaffolding and wooden components for the structure itself. The wood itself does not survive, but wood-working tools are variously associated with deposits relating to this phase in the history of individual monuments. At Wayland's Smithy (BRK 1) flakes from broken flint and stone axes were found on the old ground surface immediately under the mound, while at Hazleton North (GLO 54) the buried soil and contexts associated with the south chamber area yielded at least eight fragments of polished flint axe. In both cases some of the axe fragments may have derived from the pre-barrow occupation, but some if not all probably resulted from breakages during the construction of the chambers or mound.[109] At West Kennet (WIL 4), several of the sarsen stones used in making the chamber had previously been used for sharpening stone or flint axes, as shown by the basins and wear on their surfaces *(54)*. Stuart Piggott explicitly linked these to the resharpening of axes during the construction of the tomb. An axe-sharpening stone has also been found within the lowest levels of the mound at Gwernvale (BRE 7).[110]

Quarrying soil, rubble and bedrock and then shifting it to where it was needed would have required another set of tools, mainly picks, levers, shovels and containers. Again, much has perished over the millennia, although wicker baskets and leather buckets would have been obvious choices as containers in which to carry materials and well within the manufacturing capabilities of these communities. What have survived at some sites are the bone and antler tools either abandoned in the quarries or incorporated into the mound. On the Cotswolds, levers made from red deer antlers seem to have been the main tool used in quarrying limestone. Fourteen such tools were recovered during the excavations at Hazleton North, many with the pointed tips worn smooth or polished through

54 West Kennet, Avebury (WIL 4). Detail of an orthostat on the south side of the chamber complex that was used as a polissoir for shaping and sharpening flint and stone axes. Vertical scale totals 1m. Photograph by Timothy Darvill, May 2003

use in prizing out the highly fissured bedrock.[111] A similar tool is known from early excavations at Belas Knap (GLO 1).[112] At long barrows on the north Wessex Downs antlers with some of the tines removed to form picks seem to have been preferred by communities digging into chalk. Such picks have been found at Horslip (WIL 30), Beckhampton Road (WIL 27), where perhaps a dozen examples were represented together with at least two antler rakes, South Street (WIL 36), Wayland's Smithy and Lambourn (BRK2) among other sites. In some cases these tools were still serviceable when seemingly deliberately placed on the floor of the quarry in which they had presumably been used. Such superficially profligate actions are probably best seen as symbolic in some way, perhaps a sign that the tool had become 'unclean' through being used to cut into the earth.

FINAL APPEARANCE, SYMBOLISM AND WIDER RELATIONSHIPS

When first built, long barrows must have been large and impressive structures. It is easy to see them as being neatly edged mounds with tidy outer revetment walls, post and panel edging, or peristaliths around a central core that could well have had stepped sides and a ridged top. Posts and stones may have projected through the top, and there is no reason why there might not have been decoration or ornamentation, even though no evidence of it survives. East of the Severn these mounds would have been mainly white or silty grey in colour, and for that reason would have stood out in a landscape otherwise dominated by greens and browns. On the north Wessex Downs the red/brown sarsen would have contrasted with the white chalk. West of the Severn, the red colours of the sandstones and the greys of the carboniferous limestone would have been equally impressive. For much of the time the entrances into the chambers would have been concealed with closing slabs and temporary walling extending over the entrances.

Set against this image must be some appreciation of the squalor and decay evident at such sites, although exactly how this was perceived must in large measure depend on contemporary cultural values. All we can be sure of is that people of the fourth millennium BC saw these things very differently from our modern western gaze. The white and grey coloured mounds of limestone and chalk would soon turn dusty and green as weeds and moss took hold. Dry-stone walling and hurdles are robust enough when new, but they too start to bulge and collapse after perhaps 30 or 40 years. Scrambling across a quarry pit to reach the chambers may not have been much fun, and in wet weather would have been muddy and dirty.

Access into the passage, or directly into a chamber, from the top of the mound was certainly possible in some cases, and may well have been used as a means of entry even if that meant damaging the mound at times. Some of the material heaped up around the mound may simply have been to provide easy access onto the top of the monument to allow the capstones or covering to be lifted. At Ascott-under-Wychwood (OXF 6), all the chambers appear to have been accessible only from the surface of the mound, and this applied to other sites as well. Mention has already been made of the situation at Rodmarton (GLO 16), with its steps leading down into the chamber from a relatively high point on the side of the mound.

Getting into the dark damp recesses of the chambers at many sites would have meant removing temporary blocking and crawling through generally low narrow entrances into equally restricted passages. At Burn Ground (GLO 60), Grimes's excavations found that getting into the main chamber entrance involved digging down through temporary blocking until there was enough clearance to allow sideways movement into the central passage that gave access to the separate chamber cells. Where timber chambers were built, access from above may have been the norm, but the postholes found in excavations tell us nothing about the form of the timberwork that they held, and the idea that large solid posts blocked the entrance to these chambers must be questioned.

Symbolically, the ensemble of mound, chambers, forecourt and quarries, the shape of the overall structure, or the form of individual elements may have had a series of overlapping meanings. C.E. Vulliamy, for example, suggested that the outline of a long barrow is similar to the shape of the contemporary stone axes,[113] a layer of symbolic association made all the more interesting because axes are very rarely found at long barrows except in construction contexts. Others have seen the long form of the mound as being phallic, perhaps a monumental representation of a penis symbolizing the propagation of a male patrilineage.[114] At an altogether different scale, it has been noted that the outline of many long barrows compares well with a truncated human female body: the chambers symbolically placed in the region of the womb, the vagina being the entrance passage at the back of the forecourt opening between the horns which themselves perhaps represented the legs. As Timothy Taylor has suggested, within an agricultural community of long barrow users, bones were placed like seeds in a womb of earth as if waiting for the moment of rebirth.[115] It is powerful imagery and is perhaps supported by Julian Thomas's and Chris Tilley's contention that axes and torsos were amongst the most significant motifs used in the decoration of orthostats forming the walls of passage and chamber zones in long barrows and passage graves in Brittany.[116]

In a sense such symbolism might seem a long way from the links between houses and long barrows explored in Chapter 4. But the differences may not be so great, and more than one set of symbolic referencing may have applied to the same thing so that it could be understood at different scales or in different contexts.[117] Ian Hodder has suggested that in early farming communities in Europe the position of women was emphasized in the context of communal ritual outside the domestic sphere. 'Here women are depicted and the domestic "house" context is elaborated. Women as reproducers, as the source and focus of the lineage, are here celebrated . . . Their services are for the lineage alone and this control is legitimated by the ancestors and by higher authorities.'[118]

Following Hodder's argument, long barrows in the Cotswold-Severn region and beyond may have an architecture that in a single structure embodies the notion of the traditional long house, the female body and the womb. Symbolically, they owe their inspiration to particular views of the world and the relationships between time, space, life and death. However, aspects of the physical expression of these ideas in architectural form can also be traced back to the timber and stone structures within oval barrows, round barrows and simple passage graves within and around the area. The portal settings, simple chambers and an interest in having a forecourt may relate to the portal dolmen tradition. The long mounds may be both an elaboration and a development of the oval mounds of the area, as well as introducing ideas inherent to wider traditions of mound building from further afield along the Atlantic seaboard and across the north European Plain. Certainly, the similarity of transepted chambers in Brittany and the Cotswolds, sometimes referred to as the Notgrove-Pornic style, is uncannily close for independent development in both areas. Comparable chamber forms are also well represented in Ireland.[119] In many ways we may simply be seeing the continued network of contacts represented earlier by the simple passage graves and rotunda graves which likewise connected these areas. Thus rather than seeing long barrows as highly structured packages adopted as a totality, it may be better to see individual communities selecting elements from a wide repertoire of constructional devices past and present, to create a structure that fulfilled their needs by expressing their particular beliefs and understandings of the world. Monumentalization and elaboration are key aspects of this process; the reorganization of space in the landscape as a whole finds a reflection in the reformation of the architecture seen in the long barrows. The public spaces represented by the forecourts and the areas in front of the façades take over from the internal, essentially private spaces of the chambers.[120] Looked at in this way we can move away from traditional typological approaches to the study of long barrows towards a more interpretative perspective. As Andrew Fleming has reminded us, tombs were for the living and their architecture represents the essential framework of spaces within which people did things and expressed themselves.[121]

6

PEOPLE, CEREMONIES AND OBJECTS

The form, structure and architecture of a long barrow provided the spaces, contexts and mnemonics for its use by the living, the dead and the spirit world beyond. By analogy with ceremonial structures used by communities whose beliefs can be studied in detail, it is highly likely that the various components of a long barrow had specific symbolic meanings which were cross-referenced to key aspects of life and death: creation myths; views of the world and the place of people in it; accepted patterns of social order; community identity; age and gender structures; the passage of time; cycles of life; the origins of the cosmos; and perhaps some apparatus to cope with the end of the world as they knew it. How such things were represented can only be guessed at; the only certainty is that they were quite different from our own twenty-first-century views. Patterns and regularities amongst what can be seen at investigated long barrows are important, however, and we have to ask whether it is possible to identify anything of the thoughts and beliefs of the barrow-builders. How did they view death? What kinds of object did they place with corpses inside the chambers? What role did animals play? What were the long barrow people like? How are their remains represented inside long barrows? What activities took place inside long barrows and what happened around about and in the forecourt? And, critically, what was the relationship between the living and the dead?

ANCESTORS AND THE LIVING

One theme that is regularly discussed with reference to the use and purpose of long barrows is their association with the ancestors of the communities that built and used them. They are seen as having an active role in the perpetuation of ancestral traditions, things passed down through successive generations. Colin Renfrew linked this to the creation of group identity, the legitimation of land-ownership, and the assertion of territorial rights.[1] It can be suggested that amongst non-literate societies it is common for status to be associated with family descent patterns. People knew their genealogy and identified with particular ancestors whose relics were stored within the chambers of a nearby long barrow. However, although most long barrows in the Cotswold-Severn region contain the physical remains of human beings, not all do. It is a pattern repeated elsewhere in the British Isles and could be explained by accepting that ideas about ancestral traditions may have extended beyond the simple and obvious human chain represented by successive generations of people in the community. The progenitors of a group were perhaps seen as animals, plants, or some geomorphic phenomenon such as a rock or a spring. Here it is perhaps relevant to recall that at the Beckhampton Road long barrow (WIL 27) two ox-skulls had been placed on the ground surface prior to the construction of the mound, while a third had probably been set on a post as a highly visible reminder of the power and importance of these beasts.[2] Taking the barrow as a focus, two sets of connections help account for the evidence as presently understood. On the one hand it is possible to see a direct link between the monument and the landscape. Meanwhile, on the other hand, there is an indirect link between people and their barrow, represented sometimes by a physical presence and sometimes by a symbolic or totemic presence.

Emphasizing the role of the ancestors and their physical and symbolic association with particular long barrows may well be important, but it hinges on a number of assumptions and underlying principles that are rarely questioned. First, and perhaps most important, is the matter of whether the human remains within a given barrow do in fact derive from a single family or lineage. It is a matter that needs to be resolved through DNA testing, but, as we will see below, is currently assumed rather than documented. A second assumption is that the accumulation of human remains took place over a sufficiently long period of time that it is legitimate to speak of ancestral lines that transcend more than perhaps two or three generations. When Stuart Piggott reported his excavations at the West Kennet long barrow (WIL 4) he confidently asserted that 'the use of the West Kennet tomb, from building to final blocking, can hardly have spanned less than a millennium'.[3] It is a perspective that has endured and coloured much subsequent thinking, but needs to be fully tested by the blanket application of radiocarbon dating to the contents of several barrows. The assumptions are weak and evidence is growing that long barrows were far more transitory than Piggott imagined, even though he was right to stress the long period over which the filling and blocking of the chambers took place. Thirdly, the very idea of an ancestral lineage stretching across the centuries carries with it the notion of a linear progressive view of time, much as we use today. In this the passing of time is essentially a sequence of events that can be extended to infinity both backwards and forwards from the present. But not all societies view time in this way. One common alternative that is especially widespread among agricultural societies is a cyclical view in which a sequence of stages unfolds according to a set rhythm and pace, until the starting point is reached again and the cycle repeats: the seasons of the year or the passing of a human life. It is a kind of time that is often generated by rituals and marked through festivals and celebrations at key moments in the unfolding of the cycle.

Linear and cyclical patterns can of course be combined perhaps with a series of interlocking recurrent cycles of differing duration (e.g. solar day, lunar month, seasonal year) defining progress along a recognized trajectory.[4] The possibilities are legion and our ability to distinguish between them at more than five millennia removed is almost non-existent. Nonetheless, when we come to look at the way long barrows were used, and the things that were deposited as a result of that activity, it is important to keep an open mind about how these distant peoples viewed superficially simple matters such as the passage of time, ritual cycles and the dividing up of space.

PATTERNS OF ACTIVITY AROUND THE MOUND

Forecourts
The forecourt, defined as the area between the horns at the proximal end of most long barrows, was the scene of sporadic activity. Among the most common features represented within excavated forecourts are formal hearths and spreads of charcoal-rich soil suggesting the eroded remains of bonfires. At Nympsfield (GLO 13) there were two hollows in which there was evidence of burning and immediately outside the entrance to the chambers a small trodden platform on which a fire had been lit.[5] Similarly, at Notgrove (GLO 4), within a rather narrow partly paved forecourt there were two stone-lined depressions filled with black burnt material and evidence of several fires on the axis of the barrow 4-5m out from the entrance.[6] At the Giant's Caves (WIL 2) three closely set hearths were recorded in the forecourt, perpetuating the main axis of the mound, the innermost lying close to the false-portal in the façade wall.[7] At Hazleton North (GLO 54), two spreads of charcoal-rich soil were recorded more or less on the centre-line of the mound within the forecourt, probably the result of fires being lit on the vegetated original ground surface, with worm-action taking charcoal into the natural soil beneath.[8] Traces of burning were found on the forecourt wall and across the small area of original ground surface examined at Rodmarton (GLO 16).[9]

Pits unconnected with burning or fires have been recorded at several sites. At Nympsfield one such pit was 0.4m across and about 0.4m deep. It lay on the central axis of the barrow about 3.6m in front of the entrance *(13)*. It contained only soil and one fragment of animal bone. At Notgrove there was an oblong depression about 0.6m by 0.5m, edged with stones, over which unburnt human bones represented the fragmented remains of a young person and a child. A small-scale excavation of a section of the forecourt at Rodmarton revealed a stone-lined pit containing three deposits of pig bone, one near the top, one in the middle and one at the bottom. Each comprised the coronid process of a mandible, two from the right side and one from the left.[10] As a whole, this series of deposits strongly suggests recurrent visitations over a period of time in order to enact a specific ritual. Not all sites reveal such clear evidence, though, a small hollow and several possible stakeholes being all that could be identified from the use of the forecourt at Gwernvale (BRE 4).

Human bones are sometimes represented in forecourts, mostly of those barrows with terminal chambers, and in some cases perhaps the result of casual loss or deposition after the barrow had fallen out of use. Generally, the human remains from forecourts are very fragmentary. At Nympsfield parts of a young person and an adult were found on the north side of the forecourt; mention has already been made of the remains of a young person and a child found at Notgrove. Amongst long barrows with lateral chambers, there were no human remains in the forecourt at Hazleton North, but at the Giant's Caves a few small fragments of human bone were found on the ground surface and in a disturbed area around the northern stone of the false-portal. At West Kennet (WIL 4) a right femur was found below a stone in the centre of the forecourt, the greater part of an adult female skull lay against one of the façade stones added to the front of the forecourt, and fragments of cranial bone were also found between the stones forming the façade of the northern horn.

Animal bones are more common than human remains within forecourt deposits. They are usually found scattered on the old ground surface and in the very lowest layer of collapse and filling deposits. Such contexts strongly suggest that originally these bones, or more likely the body parts to which they relate, were fixed to the façade of the barrow or placed on steps in the barrow's profile. Cattle and pig are most commonly represented, and in most cases it is skull fragments and teeth that are found. At Hazleton North, about 179 fragments of animal bone were found within the forecourt, concentrated along the façade; all but four of the bones were from crania. Pig bones representing four heads were mainly found in the central section of the façade, while cattle bones representing perhaps two or three heads were found mainly to either side of the concentration of pig bones.[11] West of the Severn, at Pipton (BRE 8), an ox horncore was found on the forecourt surface next to the eastern upright of the false-portal, perhaps the remains of a decayed cattle-head on or above the portal setting.[12] Taking the evidence from these and other sites together, the animal heads at the back of the forecourts may perhaps be seen as protective talismans or as totemic symbols.

Surprisingly, pottery, flintwork and other deliberately placed artefacts are rather rare in forecourt contexts, except as part of the blocking deposits discussed in Chapter 7. At Gwernvale two rather special finds within the forecourt are considered to have been deposited during the use of the monument: an unusually large leaf-shaped arrowhead and a scraper made of the kind of flint usually reserved for polished axeheads.[13] Similarly, at Parc le Breos Cwm (GLA 4) there were no features in the forecourt, but two small placed deposits. The first, near the mouth of the forecourt on the west, included both burnt and unburnt flint debitage and cores, a large burnt leaf-shaped arrowhead, eight pieces of rock quartz, a single sherd of pottery and five fragments of cremated bone. A second deposit in the east half of the forecourt included five rock crystals, a flint blade and 34 potsherds.[14] Something rather similar was noted at Ty Isaf (BRE 5) where the butt of a polished flint axe was found buried in the old ground surface at the outer edge of the forecourt.[15] At Tinkinswood (GLA 9), potsherds representing most of a single vessel were found crushed on the floor of the forecourt and in the entrance to the chamber.[16] East of the Severn at Nympsfield, the broken remains of a small Ebbsfleet style bowl with impressed cord decoration were found in the lower levels of the forecourt blocking and it may once have stood on the mound near or above the entrance to the chambers *(55F)*.

Interpreting this evidence of activity in the forecourts is far from easy. That they were periodically a focus for ceremonies and rituals can hardly be doubted, but what form did these take? Recent studies suggest that they may have been rather macabre places, perhaps with severed animal heads pinned to the façade wall and objects placed on portal slabs or the natural shelves made by steps in the profile of the mound. Julian Thomas suggested that the deposits found in the forecourts were the products of feasts in celebration of the dead, possibly coinciding with the removal of human remains from the chambers and perhaps the deposition of bones.[17] Although some forecourts were quite small, as arenas for ceremonies these spaces were relatively open, public and accessible in contrast to the closed and restricted chamber areas within the mound. Looking at such things in social terms, Mark Edmonds has emphasized the way in which power and prestige could have been expressed through the social use of space within the forecourt and around the barrow generally; access to the chamber being some kind of privilege bestowed through kinship or position.[18]

Sounds are also important elements of ritual and ceremony, albeit an aspect largely inaudible to archaeologists so far distant in time from what went on in the ancient past. We can, however, be sure that the curving forecourt wall or façade of a long barrow would have served to amplify and reverberate all the sounds made during the activities there. In the case of barrows with terminal chambers, the hollow spaces within the end of the mound would have added to the acoustic effects by providing echoes from within the chambers. Perhaps such returning sounds were interpreted as the voice of an oracle.[19] Exactly what kinds of noises and sounds may have been made can only be guessed at, but one clue comes from the discovery of a broken simple pipe or end-blown flute *(55G)* made from the metapodial of a sheep in the entrance to the northeast III chamber at Penywyrlod (BRE 14).[20] It is easy to imagine the ethereal haunting tones enveloping the barrow and drawing those present into alternative worlds conjured up by the tune.

It is important, however, not to push the archaeological evidence for forecourt activity too far. Some forecourts show almost no signs of activity there at all. At Burn Ground (GLO 60), for example, no features were found in or on the original ground surface of the narrow and fairly deep forecourt, or around the façade and horns. The same applies at West Kennet. At the three chamberless barrows excavated in north Wiltshire – Beckhampton Road (WIL 27), South Street (WIL 36) and Horslip (WIL 30) – there are no forecourts or façades at the proximal ends of the barrow mounds and thus they could not have hosted ceremonies at the end of the mound in the same way that other long barrows did.

Activity around the tail of the barrow

Generally speaking, the distal end or 'tail' of most long barrows is poorly preserved and few have been investigated in detail. At Nympsfield, Elsie Clifford found what

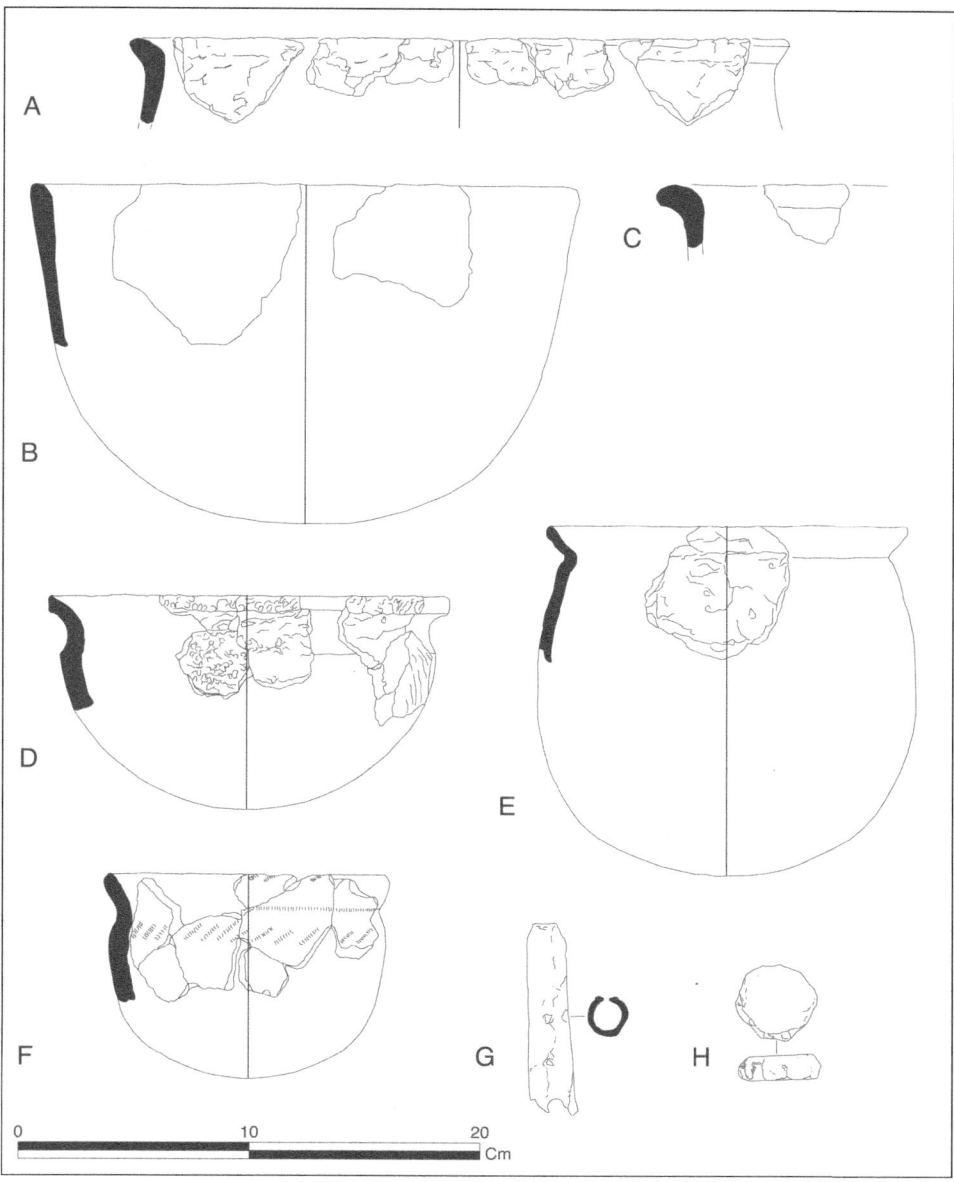

55 Finds from the forecourts and peripheral areas of long barrows in the Cotswold-Severn region. *A:* Hazleton North (GLO 54); *B* and *C:* Gwernvale (BRE 7); *D* and *E:* Burn Ground (GLO 60); *F:* Nympsfield (GLO 13); *G* and *H:* Penywyrlod (BRE 14)

she took to be a shallow 'back-court' at the west end of the mound, making the whole structure 'double-ended'. Within this area were the remains of a fire on the old ground surface and a single row of stones suggesting the former presence of some other feature. More recent work by Alan Saville has shown that Clifford's western façade was in fact an internal retaining wall, and that the supposed 'back-court' features should be seen as the remains of pre-barrow constructions.[21] At Penywyrlod, an oval pit 3.3m long by 1.5m wide by 0.6m deep was found just beyond the end of the mound, the whole feature being backfilled with carefully angled stones which the excavator believed provided a kind of buttress for the back of the mound.[22] It is not all clear what it is, but one possibility is that it was used like a step to provide access to the top of the mound.

Quarries, berms and surrounding ground

Where excavated, the quarries of long barrows usually contain evidence of activity broadly contemporary with the use of the monument. In the case of relatively deep and narrow quarry ditches they simply provided a trap for material that accidentally fell in or was deliberately thrown in. Once in position such material tended to stay where it was and is generally well preserved. It does not of course necessarily signify that people went down into the quarries to do things. Elsewhere, wide and open quarry pits were extensive enough that they did become the setting for activities rather like the forecourts. Most such evidence lies on top of the initial natural silting and infilling of the quarry, on stabilization surfaces that in some cases may have been permanent enough for vegetation to appear and thin organic soils to develop. At Hazleton North, there was considerable evidence for activity in the southern quarry. Towards the eastern end were two spreads of charcoal-rich soil and burnt stones suggestive of former bonfires, while nearby was a concentration of finds including cattle and pig bones, a cattle horncore and eight pieces of human bone. Towards the centre of the quarry was a small hearth with burnt fragmentary cattle and sheep bones together with part of a ceramic vessel *(55A)*. This pot was unusual because it was made in a fabric that included crushed bone (probably animal bone) as well as local limestone.[23] Various other small deposits were scattered across the quarry floor, but the only substantial feature was at the point where the edge of the quarry came close to the entrance to the south chamber. Here a fan of stonework from the barrow mound, fragments of human bone and charcoal-rich soil spilled over the edge of the quarry as a result of natural collapse accelerated by people scrambling up the edge of the quarry to reach the chamber.[24] By contrast, very little activity connected with the use of the barrow was found in the northern quarry.

Flanking areas of excavated long barrows outside of quarry features and the berm between the quarries and the mound, show little evidence of intensive activity; indeed they appear to have been kept relatively clean, undisturbed and free of encumbrances. Pottery is the most widely represented material found in these areas and some at least may well have originally been placed on shelves or steps in the profile of the barrow mound near significant points such as chamber entrances. At Penywyrlod a large rim fragment from a hemispherical bowl with a thickened and slightly everted rim was found outside the entrance to the northeast III chamber.[25] Similarly, at Gwernvale (BRE 7), three vessels lay on the ground surface under the blocking deposits and layers connected with the decay of the mound.[26] It is a pattern seen elsewhere, for example at Burn Ground (GLO 60) where parts of a rather unusual vessel were found outside the southern lateral entrance to the chamber.[27] At Parc le Breos Cwm, a light scatter of potsherds was found along the base of the outer revetment wall on the west side, but little else.[28]

Elsie Clifford noted that at Nympsfield 'the most striking thing was what appeared to be a continuous ring of burnt material, against the outer edge of the main construction of the barrow'.[29] Stakeholes or perhaps postholes containing burnt material were reported from some trenches, but they are not recorded on the plan and may just relate to a much more recent fence around the site.[30] At Gwernvale, the area outside chambers 1 and 2 on the south side of the mound contained shallow pits and hollows within which was broken pottery and charcoal-rich soil; in two cases these pits had been dug against the outer revetment wall, partly undermining it.[31] Around the entrances into the chambers at Penywyrlod the old ground surface contained smears of charcoal and occasional potsherds, while near the north corner of the mound a sandstone disc was found on the contemporary ground surface *(55H)*. One exception is perhaps Randwick (GLO 10), where in July 1883 G. Witts and C.A. Witchell found 'several skeletons laid close to the external wall' near the southwest corner of the mound.[32] Witts reports similar finds of four skeletons around the edge of the mound at West Tump (GLO 8),[33] but nothing similar has been found in recent excavations, and it is possible that these burials were of much later date (see Chapter 9).

The area around long barrows has rarely been investigated. Very few excavation trenches extend more than a few metres beyond the edge of the mound except to provide sections through quarries. Surface surveys or extensive geophysical surveys are extremely rare. Surface collection and test-pitting at 20m intervals around the neighbouring Easton Down (WIL 19) and Roughridge (WIL 35) long barrows revealed a light background scatter of broadly fourth-millennium BC flintwork which seemed to increase in density in the general area of the barrows.[34] Surface collection around the pair of long barrows at Hazleton (GLO 33 and 54) also produced low-density but widespread scatters of flintwork, while geophysical surveys around Stoney Littleton (SOM 1) suggested the presence of a few pit-like anomalies to the southeast of the mound.[35] Clearly, long barrows were places in the landscape that were occasionally visited, but they were hardly the focus of intensive activity, at least not of the kind that leaves strong archaeological traces. Such a view accords with the environmental evidence gathered from the accumulating silts and fills in adjacent quarries and side ditches, which suggests that, during their use, long barrows lay in relatively stable, generally open, conditions.

ACTIVITY IN THE CHAMBERS

The vast majority of long barrows within the Cotswold-Severn region contain chambers of one sort of another, these being the main areas for the deposition of human remains as discussed below. As noted in Chapter 5, many chambers were paved with stone slabs while the remainder were floored with beaten earth and clay. Fragments of pottery, crushed bone and charcoal are frequently reported pressed into the floor or trapped between the paving slabs, showing that people trampled about inside the passages and chambers without much regard for what they stepped on. Stones were sometimes placed on the chamber floors in order to demarcate specific areas and at the scale represented by individual chambers the prescribed use and treatment of space can be glimpsed from the disposition of material and occasional localized structural works. At Nympsfield (GLO 13), for example, a small section of the north side of the passage immediately outside the north chamber was marked in a way that led Buckman to refer to a cist; Alan Saville's excavations in 1974 showed what was probably more of a stone-edged box with only the slots for the side slabs penetrating the floor surface.[36] The western chamber at Ty Isaf (BRE 5) was subdivided into two sections by means of stone slabs, the inner portion being paved while the outer portion was beaten earth. Nearby, at Pipton (BRE 8), small stone slabs had been used to delimit the spread of bone relating to one of the seven piles of human remains within Chamber II on the northwest side of the barrow.[37] Slightly different is the platform of sarsen slabs on the floor of the northeast chamber at West Kennet (WIL 4) on which the crouched burial of an elderly man had been placed,[38] and the stone platform within the chamber at West Tump (GLO 8) on which the skeletons of a woman and child were found.[39]

Lighting fires inside the chambers was commonplace, and many excavation reports document the evidence in terms of scorched stones, deposits of charcoal and localized burning of human remains. At Nympsfield, the remains of fires were found on the floor of the outer passage and in the north chamber. Burnt bone was found in both areas, and charcoal and debris from these fires was also found in the south and west cells of the chamber.[40] Analysis of the charcoal showed that hazel and hawthorn had been used, both quick-burning woods that when dry would provide a bright fire to help illuminate the otherwise dark chamber. These were more than just brushwood torches, for the fires had been sufficiently fierce to discolour two of the orthostats in the outer chamber. Much the same was reported at Notgrove (GLO 4), where ash, plum/cherry, hazel and elm wood had been burnt extensively, leaving spreads of charcoal and discoloured stone on the south door jamb, in the western chamber, southeast chamber and adjacent inner passage and in the entrance zone.[41] At the Giant's Caves (WIL 2), the remains of a hearth that included burnt bone in its matrix was found in the passage of the southeastern chamber,[42] while at Hazleton North (GLO 54) burning was identified at the junction of the entrance zone and passage of the north chamber.[43]

BURIALS AND HUMAN REMAINS

The main purpose of constructing timber or stone chambers inside long barrows was to hold human remains. These have long been a major fascination for those concerned with the excavation and analysis of long barrows, providing a source of much controversy and debate not only about their interpretation but also about the ethics of disturbing them. Sir Richard Colt Hoare, for example, favoured the reburial of human remains as a moral duty towards the people they represented, but at the same time of course depriving subsequent specialists of the raw materials for new studies. Later investigators felt less bound by such scruples. John Thurnam, a medical doctor who spent most of his working life at the Wiltshire County Asylum in Devizes, opened long barrows with the explicit aim of collecting anatomical specimens for examination and analysis.[44] Biometrical studies and craniometry involving numerous detailed measurements across specified facets and processes on major bones was one of Thurnam's passions and became a widely practised field of human anatomical science in the mid-nineteenth century. It purportedly allowed the possibility of comparing and grouping ancient and modern populations, although it later fell into disrepute because of its over-emphasis on defining ethnic and racial groupings. However, substantial listings of carefully collected statistical data were accumulated and remain useful. Especially notable is the massive two-volume work entitled *Crania Britannica* published by Joseph Davis and John Thurnam in 1865, and an appendix to Canon Greenwell's *British Barrows* compiled by Professor George Rolleston and published in 1877. Subsequent trends in the analysis and examination of human remains from long barrows can be seen in the work of later specialists. Dr A.J.E. Cave and Sir Arthur Keith, for example, provided much of the medical, anatomical and scientific study of human remains from long barrows, with important contributions on the assemblages from Nympsfield (GLO 13), Notgrove (GLO 4) and Rodmarton (GLO 16). The remains from West Kennet (WIL 4) were studied by L.H. Wells, F.P. Lipowski (cremations) and Don Brothwell (dental pathology), who provide much anatomical detail and information about the pathology of the population. The development of forensic archaeology and greater concern with what is known as the taphonomy of assemblages – the way they are formed – provide the basis of the most recent work, with very detailed studies at a handful of sites: Ascott-under-Wychwood (OXF 6) partly published in advance of the main report by J.T. Chesterman and later heavily criticized by the excavator of the site Don Benson;[45] Hazleton North (GLO 54) studied by Juliet Rogers; Parc le Breos Cwm (GLA 4) studied by Michael Wysocki; Millbarrow (WIL 11) studied by Don Brothwell; and Wayland's Smithy (BRK 1) studied by Don Brothwell and Rachel Cullen. By the early 1970s Don Brothwell was able to cite over 400 individuals represented amongst the burial deposits in long barrows within the Cotwold-Severn region, a number which has since risen considerably.[46]

What all these studies show is that, in general, the human remains found at long barrows within the Cotswold-Severn region, more frequent inside the chambers than out, comprise disarticulated skeletons representing multiple collective burial. But such general statements mask extremely complicated and variable patterns of deposition and the movement of both flesh-covered and defleshed body-parts within the chambers and beyond. In part, these movements may be connected with activities in the forecourt and around the edge of the mound that sometimes result in the placement of human bones or the incorporation of bones in accumulative contexts such as ground surfaces.[47] However, our thinking about these movements should not be confined to the limits of the long barrow site itself, for human remains circulated within much wider systems that included other places within the landscape as well (see Chapter 7). As a result, there are many difficulties and uncertainties surrounding the interpretation of burial deposits from long barrows, of which two general issues deserve comment at this stage.

First, there is the possibility that corpses or skeletons were accumulated over a period of time before the long barrow was built, and that some of the bones deposited within the chambers were therefore already old and skeletonized when first interred. The presence, for example, of fragmentary human bones representing perhaps two or three individuals on the old ground surface underneath Hazleton North may support this idea,[48] as may the occasional presence of human remains below the flooring of chambers as at Pipton (BRE 8).[49] Set against this is the problem of not knowing what was typical and what was unusual within these early farming communities. Human remains may find their way into general accumulative contexts in all sorts of ways, quite possibly unbeknown to people at the time, as a result of reworking earlier deposits, the activities of animals and the movement of discarded material and waste. The presence of human remains does not in itself signify anything special about a deposit; significance can be interpreted only in relation to the context of the find and the meanings that may have been attached to its placement or deposition in the past.

Second, there is the possibility, touched upon briefly in earlier chapters, that chamber areas were periodically cleared out so that they were available to receive further interments when the need arose. This issue was discussed by Stuart Piggott, who concluded that 'these problems are ultimately bound up with the cardinal problems confronting us when we attempt to interpret collective chambered tombs in terms of likely social contexts – what members of the total population group were so buried, at what intervals and over what duration of time?'[50] The presence at Ascott-under-Wychwood of a completely empty cell within the northern chamber area may be relevant here,[51] but can be interpreted in a number of ways. Perhaps it was prepared to receive remains that never arrived, or perhaps it was cleared of remains originally placed there. Empty chambers are rare, but have been recorded elsewhere: chamber B on the south side of the mound at Lugbury (WIL 1), for example, was empty when investigated by Thurnam in 1854.[52] In some areas west of the Severn particularly, the presence or absence of skeletal remains is impossible to determine because acidic soils will have dissolved any calcareous bone that was once deposited there. At Gwernvale (BRE 7) the preservation of human bone was extremely poor, but there is some evidence that the northern chamber was empty when abandoned by its users despite the fact that a series of rebuilds in the blocking material indicates that it had been entered and resealed on several occasions.[53] No empty cells have yet been positively identified amongst long barrows in the Cotswold-Severn region with terminal chambers, and this has led Julian Thomas to suggest that part of the normal usage of lateral-chambered long barrows was the removal of skeletal material from the chambers.[54] It is, however, the case that human bone is not universally associated with long barrows, as the three chamberless examples on the north Wessex Downs and others elsewhere in southern England conclusively demonstrate.

People, Ceremonies and Objects

*56 Hazleton North, Hazleton (GLO 54). View into the south chamber from above showing the burial deposits on the floor surface. The entrance to the chamber is bottom left. Scale totals 0.3m
Photograph by Alan Saville. Copyright reserved*

Distribution and deposition

When excavated, the chamber areas typically contain abundant human remains widely distributed across the paved or earth floors as what superficially appears as jumbled spreads of bones *(56)*. Describing the deposits excavated at West Kennet (WIL 4), Stuart Piggott refers to 'a scatter of odd bones among the rubble and stones',[55] a scene more colourfully brought to life by Professor Wells who notes that the ghoulish will 'picture a visitor to the barrow picking up a partly decomposed arm, detaching the humerus and flinging the other bones into a dark corner'.[56]

Almost exclusively, the human remains lie on or above the floor of the chamber. Earthcut graves are rare from the period 3700–3000 BC, although they are known earlier and become fairly common after about 3000 BC. For most of the fourth millennium BC the pattern of above-ground burial is so marked that one wonders if this is not a reflection of fundamental beliefs, for example a taboo against disturbing the ground and the direct placement of the dead into that underworld domain.[57] Indeed, the very act of digging into the ground, although occasionally necessary, may make the tools used 'unclean' in some way (see Chapter 5).

The few occasions when specifically human remains have been found under the floor of the chambers at long barrows may be exceptional cases related to construction contexts (see Chapter 5). There are also a few discoveries of pits that had been dug into the floor of a chamber area, into which a burial had then been deposited. At Nympsfield, for example, a grave was found cut into the floor of the passage on the south side towards the western end. It contained parts of three human skeletons, one an infant, as well as bones and teeth from an ox, a flint flake and two bone tools.[58] Much less rare are cases where individual bones or small groups of bones were put into cracks or gaps between the orthostats forming the walls of the passage or chamber. At the Giant's Caves (WIL 2), for example, vertebrae from perhaps three individuals had been pushed into gaps in the wall of the passage zone of the northwest chamber.[59]

Long Barrow		Entrance zone	Passage zone	Chamber zone	Total
BRK 1	Wayland's Smithy†	★	★	8	8
BRE 1	Pen-y-wyrlod	★	★	12	12
BRE 2	Little Lodge	★	★	9	9
BRE 4	Ffostyll South	1		8	9
BRE 5	Ty Isaf	1	2	21	24
BRE 7	Gwernvale†	★	1	9	10
BRE 8	Pipton	0	0	8	8
BRE 14	Penywyrlod	0	4	13	17
GLA 4	Parc le Breos Cwm†	7		33	40
GLA 9	Tinkinswood	?3		?45	?48
GLO 1	Belas Knap†	★	★	31	31
GLO 2	Pole's Wood South	★	3	9	12
GLO 3	Eyford Hill	★	★	13	13
GLO 4	Notgrove†	1	1	7	9
GLO 8	West Tump	?1	?4	?20	?25
GLO 10	Randwick	★	★	4	4
GLO 13	Nympsfield†	3	5	9	17
GLO 14	Hetty Pegler's Tump†	2	6	7	15
GLO 16	Rodmarton	★	★	16	16
GLO 20	Bown Hill	★	★	6	6
GLO 24	Pole's Wood East	★	★	19	19
GLO 54	Hazleton North§	10	7	24	41
GLO 60	Burn Ground	1	3	8	12
GLO 93/GLO 17	Norn's Tump	★	★	11	11
GLO 94	Sale's Lot	1	6	?>6	?>13
OXF 6	Ascott-under-Wychwood§‡	16	12	18	46
SOM 1	Stoney Littleton†	★	★	6	6
WIL 1	Lugbury	★	★	26	26
WIL 2	Giant's Caves†	0	6	19	25
WIL 3	Lanhill	0	1	18	19
WIL 4	West Kennet†	2	1	57	60
WIL 6	Adam's Grave	★	★	4	4
WIL 11	Millbarrow	★	★	9	9

† Complete excavation but part of the assemblage lost in earlier robbing or previous excavations
§ Complete excavation
‡ There was no access between the elements of the chamber areas here. Three individuals were also represented in the cairn between the two innermost cists
★ Details not recorded

Table 1 Distribution of human remains within the chamber areas of Cotswold-Severn long barrows

Table 1 provides an analysis of the approximate number of individuals estimated to be represented within the chambers of excavated long barrows in the Cotswold-Severn region. Where barrows have been only partly excavated these must be treated as minimum numbers, and even where full excavation has taken place the problems of rematching disarticulated skeletal remains means that the numbers are best approximations. As can be seen, overall numbers vary between fewer than five and over 60 individuals. Typically, about 40 burials are represented in each long barrow across the region that has been fully excavated and the resulting assemblages examined to modern standards.

The predominant burial rite involved the deposition and treatment of corpses and their skeletonized remains. There is some evidence for cremation, however, with small amounts of burnt bone being deposited within the long barrows of both lateral-chambered and terminal-chambered types, including Hazleton North (? 2 or 3 individuals), Parc le Breos Cwm (? 2 individuals), Nympsfield (? 1 or 2 individuals), West Kennet (? 2 individuals) and the Giant's Caves (? 1 individual).[60] In no case is there evidence that bone was cremated within the chambers themselves, so this is an activity that must have happened elsewhere. Whittle and Wysocki suggest that much of the cremated bone in long barrows within the Cotswold-Severn region tends to be deposited late in the sequence at individual monuments, and its location within terminal-chambered long barrows focuses on areas immediately to the right-hand side after entering the entrance zone or passage. Thus at Parc le Breos Cwm the cremated bone lay in the southeast chamber, a pattern echoed at West Kennet and Nympsfield.[61] At West Kennet the cremated remains lay in a single spread in the northwest corner of the northeast chamber, stratigraphically overlying the complete crouched burial of an elderly man.

The superficial appearance of the deposits hides many strands of evidence for the way the chambers were used. Julian Thomas has proposed that there are marked differences in the treatment of human remains in lateral-chambered long barrows as against terminal-chambered examples,[62] but little if any of it stands up to closer scrutiny and the full analysis of evidence that was available to Thomas only as interim accounts. One pattern seen in all kinds of long barrow where there are multiple chambers is that those on the north side of the mound, or comprising the northern elements of nucleated chambers, tend to hold fewer burials than those on the south *(57)*. At Ascott-under-Wychwood, for example, cist-chambers 5, 6 and 7 together contained 13 burials in contrast to 33 in cells 1, 2 and 3 on the south side. In general, less than 40 per cent of burials lie in north-side chambers, suggesting perhaps that some kind of superstition applied either prejudicing the placing of bones here in the first place or favouring their subsequent removal.

Taking the threefold division of space outlined in Chapter 5 and represented within almost all chamber areas – entrance zone, passage zone and chamber zone – it is easy to see that skeletal remains are usually concentrated in two zones, the entrance and the chamber *(Table 1)*. At Hazleton North, analysis of the remains in the south chamber showed that there were fragments of the same individual in adjoining zones and a few cases of remains in the entrance linking with pieces in the chamber. The empty element of the chambers at Ascott-under-Wychwood

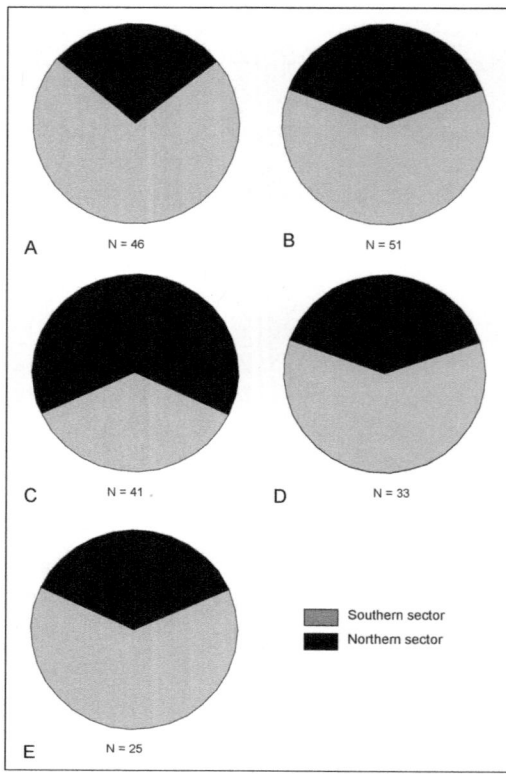

57 North-side and south-side differences in burial patterns. Lateral chambers: *A:* Ascott-under-Wychwood (OXF 6); *B:* Hazleton North (GLO 54); *C:* Giant's Caves, Luckington (WIL 2). Terminal chambers: *D:* West Kennet (WIL 4) 1955-6 excavations only; *E:* Parc le Breos Cwm (GLA 4)

would be the equivalent of the passage zone of the north chamber at other sites and so perhaps provides another reason for the lack of burials. The general poverty of skeletal remains in the passage zone of transepted terminal-chambered long barrows was discussed by Whittle and Wysocki following their analysis of Parc le Breos Cwm.[63] They highlight the fact that in this kind of tomb the passage was an artery or conduit for the introduction and circulation of ancestral remains by the living population and it was questionable whether passages were seen as resting places for the dead. Moreover, there are hints that those few burials that are found in passages may be extremely late in the sequence of use, in some cases perhaps secondary interments. This is certainly suggested by the taphonomy and radiocarbon dates on the examples from Parc le Breos Cwm.[64]

Representation and circulation

Ever since the first detailed examination of skeletal material from the chambers of long barrows took place back in the nineteenth century it has been recognized that very few complete skeletons are represented, and that most individuals represented have lost major body parts either before or after being placed in the barrow. In his summary of the evidence available to 1950, Glyn Daniel noted that there were far fewer skulls than long bones in the chambers at Randwick (GLO 10) and Nympsfield (GLO 13). At Ty Isaf (BRE 5) about 33 people were represented altogether, but while there were 22 mandibles there were only seven skulls.[65] A similar picture can be glimpsed elsewhere. At Pipton (BRE 8) there were ten mandibles but only five skulls,[66] while at Lanhill (WIL 3) south chamber there was a complete skeleton plus nine mandibles, only six skulls and enough major limbs to be the remains of at least eleven people.[67] The disarticulation and partial representation of individuals within the chambers was emphasized during anatomical studies, and naturally this led to a series of debates about the way in which burials were made and how the evidence recovered through excavation should be explained.

One idea that became prevalent in the early twentieth century is the so-called 'ossuary theory', succinctly outlined by O.G.S. Crawford who suggested that with reference to the long barrows of the Cotswolds 'the bones deposited in the burial-chambers had already been buried or exposed for a time elsewhere; and were subsequently dug up or collected for solemn re-burial in a permanent and more imposing resting place'.[68] The exposure of corpses, technically known as excarnation, prior to interment within a long barrow enjoyed a great deal of support. Indeed, Richard Atkinson was sufficiently convinced that he applied the term 'long mortuary enclosure' to a rectangular ditch-edged enclosure he excavated at Dorchester on Thames, in the belief that it was the place where corpses were exposed as part of the excarnation process prior to their incorporation into nearby long barrows.[69] A similar kind of enclosure bounded by a bank and ditch is shown immediately east of the Old Chapel long barrow (WIL 14) in an early eighteenth-century illustration by William Stukeley.[70]

In their analysis of Atkinson's excavations at Parc le Breos Cwm, Alasdair Whittle and Michael Wysocki accept that prior burial followed by a single act of deposition in the long barrow could apply at this site, but allow that successive depositions could equally well account for the evidence.[71] In an analysis of the bone assemblage from Ascott-under-Wychwood, Mary Baxter found that rather few of the small bones of the hands and feet were represented in the chambers and took this as an indicator of the fact that the bodies had been exposed elsewhere prior to the skeletonized remains being taken to the barrow for placement in the chambers. Support for this idea comes from the identification of a mass of bones deposited between the southernmost cist and the outside of the mound. This comprised over 800 bones mixed with stone rubble in a layer over 0.3m thick. Some of the skulls had been placed at the corners of the spread. During the act of placing the individual body-parts in the chambers further into the mound some elements were reassembled in ways that could not have been possible during life, and in some cases pieces from different individuals were reassembled together.[72] Ethnographic parallels provide some insights into how different communities store corpses before formal burial. The range is almost endless and any could have been used in connection with long barrow rituals: wrapped in a blanket; sat outside the house; placed on a timber or stone platform; or stored in a box are amongst the more widespread.

A second, more or less opposing view holds that whole corpses had been placed in long barrows, where they gradually became skeletonized before selected elements were removed for use elsewhere. This explanation gained weight following the investigations at Lanhill in 1938, as both Stuart Piggott and Alexander Keiller felt that the evidence they collected showed that this community at least focused on successive collective burial.[73] Much the same interpretation was applied by Stuart Piggott to the deposits within the West Kennet long barrow which he excavated a decade later, a critical line of evidence being the presence of five adults (three women and two men) and several children represented as more or less complete skeletons in the northeast and southeast chambers. One burial, that of an elderly man in the northeast chamber, was wholly intact, placed in the barrow as a corpse laid in a crouched position on a small area of sarsen paving *(58)*. Other modern excavations emphasize the importance of direct deposition of corpses inside long barrows.

The most completely recorded deposits are those at Hazleton North, where the entrance to the north chamber area contained a very well-preserved sequence of deposits. The latest interment was represented by the more or less complete extended skeleton of a male aged 30–45 years *(59)*. Below this were the remains of a crouched burial, of which the lower half of the skeleton was articulated and other bones were scatted within the entrance; it was certainly an adult, probably a male. Earlier still was a scatter of mainly disarticulated remains representing another adult male. Scattered remains representing a very young child and another pre-adult pre-dated some if not all of the more complete burials, as did the scattered cremated remains of a further adult and child. It is tempting to see in these deposits a regular pattern that involved placing corpses in the entrance zone, leaving them to decompose and then, when space for subsequent burials was needed, moving some of the bones into the interior.

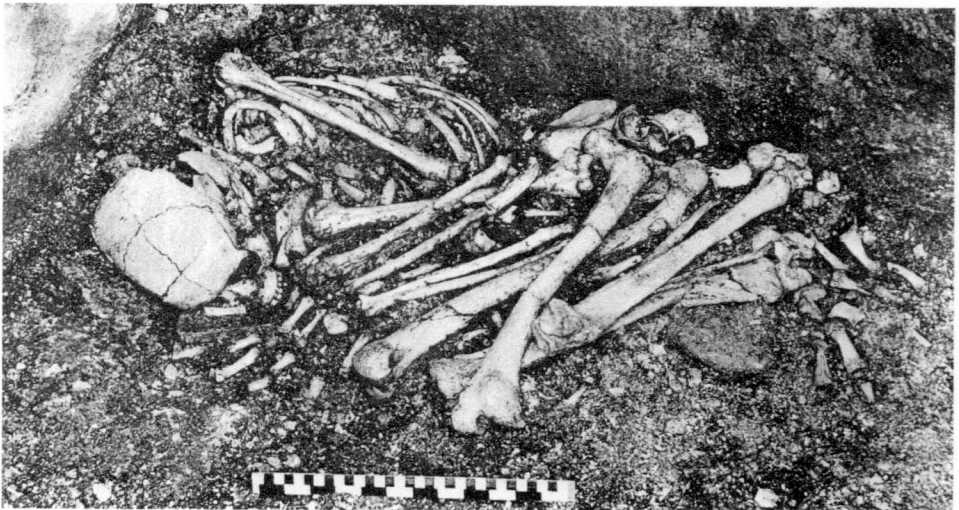

58 West Kennet (WIL 4). Elderly male inhumation in the northeast chamber. Tightly flexed on his right side facing to the southeast, this burial had been placed on a platform of sarsen slabs, partly covering earlier burials. A leaf-shaped flint arrowhead in the region of the throat may have been the cause of death. Scale totals 0.3m. *From Piggott 1962, plate xvb. Copyright reserved*

59 Hazleton North (GLO 54). Adult male inhumation in the entrance zone of the north chamber area. The head lies to the north, flexed against the temporary blocking in the entrance. A large flint core was found underlying the right elbow and a quartz hammerstone lay near the right knee. Scale totals 0.3m. *Photograph by Alan Saville. Copyright reserved*

This was indeed the scenario proposed by Alan Saville in his preliminary report,[74] and followed later by Julian Thomas.[75] Unfortunately, detailed analysis revealed that none of the missing elements of the skeletons in the entrance zone seem to have been represented in the north chamber, which rather undermines the argument and suggests that in fact skeletal elements, if not whole body parts, must sometimes at least have been taken elsewhere rather than progressively moved ever deeper into the chamber. The exceptional preservation, however, may have been the result of exceptional circumstances in this particular chamber causing the process to be truncated and halted in an unusual way. As already noted, the passage zone of the north chamber was devoid of skeletal remains, although remains representing two individuals were present in the chamber zone beyond. When excavated, however, the passage was found to be filled by collapsed walling and roofing, with a collapsed orthostat at the north (outer) end; the blocking slab at the south (inner) end was still in place. When the collapse of the orthostat and walling happened is not known, but it could have been during the life of the tomb. If so, the usual rituals could not have continued and access would have been restricted to the entrance zone. But if the north chamber area was anomalous because of rather extraordinary events, what about the south chamber? Here access seems to have been possible throughout the life of the tomb, and analysis of the scattered remains suggested a credible and coherent pattern of activity. Initially, a succession of corpses were interred in the chamber zone, the remains being confined to the area in which they were placed by blocking slabs at the entrance to the chamber and between the passage and the entrance zones. At some stage it was decided to cease burials in the chamber and to commence successive interments in the entrance zone with the blocking slab between the entrance and the passage still in place. Two burials in this area were fairly intact when excavated, perhaps a less well-preserved version of what was represented in the entrance to the north chamber area. Later still, the blocking slab was removed and bones in the entrance zone were scattered across the sill slab and into the passage. The chamber may have been brought back into use, and certainly bones from the chamber were scattered back into the passage. At what stage bones were removed from decomposed bodies in the chamber and entrance is unclear, although there is the distinct impression that it happened at intervals throughout the life of the barrow.

Using the model of burial activity suggested by the evidence from West Kennet and Hazleton North it is possible to revisit reports of earlier excavations. These generally serve to support the broad picture seen at Hazleton, while adding variations by way of local colour. Overall, the presence of whole corpses within the chamber zones is probably better attested than adherents to the ossuary theory would admit. Winterbotham's account of his work at Belas Knap (GLO 1) between 1863 and 1865 suggests the presence of a complete corpse in the northeast chamber, noting that 'in each nostril were found two phalanges of a forefinger; the top phalanx of one having been driven through the orbit into the cavity of the cranium, as if the body had been placed in a sitting posture, and the head kept erect by thrusting the fingers into the nose'.[76] The recognition of remains compatible with the deposition of sitting or squatting corpses has also been noted during antiquarian excavations at Hetty Pegler's Tump (GLO 14), the west chamber at West Kennet excavated in the mid-nineteenth century and Parc le Breos Cwm, although Whittle and Wysocki note that no evidence of burials articulated in this way has been found in recent excavations and it may in part be fanciful thinking on the part of early investigators.[77]

As would be expected with the direct deposition of corpses, the last burials to be introduced into a chamber area tend to be the most complete, presumably because less time elapsed for the dismemberment of the decaying or decayed remains through successive rituals before the barrow ceased to be used. At Lanhill, earlier remains seem to have been pushed to the back of the chamber prior to the introduction of the final corpse, a male of about 50 years of age, while at Pole's Wood East (GLO 24) George Rolleston and David Royce recorded that 'one skeleton was found undisturbed and surrounded by other human bones so disposed, and in such numbers, as to make it clear that the skeletons they had belonged to had been displaced to make room for it'.[78] Similarly, G.B Witts remarked that at West Tump (GLO 8), 'the further we got in, the more perfect we found the skeletons'. He suggested that the barrow had been raised in honour of a young female and her baby whose bones were discovered on a small semi-circular pavement in the innermost part of the chamber.[79]

Moving bones from skeletonized corpses within the chamber areas, piling them up and on occasion rearranging them, is evident at almost every site that has been investigated. At Hazleton North there is a slight suggestion that some piles of bones were originally the remains of a single individual, but as time went on the heaps became less discrete. Skulls were placed against the side walls of the chambers at Eyford Hill (GLO 3), Hazleton North, Penywyrlod (BRE 14), Cow Common Long (GLO 22), Pole's Wood East, Ascott-under-Wychwood, Ty Isaf and Lanhill. Skulls were placed in the corners of the cist-chambers at Ascott-under-Wychwood.[80] Long bones were found piled against the chamber walls at Penywyrlod. In a few cases the segregation of bones is even more marked. In the northeast II chamber at Penywyrlod skulls were placed against the north wall and long bones against the northwest side of the chamber and towards the southwest end.[81] At Wayland's Smithy, the excavators of the 1919–20 trenches reported that the bones were in groups, but not in anatomical order.[82] At West Kennet there was extensive evidence for the rearrangement of human remains, mainly in what Stuart Piggott called the 'tidying-up of the bones'. In the northwest chamber this involved long bones and vertebrae being cached against the north wall, while in the southwest chamber three skulls had been set in a row against the south wall, the opposite of the arrangement at Penywyrlod noted above. At Ty Isaf the tidying-up in the western chamber involved making groups 'consisting frequently of the cranium, lower jaw and one or two long bones carefully placed against the side-stones and sometimes pushed into angles and crevices'.[83] Chesterman has suggested that at Ascott-under-Wychwood the circulation of bones included the rearranging of previously disarticulated skeletons, on occasion bringing together pieces from the wrong individual.[84] The same has been recorded at Lanhill, where three skulls lay against the eastern side of the chamber with two in the southwest corner. Of the first three it was noted that 'each skull was furnished with a lower jaw placed in approximately the correct position, but it was subsequently proved that one of the jaws could not have originally belonged to the skull in association with which it was found'.[85]

Understanding the arrangement of burials within the timber chambers of long barrows in the Cotswold-Severn region is difficult because none has been excavated to modern standards. At Oldbury Hill (WIL 17), William Cunnington's excavation in about 1864 cut into what seems to be part of the chamber to reveal three skeletons, a male and two females, with abundant 'rude pottery and flint flakes' together with dark soil mainly on the north side of the 'grave'.[86] At Shepherd's Shore (WIL 18), excavations in 1914 by Maud Cunnington revealed what seems to be an oolitic limestone platform forming the floor of a timber chamber in which were the remains of three adults, a child and the cremated remains of another adult.[87] The Kings Play Down long barrow (WIL 31) appears to have had the contracted burial of a single adult male within its timber chamber.[88] From these snippets, however, it is clear that activities within and around these timber chambers broadly parallel what can be seen more clearly at other long barrows in the Cotswold-Severn region.

Further evidence for concerns about the deposition and movement of corpses and skeletonized material within long barrows comes from the temporary blocking slabs and removable sections of walling that seem to have been used to prevent or limit movement between the three main zones within chamber areas. These may also have controlled access and/or egress by forces of the supernatural world. Most commonly these barriers were stone slabs placed across the projecting jambs of key junctions between the entrance and passage or between the passage and chamber. The outer edge of the entrance may also be covered or concealed in similar fashion. At Parc le Breos Cwm careful examination of the human remains from the chambers revealed that about 50 per cent of fragments showed evidence of damage in the form of gnawing marks left by large mammals, both carnivores and omnivores. Upper and lower limb bones were the most frequently damaged, the evidence of teeth-marks being consistent with flesh-covered corpses being scavenged by carnivores. Whether this took place in the chambers or while corpses were temporarily stored or exposed elsewhere cannot easily be determined, although the latter seems more likely.[89] At Hazleton North, by contrast, less than one per cent of bone fragments showed evidence of animal gnawing, the majority of these being from the north chamber area.

On balance, no single model accounts for the rich variety of evidence visible in the mortuary assemblages at long barrows, although in general it seems the human remains accumulated as a result of the periodic deposition of corpses and the sorting and selective removal of bones or body-parts for use or deposition elsewhere. What was brought to the barrow – fresh corpses, partly decomposed corpses kept elsewhere for a period, or cremated remains – probably varied from site to site and from time to time. Indeed, if the timing of ceremonies at long barrows was significant, as we should expect it to be, it is possible that human remains were brought to the site only at particular days in the year, or to coincide with recurrent solar or lunar events. As such, the state of the remains would be heavily dependent on how long the individual had been dead and how the corpse had been treated in the meantime.

Whatever their state, manoeuvring human remains into position within a barrow can hardly have been a comfortable activity. In most barrows the entrances were low, the passages narrow and the chambers small. In a few cases, the constricting slabs separating out the different spaces within the chamber area may have created such narrow openings that whole corpses could not be taken into the deepest parts; only defleshed bones or body-parts could have been taken through some of the porthole entrances for example. It is hardly surprising therefore that bones were sometimes broken and trodden into the floor. Fires may well have been needed to provide light and perhaps mask the stench of rotting flesh. In 1938 Alexander Keiller and Stuart Piggott made a full-sized reconstruction of the south chamber at Lanhill in order to experiment with the way that corpses could have been placed in the chamber. Using as a guide the remains of the last individual to be added to the chamber, they showed that:

> an individual of the same height as that estimated from the skeleton could be inserted through the aperture by tightly flexing his legs against his body, which accounts for the contracted position of the burial. On insertion into the tomb the corpse would still be lying upon its back, while the legs, if they did not naturally

fall into the position in which they were found, would take this up as a result of a slight push from without. Finally, the right arm of the corpse, bent at the elbow, was forced into the chamber and the upper arm pressed almost at right-angles to the body against the eastern wall.[90]

Gender, age and place

Widespread evidence for the circulation and movement of skeletal elements within the chamber areas and beyond makes it difficult to identify meaningful patterns in the way space may have been used in terms of the final resting place for different categories of people. Both sexes are represented at long barrows, generally in about equal number. At Ascott-under-Wychwood, for example, Chesterman reports the presence of 13 males and 15 females,[91] while Wells's analysis of the human remains from the 1955–6 excavations at West Kennet documented the presence of about 12 males and 13 females.[92] Females were mainly represented in the northwest and southwest chambers, while John Thurnam's analysis of the six burials he recovered from the western chamber excavated in the summer of 1859 suggests that all the adults present were male *(60A)*.[93] At Parc le Breos Cwm males tend to dominate the assemblages from deeper inside the tomb *(60B)*, while at Hazleton North there seems to have been a fairly balanced gender distribution with two males and two females represented in the north chamber and perhaps three males and one female in the southern chamber *(60C)*. In the north chambers at Giant's Caves, Luckington, males dominate the assemblages from the chamber zones, but this is not repeated in the southern chamber areas *(60D)*. A similar pattern has been suggested for Notgrove,[94] and at Lanhill there was a slight preference for females in the south chamber and males in the north chamber. Overall, there is thus only slight evidence for the preferential placement of males and females in particular cells within the chamber area. Although perhaps overstating the case slightly, Ian Hodder has tentatively proposed that male-centred rituals were associated with the use of the chambers in many long barrows.[95]

Separation by age within the chambers of a single barrow seems to be more marked than gender distinctions *(61)*. Children are well represented at excavated sites, also infants, neonatals and foetuses at Notgrove and West Kennet amongst others. A cache of bones between the uprights in the east wall of the northeast chamber at West Kennet contained parts of the skull of a newborn or stillborn child.[96] At Hazleton North there were estimated to be 22 adults and 19 children. Of the adults at least two were probably over 45 years of age and another five between about 35 and 45. The children showed a complete range from six months to 16 years. There were at least two foetuses of less than five months. At Ascott-under-Wychwood, the proportion of sub-adults represented was lower than elsewhere according to Chesterman (8 out of 49 individuals).[97] West Kennet shows some evidence for clustering, with the majority (55 per cent) of all children and infants found in the southeast chamber while the mature adults were fairly evenly spread between the two northern chambers; adult males alone were found in the western chamber.

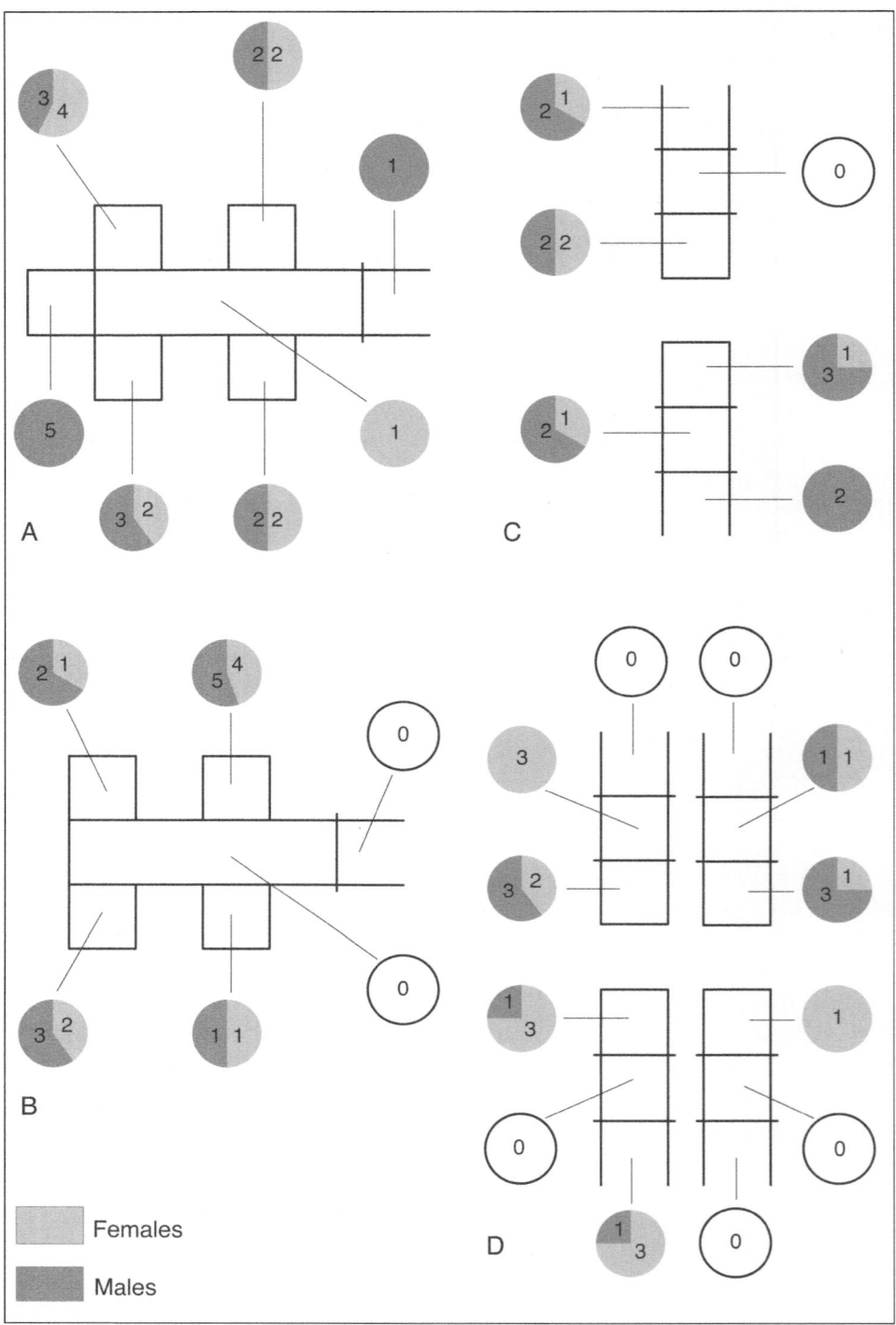

60 Male-female distributions in the chamber areas at a selection of long barrows in the Cotswold-Severn region. *A:* West Kennet (WIL 4); *B:* Parc le Breos Cwm (GLA 4); *C:* Hazleton North (GLO 54); *D:* Giant's Caves, Luckington (WIL 2)

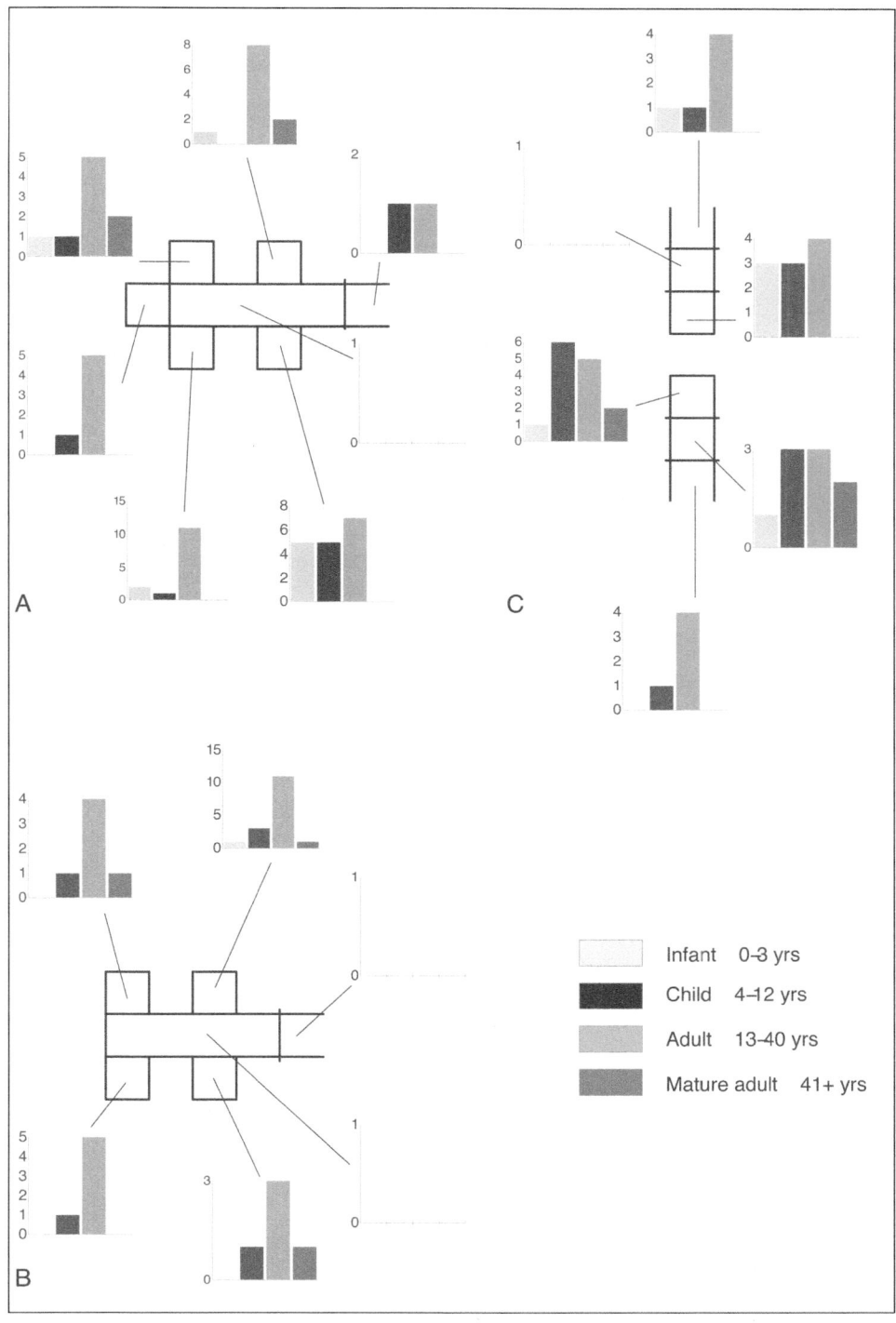

61 Age distributions in the chamber areas at a selection of long barrows in the Cotswold-Severn region. *A:* West Kennet (WIL 4); *B:* Parc le Breos Cwm (GLA 4); *C:* Hazleton North (GLO 54)

Taking the predominant character of the human remains found within the chambers in terms of the gender of the adults and distinguishing children as a separate group, Julian Thomas has proposed a fairly regular distribution pattern amongst four- and five-cell terminal-chambered long barrows.[98] In this, adults tend to concentrate in the innermost, mainly western, cells, with old people and young people predominating in the outermost cells. It is a pattern that seems to hold fairly well amongst lateral-chambered long barrows with dispersed chambers too *(62)*. It must always be remembered, however, that the pattern found through excavation is actually a process frozen in time. We cannot be sure that the circulation of bones had reached a conclusion, or that the full consequences of whatever logic underlay the movement of remains had played itself out. It is tempting to invoke Hodder's idea of parallel systems connecting the use of space inside long barrows with the arrangements used in houses occupied by the living,[99] but insufficient detail is known about either to progress the comparisons very far. What is clear is that, within long barrows, the movement and circulation of human remains were important elements of the scheme, and that sometimes particular bones, mainly skulls and long bones, left the closed environment of the long barrow altogether. Exactly what was done with the bones once out of the chamber is not known, but despite occasional claims to the contrary there is no evidence for cannibalism.

Rates of accumulation

One of the critical questions surrounding the use of long barrows, and the accumulation and circulation of the human remains within them, is how long they were open for. This can really only be judged by dating the remains within the chambers, always bearing in mind the caveats expressed at the head of this chapter about periodic clearing out of the chambers. At Hazleton North, 14 carefully selected samples of human bone from both the chamber areas were dated using the AMS system at Oxford University. All the dates fell within a narrow band representing, at most, about 300 years; statistically all the burials could have been made over a period of about a century.[100] What the dates confirm is that, within the limitations of the dating technique, both chambers were in use at broadly the same time, that the use of the chambers was not significantly later than the construction of the mound, and that the period represented by the accumulation of corpses buried in the chambers was short. A very similar picture emerges from the equally comprehensive dating programme applied to remains from the Parc le Breos Cwm long barrow. These were also determined at Oxford University using high-precision AMS measurements, and with the exception of two burials from the passage, all the sampled skeletons appear to be of broadly the same date and could have accumulated within one or two centuries.[101] No other long barrows have anything like the number of relevant radiocarbon determinations to assess the duration of use, although the four on human skeletal remains from West Kennet are well bunched and wholly in keeping with the short chronology suggested by Hazleton North and Parc le Breos Cwm. Taking all available dates together (see *32* in Chapter 4), the overall duration of long barrow use represented by the

People, Ceremonies and Objects

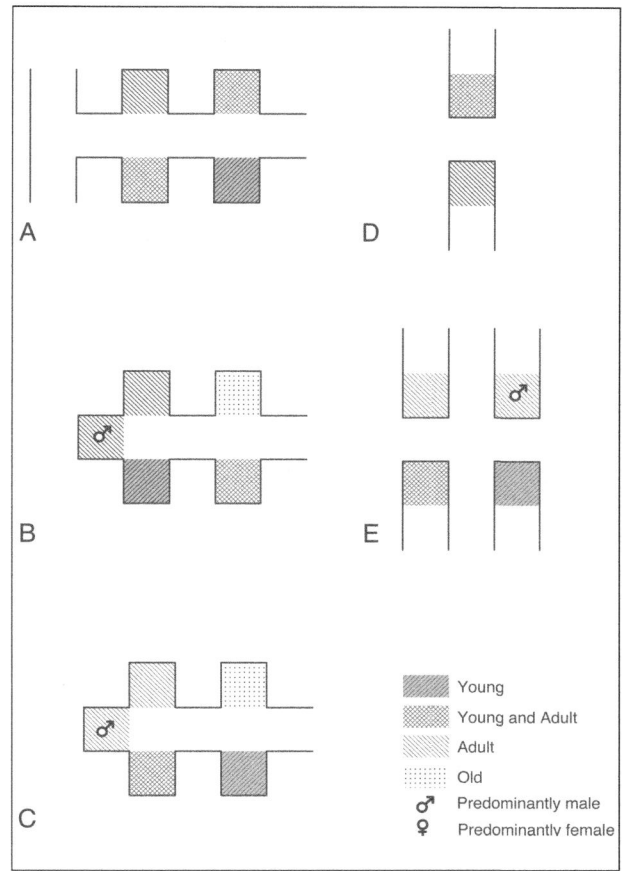

62 Age-gender patterns within the cells of the chamber zones at a selection of long barrows in the Cotswold-Severn region. *A:* Burn Ground (GLO 60); *B:* Notgrove (GLO 4); *C:* West Kennet (WIL 4); *D:* Hazleton North (GLO 54); *E:* Giant's Caves, Luckington (WIL 2). *After Thomas 1998, fig. 6, with additions and amendments*

human remains from the chambers is no more than a few centuries. Alasdair Whittle has expressed concerns over the idea of a relatively short period of use for long barrows in the Cotswold-Severn region, hinting that what we see may be the product of the dating method as much as a real pattern.[102] The weight of evidence for short-duration usage is, however, now very strong and needs to be tempered only with the widely supported view that far more carefully selected samples need to be properly dated before the picture can be better focused.

THE LONG BARROW PEOPLE

Accepting that the deposits of human remains in the chamber areas of long barrows represent snapshots of human populations, it is instructive to consider what they tell us about the nature and character of the small-scale communities from which they derive. Naturally, there are issues of interpretation that affect how the sample of remains may be seen. For example, was everyone ultimately buried in a long barrow? These and related questions are considered below.

157

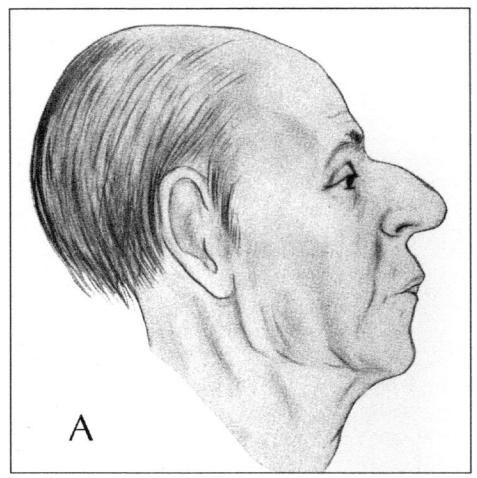
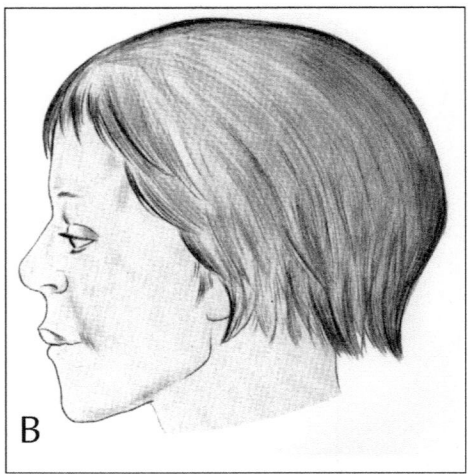
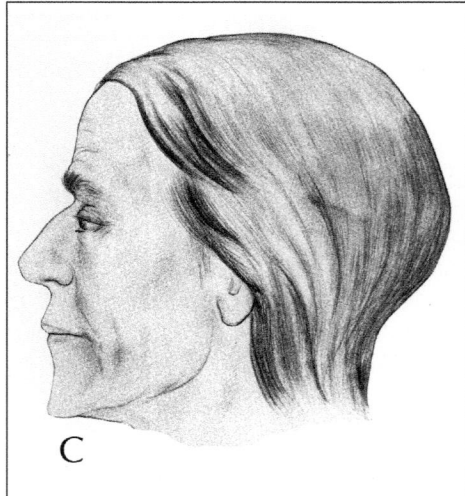
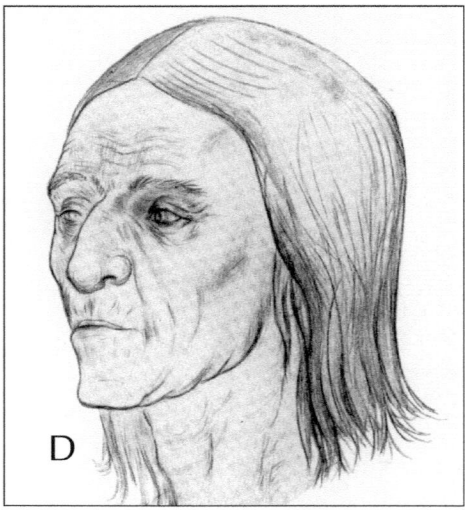

63 Lanhill (WIL 3). Facial reconstructions of the Lanhill people based on skulls recovered from the northeast chamber. A: Elderly male (skeleton 1); B: Child aged 12-13 years (skeleton 4); C: Elderly female (skeleton 2); D: Adult male of about 50 years (skeleton 7). Drawings by Miss D.E. Chapman, reproduced courtesy of the Prehistoric Society

In his report on the burials from the south chamber at Lanhill (WIL 3), Dr A.J.E. Cave pronounced that in their physical form this small population represented examples of the Mediterranean frame, with smallish bones and a gracile architecture to the skeleton. Using information gained from the careful analysis of the crania of four of these people, facial reconstructions were attempted *(63)*. These are amongst the earliest examples of a tradition of forensic science that remains familiar today, albeit in a more developed form using computer imaging as well as physical reconstruction.[103] While the drawings made by Miss Chapman for Dr Cave in one sense reflect 1930s images of people imbued with a sense of modernity, they also betray at least a shadow of the ancient past. Long before Cave's work on the Lanhill population, it was recognized that the skulls from long barrows were long in proportion to their width – so-called dolichocephalic – suggesting a distinct and fairly unified population group. Davies and Thurnam provide abundant data on such matters in their *Crania Britannica* with studies on remains from West Kennet (WIL 4), Hetty Pegler's Tump (GLO 14), Stoney Littleton (SOM 1) and Rodmarton (GLO 16), amongst others. Human remains from recent excavations have confirmed the general pattern, the three measurable skulls from Hazleton North (GLO 54), for example, all being dolichocephalic, with cranial indices of less than 75.00. The implication of these statistics is that, as in Chapman's pictures, these people would have had slightly elongated heads and rather oval faces.[104]

It is often supposed that the builders of long barrows were short, but this was not really the case. Analysis of the Parc le Breos Cwm (GLA 4) assemblage and comparisons with other material of comparable age and origin suggest, albeit subjectively, that the population comprised short rather gracile females and considerably more robust males. Three females from the site had estimated heights of 143–152cm, 155–163cm and 154–162cm.[105] At Hazleton North a selection of five adults ranged in height from 159cm through to 177cm.[106] A large sample of 19 adults at West Kennet showed that males included tall and well-built individuals as well as individuals of more slender build in the overall height range 164–179cm; females, accordingly to Wells, were generally shorter (average 148cm) than the males (average 164cm) and in general rather slenderly built.[107] Taking all available estimates for adults in long barrows within the Cotswold-Severn region together, the mean height of the population is about 161cm *(64)*, with a distribution that is well within the expected range of pre-industrial north European populations of almost any period.

The mortuary evidence of the long barrow burials provides useful information on the age at death, although there are considerable technical difficulties in determining the lifespan of longer-lived individuals. Using bone development, tooth eruption and tooth attrition as broad indicators of age, it appears that 43 per cent of those interred in Hazleton North died below the age of five. At West Kennet some 25 per cent of those interred were below the age of ten and, similarly, at Parc le Breos Cwm about 22 per cent of the reported burials had not yet reached their tenth birthday.[108] Compared to many simple agricultural societies, even these superficially horrific figures seem low; infant mortality rates in which upward of 50 per cent of live births were lost within the first year would be more typical.[109] Taking all the burials from long barrows in the Cotswold-Severn region for which appropriate data exist, a rough age at death profile can be developed (65). This cumulative frequency chart effectively shows the percentage of the total born population that is dead after set intervals (in years), based on the assumption that all are dead after 70 years. As expected, there is a heavy death toll in the early stages, with a more regular and rather lower rate of loss later on.

Translating age at death data back to the structure of the living population is far more complicated than might at first appear, not least because all sorts of

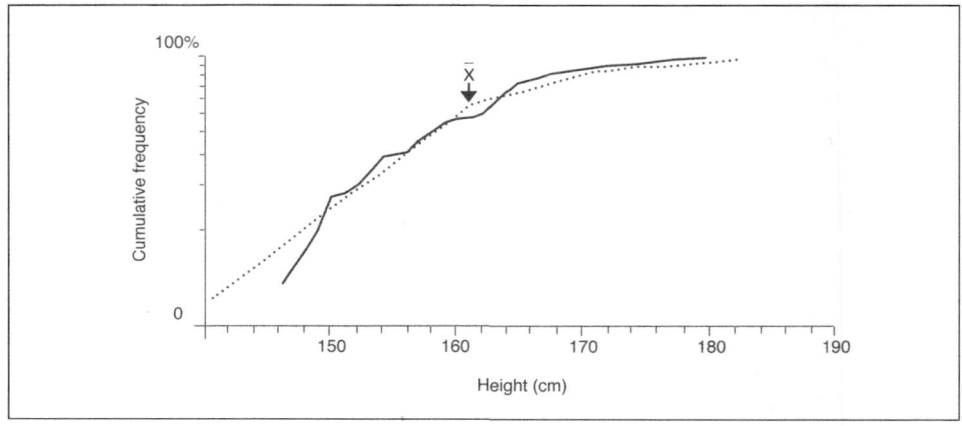

64 Cumulative frequency chart showing the stature of the human population buried in long barrows within the Cotswold-Severn region (solid line) compared with a normal distribution (dotted line) calculated at two standard deviations around the mean (mean = 161cm)

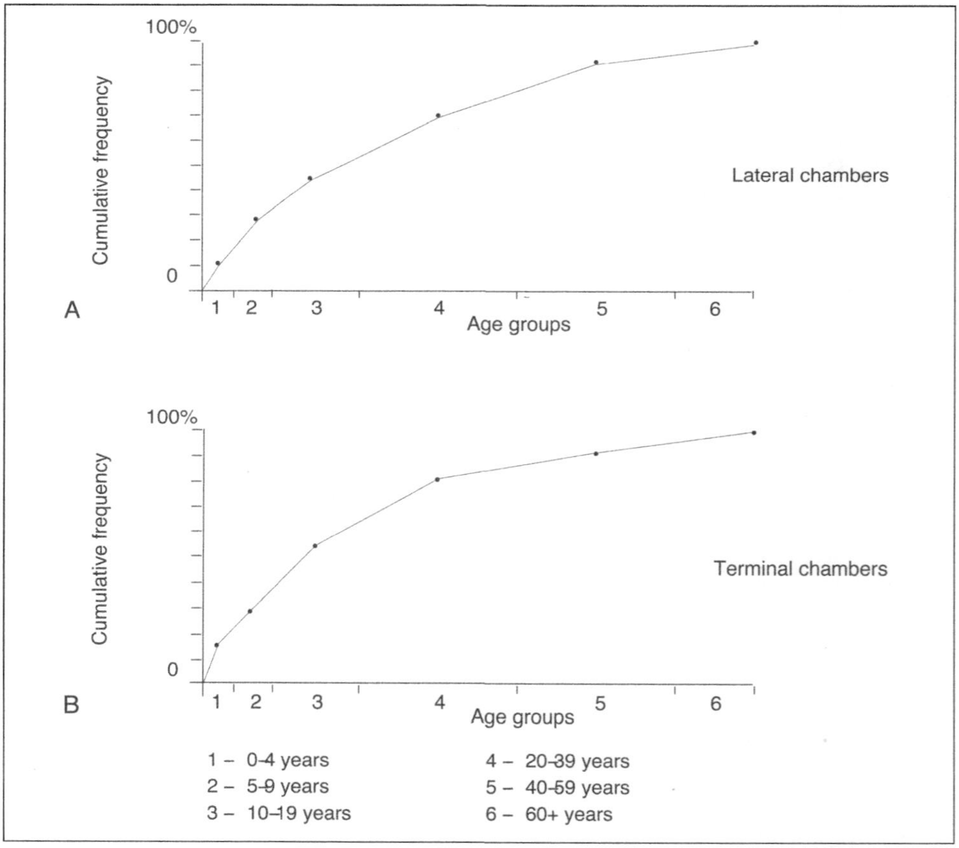

65 Cumulative frequency chart showing the age at death of the population buried in long barrows within the Cotswold-Severn region. *A:* Barrows with lateral chambers; *B:* Barrows with terminal chambers

assumptions have to be made about rates of death within different sectors of the population. What we can say with some certainty about the communities who built and used long barrows is that there are certainly individuals whose life spanned more than 45 years in many barrows, and some of these could easily have been 60 or over when they died. Life may have been short and brutish for many, but some survived into old age and must have seen their long barrow gradually change as it gradually filled up with the remains of their peer group.

Skeletal remains preserve a great deal of information about the health of the population. Evidence of various ruptures, bumps, falls and misadventures can be seen as healed fractures, ossification exostosis and osteophytic growths on skeletal components. At Parc le Breos Cwm about 10 per cent of the interred population displayed such evidence.[110] At Hazleton North, broken ribs were the most common evidence of injury amongst the 14 bones with evidence of healed fractures. The near-complete skeleton in the north entrance showed evidence of fractures on two bones: the distal part of the left fibula and the second left metatarsal.[111] At Parc le Breos Cwm, Hazleton North and West Kennet, dentition was in a generally good although worn state, with relatively little evidence of caries. Two toothless jaws were recorded at West Kennet.

Wells's analysis of the West Kennet remains suggests that osteoarthritis was the plague of the community, with hardly a single individual over 30 years of age failing to display at least some signs of vertebral arthritis.[112] Three of the eight members of the Lanhill population studied by Cave suffered from osteoarthritis.[113] By contrast, Juliet Rogers reported that at Hazleton North there was evidence of various joint diseases on 14 separate bones but that the incidence of osteoarthritis seemed to be less than might be expected.[114]

Various deformities have been recorded. The skull of a young woman in the southwest chamber at West Kennet showed excessive elongation and narrowing of the skull owing to the obliteration of the sagittal suture in early childhood. Two cases of spina bifida were also reported at West Kennet, both on female skeletons from the southeast chamber.[115]

A skull that was probably found in the Bisley Barrow (GLO 74) has an uncompleted trephination *(66)*. The removal of a disk of bone from the cranium in order to relieve severe headaches, to reduce pressure on the brain and perhaps as a treatment for fits and seizures is a relatively common practice and well represented in the archaeological evidence; in 1940 Stuart Piggott listed nearly a hundred examples from prehistoric Europe.[116] Exactly what the person from Bisley was suffering from is not known, but to judge from the evidence before us he or she either died before the operation was completed or the pain of having a hole cut into the skull overwhelmed whatever else was wrong to the extent that further work was unnecessary.

Injuries likely to have been the cause of death and which leave traces on the skeleton have been recorded at several barrows. John Thurnam reported that two of the six skulls he recovered from West Kennet in 1859 showed distinct traces of fractures unequivocally inflicted before death, although he does not speculate further on whether they might have been the direct cause of death.[117] He notes

66 Bisley Barrow (GLO 74). Trephined skull probably from the excavations at this long barrow in 1863. *From Crawford 1925, plate opposite p.80. Copyright reserved*

other cleft skulls amongst remains from Lugbury (WIL 1), Hetty Pegler's Tump (GLO 14) and Rodmarton.[118] More recent investigations by Rick Schulting and Michael Wysocki suggest that what Thurnam saw is more widespread than previously thought, and that as many as 7.5 per cent of the skulls they examined show evidence for significant trauma, about 2.6 per cent of skulls having evidence of mortality through cranial injury. In one case, a child from Belas Knap (GLO 1), the cranial injuries are massive and would have resulted in instant death.[119] Far more common, however, would have been soft-tissue injuries and damage to critical organs which leave no direct evidence on the skeletal frame. The presence of projectile points within body cavities provides a useful line of evidence for this, and a number of cases are considered in detail below.

Diet and nutrition

Something of the diet and the main sources of nutrition used by the populations in long barrows can be reconstructed by examining the ratios of various stable isotopes in the collagen found within human bones. This well-established technique has been widely applied to archaeological populations, especially using two stable isotopes of carbon, namely ^{12}C and ^{13}C, the ratio of the two being denoted by the symbol $\delta^{13}C$. Mike Richards has examined a sample of individuals buried in long barrows within the Cotswold-Severn region in order to assess the relative contributions of marine as against terrestrial sources of foodstuffs, and whether their protein intake derived from plants, animals or a combination of the two. Ten samples from the Parc le Breos Cwm population showed that although the site is near the coast, marine resources did not figure significantly in their diet. The average $\delta^{13}C$ value was −20.5±1.0‰ showing that the dietary protein came mainly from animal sources (flesh, milk and perhaps blood), with rather little input from either gathered wild plants or cultivated grain.[120] Similar values have been obtained from samples taken from Hazleton North, Ascott-under-Wychwood

(OXF 6), Millbarrow (WIL 11), West Kennet and Lambourn (BRK 2).[121] These contrast sharply with values of around $-14\pm1.0\permil$ obtained from bone taken from fifth- and sixth-millennia BC coastal sites in the same area which suggest the heavy use of marine resources.[122]

Relationships, family ties and status

General similarities between the populations interred in long barrows revealed by biometric statistics such as skull shape have already been noted and have long been cited as evidence for the genetic unity of the population at the time.[123] Many incredibly detailed data relating to skeletal remains from long barrows were gathered in the nineteenth century by Joseph Davies, John Thurnam and others. Although their aim was often to try to use it in order to establish racial affinities as part of a search for the aboriginal populations of the British Isles in a way that might today seem almost nationalistic, the data themselves are useful and of more general interest. Accepting a general link between genetics and skeletal characteristics, powerful modern multivariate statistics provide a way of reanalysing existing datasets.[124] Illustration 67 shows a principal components analysis of biometrical data collected by Davies and Thurnam for five long barrows of fourth-millennium BC date in Wiltshire and south Gloucestershire as well as six burials variously from round barrows and cist graves of third-millennium BC date. All of the examples from long barrows lie close together within the x = negative quadrants, suggesting a closely related and fairly uniform population. The later specimens are more scattered and suggestive of greater genetic diversity. The most separated cases (3 and 4) both come from Roundway Down in north Wiltshire and may be people who have moved into the area from some distance away.[125]

At a more detailed level, various anatomical characteristics have been proposed as evidence for family relationships within studied assemblages. At West Kennet, Wells suggests that five skeletons, two female, two male and one of uncertain sex, scattered through three separate chambers, may be from the same family line because of defects in the sacral vertebrae, in two cases manifesting themselves as the cases of spina bifida noted above.[126] At Lanhill, the frequency of wormian ossicles at the lambdoid on the crania of all but two of the skulls was taken by Cave to indicate familial relationships between the members of this population.[127]

Recognizing the presence of family groups in long barrows naturally raises the question of whether or not everyone in the community was eventually buried in a long barrow. Since the days of John Aubrey, scholars have pursued the line that long barrows 'were the mausolea or burying places for the great persons and rulers of their times'.[128] It is a view that became deeply entrenched, so that in the 1940s Gordon Childe proposed that amongst early farming communities in central southern England 'their chiefs at least were sometimes buried in communal ossuaries – long barrows'.[129] In the late 1960s, Richard Atkinson calculated that the number of people represented in long barrows within the Cotswold-Severn region fell well short of the number of people needed to build them, reinforcing the view that long barrows 'were used for the burial of selected members of the population only, and not for the population at large'.[130]

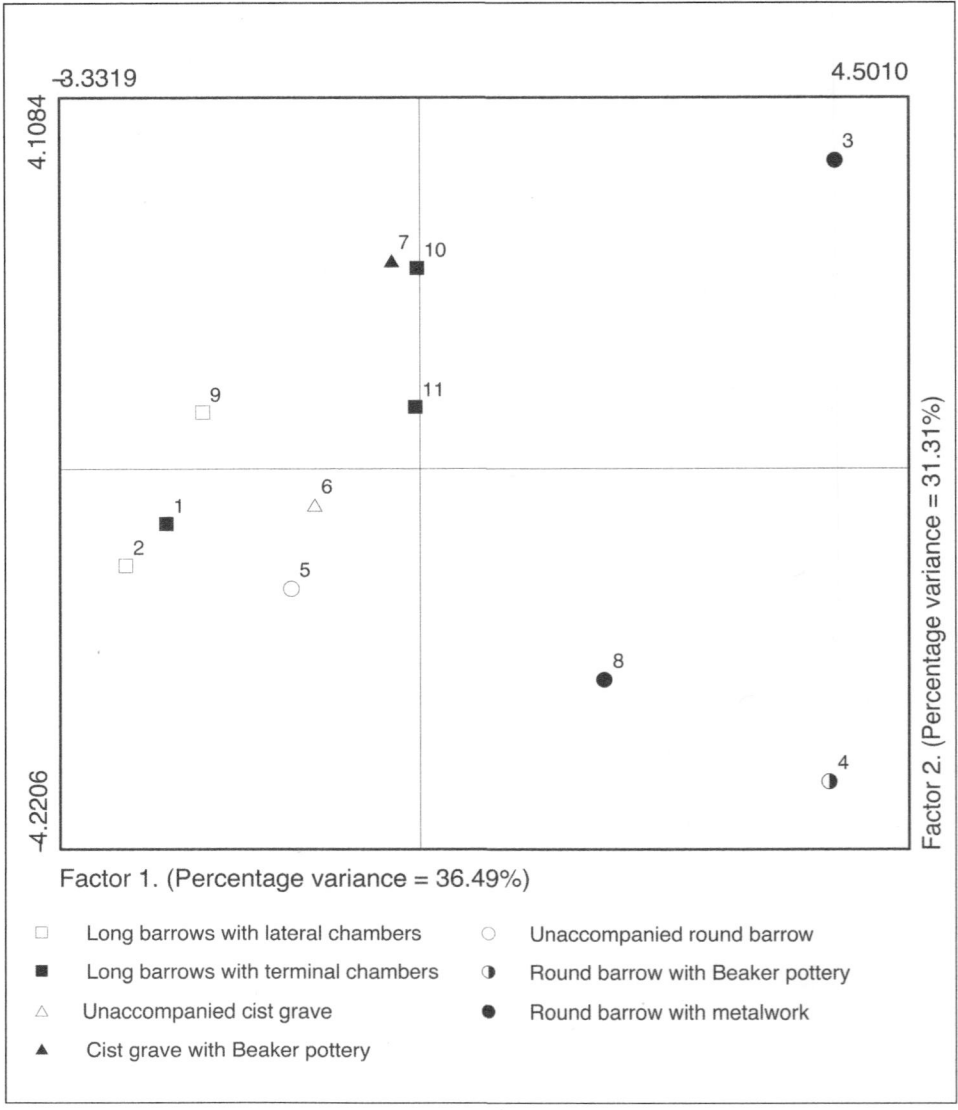

67 Principal components analysis of variations in craniometric characteristics represented in a selection of human skulls from long barrows and other monuments in the Cotswold-Severn region. *1:* West Kennet (WIL 4); *2:* Lugbury (WIL 1); *3:* Roundway Down round barrow, Wiltshire; *4:* Roundway Down round barrow, Wiltshire; *5:* Morgan's Hill round barrow, Wiltshire; *6:* Winterbourne Monkton cist grave, Wiltshire; *7:* Winterbourne Monkton cist grave, Wiltshire; *8:* Kennet Hill round barrow, Wiltshire; *9:* Rodmarton (GLO 16); *10:* Hetty Pegler's Tump (GLO 14); *11:* Nympsfield (GLO 13). *Source data from Davies and Thurnam 1865*

Set against this is the wide age range and gender structure of the deceased population which strongly suggests the remains of a fairly normal human community. Assuming a typical dead population of about 40–50 in each barrow, and allowing these to accumulate over a period of perhaps 150 years, the average rate of death would be one person every two to three years. Bearing in mind the high level of infants represented in the dead population, a living community of perhaps 10–15 people could be expected to yield this number of deaths.[131] As we have seen (Chapter 5), such a community represents just about enough people to build a long barrow in the first place, especially if helped in their efforts by neighbouring groups from time to time. Moreover, as will be discussed in Chapter 8, long barrows were not the only places where human remains were deposited during the fourth millennium BC, and when these are taken into account it is easy to see a pattern of numerous widely distributed, small-scale, biologically viable communities, each with their own long barrow serving in part at least as a family vault.

GRAVE GOODS AND PLACED DEPOSITS

In general, finds other than human bones are rather rare in the chambers of long barrows in the Cotswold-Severn region, as indeed in long barrows generally. It is possible that objects in organic materials such as wood, leather, cloth, or feathers in the form of clothes, containers, or decorative items were originally present, but all have long since disappeared. All that is usually left is things made from inorganic materials, bone or shell. Elsie Clifford published an extensive review of recorded artefacts from long barrows in the Cotswolds in 1950, since when there have been further finds. In the main, however, these have increased the number of recorded examples rather than widened the range of material represented. As will be shown in Chapter 7, the blocking deposits within the chamber areas and in the forecourts are often far richer in artefacts than the deposits within the chambers. Here attention is focused on what has been found in the primary deposits within chambers, passages and entrance zones from the period when the barrows were in use *(68* and *69)*.

Pottery
Pottery from primary deposits almost always comprises small plain bowls and cups, often with thickened or rolled rims. At Parc le Breos Cwm (GLA 4) about 100 small sherds from a single vessel were found widely scattered through the chambers, the passage and the floor of the forecourt. Sherds representing a single, more or less complete, undecorated cup were found scattered through the south chamber area at Hazleton North (GLO 54; *68Q*). Cups of very similar form have been found at Pole's Wood East (GLO 24; *68P*) and Pole's Wood South (GLO 2). Single bowls, whole or fragmentary, were represented in the west chamber at Ty Isaf (BRE 5; *68B*), the main chamber at Eyford Hill (GLO 3; *68A*), chamber B at the Giant's Caves (WIL 2), the chamber and forecourt area at Parc le Breos Cwm and the southernmost part of the chamber area at Ascott-under-Wychwood (OXF 6).

Larger collections of pottery have occasionally been recorded. Chamber 2 at Gwernvale (BRE 7) contained fragments of six separate pots, all round-bottomed

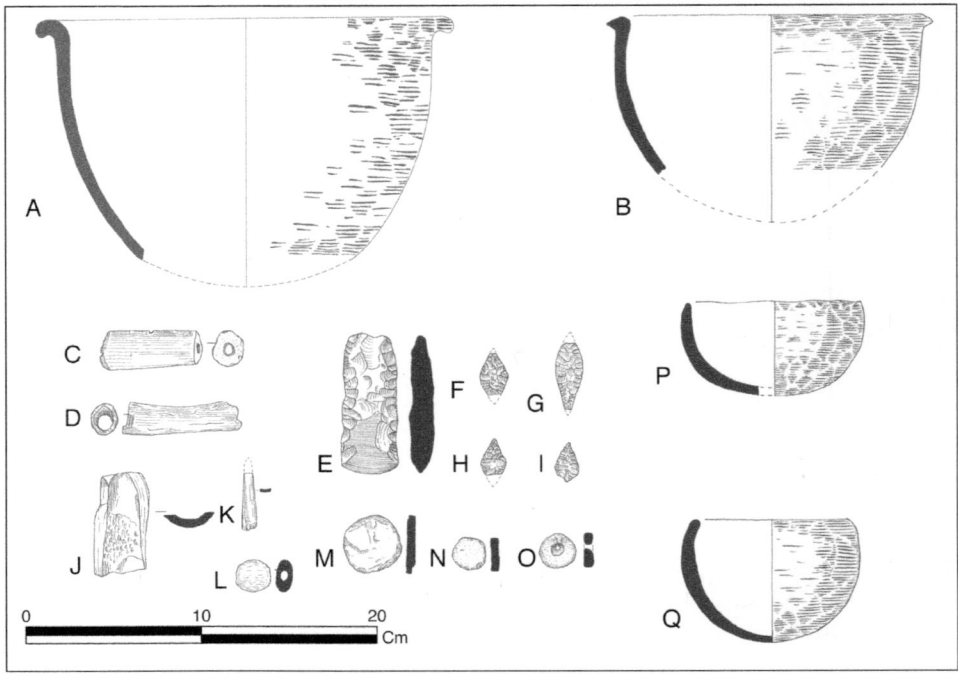

68 Objects from the chamber area within long barrows with lateral chambers. A and L: Eyford Hill (GLO 3); *B, E, H, I, M, N* and *O:* Ty Isaf (BRE 5); *C, D* and *G:* Rodmarton (GLO 16); *F:* West Tump (GLO 8); *J* and *P:* Pole's Wood East (GLO 24); *K:* Pole's Wood South (GLO 2); and *Q:* Hazleton North (GLO 54)

simple vessels, probably two bowls and four small cups. A collection of similar size was found amongst the burials at West Kennet (WIL 4), mainly in the southeast chamber although with some in the northeast chamber (e.g. *69A* and *B*). These sherds represent classic Windmill Hill style bowls and cups. The east chamber at Ty Isaf contained little by way of human remains but parts from at least six pottery vessels, many of the sherds being associated with black material rich in finely comminuted charcoal. This suggests that the pots had served as cooking vessels or fallen into a fire before being deposited in the barrow. Part of a seventh vessel was found in the entrance zone to the same chamber. At Tinkinswood (GLA 9) sherds representing at least four vessels were found scattered through the single terminal chamber. Similarly, at Belas Knap (GLO 1), Bown Hill (GLO 20), Gatcombe Lodge (GLO 15), Hetty Pegler's Tump (GLO 14), Randwick (GLO 10), West Barrow (GLO 18), West Tump (GLO 8), Notgrove (GLO 4) and Rodmarton (GLO 16) sherds representing the broken remains of several vessels were found scattered through the chamber fills in each case. At Nympsfield (GLO 13) several parts of a rather unusual necked jar were found in the entrance zone during the 1937 excavation *(69C)*. Although locally made, the shape of this vessel has analogies with pots found in the Loire-Inférieure of northern France where they are associated with monuments of very similar design.[132]

People, Ceremonies and Objects

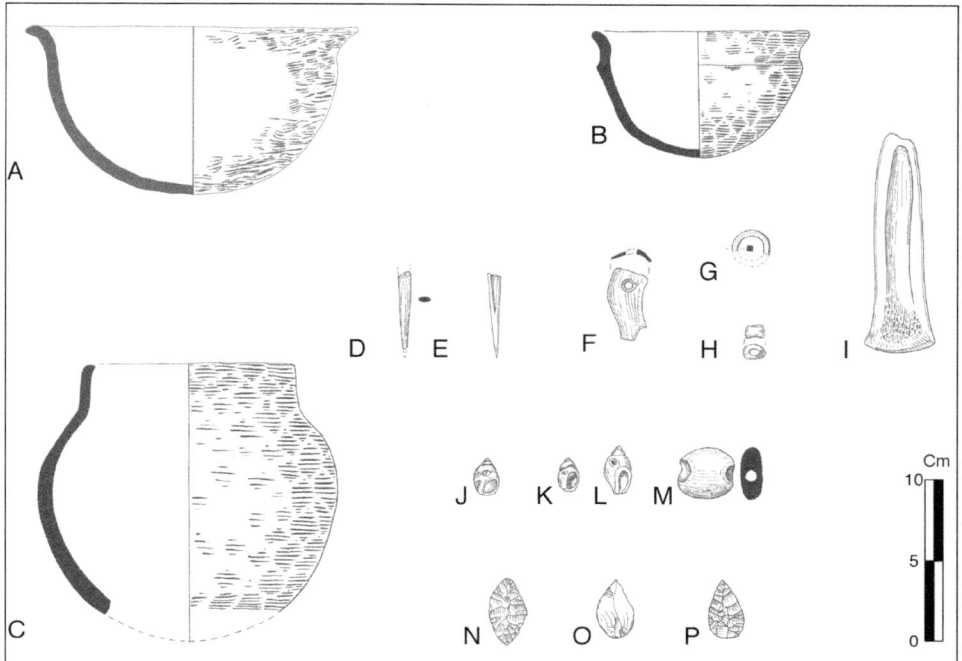

69 Objects from the chamber areas within long barrows with terminal chambers. A, B, E, K, L and O: West Kennet (WIL 4); *C, J and P:* Nympsfield (GLO 13); *D, G, H, M and N:* Notgrove (GLO 4); *F:* Hetty Pegler's Tump (GLO 14); *and I:* Bown Hill (GLO 20)

Stylistically, all of these pots from chamber deposits and also those from other contexts associated with the use of long barrows (see above), fall within the general family of Southern Decorated Wares,[133] although few are in fact decorated and most belong to forms that can easily be matched amongst the assemblages from Windmill Hill, Wiltshire, or Abingdon, Oxfordshire. Functionally, all these vessels are probably best seen as small cooking pots and personal eating and/or drinking cups. Most were probably introduced into the chamber with particular individuals, subsequent activity within the chambers and the movement and reorganization of body-parts accounting for the breaking and scattering of the pots, which gradually became dissociated from specific individuals and the rituals associated with them. One has the general feeling that pottery and indeed other artefacts yet to be discussed were treated with less ceremony and respect than the human remains.

Spoons
The fragmentary remains of a pair of ceramic 'spoons' were found at Cow Common Long (GLO 22) in 1874, 'towards the west end of the mound and not much below the surface'.[134] Although the context is unclear, the fragments are typical of other such objects from southern England that can be dated to the fourth millennium BC.[135] The pair comprises one implement with the bowl in line with

the handle like a modern spoon and the other with a very slight bowl turned at right angles to the handle. At less than 12cm long, these items may well have been used in association with the small ceramic cups. To judge from their general scarcity amongst contemporary assemblages, they were perhaps used during particular ceremonies to dispense special food or drink to the celebrants.

Flint and stone tools and weapons

Worked flint is well represented amongst the finds from within chamber areas, perhaps a reflection of the importance of this activity for the production of edged tools and weapons during the fourth millennium BC. At Hazleton North the near-complete skeleton deposited in the entrance zone to the north chamber area was equipped with a quartz hammerstone that had probably been held in the left hand when the corpse was deposited in the barrow. In the right hand was a large flint core *(59)*. Taken together, these finds suggest that this adult male was a left-handed flint-knapper. A second quartz hammerstone was found outside the edge of the mound on the north side and a third came to light in the entrance to the south chamber area, suggesting that perhaps one of the persons buried here was also a flint-knapper. Twenty other pieces of struck flint were found within the two chamber areas, of which nearly half were unretouched flakes. A second core, a serrated flake, two edge-trimmed flakes and two flakes with edge-gloss could have been intentionally included with burials.[136] A flint-worker may also be represented at Lyneham (OXF 8), where excavations in the later nineteenth century brought to light two large multi-platform flint cores associated with burials.[137] A flint core and three flakes were also found at Rodmarton,[138] while Elsie Clifford records the discovery of sandstone hammers and pounders at Bown Hill and Rodmarton.[139] A very neat sandstone hammerstone was found near the northeast corner of the mound at Penywyrlod (BRE 14).[140]

Finished products are less well represented in chamber areas than the raw material and flint-working equipment for their manufacture. In addition to the items already noted, a complete flaked and polished flint axe was found in the west chamber at Ty Isaf *(68E)*, one of very few such implements associated with long barrows in Britain. Belas Knap yielded a serrated flint blade; Tinkinswood a broken scraper. A broken awl came from chamber D at the Giant's Caves; a broken knife from the northeast III chamber at Penywyrlod; a knife and a rather poor serrated blade from the southeast transept and passage at Burn Ground (GLO 60); a scraper and three broken knives from Lanhill (WIL 3); and four edge-trimmed flakes from Hazleton North.

The most numerous class of finished artefacts is leaf-shaped arrowheads, more than a dozen of which have been recovered from primary deposits within chamber areas *(68F–I* and *69N–P)*. The tip of a bifacially worked leaf-shaped arrowhead from the entrance zone in the north chamber at Hazleton North is exactly the kind of fragment that would remain in the body of a victim of an arrow-wound and quite possibly arrived in the barrow within one of the corpses placed therein.[141] A similar interpretation probably applies to arrowheads found in the northeast II chamber at Penywyrlod, the west chamber at Ty Isaf, Adam's Grave

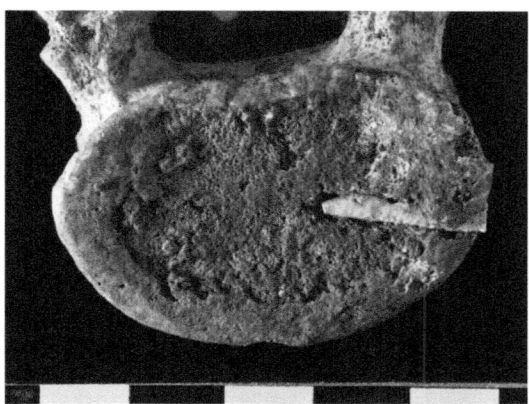

70 Ascott-under-Wychwood (OXF 6). End-on view of the third lumbar vertebra of a robust adult male with a leaf-shaped flint arrowhead embedded in the bone. *Reproduced courtesy of Don Benson, Alasdair Whittle and the Oxfordshire County Museum Service*

(WIL 6), Notgrove, West Tump, Rodmarton and Nympsfield. At West Kennet the evidence is perhaps more clear still. Two leaf-shaped arrowheads were found, one on the floor of the passage, the other lodged in the region of the throat of an elderly man laid to rest in a crouched position on a small sarsen pavement in the northeast chamber. He had a fractured left radius and an abscess cavity at the head of the left humerus that was probably the result of a wound through the deltoid muscle.[142] Still more secure is a case at Ascott-under-Wychwood where a leaf-shaped arrowhead was found embedded in the third lumbar vertebra of a robust male adult *(70)*. The projectile to which the arrowhead belonged had pierced beneath his ribs and then broken off.[143] The arrow must have been released from close range to have penetrated so deep; assuming the man was alive at the time, the impact of this shot must have caused excruciating pain. All these finds have implications for the nature of life and death in the fourth and third millennia BC, not least in emphasizing the role that arrow-shot played in killing people rather than hunting wild animals.

Pebbles

Natural exotic pebbles have been reported from a handful of barrows, some of them brought from quite a distance away. At Parc le Breos Cwm a flint beach pebble was found in the north end of the passage, while Nympsfield, Notgrove and Rodmarton each produced a pebble, two brown and one white quartzite, perhaps from the local Bunter Drift that can be found scattered across several parts of the central Cotswolds.[144] White quartz pebbles in particular have been found in many long barrows and related monuments in western Britain, a practice that may stand at the head of the long-lived tradition that can be traced down into relatively recent times in which the pebbles are believed to contain a human soul or a person's spirit.[145]

Other pieces of unusual, and in a sense exotic, stone have been found at a few barrows, for example pieces of haematite at Nympsfield and Rodmarton and a block of Old Red Sandstone at Rodmarton.[146] The haematite may just conceivably have been used to decorate or colour orthostats forming the chamber walls, or to colour human remains in a manner that finds echoes in many periods of early prehistory in northwest Europe and beyond.[147]

Stone discs

Simple round stone discs made by flaking tabular pieces of rock into a roughly circular outline have been found at four sites, some from within the chambers *(68F–I)*. The largest group is from Ty Isaf, where a total of ten discs of various sizes were found within and around the long barrow and its predecessor the simple passage grave (see Chapter 3). Three examples were found in the chambers of the long barrow, two in the west chamber and one in the east chamber.[148] Comparable discs have been found at Penywyrlod just outside the edge of the mound near the northeast corner,[149] at West Kennet in the façade to the east of the chambers,[150] and at Ascott-under-Wychwood. The purpose and meaning of these objects is not known, although it has been suggested that they were weights of some kind.

Ornaments and personal items

Beads have been found at more than a dozen sites in a variety of materials and in a range of sizes *(68C–D* and *O; 69F, H* and *J–M)*. Perhaps the most impressive are the shale beads from Eyford Hill and Notgrove. Both of these would have been shiny and black when new, exotic imports from the Kimmeridge area of the south coast and presumably rather prized possessions *(68L* and *69M)*. Both are less than 30mm across, oval in cross-section and slightly D-shaped in outline with a central horizontal perforation. It is tempting to imagine that they were suspended round the neck and worn as pendants, but the position and context of the finds in relation to the associated human remains provides no help in confirming this. Beads of very similar shape and design made of amber have been recorded from Scandinavia.[151]

Other items that may also be considered as pendants of various sorts have been found at several other sites: a sandstone example in the entrance zone to the east chamber at Ty Isaf; perforated boar's tusks at Hetty Pegler's Tump and Belas Knap; and a perforated sea shell (*Nucella*) from Nympsfield. Two similar shells, also perforated for suspension, were found with the primary burials in the northeast chamber at West Kennet.[152] These may well have been amulets of some kind, but attest a link to coastal areas some distance away.

At Hazleton North a tiny perforated stone bead was found in the entrance zone of the north chamber area while four tubular bone beads were found in the south chamber area. None could be associated with a specific individual. A spherical bone bead was found at Notgrove, and what may be two tubular bone beads polished from use come from Rodmarton. What appears to be a bone ring, just possibly a finger ring given an internal diameter of 15mm, was found on the floor of the forecourt at Notgrove *(69G)*.[153]

Bone pins have been found in the west chamber at Ty Isaf, at Pole's Wood South *(68K)*, at Notgrove *(69D)* and at West Kennet *(69E)*. These were perhaps originally dress fittings or for holding hair arrangements in place.

Bone scoops and chisels

A handful of barrows have yielded bone scoops or chisels, formed by rubbing down the split leg-bone of a large animal *(68J, 69I)*. Examples come from Bown Hill, Pole's Wood East, Pole's Wood South, Rodmarton and Notgrove. Their purpose is unknown.

Whistle or flute

One of the most remarkable finds is from near the entrance to the northeast II chamber at Penywyrlod. It comprises part of a sheep's long bone that has been hollowed out and perforated with three small holes to form a simple whistle or end-blown flute *(55G)*. As such, it has a fair claim to be the earliest musical instrument from the British Isles.[154]

Animal remains

Animal remains are commonly found mixed with the human remains in chamber deposits, although typically in small quantities. The presence of some animals, for example cat and fox, may relate to these creatures using the chamber as a refuge or home. Slightly unusual are the remains of at least eight neonatal and juvenile dogs in the passage of Parc le Breos Cwm, although judging by the human remains from the same area these may have been introduced during secondary disturbances. At the same site, however, some animal bone of early post-glacial date found its way into the passage, perhaps as part of the blocking up of the site (see Chapter 7).[155] At Hazleton North, very few animal bones found their way into the north chamber area, but nearly 30 pieces were found in the south chamber area, mainly in the passage and chamber. The most extensive included the scattered remains of a perinatal sheep or goat together with fragments of cattle, pig, roe deer and dog. Animal remains at Penywyrlod were mainly concentrated in the entrance zone of the northeast chambers and included red deer as well as pig and sheep. Horse has been identified amongst the remains in chambers at Penywyrlod, Tinkinswood, Belas Knap, Bown Hill, Eyford Hill, Notgrove, Nympsfield and Rodmarton. At West Kennet, a roe deer antler lay in the entrance to the northeast chamber. At Notgrove the almost complete skeleton of a calf was found in chamber E at the far east end of the passage; the remains of a calf were also found at Bown Hill.[156]

Marine shells (*Ostrea edulis*) have been reported from Rodmarton, presumably imported from the coast.[157] Bird bones have been recorded at Nympsfield and Randwick (GLO 10), perhaps the remains of wildfowl caught in the excellent fowling environments along the River Severn.

The majority of animal remains from chamber fills appear to derive from domesticated creatures. Among these, Clifford noted that at least two breeds of dog were represented amongst the remains, one the size of an Irish wolfhound, the other the size of a collie.[158] The wolfhound from Nympsfield is the largest dog so far recorded from a fourth-millennium BC context in Britain. Overall, cattle appear to dominate the spectra of animal species deposited within the chambers, being noted in more than 90 per cent of reports dealing with the representation of animal remains from long barrow chambers. This is a point that Ian Hodder has taken up, suggesting that it may be linked to the fundamental symbolic significance of cattle in early farming cultures in Europe and the ability, in symbolic terms, of cattle to 'stand' for humans.[159]

PEOPLE AND OBJECTS

In many senses, long barrows were alive; they were places where people did things. What exactly they did, how and when, remain far from certain, but that it involved corpses, skeletons and bones from those that today we might consider 'dead people' as well as a selection of artefacts and parts of non-human animals is clear enough. In thinking about the human remains we must beware of blandly applying our own distinctions between life and death, especially our belief that life expires with someone's last breath. As Julian Thomas, Mike Parker Pearson and others have illustrated,[160] ethnographic studies show that our perspective is just one amongst many different ways of seeing and rationalizing an individual's demise. For many communities, someone's last breath is just one point in a long process of 'passing-on', in which the decay of the flesh and the disintegration of the skeleton are just as significant as the loss of sentience.

The evidence from the long barrows suggests an interest in an extended understanding of death through a variety of practices that included: excarnation followed by the deposition of defleshed and disarticulated remains; the deposition of corpses into the outer parts of long barrow chambers followed by the systematic movement of elements into the inner recesses of the chamber area; the placement of a corpse in a chamber followed by the removal of significant elements as it decayed; and the periodic removal and social use of disarticulated remains. Everyday objects do not seem to have been given an especially central role in the activities represented at long barrows, many of the finds being explicable as the possessions of the deceased. Only the pottery and animal remains placed on the mound or in entranceways can easily be interpreted as ceremonial deposits, although there may have been others, including organic materials which over time have become archaeologically invisible. Apart from the obvious differences that apply in the case of long barrows that lack internal chambers, there is little or no evidence for any significant differences in the way that human remains or objects were treated in relation to the different kinds of chambers represented. In all cases, the pattern of activity was complicated and is difficult to recover through archaeological evidence. Indeed, it is far from clear whether the excavated remains represent the conclusion of the various processes, or the remains of ongoing activity that for some reason became frozen in time. What is perhaps more certain is that the internal spaces within long barrows were used only periodically, and that between uses, and also at some pre-determined or assumed final point in time, access to the chamber areas and forecourts was prevented by blocking deposits and deliberately placed fills.

7

BLOCKING BARROWS AND BREAKING TRADITIONS

For about four or five centuries, long barrows were places for periodic visits and occasional use. Between the times when access into the interior was needed, the chamber entrances were temporarily closed off with blocking slabs and sections of removable walling, some of it impressive and robust *(71)*. The low incidence of animal scavenging visible on the preserved bones attests to the effectiveness of these temporary blocking arrangements in keeping unwanted visitors out. But the very act of blocking up access routes into the chambers takes us beyond the practical and the mundane. Perhaps these same barriers were also intended to prevent the spirits of the ancestors leaving the sanctuary of their 'house of the dead'. Still more significantly, preventing admittance to the inner concealed areas of a long barrow implies the existence of an abstract knowledge about the contents of barrows generally, and realization of deliberate attempts to hide, mask, or restrict that knowledge at particular sites.[1] So what happened when the internal elements of a long barrow were no longer needed? Were all barrows treated in the same way? Is there any pattern to the way barrows were sealed and closed off? And did it happen across the region at a particular time?

BLOCKING UP THE ACCESS

As we saw in Chapter 5, long barrows comprised a complicated set of constructed spaces, some internal and some external, variously accessible to large or small groups of people at a time. Movement within the monument was in part controlled by architectural features such as portals, entrances, projecting jambs, sill-stones, septal slabs, portholes and the generally rather limited space. Some of these features facilitated the insertion of temporary blocking material, often stone slabs or sections of dry-stone walling, especially at the outer entrance to chamber areas and the junctions between the entrance zone and the passage zone and between the passage zone and the chamber zone. As time went by, however, the blocking

Long Barrows of the Cotswolds

71 Rodmarton (GLO 16). Dry-stone walling forming a blocking within the porthole entrance between the chamber zone and the passage zone of the south chamber area. *From Clifford and Daniel 1940, plate xii; reproduced courtesy of the Prehistoric Society*

arrangements at individual barrows seem to have become more and more substantial, until a time came when further access was prevented altogether as chambers and passages were filled with soil and rubble, entrances were enveloped by heaps of stones and forecourts were filled.[2] These things did not necessarily happen all at once, and in many cases went hand-in-hand with the natural decay of the structure. Neither did all long barrows in the region undergo the same pattern of abandonment and sealing up; indeed some may have simply fallen out of use with little or no deliberate closing up. Where there is evidence of closure, attention seems to focus on one or more of three key areas.

Chamber and passage zones

Determining the state in which chambers and passages were left by fourth-millennium BC communities is not always easy, and when using the results of antiquarian excavations can sometimes be confusing and inconclusive. When examined, however, the archaeological evidence typically falls into one of two main kinds. First, there is no doubt that when some chambers were abandoned they were completely empty except for their burial deposits spread across the floor. Where preservation is good and the roofing has remained intact, discovering such cases can be alarming, as for example at Pole's Wood South (GLO 2) where a man building stone walls in the area began taking stone from the mound and 'all at once dropped into a cavity and found himself to his horror amongst a mass of human bones'.[3] Where preservation is less good it is often possible to recognize the presence of collapsed orthostats, broken roofing slabs and collapsed mound material within the chamber or passage. Not all of these are necessarily of modern origin as long barrows started collapsing almost as soon as they were finished. At Hazleton North (GLO 54), for example, part of the passage in the northern chamber area collapsed during the time the barrow was in regular use, possibly with calamitous effects on the deposition and circulation of human remains at the site.[4] Natural processes leading to the decay and collapse of the walls and roofing are sometimes accelerated by human interventions of various kinds. Rifling during later prehistoric, Romano-British, or more modern times was fairly common (see Chapter 9) and usually resulted in the collapse of original architectural features and the natural or deliberate accumulation of back-fill. The perpetrators of such invasions were usually rather messy and they almost invariably left behind tell-tale traces from their own times to fix the date of the damage. Second, there are barrows where part or all of the passage and chamber are found upon examination to contain varying amounts of deliberately introduced fill. Whether revealed by modern systematic excavations or brought to light through antiquarian diggings or casual investigations, these deliberate fills are generally fairly compact and contrast with the matrix of the mound in terms of the nature of the material used and the way it was placed.

Accepting these various difficulties of interpretation, there seems to be little overall regularity to the way that chamber and passage zones were left when the original purpose of the barrow was abandoned. In some cases barrows were left with both the chamber and passage zones exactly as they had been during use, allowing natural processes of decay and collapse to take over. In other cases either the chamber zone, or the passage zone, or both were deliberately infilled. However, when looked at in relation to specific kinds of chamber, some slight patterning can be glimpsed.

Amongst transepted terminal chambers, all but one example for which detailed records exist seem to have had all the chambers and the passage filled. The exception is the Fairy's Toot at Nempnett Thrubwell (SOM 2), where there is good reason to believe that none of the chamber area was infilled prior to its abandonment, although the site is usual in other ways with its 16 separate chamber elements.[5] The most fully investigated chamber and passage fills are those at West Kennet (WIL 4). Here, Stuart Piggott found that a layer of slabs and stones, perhaps derived from the collapse of temporary blocking walls and the deterioration of the chamber walls, had formed over the top of the burial deposits before the filling was introduced. This layer suggested a period of inactivity between the last insertion of a burial and the decision to infill the chambers and passage. The filling itself was up to 2m thick in places, and in volume represented 65-70 cubic metres. It extended from floor to ceiling (72), and its insertion almost certainly involved lifting some capstones over the chambers. Two types of fill were recognized: a clean coarse chalk rubble which accounted for the majority of matrix by volume, in amongst which were lenses of dark humic material containing cultural material such as pottery, worked flint, ornaments and bone and stone tools. In his report on the excavations, Stuart Piggott suggested that this material had been deposited within the chamber area as a single act, utilizing locally derived chalk rubble (perhaps from recutting the ditch) as well as material from a nearby midden or ceremonial centre of some kind where a wide range of debris had accumulated over several centuries.[6] Various possible sources for this midden material have been suggested, amongst them a spread of occupation debris later covered by the

72 West Kennet (WIL 4). Filling in the northwest chamber viewed from the passage. The capstone is at the top of the picture. Scale graduated in 1-foot (c.0.3m) intervals. *From Piggott 1962, plate xviiib. Copyright reserved*

Avebury G55 round barrow some 300m to the northwest of the long barrow.[7] It may also be noted that West Kennet lies within a landscape that during the third millennium BC would have been a relatively busy place. It is only 750m southwest of a series of the massive palisaded enclosures in the valley of the River Kennet where midden deposits would certainly have accumulated.[8]

Since the publication of Piggott's report in 1962 there has been much debate and speculation about how the filling was inserted and its relationship to the use of the monument. Following a detailed and extensive re-examination of Piggott's records, Julian Thomas and Alasdair Whittle argued that the chamber fills at West Kennet accumulated over a long period of time and in three main stages.[9] However, the stratigraphic sequence in all four chambers suggests a high degree of unity to the accumulation of material, and there are joining sherds scattered through the fill that seem more abundant than could be explained by animal activity moving material around. For these reasons, Humphrey Case has reinterpreted Piggott's original single-episode arguments, with modifications that add a degree of pragmatism. In particular he notes that the majority of the fill could have been obtained locally from the reuse of the quarry ditches, with only perhaps 4–5 cubic metres of occupation debris needing to be brought to the barrow from some distance away. Presumably such material had some special symbolic meaning, but transporting such a modest amount would represent no great effort on the part of communities that were demonstrably capable of shifting thousands of tons of soil and rock to build nearby structures like Silbury Hill and Avebury.[10]

Although less well preserved, other barrows with transepted terminal chambers show similar patterns, although not all were necessarily full to the roof with blocking material. At Wayland's Smithy (BRK 1), for example, relatively clean chalk rubble, perhaps derived from the flanking ditches, seems to have been used to infill the passage and three chamber cells, the excavator drawing specific attention to a deposit of calcium carbonate well up the walls of the west transept and suggesting that this indicated the thickness of the blocking deposit.[11]

If the excavated simple terminal chambers at Randwick (GLO 10) and Tinkinswood (GLA 9) are representative, then a high proportion of these long barrows also had their chambers filled. Tinkinswood is the most fully investigated and certainly had some fill within the chamber, but the excavator, John Ward, did not have time to examine completely the structure of the filling beyond noting that it was up to 0.6m thick in places.[12] Excavations at Millbarrow (WIL 11) revealed some circumstantial evidence of blocking or filling in the chamber area, but the monument was too heavily damaged to allow a full interpretation.[13] No reliable evidence at all is available from long barrows in the region with timber chambers.

The greatest variation in the way that chambers and passage zones were infilled can be found amongst the barrows with lateral chambers. A few, for example Pole's Wood South and the Giant's Caves at Luckington (WIL 2), seem to have had their chambers left empty and their passages filled. Ffostyll North (BRE 3) by contrast seems to have had the chamber filled but the passage empty, while the rest either have both zones filled or both left empty. At West Tump (GLO 8) limestone rubble was used to pack the passage and chamber in a manner described by Witts as being in a 'very disorderly or confused state'.[14] At Pipton (BRE 8) there were two layers of fill. Immediately above the burial deposits was a 0.3–0.75m thick deposit of dry red-brown soil that became thicker at the chamber entrance. Interleaved in places, but stratigraphically above this, was a layer of stones that bonded with the blocking in the entrance (see below). At Penywyrlod (BRE 14) the excavator noted that the main chamber was filled up evenly to the top of the orthostats with small stone chips. This chamber was not, however, excavated because of its intact condition.

Entrance zone blocking

The most common form of blocking occurs in the entrance zone, often utilizing constructional elements put in place when the barrow was built. At Hazleton North, the entrances to both chamber areas were closed by building a section of dry-stone walling into the entrance hole, its outer face being flush with the outer revetment wall *(73A)*. At Belas Knap (GLO 1) something rather similar was observed for the southeast chamber, which 'had been deliberately and carefully blocked', the outer revetment wall having been continued across the entrance as a low sill three courses high. This blocking extended about 0.45m into the entrance zone.[15] Other chambers at the site were dealt with in different ways, emphasizing the idiosyncrasy of what went on even within the separate elements of a single barrow. Reusing the outer or inner revetment wall is, however, common at lateral-chambered long barrows. At Lanhill (WIL 3) the passage into the northwest chamber was not filled, but 'the end of the passage was blocked with horizontal

Long Barrows of the Cotswolds

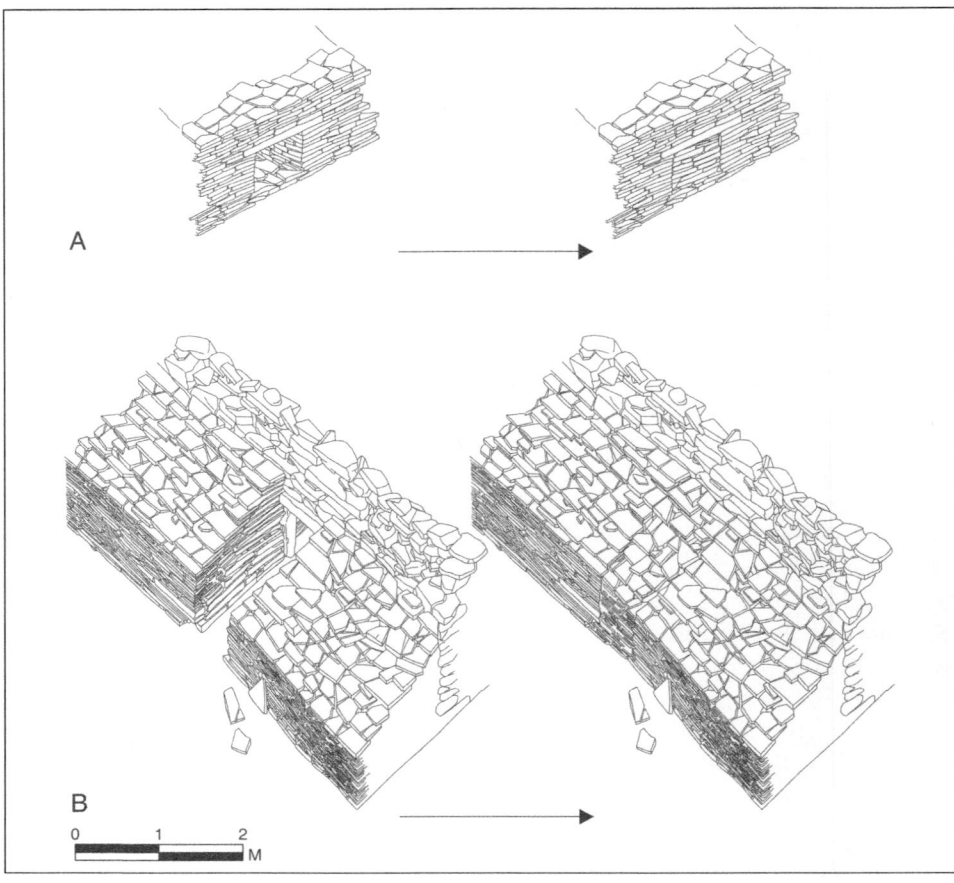

73 Entrance zone blocking at long barrows with lateral chambers. *A:* Hazleton North (GLO 54), entrance to the north chamber, open (left) as when in use, and closed (right) as when blocked between burial episodes and at the end of the use of the site. The lintel slab shown is entirely hypothetical. *B:* Gwernvale (BRE 7), entrance to the north chamber (chamber 3), open (left) and blocked (right). *A: after Saville 1990, fig. 232; B: after Britnell 1984, figs. 66 and 67*

slabs perhaps like a wall, but not extending into the passage proper'.[16] At Ty Isaf (BRE 5) the outer revetment wall appears to have been slighted outside the northeast chamber and then rebuilt to form the entrance blocking.[17] A contrasting picture can be seen at Giant's Caves (WIL 2), where there was filling in the passageway and 'the entrance was blocked by tightly packed horizontally arranged small stones'.[18] At Penywyrlod (BRE 14) the passage of the northeast II chamber was tightly filled and the outer revetment wall carried across the entrance. Access was probably gained through the roof of the entrance zone, and in this sense there is really very little difference between such an arrangement and the construction of the chamber area at Ascott-under-Wychwood (OXF 6), where two groups of three-celled closed chambers were set back to back in the central portion of the mound with no direct access from the side of the mound.[19]

At Gwernvale (BRE 7), the blocking deposits extended through the entrance zone and into the passage in at least two of the four chambers; the same probably applied to all the others. During the life of the barrow the entrances were concealed by the reinstatement of the outer revetment wall between episodes of activity *(73B)*. After the chambers were used for the last time, however, soil and stones were packed into the entrance zone and outer passage, with further soil and stone piled up around the outside of the entrance *(74)*. Further blocking deposits may later have been added to the edge of the mound perhaps to camouflage it and make it look more rounded and ancient. Around the well-preserved chamber 3 on the north side, a sequence of three layers was detected: heaps of specially introduced stone and soil piled against the outer revetment wall; a middle layer possibly formed by the collapse of the outer revetment wall; and an uppermost spread of stone of uncertain origin.[20]

At long barrows with terminal chambers the entrance zone blocking takes slightly different forms. At Tinkinswood (GLA 9), a single massive slab was placed in the entrance to the simple terminal chamber at the rear of the forecourt. At Burn Ground (GLO 60) the entrance zone blocking comprised a rubble filling and what Grimes describes as a vertical shaft immediately in front of the entrance and extending into the forecourt for a distance of about 1.5m. When access into the chambers was needed this blocking was removed and then later replaced *(75)*. It was quite distinct from the forecourt filling, and was separated from it by a series

74 Gwernvale, Crickhowell (BRE 7). View of the northeast chamber during excavation in 1978 with the blocking deposits in the entranceway and passage revealed. The revetment wall can be seen running left to right across the lower part of the picture with the barrow stonework above. Scale totals 1m. *Photograph by Bill Britnell. Copyright Clwyd-Powys Archaeological Trust*

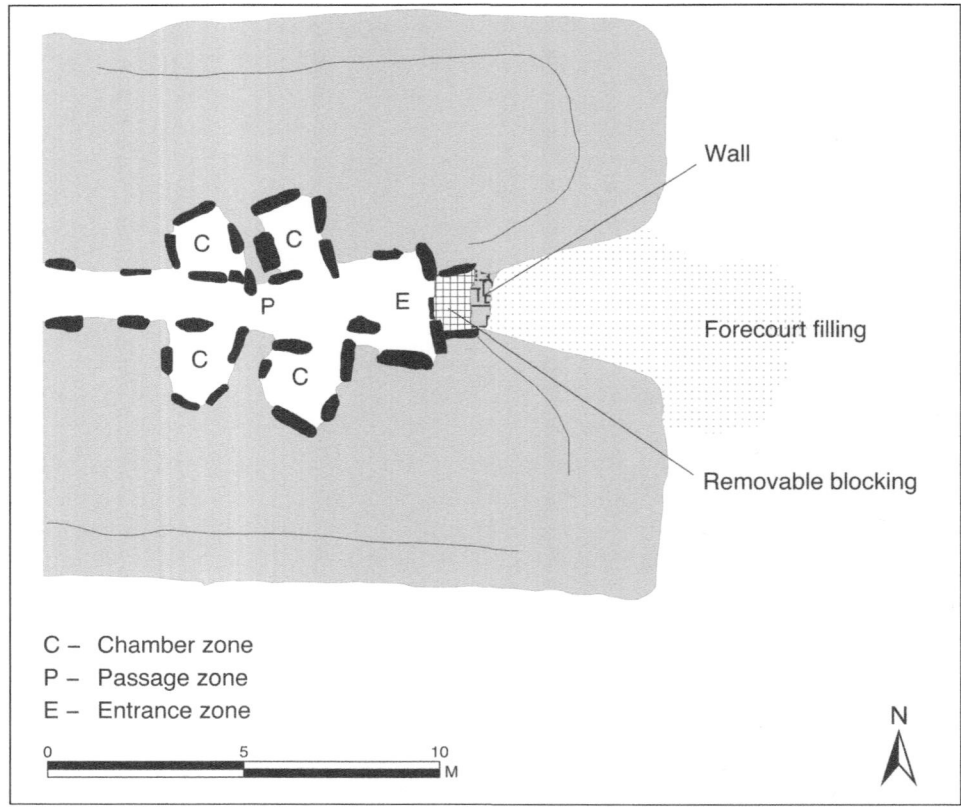

75 Entrance zone blocking at a long barrow with a terminal chamber: Burn Ground (GLO 60) showing the east entrance with removable blocking deposits and forecourt filling. *After Grimes 1960, figs 29 and 38*

of horizontally laid stones.[21] In other terminal-chambered long barrows, for example Nympsfield (GLO 13), the blocking of the entrance zones seems to have spilled beyond the entrance zone itself and become integral with the forecourt filling (see below).

Forecourt filling

Whereas the fills placed within the chambers, passages and entrance zones are relatively easy to recognize, deliberately placed stonework within and around the forecourt is far harder to identify. This is mainly because deliberate filling can easily be confused with accumulations of debris from the collapse of the façade walls or the decay of the mound around the horns. At Hazleton North, for example, Alan Saville showed that all the stonework found in the forecourt resulted from natural processes of decay and the gradual collapse of the external revetment wall. Two distinct layers were noted: a deposit of rock flakes and spalls from the weathering of the forecourt walls, over which were displaced stones from the collapse of the upper part of the forecourt wall and the decay of the mound behind.[22] With the results of the Hazleton excavations to hand it is possible to reinterpret observations set out in some earlier reports. At West Tump (GLO 8), for example, Witts notes that the 'mass of stones' filling the forecourt had been 'placed at an angle of 45 degrees against the upright wall'.[23] Similarly, at Pole's Wood South (GLO 2) George Rolleston recorded that 'the concavity of the horns at the east end was filled up for a space of 2 feet depth with fine small stones, outside of which again came larger stones all evidently arranged intentionally'.[24]

At many barrows the distinction between deliberately placed stonework and collapsed walls or mound material is fairly marked, and at a few sites contrasting kinds of stone were used as forecourt fill. At Notgrove (GLO 4), for example, slabs of shelly Stonesfield Slate were used in the forecourt filling, contrasting with the lighter stone used elsewhere in the barrow mound.[25] This suggests that perhaps colour and texture were important in the way that blocking deposits were perceived and understood. At Gwernvale (BRE 7), the forecourt filling was composed of slabs of different kinds of sandstone. Some were green and micaceous, similar to the stone forming the outer revetment walls, but approximately 40 per cent of the filling was white quartzitic sandstone of a type rarely found elsewhere in the mound.[26]

Forecourt fillings tend to be more marked and more obvious at terminal-chambered barrows, and nowhere are they more spectacular than at West Kennet (WIL 4). Here the small cuspate forecourt was filled rather haphazardly with sarsen boulders, quite unlike the chalk matrix of the mound and chamber fills. Two upright stones had been positioned to extend the line of the passage into the forecourt area and perhaps provide access into the chamber from above in a similar way to what Grimes described at Burn Ground (GLO 60). In front of the forecourt fill, three very large sarsen slabs were set upright to create a continuous, slightly convex façade on the line already established by the stones forming the façade of the two horns. Human bone, including a skull and a femur, was found in the forecourt fill. Like the stones of the original façade, the additional blocking stones were large, up to 4m high, perhaps selected for their distinctive shapes. The one in the centre has a fairly rounded top, the one to the left is flat-topped and the one to the right is lozenge-shaped or pointed. The presence of a vertical elongated oval hollow on the eastern, outward, face of the central blocking stone is seen by some commentators as the symbolic representation of a vulva on what might appropriately be considered a 'female' stone. In origin this feature seems to be a natural hollow, although whether the stone was deliberately selected and positioned because of it is impossible to say.

There is great variety in the way forecourts were filled. Not all were filled immediately, as at some there is evidence for a period of inactivity and natural decay before the construction of forecourt blocking. At Penywyrlod, for example, a primary triangular-shaped heap of stones was piled up near the false-portal. This in turn was sealed by a second layer of stone filling the gap between the primary heap and the false-portal and extending out in front of the horns of the forecourt.[27] Rather different is the situation at Rodmarton (GLO 16), although the evidence is susceptible to more than one interpretation. Excavations in 1863 revealed a huge slab of local limestone seemingly propped against the uprights of the false-portal and supported on short stub-walls. All around were carefully placed blocking deposits, which consisted of large flattish stones. How exactly the stones got to be like this is uncertain, but it is possible that in origin the huge slab was the lintel of the false-portal (or perhaps even the capstone of an earlier portal dolmen) which fell during the life of the barrow and was later secured by the stub-walls before being incorporated into and covered by the forecourt blocking.[28] The entrance to the simple terminal chamber at Tinkinswood was also sealed by a large slab that was later covered by forecourt blocking.[29] However, at Burn Ground, the forecourt filling was fairly even and undisturbed except adjacent to the entrance zone blocking where it had been disturbed by continued use of the entrance after the filling had been inserted.[30]

The final effect of filling the forecourt would have been to make the proximal end of the mound appear rounded and decayed. At Notgrove the forecourt blocking extended 9.4m from the entrance to the chambers, while at Rodmarton blocking extended for a distance of 11.5m from the false-portal. Similar spreads are recorded at Burn Ground and Penywyrlod. What the upper surface of the blocking deposits looked like is generally uncertain because of later erosion, but a preserved section at Notgrove suggested to Elsie Clifford that it was roughly paved, with small hollows and hearth pits cut into the surface.[31]

FINDS FROM BLOCKING DEPOSITS

Cultural material such as pottery, worked flints, ornaments and animal bone that was included within blocking deposits derived from a number of different sources, but two predominate. First there are objects associated with the use of the long barrow that in a broken or dislodged form become incorporated into the soil and rubble filling. This especially applies to deposits found in forecourts and around the entrances to lateral chambers where it seems likely that pottery, animal remains and personal ornaments were stacked up or displayed. Much of this material has already been discussed in relation to the way long barrows were used (Chapter 5) and is not repeated here. Second, objects were deliberately added to or incidentally incorporated within the blocking deposits at the time these were being put in place. In general these are later in date than the things associated with the use of the barrow, although sorting out which is which can be extremely difficult. In general, however, the datable material in this second category belongs to cultural traditions that flourished during the third millennium BC. As such it contrasts rather markedly with material associated with the construction and primary use of the long barrows.

By far the richest assemblage of cultural material incorporated within blocking deposits comes from the fills in the chambers and passage at West Kennet (WIL 4). Humphrey Case has estimated that about 4–5 cubic metres (6–7 per cent of the overall fill) of dark soil contained a wide range of cultural material,[32] including more than 850 sherds of pottery from perhaps 250 or more vessels, about 25 flint implements, a dozen or so bone objects, 20 beads and related objects and a substantial collection of human and animal bones. Most of the pottery was Peterborough Ware (mainly in Mortlake and Fengate styles), but Grooved Ware and Beaker Ware were also well represented. In their analysis of the way the West Kennet fill accumulated, Julian Thomas and Alasdair Whittle considered that in the initial deposits the distributions of pottery, animal bones and human remains were relatively uniform, but higher up the sequence the deposits appear increasingly to emphasize the northern chambers and especially the northeastern chamber, in terms of the quantity of cultural material included.[33]

West Kennet is unique in terms of the quantity and variety of material culture within the blocking deposits. It may be explained, in part at least, by its situation within one of the most dense concentrations of third-millennium BC occupation in southern England and the fact that these fills were being introduced at a time of great change in the landscape, when Avebury was being elaborated and Silbury Hill constructed.[34] Elsewhere, finds are more limited in number and variety, although, as at West Kennet, pottery represents the most distinctive material present. At Gwernvale (BRE 7) parts of four pots appear to have been incorporated within the blocking deposits (including 76A and B). All the sherds are small and only a little of each vessel is represented, suggesting that their presence in the blocking outside chambers 3 and 4 may be accidental, the sherds being incorporated in soil brought in to provide the blocking.[35] In form and decoration, one of the fragmentary vessels (not illustrated) from Gwernvale is rather similar to a Peterborough Ware vessel from Burn Ground (GLO 60) found near the southeastern horn of the mound *(55D)*.[36] Another broadly similar vessel was found over the north horn of Pole's Wood South (GLO 2), 'not much below the present surface of the mound', perhaps within some kind of blocking deposit or forecourt filling *(76C)*.[37] At Nympsfield (GLO 13) dark-coloured sherds of heavily decorated Mortlake style Peterborough Ware representing perhaps three or four vessels occur sparsely within the chamber area and more commonly in the forecourt filling.[38] A rather similar sequence is represented at Notgrove (GLO 4) where a large fragment from a heavily decorated Mortlake style bowl was found in the entrance blocking.[39] At Gatcombe Lodge (GLO 15) the skull of an adult female was found with sherds of Peterborough Ware in the forecourt blocking immediately in front of the false-portal.[40]

Human bone is also well represented, strengthening the idea that the material used to fill the chambers and passage was derived from around the mound or somewhere close-by. At least two burials in the passage at Parc le Breos Cwm (GLA 4), an adult female and a sub-adult, seem to have been added during the filling of the passage in the third millennium BC, and it is possible that the other four or five individuals in the passage are of the same date.[41] Similarly, at West Kennet, a child aged about one year appears to have been buried on top of the filling in the southeast chamber,[42] further strengthening the argument that some of the capstones were removed in order to block up this tomb.

Long Barrows of the Cotswolds

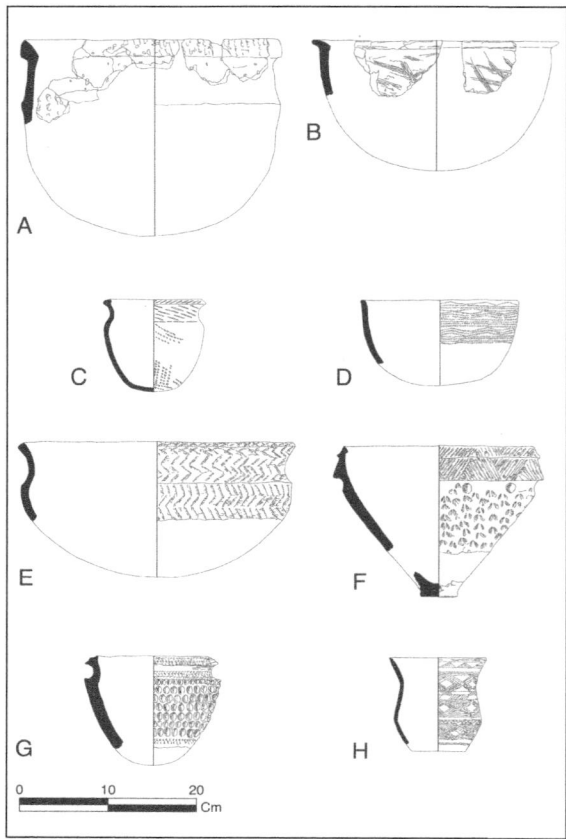

76 Pottery from the blocking deposits in long barrows within the Cotswold-Severn region. *A* and *B:* Gwernvale (BRE 7); *C:* Pole's Wood South (GLO 2); *D:* Tinkinswood (GLA 9); *E-H:* West Kennet (WIL 4)

DATING THE END OF USE

When exactly these blocking deposits were put in place and the original use of the long barrows ended is very hard to say, for it did not happen simultaneously at all sites. No burials later than about 3200 BC have been found in the chambers of long barrows, except for certain and probable secondary additions. Thus, as suggested in Chapter 5, the period from about 3700 BC down to 3200 BC may be seen as the main phase of long barrow currency. On the basis of pottery finds from blocking deposits, and a handful of relevant radiocarbon dates, long barrows were already being deliberately blocked up by the middle centuries of the third millennium BC and most had fallen completely out of use by about 3000 BC. Only a few sites, West Kennet (WIL 4) prominent amongst them, rather atypically witnessed some continued activity over the following centuries down to perhaps 2500 BC.

Pottery from blocking contexts belongs to three main ceramic traditions of the third millennium BC: Peterborough Ware, Grooved Ware and Beaker Ware *(76E–H)*. None of these traditions is represented amongst pottery recovered from certain primary contexts, and as hinted above this might suggest a cultural as well as a chronological difference between the communities that built and used long barrows and those that blocked them up. Peterborough Ware is well represented in Mortlake styles at West Kennet, Notgrove (GLO 4), Pole's Wood South (GLO 2), Wayland's Smithy (BRK 1), Millbarrow (WIL 11), Burn Ground (GLO 60), Sale's Lot (GLO 94) and Randwick (GLO 10); and in Fengate styles at West Kennet. Grooved Ware is far more restricted, being found only at West Kennet, in relatively small amounts. The latest ceramics represented are Beaker Wares, which occur in blocking deposits at West Kennet, Wayland's Smithy, Notgrove, Pen-y-wyrlod (BRE 1), Ty Isaf (BRE 5), Eyford Hill (GLO 3), Pole's Wood South and Tinkinswood (GLA 9). As noted above, the largest and most significant group of ceramics is that from the filling of West Kennet which collectively spans much of the early and middle third millennium BC. It is notable, however, that the Beaker Ware within the assemblage falls mainly within Group D of Humphrey Case's regional sequence, all three styles of beaker from that Group being represented.[43] In this view the latest pottery present must therefore date to the last quarter of the third millennium BC, perhaps as late as 2200 BC.[44] It should be emphasized, however, that West Kennet is exceptional in many ways, one of which may be that activity here continued rather later than elsewhere because of the high level of occupation and ceremonial activity in the area.[45]

Radiocarbon dates relating to the closure and early secondary use of long barrows in the Cotswold-Severn region are available from Gwernvale (BRE 7), Parc le Breos Cwm (GLA 4) and Lambourn (BRK 2). The Gwernvale dates, which focus on 3000 BC, relate to charcoal from pits immediately below the blocking deposits outside chamber 2 in the southwestern part of the mound. Dates for Parc le Breos Cwm span the period from 2290 down to 200 BC and derive from two human burials and a piece of deer bone in the passage zone. Some of these bones were perhaps introduced into the chamber area with blocking material from elsewhere, as there are also two further samples which are very much earlier than the construction of the barrow (see Appendix B); the roe deer bone of the late first millennium BC may be intrusive. Alasdair Whittle and Michael Wysocki suggest that perhaps the blocking material was brought to the barrow from the Tooth Hole Cave situated not far away to the north.[46] At Lambourn the uppermost of two superimposed interments at the east end of the barrow dates to 3340-2880 BC and probably reflects a late insertion or a momentary resurrection of the site as a burial ground sometime after its initial abandonment.[47] The only other relevant date currently available is from the secondary fill of the quarry ditch at Easton Down (WIL 19), where a date of 2480-2140 BC is wholly compatible with the idea that this long barrow was out of use well before 2500 BC.

BREAKING WITH TRADITION

With the final blocking up of long barrows in and around the Cotswolds a centuries-old tradition came to an end. As individual long barrows reached the blocking and abandonment stage in their lifecycle they joined the increasing ranks of monuments that must all have looked more or less the same, regardless of whether the internal chambers were at the end or the sides of the mound. Even the chamberless long barrows of the north Wessex Downs would have blended in with all the others, and perhaps achieved their builders' ultimate aim of creating a fake antiquity. Natural decay coupled with the deliberate placement of blocking deposits in forecourts and around the chamber entrances would create a structure in the landscape that could be interpreted as something archaic – a tomb that had ceased to be used for formal mortuary activities, as Bill Britnell once put it.[48] In Julian Thomas's view, the final blocking of the barrows served to distance and make unassailable their contents.[49] But their abandonment in this way may have been still more fundamental, as all the things that these structures stood for were propelled into oblivion. At Wayland's Smithy (BRK 1) the blocking up of the barrow coincided with the point in the ditch sequence at which molluscan analysis indicates woodland regeneration and a relaxation of activity around the site.[50] Much the same happened at other sites, where changes to the local environment can be charted;[51] metaphorically at least the unquiet barrows of the fourth millennium slowly became the sleeping giants of later ages. Long barrows did not stand alone, however; they were just one element within much wider patterns of social life and these deserve brief exploration before turning to how the long barrows fared in the millennia after 2500 BC.

8

COTSWOLD-SEVERN LONG BARROWS IN CONTEXT

Long barrows did not exist in isolation. Physically, they were part of diverse and extensive landscapes comprising the places and spaces that people used; socially, they lay within intricate and complicated mindscapes comprising ideas and beliefs that structured and justified what their builders and users thought and did. The evidence of temporary blockings and relatively small-scale activity around the mounds suggests that they were not a focus for major activities and ceremonies very often, even if they were visited more frequently for encounters and experiences that left little or no archaeological trace. Just passing by the house of the dead, home of the ancestors and refuge of guardian spirits, would no doubt have been an emotional experience for members of the community that built it, if that is how long barrows were perceived. Overall, how did long barrows fit into wider patterns of society? Where else did these visitors spend their time? Where did they live? What other kinds of monuments did the users of long barrows build and use? And were long barrows at the centre of their worlds or marginal to the focus of activity?

LONG BARROWS: CENTRE OR PERIPHERY?

The idea that long barrows were somehow central places to the lives of a community is widely held, and has been discussed in earlier chapters; how this significance was realized has become a matter of considerable debate. For Colin Renfrew long barrows and various other kinds of contemporary monuments were the territorial markers of segmentary societies, constructed in a climate of social stress as pioneering farming communities filled the landscape and brought upon themselves increased competition for land and resources.[1] This is a theme that I developed with specific reference to the Cotswold-Severn region some years ago, arguing that architectural devices embedded in the design and construction of the long barrows provided a symbolic scheme that could be decoded by contemporary people to reveal information about identity, ownership and control.[2] In such a scheme, communities occupied defined settlement areas for appreciable periods, in some cases constructing enclosures to contain and define their activities and act as foci for the living. Simple distinctions between settlements and ceremonial sites of the kind that seem obvious to us today do not really work for the kinds of small-scale societies that must be envisaged for early farming communities in Britain. Elman Service referred to such societies as 'tribes' – groups of families or clans who believe they have descended from common ancestors and who form a close-knit community under a defined leader.[3] The land occupied by such a group becomes a territory, perhaps physically subdivided and fractured along kinship lines. In such communities everyday life is shot through with what to modern eyes seem like strange patterns of behaviour involving degrees of reverence, taboo and beliefs that transcend everything that is done; all of life in this sense is deeply embedded in the ideas that structure the way things are done.[4] Thus although communities live in one place and bury their dead somewhere else, these should not be seen as corresponding to our particular notions of ordered existence; rather, barrows and enclosures were nodal points in a scheme of the world which we have to try to understand in its own terms.[5]

During the 1980s an alternative model of early farming communities developed in which communities are seen as being highly mobile. In this view, long barrows were fixed points in extensive patterns of movement, perhaps with communities periodically meeting together at large enclosures and visiting their ancestral barrows in the neighbourhood for ceremonies and the placement of human remains belonging to those who had died since the last visit. The monuments in this scheme become permanent nodes within an impermanent world. For John Barrett, 'the temporal and spatial referents of these lives would have been known in terms of the seasons and of the distances between places . . . sites did not occupy the centers of territories so much as lie at the end of one path and the beginning of the next'.[6] Alasdair Whittle described this in terms of what he called 'tethered mobility', periodic returns to a small number of fixed points,[7] while for Julian Thomas it was engagement in such mobility and the various cycles of movement that went with it, including seasonal movements from place to place, that contributed to the development of personhood – the quality or condition of being an individual.[8] It is a tempting and seductive model, which by its nature requires relatively little archaeological evidence to support it. Indeed, its origins owe much to the apparent poverty of evidence for structures that could be considered as long-term houses or settlements. But so far as the fifth and fourth millennia BC in Britain as a whole are concerned there are certain difficulties with the peripatetic community model, not least the existence of fairly marked regional styles of material culture – pottery and long barrows are obvious cases – which at the very least suggest that perhaps the areas within which communities might have moved around were of fairly limited compass. In some areas, and the Cotswold-Severn region is certainly one, there is increasing evidence of more established settlement patterns that deserve to be considered.

Cotswold-Severn Long Barrows in Context

ENCLOSURES AND CAMPS

Within the Cotswold-Severn region more than a dozen certain and probable ditched enclosures dating to the fourth millennium BC have been identified through fieldwork and aerial photography *(77)*. Generally known as causewayed enclosures or interrupted-ditch enclosures, the rate at which previously unrecorded examples have been discovered has risen steeply in recent decades, at the same time increasing the distribution of sites into a wide range of landscapes and emphasizing the variety of shapes, sizes and construction methods.[9] Three main clusters of enclosures can be identified within the Cotswold-Severn region *(78)*: the north Wessex Downs, the upper Thames valley and the Cotswold Hills. Like the long barrows, all of these enclosures form part of much wider traditions that can again be traced back to continental Europe, to origins amongst the ditched enclosures built by *Linearbandkeramik* communities of the Rhine valley in the middle and later sixth millennium BC.[10]

North Wessex Downs

Windmill Hill lies at the heart of a cluster of enclosures on the north Wessex Downs. It was one of the first causewayed enclosures in Britain to be extensively excavated, and has since become the type-site against which other examples are compared. Alexander Keiller's excavations between 1925 and 1929 revealed that the enclosed area was massive: 360m across and covering an area of nearly 8.5ha. Three roughly concentric circuits of earthworks defined three discrete spaces or

77 Eastleach, Gloucestershire, on the eastern Cotswolds. Aerial view of a causewayed enclosure with four circuits of ditches arranged in two pairs. Looking northwest. *Photograph by Timothy Darvill, July 1986*

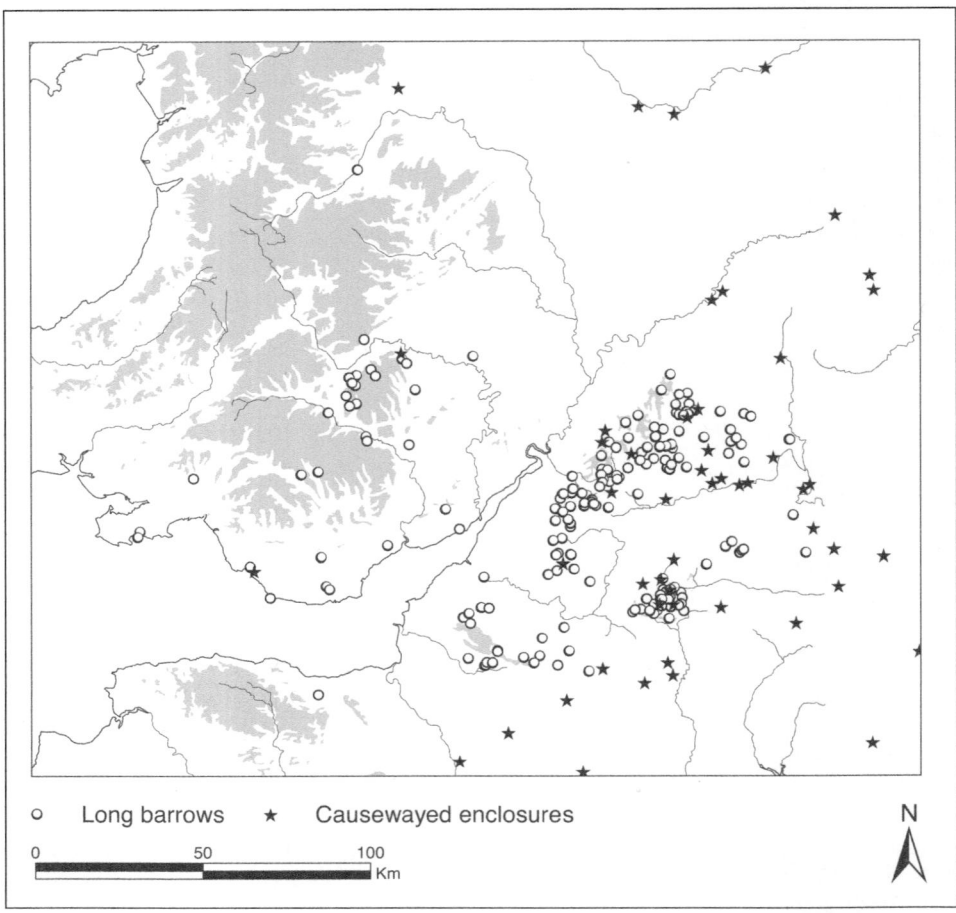

78 Causewayed enclosures and long barrows in the Cotswold-Severn region. Land over 244m OD is stippled. Enclosures after Oswald et al. 2001

zones, the outer earthwork comprising a substantial bank and outer ditch while the inner earthworks were more modest in scale. The inner enclosure appears to have an entrance that opens to the northwest, but it is not known where the entrances through the middle and outer circuit lay. The ditches had been constructed as a series of elongated pits with the result that they appeared 'causewayed' or 'interrupted', so providing a convenient descriptive term for what has become a whole class of monuments. Within the fills of the ditches were substantial assemblages of pottery, worked flint, worked stone, animal bone, human bone, personal items and carbonized plant remains. Some of this may have been deliberately placed where it was later found, especially around ditch terminals. However, much of it found its way into the ditches in a less structured way, the accumulating fills serving to trap deposits and protect them from erosion and damage. Although little was found in the areas between the ditches, it is clear that long periods of cultivation in later prehistoric, Roman, medieval and later times had truncated earlier deposits. Keiller interpreted Windmill Hill as a settlement site, although he mistakenly thought that the ditch segments represented dwellings. In bringing Keiller's work to publication, however, Isobel Smith re-interpreted the evidence and concluded that the site was a 'centre or rallying point for the population of a fairly wide area'.[11] Critical to this interpretation was the presence of pottery and stone implements brought to the site from surrounding areas. More recently still, a re-examination of the rich assemblage of finds and some new excavation led Alasdair Whittle to emphasize the symbolic nature of the site in terms of the activities that went on there – a harmony of symbols – in which space was divided up and gathering, feasting and depositing took place within a social setting that linked the past and the present, myth and memory, life and death, culture and nature.[12] Meanwhile, new studies of the local environment showed that the enclosure was originally constructed in a woodland clearing. Fieldwalking, test-pitting, geophysical surveys and small-scale excavations in the fields immediately south of the enclosure in 1992–3 revealed that activity was by no means confined within the area defined by the ditches but spilt down the sides of the hill towards the Winterbourne Stream below.[13]

Contemporary with Windmill Hill were two other enclosures: Knap Hill and Rybury. Both are less than a quarter of the size of Windmill Hill (2.4ha and 2ha respectively) and less fully explored. Knap Hill has commanding views over the Vale of Pewsey and southwards to Salisbury Plain. Its single earthwork boundary comprises an irregular heavily segmented ditch up to 3m deep and an internal bank. The enclosure lay within an area of open scrub. Even less is known of Rybury, which is situated on a spur projecting into the Vale of Pewsey, access to the main hilltop enclosure being defended on the southeast by a cross-ridge outwork.

Around these three enclosures there are about 20 long barrows *(79)*, including the three chamberless examples which all lie on the lower slopes of Windmill Hill. Adam's Grave (WIL 6) lies just 800m to the southwest of Knap Hill, set in an imposing position on the summit of Walker's Hill. Establishing the relationships between these sites from archaeological evidence is not as straightforward as it might seem. In purely human terms, there are long barrows within 10-15 minutes' walk of all the known enclosures; indeed long barrows are visible from the interior of the enclosures. Isobel Smith raised the possibility of a connection between the West Kennet long barrow (WIL 4) and the Windmill Hill enclosure by suggesting that the kind of bones missing from the long barrow (mainly skulls and upper limb bones) appeared in the ditch fill of the enclosure.[14] Drawing heavily on anthropological analogies, Julian Thomas has suggested that the circulation of human remains in this way was bound into beliefs in the potency of ancestral relics.[15] Recent studies of the animal bone and human bone assemblages from Windmill Hill side by side with each other suggest that, in terms of their deposition, animal remains were treated in the same way as human remains, as if the conversion from flesh-covered corpse to dry bones in the dark cells of a long barrow paralleled the process whereby animals were butchered, consumed and reduced to bone.[16]

Long Barrows of the Cotswolds

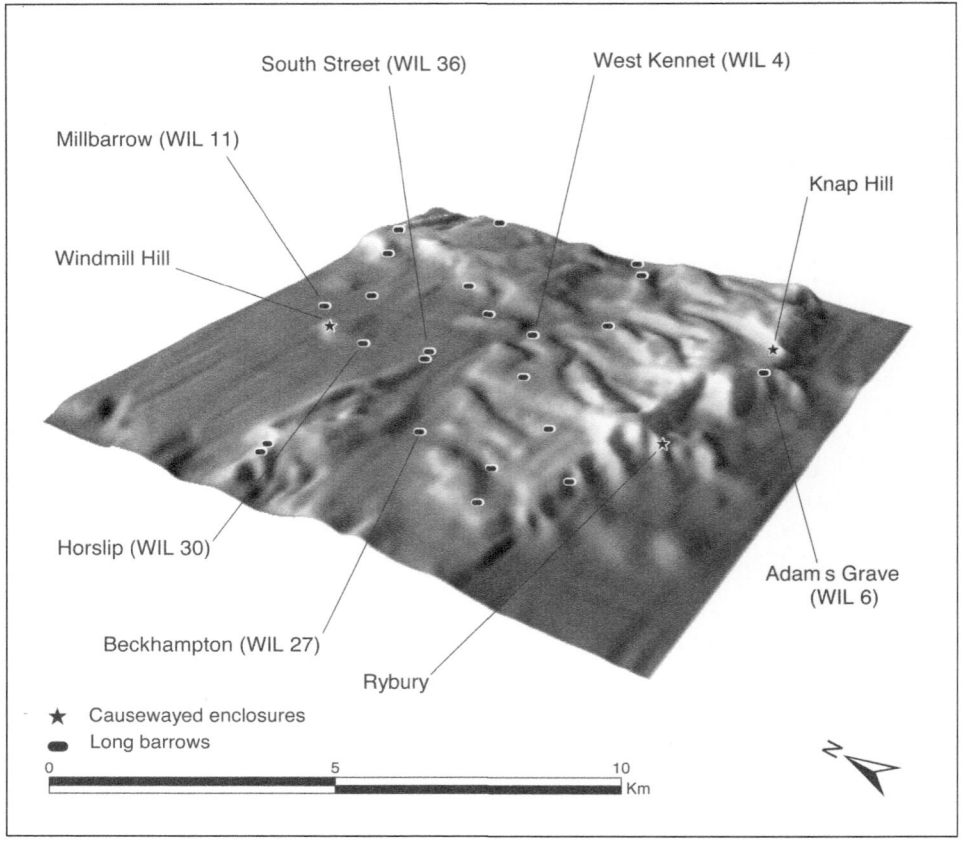

79 Topographic model of the north Wessex Downs around Avebury, Wiltshire, showing the position within the landscape of known long barrows and causewayed enclosures

Upper Thames valley

A string of ten enclosures lies mainly along the north bank of the upper Thames and its tributaries from Radley in the east to Down Ampney in the west. Of these, only the example at Abingdon has been excavated.[17] Set on a slight spur bounded by the valleys of two small streams that ran to the Thames about 1km to the south, the enclosure of about 3ha was defined by two roughly concentric earthworks running across the higher ground between the streams, the streams themselves providing the boundary on two sides. Abundant pottery, worked flint, animal remains, querns, bone and antler tools, stone axes and at least three deposits of human remains suggested to Humphrey Case that this was the farmstead settlement of perhaps five or six nuclear families,[18] a suggestion perhaps supported by Bill Startin's calculation that the inner enclosure boundary at Abingdon could have been built by a group of about 27 people over a period amounting to about three weeks.[19]

Relationships between these Thames valley enclosures and long barrows are not well documented. Abingdon has a classic oval barrow of the early third millennium BC about 100m to the east, just beyond the small stream on this side of the causewayed enclosure, the two monuments having overlapping histories because the barrow overlies what is defined below as a sanctuary-enclosure.[20] Less is known of the monuments contemporary with the mainly fourth-millennium BC occupation inside the causewayed enclosure, although about 5km to the southwest is the Drayton long barrow (OXF 21) discovered in a heavily arable landscape through aerial photography.[21] Further west these Thames valley enclosures seem to have an almost mutually exclusive distribution in relation to recorded long barrows. However, the lesson to be leant from Drayton is that because the enclosures are on low-lying and heavily cultivated land it is possible that any associated barrows have yet to be identified. Alternatively, other styles of burial monument may have been used in the area in place of long barrows during the fourth millennium BC, perhaps round barrows that are now represented archaeologically by some of the numerous ring-ditches identified through aerial photography.[22]

Central Cotswolds

Three enclosures in the central Cotswolds – Southmore Grove, the Peak Camp and Crickley Hill – are all closely associated with long barrows. Crickley Hill was discovered in 1971 during the excavation of the Iron Age hillfort on the same hilltop and was extensively excavated over 21 summer seasons down to 1993.[23] It lies on a roughly triangular spur projecting westwards from the main Cotswold escarpment into the Severn valley. Two main phases of use can be recognized, each with several sub-phases, probably spanning much of the fourth millennium BC. The earlier phase comprised a pair of roughly concentric earthworks with causewayed ditches. Later, the inner boundary earthwork was partly covered by a more substantial enclosure boundary comprising a continuous ditch with an internal stone rampart. This second phase had at least three entrances, two opening to the east and a third to the northwest. These enclosures bounded a small fortified village *(80)*. There was evidence of fences defining roads and paths, a group of at least three rectangular timber-framed houses and, towards the western end of the hill, a small shrine that started life as a paved circle. Amongst the material recovered during the excavations was a substantial amount of flint-working waste in clusters around the edge of the main settlement area.[24]

Just 1km south of Crickley Hill is another roughly triangular promontory projecting into the Severn valley, known variously as the the Peak Camp or Birdlip Hill. Here there was another enclosure, also bounded by two roughly concentric rings of earthworks. Small-scale excavations in 1980 and 1981 confirmed that the site underwent a series of remodellings and changes, here closely dated to the mid-fourth millennium BC.[25] The third site in the group, Southmore Grove, is known only through aerial photography, although fieldwalking over the area in 1985 revealed extensive spreads of worked flint.[26]

All three enclosures are spatially linked to nearby long barrows. About 1.5km north of Crickley Hill is the Crippetts Barrow (GLO 7), a very large barrow that was poorly investigated sometime before 1779 and was probably a terminal-chambered example. Some 2.2km south of the the Peak Camp is West Tump (GLO 8), excavated by George Witts in 1881 and shown to be a lateral-chambered

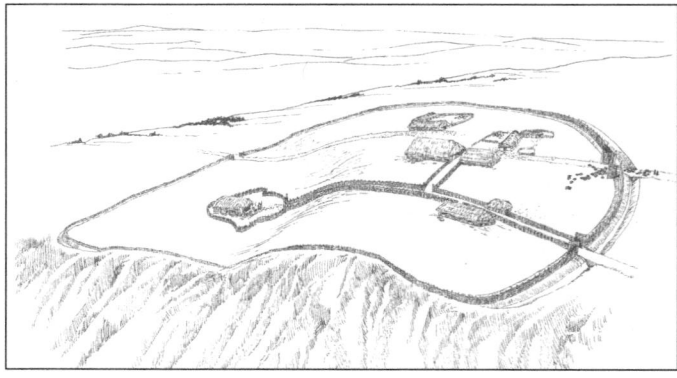

80 Reconstruction drawing of the second main phase of the enclosure on Crickley Hill, Gloucestershire, c.3200 BC. Drawing by Neville Stokes, based on illustrations and plans in Savage 1988

example. About 1.4km west of Southmore Grove there is the North Cerney II long barrow (GLO 96). It was discovered as recently as 1977,[27] less than a decade before the enclosure was recognized, but its type and layout is not known. Although the density of long barrows and enclosures in the central Cotswolds is not as great as on the north Wessex Downs, the pattern is very comparable, especially along the escarpment edge *(81)*.

Enclosures between the clusters

Around and between these three clusters of enclosures there are many other more isolated enclosures that in due course may come to represent the core of other groups. On the Cotswolds these include examples at West Kington near Nettleton, Wiltshire and Salmonsbury at Bourton-on-the-Water, Gloucestershire, both of which appear to be classic causewayed enclosures and both of which are associated with long barrows less than 3km away (GLO 90 and GLO 53 respectively).

West of the Severn, a possible enclosure at Dorstone Hill, Herefordshire,[28] lies 2.2km southeast of Arthur's Stone (HRF 1) and less than 1km northwest of the Cross Lodge (HRF 4). This extensive site covering perhaps 7ha has yielded more than 4,000 pieces of struck and worked flint and 60 fragments of polished stone axe.[29] Two enclosures discovered through aerial photography in the Ogmore valley of Glamorgan show that long barrows along the north coastlands of the Bristol Channel may also be closely associated with enclosures.[30]

The only areas within the Cotswold-Severn region where long barrows are found but enclosures appear to be absent are within the Black Mountains of Powys and the southern coastlands of the Bristol Channel and Severn estuary south of Bristol. Further reconnaissance in both these areas is likely to reveal contemporary enclosures, but care is needed because not all fourth-millennium BC enclosures look alike. The special attention given to Windmill Hill during the later twentieth century has, in many ways, distracted research from other kinds of potentially contemporary enclosures and boundary works. At Randwick, for example, the long barrow (GLO 10) lies on an upland plateau cut off from the main hill by a cross-ridge dyke of the sort that elsewhere in the country has been dated to the fourth millennium BC.[31]

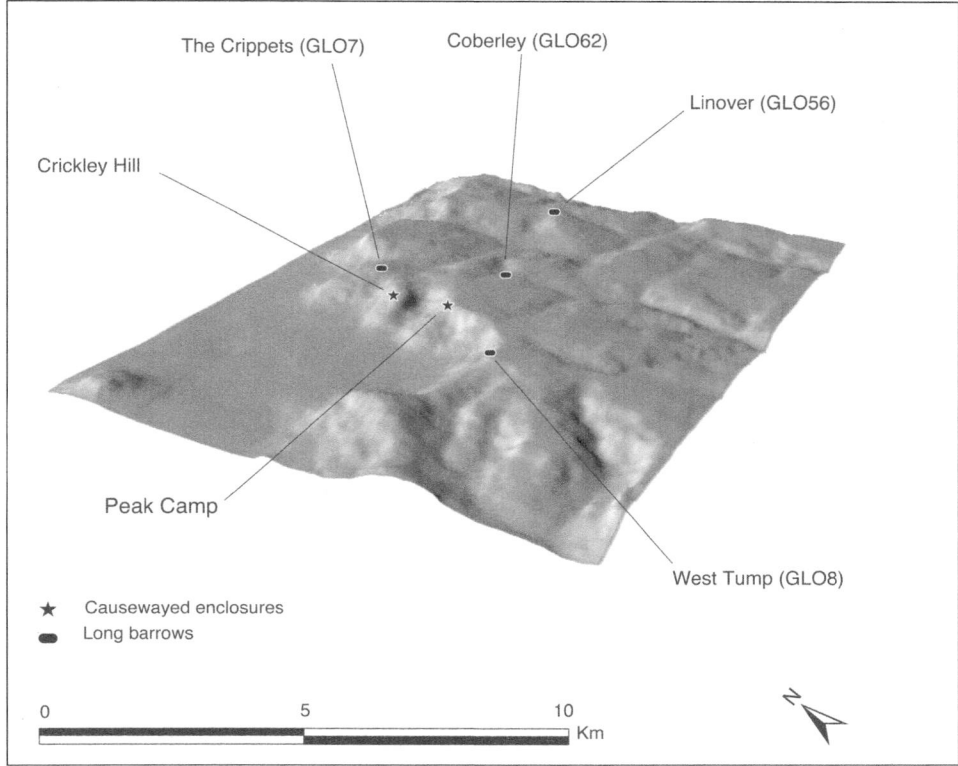

81 Topographic model of the Cotswold escarpment east of Gloucester showing the position of the causewayed enclosures at Crickley Hill and The Peak Camp in relation to nearby long barrows

NEW ENCLOSURES OF THE THIRD MILLENNIUM BC

Like long barrows, many of the enclosures constructed in the fourth millennium BC seem to have been abandoned for their primary purposes by about 3000 BC, although material from the upper ditch fills suggests some continuing small-scale activity. Already the focus of attention had moved elsewhere, in particular to new kinds of enclosure that began to appear in southern England from about 3200 BC onwards. Closely associated with these new kinds of site are exactly the kinds of pottery – Peterborough Ware, Grooved Ware and Beaker Ware – found within the blocking and final closing of many long barrows (see Chapter 7).

The most distinctive of these new kinds of enclosure are known as 'henges', circular earthworks with a bank set outside of a ditch, often associated with one or more internal stone circles, which are generally believed to be ceremonial centres. Henges are widely scattered through the Cotswold-Severn region east of the River Severn, but rather sparse west of the river. The most well-known example is Avebury, also the largest classic henge in the British Isles. This site and its landscape evolved over several centuries, with three internal stone circles, avenues approaching from the south and southeast, and connections with stone settings, timber circles, and perhaps smaller enclosures nearby. Set in the heart of a substantial group of third-millennium BC monuments, these structures perhaps continue the focal role established by the cluster of long barrows and earlier enclosures in the area.

Northwards, on the Cotswolds, there is a smaller concentration of henges and related structures around Condicote that perhaps continues the significance of the Swell area. In the upper Thames valley there are ceremonial centres of the third millennium BC that variously include classic henges, mini-henges, pit circles and cursus monuments, around Lechlade, Cassington and Dorchester on Thames, also perhaps echoing earlier concentrations of enclosures. On the Mendips there are yet more concentrations of henges around Priddy and in the valley of the River Chew is the cluster of stone circles and henges at Stanton Drew. Perhaps these sites also perpetuated the significance of ancient landscapes marked by clusters of long barrows in the neighbourhood. West of the Severn, the only reasonably certain henge is at Newton in the Ogmore valley of Glamorgan,[32] an area already noted for its third-millennium BC enclosures and long barrows.

A second group of enclosures that overlap chronologically with the later use of long barrows is the recently recognized class known as palisaded enclosures.[33] These large enclosures are distinctive in being bounded by timber walls. Little is known about them, although like the earlier causewayed enclosures they may well represent settlement of some kind. Two such enclosures were recognized in the Kennet valley south of Avebury during the late 1980s and investigated through excavation.[34] The southernmost enclosure lies just 750m to the northeast of the West Kennet long barrow (WIL 4); indeed, as noted in Chapter 7, the close proximity of these enclosures and other contemporary monuments may go a long way towards explaining the unusually high level of activity and rich third-millennium BC material culture represented at the long barrow. A pair of similar enclosures has been investigated in the Walton Basin, Radnorshire, some 25km to the north of the long barrows in the Black Mountains. For just as some centres of third-millennium BC ceremonial activity lie within earlier clusters of long barrows, others seem to be established within previously little-used areas nearby.

FLINT SCATTERS, ACTIVITY AREAS AND SETTLEMENT SITES

Natural erosion and cultivation over many millennia have combined subtly to alter the way in which archaeological sites are represented in the modern landscape. One of the most commonly recovered kinds of archaeological remains relating to the period when long barrows were used is what are generally known as 'flint scatters'. These are the transformed remains of a whole range of different kinds of activity, represented now by spreads of flint in the present topsoil. Some represent material that became scattered on an ancient ground surface, perhaps as a result of working flint, the scattered material gradually being taken down into the soil beneath through worm action and cultivation. Other flint scatters represent material that was originally incorporated in the fills of pits, ditches, postholes, or hollows in the ground but that has been moved upwards into the topsoil by ploughing and erosion. Yet other flint scatters represent previously upstanding structures that have been levelled either deliberately or through natural processes, scattering objects once in their matrix into the surrounding soil. Flint scatters then are very hard to interpret, because they are not sites in the conventional sense but only blurred manifestations of a whole host of different things that were once complete and distinctive. Thus many researchers have been disappointed when excavating flint scatters because there is often little or nothing of substance under the topsoil. To understand them fully, it is necessary to throw away the idea of discrete sites and instead think of a landscape in which every part was used in one way or another. Some places reveal themselves as 'hot-spots' of activity when measured in terms of the quantity and variety of material deposited: occupation areas, flint-working sites, rubbish disposal places and so on. Other areas seem comparatively 'cold', with only a light scatter of material resulting from casual losses and extensive activities such as manuring garden plots with household waste. Using these kinds of model, off-site archaeology as it is sometimes called,[35] it is possible to interpret some of the flint scatters and spreads found during landscape surveys that have been carried out over many years.

The Cotswolds

Robin Holgate analysed all the available large collections of worked flint from the Cotswolds and surrounding areas, suggesting as a result that amongst an extensive background scatter of low-density spreads of worked flint it was possible to identify areas used for occupation because of the presence of distinctive assemblages that included leaf-shaped arrowheads, cube-shaped two or three platform cores, ground flint axe fragments reflaked into cores, ovates, scrapers, knives, piercers, microdenticulates and other implements manufactured on blades detached from cores using soft hammers.[36] Applying this template, he found that across the eastern and central Cotswold uplands there were about 20 concentrations of worked flint suggestive of occupation sites. Taking this evidence as a whole, and recognizing that in spatial terms Holgate's samples relate to less than 10 per cent of the total landscape, it is easy to envisage a situation where each long barrow could be linked to a nearby occupation area.[37]

Support for Holgate's analysis comes from a detailed case study in the northern Cotswolds carried out by Alistair Marshall and the Cotswold Archaeological Research Group. Here, a non-selective sampling programme using a range of random, transect and grid collection patterns recognized four kinds of flint scatter, classified in this study as ranging from Grade 0 (diffuse low-density spreads peripheral to settlement areas) through to Grade 3 (intensive non-domestic flint-working areas or settlement areas). Within the study area of 19 square kilometres there were two long barrows (Belas Knap (GLO 1) and Notgrove (GLO 4)). A large Grade 3 flint scatter lay 300m south of Belas Knap on a hill spur, but being on the eastern edge of the study area it is not possible to say whether a similar association also obtained at Notgrove.[38]

Broadly similar patterns can be seen in the distribution of flints recovered by the Revd David Royce, rector of Lower Swell between 1850 and 1902. Although these were amassed over a long period and through personal collection, gifts and purchases, much is known about the provenance of the finds and these have been classified and plotted.[39] Taking the thousand or more leaf-shaped arrowheads, for example, a high proportion of them come from fields within 300m or so of a recorded long barrow. More recent studies of the flint assemblages from Cow Common and the Park suggest a substantial fourth- and third-millennium BC scatter south and east of Cow Common Long (GLO 22).[40] Unfortunately, rather little excavation has been carried out to discover what some of these intensive flint scatters result from. It is a common problem. At Birdlip, intensive fieldwalking in 1983-4 along the line of the proposed Birdlip Bypass revealed a series of low-density flint scatters, one of which lay within an area later investigated through excavation when the bypass was built. Although more worked flints were found during the excavation, all were unstratified or residual in Iron Age and Romano-British contexts.[41] Some years later, during the construction of the A419/417 from Cricklade to Birdlip, further opportunities for survey and excavation presented themselves along a much longer linear transect.[42] On this occasion, six areas containing features broadly dated to the fourth millennium BC were identified, all but one of them on the dip slope of the Cotswold Hills overlooking the upper Thames valley. Two of the sites, Hare Bushes and Norcote Farm, lay within defined flint scatters but neither yielded substantial remains. Of the remaining four sites, that at Duntisbourne Grove revealed a cluster of six pits and five postholes, while the others revealed small collections of struck flint and occasional, largely undated, bedrock-cut features. The overall impression created by the examination of the roadline is one of relatively sparse activity in which evidence relating to the fourth millennium BC occurs, on average, about every 4km.

South of the Bristol Avon and the Severn valley

South of the River Avon, extensive flint scatters have been recorded on the Failand Ridge between the Avon and the Kenn, and more sporadically along the valleys of the Yeo, Axe and Chew.[43] During the construction of the Chew Valley Lake in 1953–5, the postholes of a small timber-framed house were found below the floors of a Roman villa in Chew Park.[44] The site lies less than 5km from the Fairy's Toot (SOM 2) at Nempnett Thrubwell. Pits and spreads of settlement debris have been recorded at several other sites in the south Cotswolds, Avon valley and Mendip area, including Sandford Hill at Winscombe,[45] Charmy Down near Bath,[46] and Camerton,[47] among others. As elsewhere, most of these finds lie within 2–4km of a recognized long barrow.

In the Severn valley, flint scatters and occasional finds of pits containing pottery and worked flint of the fourth millennium BC are fairly numerous on main gravel islands and low terraces. One of the more substantial assemblages is from beside the River Severn at Gloucester, although little is known of its extent because of intensive occupation in later periods.[48] Further south, John Allen has noted the presence of flint scatters spanning the fourth to the second millennia BC on the Severn estuary levels at Oldbury-on-Severn,[49] and many more sites no doubt await discovery in the area.

The wetlands of the Somerset Levels at the southern end of the distribution of Cotswold-Severn long barrows were heavily exploited through the fourth millennium BC, with flint scatters representing probable settlements on the Polden Hills at Butterwell, Shapwick and Ashcott amongst others.[50]

North Wessex Downs and upper Thames valley

Across the north Wessex Downs around Avebury, Robin Holgate recorded six possible and eight definite domestic-type concentrations of worked flint datable to the fourth millennium BC. These lay mainly on hill-crests and the slopes of downland spurs, but included some on valley floors. Subsequently, the picture has been fleshed out through fieldwalking, test-pitting, geophysical surveys and targeted excavations around Windmill Hill. As well as confirming the geographically continuous nature of land-use in the fourth millennium BC, this work revealed a cluster of partly intercutting pits within an area showing a high concentration of worked flint in the ploughsoil.[51] Numerous similar spreads of occupation debris and small features, mainly pits and postholes, have also been recorded within or under the buried ground surfaces protected by round barrows of the second millennium BC in the area, including Avebury G55,[52] Bishops Cannings G61 and G62a on Roughridge Hill,[53] Hemp Knoll,[54] and West Overton G6b.[55] It has sometimes been suggested that the coincidence of fourth-millennium BC settlement and second-millennium BC barrows resulted from some kind of sustained memory about the significance of a particular place. But a more practical explanation is simply that the area below the round barrows is amongst the best-preserved earlier landscape we have available and, as a sample of what once existed more widely, is bound to contain fourth- and third-millennium BC material. As around Windmill Hill, there are cases where occupation evidence has been found even where not sealed by a later barrow, as at Wayden's Penning on Hackpen Hill,[56] and Waden Hill,[57] both to the southeast of Avebury and at Cherhill to the west. Cherhill lies in the bottom of a valley and upon excavation was found to comprise a series of irregular hollows that Isobel Smith and John Evans interpreted as quarries for marl to be used as daub when making the walls of houses.[58]

On the Berkshire Downs fieldwalking revealed scatters of worked flints associated with the exploitation of clay with flints, as well as possible occupation areas on the chalk uplands.[59] As around Avebury, land-use on the uplands seems to have been fairly continuous with discrete concentrations amid the background noise.

North of the Downs, in the upper Thames valley, there is widespread evidence for occupation areas around and between some of the enclosures, although they are not as numerous or substantial as the flint scatters on the Cotswolds to the west.[60] Flint scatters have been recognized around Iffley, Cumnor, Tackley and Brize Norton, for example.[61] But by far the most important evidence of fourth-millennium BC occupation has been found at Yarnton, in the upper Thames valley northwest of Oxford. Here, excavations between 1990 and 2000 in advance of gravel extraction allowed the systematic investigation of a massive area of gravel terrace on the north bank of the Thames.[62] On the lower-lying land were the postholes of a rectangular timber-framed structure 20m long by 10m wide, radiocarbon dated to 3950–3640 BC, and best interpreted as the remains of a long house *(29)*. An isolated pit nearby yielded the charred remains of what can now be recognized as the earliest bread from the British Isles, radiocarbon dated to 3620–3350 BC. And about 300m east of the house was a rectangular ditched enclosure, 60m by 30m, with a single entrance in the middle of the long southern side, similar in form to a class of monument found outside two causewayed enclosures in the region discussed further below. Only 3km west of the Yarnton house is the oval barrow at New Wintles Farm discussed in Chapter 3,[63] while less than 8km to the north is the cluster of three long barrows on the west side of the Cherwell around Shipton-on-Cherwell.[64]

West of the River Severn

Understanding settlement patterns west of the River Severn through the evidence of flint scatters and material from fieldwalking is more difficult, as opportunities are far fewer in predominantly pastoral landscapes. Diligent surface collecting in the 1930s by R.S. Gavin Robinson in and around the Golden Valley of eastern Herefordshire brought to light about 30 flint scatters, some of them very extensive.[65] It is notable that the enclosures in the Ogmore valley have yielded substantial amounts of worked flint as a result of surface collections.[66] Although evidence for half a dozen timber houses of the third millennium BC has been found in southeastern Wales, apart from the structure below the long barrow at Gwernvale no other houses of the fourth millennium BC have yet been found.[67]

MODELLING SETTLEMENT

The enclosures, flint scatters, other kinds of settlement site, and of course long barrows, are all broadly contemporary. They must ultimately have fitted together in some way, bonded together through the lives lived out by those who built and used them. We will probably never know exactly how things worked, but it is nevertheless worth attempting a general model which serves to illustrate the possibilities.[68] Many of the main relevant strands of evidence have already been introduced in this or previous chapters, all of which serve to emphasize the role of topography and environment as important considerations. Variations in landscape type and environmental diversity are key factors that influence the nature and distribution of archaeological evidence throughout the Cotswold-Severn region and both need to be taken into account. No one model will fit all situations, although the size of populations, the number of sites used and the scale of land-use may be more important than the fundamental articulations.

In topographic terms, Graeme Barker and Derek Webley have observed that many causewayed enclosures in southern England lie on or near the interface between contrasting environments,[69] and certainly this is true of many examples within the Cotswold-Severn region (see *79* and *81*). In some cases the interface is between upland and valley land; in other cases it is between a river flood-plain and the raised terraces above. One implication throughout is that the populations who used these enclosures were in the optimum situation for the effective exploitation of a wide range of resources. Equally, the enclosures were optimally situated to bring together communities whose everyday existence focused on different environments and who might therefore make complementary contributions to the overall well-being of the tribe as a whole.

Implied in this is some kind of hierarchy to the connections between sites, and certainly there are differences in the number of recorded examples of different kinds of site that may be relevant here. Although undoubtedly biased by the way that different kinds of site are recognized and brought to attention, the proportion of each is perhaps instructive: enclosures are the least numerous; long barrows are about four times as common; and major flint scatters and other kinds of settlement are perhaps twice as numerous as long barrows. Movements between these different kinds of site were undoubtedly important, whether at the everyday level of farming and carrying on essential life-sustaining tasks, or through periodic visits to more distant places and the participation in less mundane activities. The idea of fully peripatetic communities does not easily fit the archaeological evidence and even the idea of tethered mobility seems to require an ever-shortening tether.

Condensing out the archaeological patterns, it is possible to explore and illustrate the possibilities at two related scales, albeit in a very tentative and provisional way *(82)*. At a general level, it can be suggested that sub-tribal communities occupy interlocking geographically definable areas or territories, the boundaries of which may be rather fuzzy but locally known to those who directly encounter them and their neighbours. The notional centre of each territory would be an enclosure, some of which were permanently occupied, but all of which acted as periodic gathering places for the whole community *(82A)*. These enclosures were not necessarily in the geographical centre of the territory, but rather in convenient locations with good access to the range of environments accessible to the particular community. Scattered around the territory there were other settlements, variously occupied on a permanent or temporary basis. Around the enclosures and the other settlements there would be long barrows, perhaps one for each lineage or kinship group within the community. Moving in closer to the more detailed scale of particular communities *(82B)*, the location and position of the enclosure, settlements and barrows would have reflected sensitivity to the landscape, the local environment and the extent of cleared land. There is some reason to think that the barrows may have been on the edge of the cleared ground while the enclosures lay on or near the interface between critical environments. Trackways and paths connected the main elements in the settlement system and in turn linked these with the wider environment and neighbouring communities.

Crude as they are, such models help focus attention on what is known and how gaps in our knowledge about the lives of these communities might be filled. But archaeological evidence suggests that there is much more even than the basic elements of the system discussed so far. Some of these have been included on the diagrams and are discussed further in the following sections.

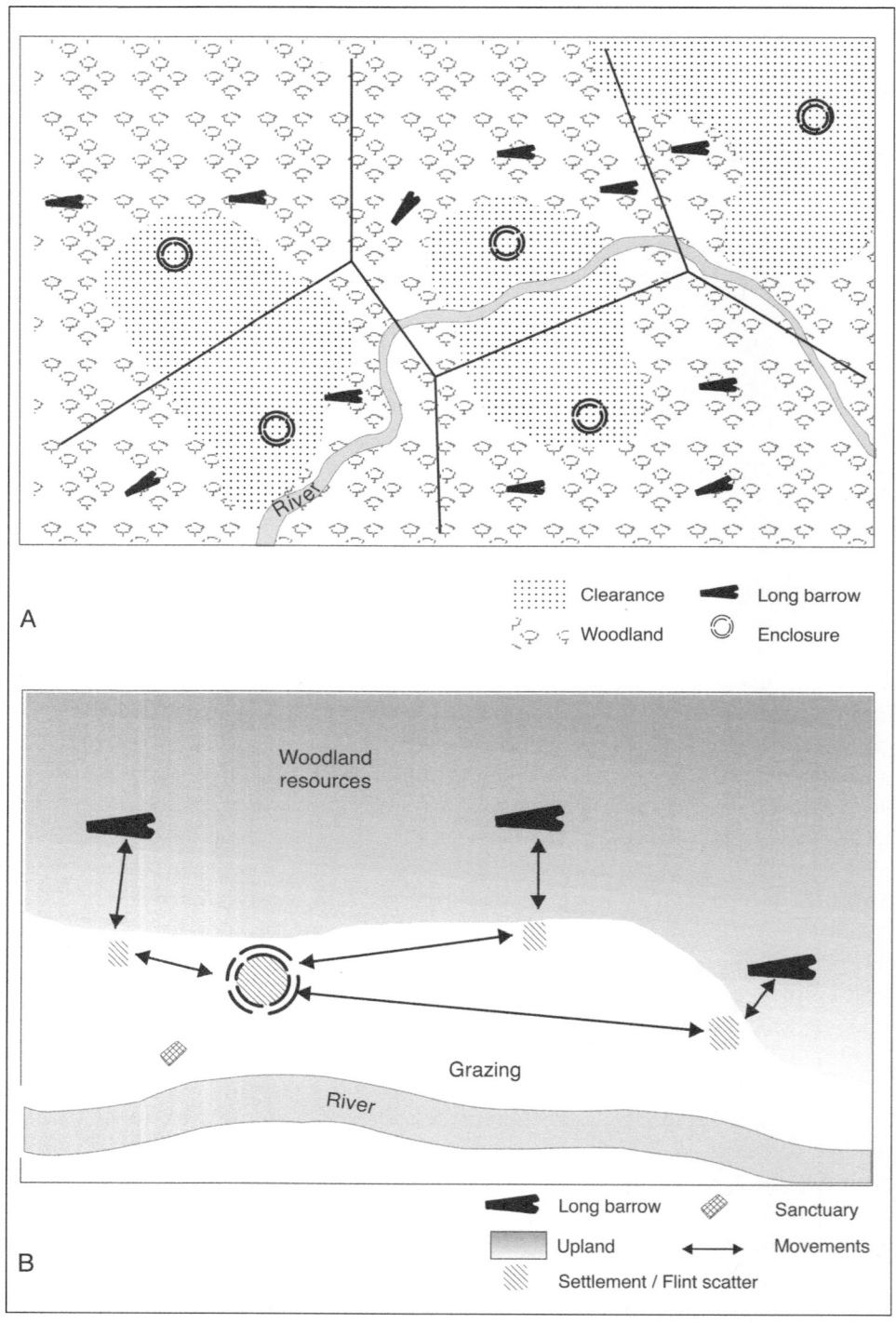

82 Idealized settlement pattern in the Cotswolds and surrounding areas. *A:* Regional system; *B:* Local system. *After Case and Whittle 1982, diagram 1 and Barker and Webley 1978, fig.3, with additions and amendments*

FLINT MINING AND AXE MAKING

One factor that will have influenced the nature and distribution of settlement on the north Wessex Downs is the availability of natural sources of flint. These were exploited through surface working and perhaps mining as well, and leave quite different yet equally distinctive signatures in the ploughsoil from the occupation debris already discussed. At flint-extraction and primary working sites, waste debris, broken nodules and part-made or broken unfinished implements predominate. Flint sources around Knap Hill, for example, seem to have been exploited from at least the later fifth millennium BC, and substantial assemblages of worked flint and working waste from the enclosures at Knap Hill, Rybury and Windmill Hill suggest that this continued down into the fourth millennium and beyond. On the Berkshire Downs, flint nodules within superficial clay with flint deposits were exploited and worked at the time.[70] The Revd Kendall published possible flint mines on Hackpen Hill, Wiltshire, in the early twentieth century, but these have since been discredited.[71] There are also suggestions of flint mines at Liddington and along the Ridgeway but again these have been questioned and rejected by recent studies.[72] The collections in Avebury Museum include many roughouts for flint axes collected on Avebury Down, suggesting that a flint-mining complex should exist in that area if ever it could be pinned down, while on Overton Down one large earthfast sarsen boulder shows clear evidence of having been used as a *polissoir* for the manufacture of flint axes *(83)*. As noted in Chapter 5, some of the stones used as orthostats in the West Kennet long barrow (WIL 4) had also been used as polishers before or during the construction of the barrow *(54)*. These industrially orientated features of the landscape add yet another layer to the range of activities happening around the long barrows.

BURIALS BEYOND LONG BARROWS

Long barrows were not the only monuments used for the disposal of the dead by communities living in the Cotswold-Severn region during the fourth millennium BC. When not covered by a long barrow, some of the early monuments discussed in Chapter 3 no doubt continued in use, and communities which did not adopt the long barrow tradition may well have built new ones. Amongst those who did use long barrows, human remains in the form of discrete burials and disarticulated skeletal elements deposited in other contexts serve to link long barrows with many other kinds of contemporary site. Indeed, there are few excavated sites of the fourth millennium BC that do not yield at least some human bone, and it is generally futile to think only in terms of 'living' sites and 'burial' places. As Martin King has emphasized, 'the dispersed patterning of human skeletal material in and around the major constructions can be viewed as the "fall-out" of a dispersed, mobile pattern of occupation where there was no strict spatial disparity between the living and the dead'.[73]

All of the excavated causewayed enclosures have yielded human remains, some in large quantity. At Windmill Hill the 1926–39 excavations revealed that perhaps

83 Overton Down, Avebury, Wiltshire. A sarsen *polissoir* in open downland within the Overton Down Nature Reserve. Scale totals 1m. *Photograph by Timothy Darvill, May 1981*

as many as 20 individuals were represented in the ditches examined, in all three circuits. A child aged two or three years of age was buried in a crouched position in the bottom of segment III of the outer ditch, while an infant aged about seven months had been placed in segment V of the outer ditch. Investigations in 1988 revealed a further burial in a pit underneath the outer bank in the southeast quarter of the circuit. The deceased was an adult male who had been deposited in a contracted position on his right side, orientated northeast to southwest.[74] Remains from at least six other people were represented by fragments from the pre-bank surface and the upper fills of the inner and outer ditches. Most odd was the immature femur of a child aged between five and seven years which had been pushed into the medullar cavity of a cattle humerus.[75]

Pit burials like the one underneath the outer bank at Windmill Hill appear rather infrequently in the archaeological literature, although this may in part be because such evidence is notoriously difficult to date in the absence of grave goods or a radiocarbon determination. More common is the presence of human bone within pits of the period, as at Roughridge Hill, Wiltshire, where human remains were found in two of the excavated pits.[76]

Interest in rivers and wet places is a well-established feature of later prehistoric ritual in Britain, but its origins lie well back in the fourth millennium BC. Numerous stone and flint axes have been found in the River Thames,[77] while one of the six human skulls from the Thames that was radiocarbon dated as part of a study by Richard Bradley and Ken Gordon proved to be of fourth millennium BC origin.[78]

Another context for the deposition of burials that to our eyes may seem entirely natural is in rock fissures and caves; to earlier communities they may have had rather different and special meanings. Two areas around the edge of the Cotswold-Severn region are well known for their caves, and both have yielded burials of the fourth millennium BC. In the Mendips, finds include remains at Chelm's Combe,[79] Sun Hole Cave,[80] Outlook Cave,[81] and Tom Tivy's Hole. At this last-mentioned site the remains of a woman aged 40–45 were found accompanied by a bone point and a small bowl very much in the style that elsewhere would be found in the chamber of a long barrow.[82] On the Gower, the main chamber of Worm's Head Cave seems to have contained scattered human remains along with worked flints and animal bones,[83] while less securely dated are the human remains from the Tooth Cave which included at least eight individuals: four adult males, three adult females and a girl.[84] Slightly more unusual is the group of human skulls representing at least six people, perhaps as many as ten, found on a ledge within a fissure in limestone rock at Ifton Quarry, Rogiet, Gwent.[85]

SANCTUARY-ENCLOSURES

Closely associated with a number of causewayed enclosures and houses in unenclosed settlements are relatively small rectangular, square, or U-shaped structures. These currently lack a name in the archaeological literature but might be regarded as sacred places and are here referred to as 'sanctuary-enclosures'. They are usually defined by a ditch, and in some cases perhaps also an internal bank, but typically they lack much by way of internal features *(84)*. Three examples within the Cotswold-Severn region are known though excavation, while another four have tentatively been recognized through aerial photography in the Avebury area.

The best-studied sanctuary-enclosure is at Barrow Hills, Abingdon, Oxfordshire, excavated in 1983–4.[86] It was found beneath the remains of an oval barrow of the early third millennium BC (see Chapter 9), the enclosure itself originating in the late fourth millennium BC, with at least three phases of recutting and remodelling *(84A)*. Initially, the enclosure was rectangular in outline, a narrow flat-bottomed ditch about 1m wide and 0.5m deep defining an area 15m by 9m. Posts had been set up at intervals around the ditch, perhaps to make the enclosure more easily recognizable to those approaching on foot.[87] This modest structure was later replaced by a slightly more substantial earthwork, U-shaped in plan, originally with two large posts set in the open end. Finally, a short curved ditch was cut across the open end of the earthwork and additional posts set up and a pit cut into the ground. Many of these features contained pottery that is contemporary with that from the Abingdon causewayed enclosure about 100m to the west. One piece of human cranium was found in the fill of the final ditch added to the southwest end of the monument, and in general the distribution of finds in the ditch fills clustered towards the southwestern end of the earthwork, suggesting that here was the focus of activity.

A rather similar small square-shaped enclosure lies about 50m east of the outer ditch of the Windmill Hill causewayed enclosure and 1,700m southwest of Millbarrow (WIL 11). About 10m square, it was surrounded by a flat-bottomed

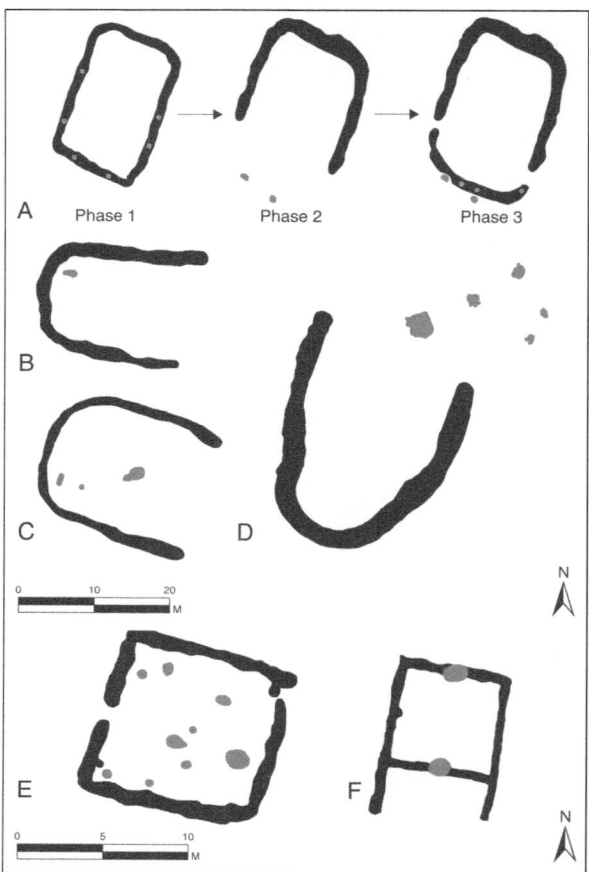

84 Sanctuary-enclosures in England and Denmark. *A:* Barrow Hills, Abingdon, Oxfordshire; *B:* North Stoke, Oxfordshire; *C:* Barford, Warwickshire; *D:* West Hill, Uley, Gloucestershire; *E:* Windmill Hill, Wiltshire; *F:* Herrup, Denmark

ditch about 1m wide *(84E)*. There were gaps in the west side and the northeast corner. Inside were about a dozen rock-cut pits, but these are generally thought to pre-date the enclosure. Finds from the ditch and the interior were very mixed in date and extend down to the Roman period, but a late fourth- or early third-millennium BC date for its initial construction seems highly likely.[88] The third excavated sanctuary-enclosure is at Uley on the Cotswold escarpment *(84D)*. Also U-shaped in plan, this enclosure is slightly larger at 25m long by 18m wide and beyond its open northeast end there are perhaps half a dozen pits and a bedrock-cut socket that may have supported a standing stone.[89] Dating evidence for the enclosure is poor, but its plan is distinctive and stratigraphically it represents the earliest phase in a long sequence of religious structures that include a shrine of the late first millennium BC, a Roman-British temple probably dedicated to Mercury and a fifth-century AD Christian basilican church.[90] The site lies just 700m south of Hetty Pegler's Tump (GLO 14) and perhaps 400m northeast of Uleybury, where there are strong indications from surface finds of flint and stone implements that a causewayed enclosure, or substantial fourth-millennium BC settlement, underlies the magnificent late prehistoric hillfort.[91]

Possible sanctuary-enclosures recognized through aerial photography include a pair of examples about 40m apart beside the Beckhampton Road southwest of Avebury. These two are 300m east of the South Street long barrow (WIL 36) and 450m northeast of the Longstones long barrow (WIL 34). Another lies north of the River Kennet, 2km southwest of the Devil's Den (WIL 8) and the final example is 100m west of the East Kennet long barrow (WIL 5).[92] The examples at North Stoke, Oxfordshire *(84B)* and Barford, Warwickshire *(84C)* were identified through aerial photography and subsequently excavated.[93]

Although relatively few in number, the excavated sanctuary-enclosures, and at least one or two of the rather less certain examples known from aerial photography and as earthworks, show a remarkable consistency in their fairly close proximity to settlements and long barrows. Several other similar structures have been recognized in other parts of southern Britain,[94] and broad parallels may also be drawn with the Tustrup-type cult houses sometimes found within a few hundred metres of long barrows and passage graves in Denmark *(84F)*.[95] Within Britain, these small apparently open enclosures may be related to a range of oval settings recognized in stone-edged, timber-edged and earthwork-edged form which appear to be connected to mortuary rituals.[96] Moreover, both the sanctuary-enclosures and the oval settings/enclosures may themselves link into a still wider set of late fourth-millennium BC traditions that focus on long narrow monuments: the rectangular enclosures christened by Richard Atkinson as 'long mortuary enclosures'[97] (typically 50–150m long) which may somehow be connected with excarnation (see Chapter 6) and the still larger elongated 'cursus monuments' (typically 170m up to 4km long) which are sometimes interpreted as ceremonial passageways through the landscape.[98]

No certain long mortuary enclosures are known within the core of the Cotswold-Severn region, although there are a number around the edge and in adjoining areas, for example at Yarnton, Oxfordshire,[99] Dorchester on Thames, Oxfordshire,[100] Barford, Warwickshire,[101] and Fengate, Cambridgeshire.[102] Cursuses also seem to lie around the periphery of the Cotswold-Severn region, for example in the middle Thames valley east and southeast of Oxford,[103] and in the valley of the Warwickshire Avon.[104] The only known examples within the main distribution of long barrows in the region are at Lechlade and Buscot in the upper Thames valley near Lechlade.[105] A possible example has been recorded in Yatesbury Field, 3km west of Avebury,[106] and more no doubt await discovery elsewhere.

WARFARE AND COMPETITION

Traditionally, the fourth millennium BC has been seen as a relatively settled, peaceful period. Increasingly, however, such a view is being called into question as evidence mounts for traumatic deaths and inter-group hostilities.[107] The evidence has two main strands: burials and enclosures.

As discussed in Chapter 6, a substantial number of burials within long barrows show evidence that the cause of death was wholly or substantially wounds inflicted by physical assaults or by arrow-shot. Amongst the most poignant is a vertebra from Ascott-under-Wychwood (OXF 6) which has an arrowhead fully piercing the person's backbone (see Chapter 6). In other cases the presence of arrowheads with damaged tips may be enough to suggest that corpses laid in the barrows originally had arrow-shot lodged in the soft tissue. By contrast, arrow-shot is very rarely found embedded in animal bone and there is little evidence for skeletal damage to animal remains as a result of hunting activities. With particular reference to the abundance of arrowheads from surface collections around Stow-on-the-Wold in the north Cotswolds, Stephen Green has argued that the density of settlement in this area was high and that the incidence of warfare increased markedly through the later fourth and third millennia BC.[108] While it seems highly likely that bows and arrows were used in the chase as well as for war, the balance of evidence suggests that human beings were the intended targets more often than animals. It can of course be argued that dispatching people by shooting them with a bow and arrow hardly proves that war was endemic; perhaps they were executed for some misdemeanour or were sacrificed during some ritual or ceremony. This is possible. Indeed, in the eyes of these early farmers there may have been no difference between ceremony and war in the way that our western way of thinking separates the two. The picture that can be built up from the individual burials must, however, be added to the evidence from enclosure sites where a much wider perspective comes into focus.

At Crickley Hill, occupation within the final enclosure appears to have come to an end in a violent fashion. More than 400 arrowheads were found choking the entrances and fanning out along the roadways into the interior. As Philip Dixon, the excavator of the site noted:

> the enclosure had quite obviously been defended against archery attack, and it is highly likely that it was built with this intention, for the low palisade formed no more than a breastwork. The ditches were presumably designed to break-up and slow down an assault and the low bank, or rather platform, would then serve as a killing ground, at point-blank range, against aggressors clambering out of the ditch.[109]

Sometime after the attack on Crickley Hill, a long mound that shows many similarities with a long barrow was built over the top of the abandoned defences, with its eastern terminal outside the former enclosure and its western terminal over the area formerly occupied by a small shrine inside the enclosure.

Arrowheads are well represented at other enclosure sites in southwestern Britain, including Hembury, Devon,[110] and Carn Brea, Cornwall, where 35 per cent of the identified flint implements were arrowheads.[111] At Hambledon Hill, Dorset, 40km south of the Cotswolds, an enclosure on the Steepleton Spur was defended by a stout timber-framed rampart through which were three entrances, each with provision for massive timber gates. The enclosure was attacked several times during its history and on at least one occasion the rampart was set alight. In two instances during excavations in the early 1980s the remains of young male attackers were found sealed underneath rubble resulting from the collapse of the rampart during raids or attacks. In one case an attacker appears to have been carrying an infant against his chest, crushing it as he fell.[112]

It would be easy to get carried away on the evidence now available, but in parts of Britain at least some inter-community warfare during the fourth millennium BC seems likely. The fact that enclosures like Crickley Hill were designed with defence in mind, as Philip Dixon suggested, perhaps shows that the idea of war was sufficiently deeply embedded within patterns of social behaviour that time and resources were invested in preparing for it. Studies of conflict and war amongst small-scale agricultural groups at other times and in other places show that such behaviour amongst fourth-millennium BC communities living in Britain should come as no surprise. Marshall Sahlins discusses how, within tribal societies, the scope for conflict is immense and is often embedded in the very fabric of society, and that peacemaking is the traditional wisdom that tribal institutions can bring to bear in order to sustain their authority and power.[113] It may be pushing things too far to follow Hobbes in believing that life in the fourth millennium BC was 'nasty, brutish and short', although Marvin Harris notes that most band-level and tribal communities engaged in some kind of inter-group combat and that in large measure this has something to do with perceived imbalances in the distribution of resources (land, cattle, women, etc.).[114] Looking across the many different strands of evidence relating to life in the Cotswold-Severn region in the fourth millennium BC, one cannot help but wonder whether the regard in which human remains were held and their placement in long barrows, pits, ditches, caves, rock fissures and rivers is not something to do with the power of the dead as trophies protected from others but occasionally liberated through combat and raiding.

SOCIETY, SETTLEMENT AND LONG BARROWS

The robustness and longevity of the long barrows stands in marked contrast to the fragility of life and the precarious social existence of the builders and users of these quite marvellous structures. For us they are fixed points in an ancient world, beacons that guide us while exploring the life and times of communities living more than 5,000 years ago. Yet to people living in the fourth millennium BC these great earth and stone structures were quite different. Amongst the questions we now have to ask is: What were these monuments for? And what did they mean to the people who built and used them? In many ways we shall probably never know, but various strands relevant to at least trying to answer these questions thread their way through the discussion of the last four chapters and can now be brought together.

Physically, the world in which the long barrows were built was a wooded landscape punctuated by clearings. Greens, browns and yellows would have been the dominant natural colours; the surface textures would have been soft and damp, and the sounds in the woods must have been muffled and disorientating just as they are in similar environments today. Clearances in the woodland, whether natural glades or hard-won breaks in cover created by the communities themselves, would have been valuable as places for occupation, building monuments, making gardens and penning livestock. Rivers and streams as well as overland tracks and pathways divided up the world into blocks, but also served to glue the blocks together by providing lines of movement and communication. Quite naturally, small clearings that are heavily used tend to get larger because regeneration is stunted and the edges of the woodland are pushed back through exploitation and manipulation. In this way the expansion and spread of settlement preserves a record of changing human relationships and social organization.

The upper Kennet valley and the north Wessex Downs are the most intensively studied part of the Cotswold-Severn region in terms of the changing environment, cultural sequence and patterns of monument distribution.[115] Alasdair Whittle has shown that the basic settlement pattern of the area was established during the sixth and fifth millennia BC by hunter-gatherer groups based along the main river valleys but periodically exploiting the adjacent uplands in a fairly low-intensity way. During the early fourth millennium BC this changed, with the gradual expansion and infilling of the landscape starting in the uplands, especially around the headwaters of the Kennet, before spreading down into the river valleys. In this process, Whittle suggests, the area was effectively colonized from the outside by people who took over what were presumably perceived as under-used areas of land for the construction of monuments and settlements 'either offshoots from a primary colonizing population coming in from abroad or part of an indigenous population pressured into change, or some mixture of the two'.[116] It cannot be assumed, however, that the same processes happened elsewhere in the Cotswold-Severn region. In the upper Thames valley Robin Holgate has found that occupation areas rich in fifth-millennium BC flintwork broadly coincide with the areas used during the fourth millennium BC, suggesting perhaps a high degree of continuity. It is also notable that on the Cotswold Hills some of the areas with dense concentrations of long barrows are the same areas in which early styles of monument are common, and which also coincide with concentrations of sites of the fifth millennium BC.[117] Continuity may again be the norm here and, as suggested in Chapter 4, some of the earliest monuments may indeed have been built by hunter-gatherer groups.

By the middle of the fourth millennium BC, long barrows were regularly constructed and used throughout the Cotswold-Severn region by communities who also built and used large earthwork enclosures for short-term and long-term occupation. In some cases they lived in small defended hilltop villages. Ian Hodder has suggested that the physical separation that exists between the long barrows and the concentrations of habitation may have been part of the very changes in the way that people saw the world around them and the reason that people built long barrows at all. He suggests that 'the drama of the control of nature would thus be enhanced by the very construction of the tomb in more distant and marginal places . . . the gradual extension of the domus away from the domestic sphere'.[118] But scale is also an important issue. A few long barrows are certainly massive and must have been incredibly impressive structures. Most though are more modest and, while certainly monumental, were hardly awesome. Many lie in impressive positions within the landscape, but they rarely exploit truly magnificent locations such as hilltops and vantage points. If the environmental evidence is right, most lay in woodland clearances rather than in open country, and thus people must have stumbled upon them rather than admired them from afar.

It is easy to romanticize the experience of visiting a long barrow in the fourth millennium BC. For most of the time these were deserted and perhaps rather spooky places out in the wild. Activity at barrows seems to have been periodic and not especially intensive. Evidence for funerary feasts and ceremonies is at best scant and in many cases almost non-existent. When they were not in use, access to the internal spaces was blocked off by walls and closing slabs. Anyone lighting upon a barrow more than a few years old would have found a crumbling mound, perhaps with a few rotting animal heads pinned to the outer revetment wall and the remains of some broken pots on the mound or scattered on the floor around about. Getting into the barrows probably meant shifting stones and rubble, dismantling sections of wall, lifting off a capstone or two, or removing timber planking. Getting inside the deeper spaces inside the barrow was made difficult by architectural features embedded into the very design of the passages and chambers. Accessing a long barrow was not glamorous. But the architecture almost certainly embodied what might be termed a discursive knowledge – myriad messages to those who encountered it.[119] Here scale may again be important, as such referencing was probably overwhelming and nested in the sense of embracing a scheme of interlocking and overlapping meanings ranging from the very general to the highly particular. We cannot know them all, but from what can be seen in these monuments a few informed guesses may be made. At a very broad scale, the barrow may have been a symbol of identity marking an attachment between a specific community and its land, tying human or spiritual ancestors to the earth in a particular place and physically demonstrating issues of ownership, identity and access for anyone that needed reminding. More particularly, the structure of the barrow and its architecture may have carried a basic set of cosmological references explaining the very fact of existence and the nature of the world – the cycle of birth, adolescence, adulthood and death – clearly visible in human life and mirrored in the lives of plants and animals, movements of celestial bodies and the passing of the seasons. As part of this, it may metaphorically represent a contemporary or a remembered domestic house, highlighting a parallel provision for the well-being of the living and the dead. By being placed in the barrow, people may metaphorically have been returned to their ancestral home or spiritual home.

At a more intimate level the barrow may represent the female body and its role in biological and social reproduction. Finally, at the most detailed scale of all, individual architectural elements may be identified with simple opposing categories, for example male :: female; wild :: domestic; back :: front; life :: death; light :: darkness; public :: private, which collectively gave life its meanings. Anyone visiting the barrow would be able to read such meanings in what was before them – the shape of the stones, the symmetry of the entrances, the form of the mound and so on – in the same way that today we can read the architecture of a Christian church or a Muslim mosque. But it was those same meanings embedded in the architecture that also structured movement around and within the monument, and which gave potency to the actions and events that unfolded in particular locations.

One feature that is central both to the physical manifestation of long barrows and to the activities that took place within and around them is an association with deposits of human remains. Although not all examples contain purpose-made repositories for these remains, most do. A hundred years ago, burial was seen as the primary function of long barrows; now it is seen as an ancillary function. Ian Kinnes has suggested that the chambers should not be seen as burial places *sensu stricto*, but rather as temporary housing or storage for the dead, removal being as common as deposition.[120] It is a theme taken up by Mary Baxter, who notes that these communities 'did not simply dispose of their dead; they handled them repeatedly and shifted them about'.[121] Inside the barrows, there were carefully constructed spaces that allowed the separation of men from women and children from adults. But our categories for thinking about the quick and the dead are undoubtedly inadequate to deal with such partitioning in the fourth millennium BC. Mortuary rituals such as we find evidenced in long barrows may be concerned with one or more of all sorts of activity: creating passages along which people could pass in the journey between life and death; the intervention of the ancestors in the world of the living, perhaps through necromancy or the prediction of the future by supposed communications with the dead; or simply a repose appropriate to certain specific stages in a much bigger cycle involving birth, life, death and rebirth. Drawing on anthropological and sociological studies of small-scale agricultural societies, Julian Thomas has argued that there is a difference between the dead and the ancestors, and that defleshing of the dead must occur 'before the individual can join the community of the ancestors'.[122] Thus we might suggest that as the body decays so does its attachment to the social life of which it was a part. Once fully detached from that life the disembodied person becomes part of another world which is accessible to living people only at particular places where the ancestral and the contemporary can meet. This perhaps is the social role of the long barrow – a place where worlds collided and the inhabitants of each could move freely from one to the other. But what kinds of worlds were they?

Archaeological evidence inevitably focuses our attention on structures, objects and physical remains of past actions, but as Aeron Watson has emphasized, for the people who attended long barrows for ceremonies and rituals it was the *sensations* they experienced that were important – a world of sounds, smells, real or perceived images and heightened emotions.[123] Whether witch-doctors, shamans, or priests of some kind led people on journeys out of themselves we cannot say for sure, but it is easy to imagine the effects of music, dance, flickering fires, fasting and perhaps ingested hallucinogens gradually drawing people into altered states of consciousness, away from everyday existence into mysterious, mythical, magical worlds beyond.[124]

People of the Cotswolds and surrounding areas were not alone in having these experiences. The widespread occurrence of long barrows and related monuments across northwest Europe and the off-shore islands along the Atlantic coast suggests that whatever these structures meant, and whatever transformations of body and mind they led to, it was an understanding and encounter shared by many small-scale dispersed populations of the period. Local and inter-regional exchange was most likely the means by which a great deal of knowledge was spread and beliefs reinforced. Such exchanges are evident not only in the design of the long barrows but also in the spread of exotic stone and flint axes transported many kilometres from their sources, pottery that was moved over considerable distances, ornaments and personal items in exotic materials and occasionally even the stones used to build the monuments themselves.[125] People moved between areas, using rivers and tracks carrying ideas and ways of seeing the world as well as objects and possessions. In the Somerset wetland some communities invested heavily in the construction of tracks down into the lower ground, implying yet again that these were probably fairly settled populations based within an established territory.[126] On a broader scale, the identity of these people can perhaps be glimpsed in their treatment of common kinds of material culture. The pottery used within the Cotswold-Severn region is rather similar from the upper Thames valley across to the Gower Peninsula, but contrasts with that used by communities living, for example, in the Southwest Peninsula, in the middle and lower Thames valley, or in the Midlands.[127] Equally, the long barrows that each group built individually translated widely held principles into local traditions.

The existence of broad social groupings promotes rather than obviates the need for regional gatherings of various sorts and some of the earthwork enclosures would have provided very suitable arenas for such events. Nor does large-scale social cohesion preclude hostility and warfare. Indeed, coming together and breaking up – social fusion and fission – is a common feature of small-scale societies, especially when there is increasing competition for relatively scarce resources such as women, cattle, or crops. Taking them from a neighbour is seen as a more effective way of acquiring such resources than waiting for them to reproduce. In the end such a system may in a sense have been too successful. With the pace of change quickening, external pressures and influences building and the role of a few individuals shifting from simple leadership to that of a chieftain, by the turn of the third millennium it was time to turn away from the traditional ancestral authority and embrace new ideas and different ways of life in which long barrows could no longer play a significant role.[128] Because of their robust construction, however, long barrows remained highly visible features in the landscape and contributed to the lives of future generations in ways that their builders could never have imagined.

9

AFTER THE LONG BARROW TRADITION

There is no good evidence that long barrows in the Cotswold-Severn region, or indeed anywhere else in Britain, were constructed much after 3000 BC, and any lingering interest in their original purpose and role seems to run out a few centuries later. As discussed in Chapter 7, the latest ceramics relating to the use of long barrows are Peterborough Ware,[1] while various ceramic traditions of the middle and later third millennium BC are found in blocking deposits inserted into entrances, passages, chambers and forecourts. But while the early third millennium BC marks the end of the long barrow tradition itself, it was not the end of interest in them. As discussed in Chapters 1 and 2, long barrows have remained visible features in the landscape since their abandonment, and have played an active role in the making, shaping and understanding of the world as seen by many generations since. So what caused their demise? How did communities of the third and second millennia BC treat them? And how did later societies regard them and use them?

3000 BC: THE CHANGE OF AN ERA

The centuries either side of 3000 BC seem to mark a period of rapid change within the Cotswold-Severn region and beyond. Not only did long barrows fall out of use, but much the same also happened to causewayed enclosures and other kinds of contemporary settlement. Long barrows were caught up in much wider patterns of social metamorphosis. They were replaced by new kinds of monuments and the reawakening of interest in earlier styles of structure such as round barrows and oval barrows (see below). Culturally, these changes were initially associated with the appearance of impressed ware pottery, Peterborough Ware and Grooved Ware, and later the spread and adoption of corded ware, including Beaker Ware. Henges, stone circles, pit circles, timber circles, hengi-forms and ring ditches all appear as part of this horizon, perhaps the physical expression of intellectual challenges to long-held and deeply felt beliefs and the final blow to the long barrow tradition.

Using the evidence of tree growth represented by the ring patterns preserved in ancient timbers, Mike Baillie has argued that around 3200 BC there was some kind of catastrophic event in the northern hemisphere, perhaps a major volcanic eruption, that adversely effected environmental conditions and climate.[2] On its own such an event may not have contributed much to changes in belief systems and ways of looking at the world, but as part of a series of cumulative processes it could have been decisive. Across much of Europe this was the period when people as individuals became more important than places. Personal possessions took over from communal effort. On a continental scale, objects in gold and bronze began to circulate, and drinking took centre stage in many rituals. The changes are well represented in the design and orientation of ceremonial monuments. They tended to be round rather than long, and cosmological references shifted towards an interest in the sun and its movement across the heavens.[3] In the upper Thames valley these changes can be seen in the evolution of one specific ceremonial centre: Dorchester on Thames. Here a long mortuary enclosure and various relatively small associated elongated enclosures and barrows dating to the late fourth millennium BC were replaced in the centuries after 3000 BC by a large cursus monument on a revised alignment. The early monuments share a common alignment and could have been directed towards the rising moon. The cursus has a clear solar alignment and the easterly section of the monument appears to have been directed towards the midwinter sunrise. Small hengi-form monuments and a large double-entranced henge were then added to the cluster of monuments, variously perpetuating and expanding alignments on solar events.[4] A similar shift in orientation and design is visible at one of the most well-known henges in Europe: Stonehenge, Wiltshire. Here the entrance of the early earthwork was moved a few degrees eastwards to open towards the midsummer sunrise, while a stone circle made of bluestones from southwest Wales was constructed within the enclosure.[5] What happened at Dorchester on Thames and Stonehenge was part of a pattern that was repeated around the British Isles: not a rapid change but rather, as Richard Bradley has suggested, 'the culmination of a process of interpretation and reinterpretation that in some areas had been going on for hundreds of years'.[6] Thus the end of the long barrows should be seen not as a short-fire rejection of earlier traditions, but rather as a gradual disenchantment with what they represented.

LONG BARROWS IN THE LATER THIRD AND EARLY SECOND MILLENNIA BC

Not surprisingly, blocked and eroding long barrows throughout the Cotswold-Severn region seem to have attracted very little attention during the middle and later third millennium BC. Although Beaker pottery has been recorded in the fills of chambers, passages, entrances and forecourts at about ten long barrows in the region, only one formal single grave with associated Beaker pottery has been found. This is at Sale's Lot (GLO 94) where a grave had been dug into the top of the mound about half way along its length. In the grave was the skeleton of an adult male about 40 years old, laid with his head to the east and a short-necked style beaker by his feet to the west. A small fragment of copper adhering to a piece of bone may be part of an earring.[7] Of comparable date, but not directly associated with Beaker pottery, is a burial at the West Kennet long barrow (WIL 4). Here the complete skeleton of a child less than one year old was found on the top of the fill in the southeast chamber. It had almost certainly been placed there by lifting the original capstone.[8] At Ascott-under-Wychwood (OXF 6), human bone from outside the chamber area was dated to 1930–1680 BC and must therefore relate to a similar horizon, but we must await the full publication of the excavations to understand the context.

Less well dated is a slab-lined cist cutting through the outer revetment wall of the southeast horn at Penywyrlod (BRE 14), found during excavations in 1972. Although damaged when the site was discovered by quarrying, the skull of a child and various other bones belonging to several adults were recovered.[9] A late third- or second-millennium BC origin for this cist seems likely, although dating such structures in the absence of grave goods is extremely hazardous. At Wayland's Smithy (BRK 1) a single grave about 4m to the west of the long barrow, between the mound and the quarry ditch, contained the partially disturbed crouched inhumation of an adult male with his head to the north. No accompanying grave goods were found, but a date in the later third or early second millennium BC has been suggested, perhaps contemporary with burials made in nearby ring-ditches.[10] Finally, at Hetty Pegler's Tump (GLO 14), workmen putting up a fencepost in 1965 brought to light parts of a female skeleton outside the western end of the mound, but yet again no details of its precise context and date are known and it may well be much later.[11]

The insertion of these burials into earlier mounds suggests some continuing reverence for their special character and symbolic meaning, but the relatively small number of identified cases suggests it was a minority interest. Perhaps a few scattered communities, or a sub-culture within them, were trying to perpetuate the 'old way' and maintain some kind of traditional identity within a 'remembered' or mythical past. Or maybe these mounds were occasionally just convenient places to dig graves, out of the way of cultivation and the demands on land that farming made.

Some evidence for the marginal position of long barrows, and a degree of disregard for their earlier importance, can be seen in changes to the local environment. Bob Smith noted that in the Avebury area many of the earlier clearances show evidence for an upsurge in bracken, hazel and thorn-scrub after about 3000 BC.[12] Through studying the snail shells represented in the gradually filling quarry ditches and pits of long barrows across southern and eastern England, John Evans has noted a great deal of regularity in the way that the environments around these sites change after their abandonment. Using data from the fills of ditches at sites in north Wiltshire, Dorset and Lincolnshire, he noted the formation of marked stabilization horizons after brief periods of initial natural erosion. These horizons represent up to a millennium of accumulation and typically show a period of woodland regeneration during the early third millennium BC followed by periods of cultivation and grassland from about 2500 BC onwards through into the mid-second millennium BC.[13] At South Street (WIL 36), the unfilled ditches of the long barrow were ploughed over by about 2000 BC, Beaker pottery being introduced into the accumulating fills along with soil and chalk eroding from the exposed broken ground around about. Ploughmarks relating to this cultivation were revealed in trenches east of the barrow.[14] As elsewhere, cultivation in this period showed no reverence or concern for the long barrows, and John Evans has associated these changes with widespread land reorganization.[15] Something similar has been noted at Wayland's Smithy, where field boundaries and an essentially agricultural landscape established in the early second millennium BC prevailed by about 800 BC.[16] At Hazleton North (GLO 54), a stabilization horizon in the fill sequence of the quarry pits can be equated with the use and abandonment of the long barrow and the local regeneration of woodland. Above this horizon the deposits were quite different: colluvial sediment resulting from soil erosion prompted by cultivation in the vicinity. The snails living in the quarries at this stage show that the area was essentially open country, the clearance of the woodland in the second millennium BC perhaps being linked with increased agricultural activity in the area.[17]

BARROW BUILDING AND BURIAL AFTER LONG BARROWS

Parallel with the decreasing interest in long barrows was a revival of interest in other kinds of burial monument. Within the Cotswold-Severn region two kinds of structure found as far back as the early fourth millennium BC, and certainly pre-dating the construction of long barrows, namely oval barrows and round barrows, enjoyed a new popularity after the tradition of building long barrows faded. It seems likely that in some areas of Britain the use of oval barrows and round barrows continued through the later fourth and early third millennia BC, contemporaneously with the construction of long barrows elsewhere, and this may have preserved their appeal. Thus their reappearance in the Cotswolds and around about is perhaps to do more with social dynamics, alliances and shifting patterns of belief than with continuity of earlier traditions. Indeed, as already noted, during the early third millennium BC there is an extremely widespread interest in circular designs for monument construction across northwest Europe and this may provide the inspiration for their adoption in the Cotswolds and surrounding areas.

Oval barrows
Oval barrows were never common in the Cotswold-Severn region and the only certain example of third-millennium BC date lies right on the eastern margin of the area at Barrow Hills, Abingdon, north of the River Thames, immediately east of the Abingdon causewayed enclosure. Excavations in 1983–4 revealed that the site developed through at least five main phases of building and rebuilding, starting

Long Barrows of the Cotswolds

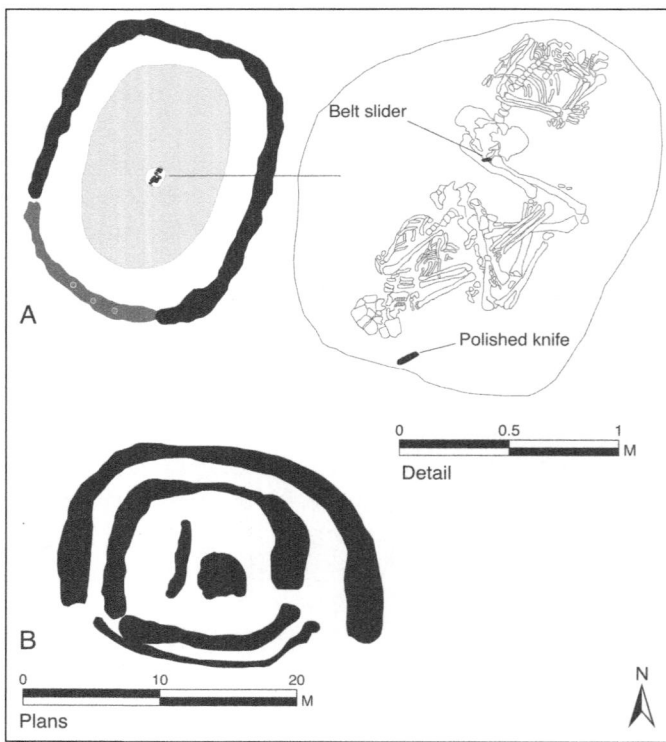

85 Oval barrows of the third millennium BC in the upper Thames valley and north Wessex Downs. *A:* Barrow Hills, Abingdon, Oxfordshire; *B:* Avebury, Wiltshire. *A:* after Bradley 1992, figs 4 and 5; *B:* after Bewley et al. *1996*

with a sanctuary-enclosure in the later fourth millennium BC (see Chapter 7).[18] In the early third millennium BC the enclosure was replaced by an oval barrow *(85)*. At least two phases were recognized in the construction of the ditch. Initially the low gravel mound was surrounded on three sides by a U-shaped ditch, but later a short arc between the original terminals closed the open western end to complete the circuit in a manner that is wholly characteristic of oval barrows built in the third millennium BC. As with the sanctuary-enclosure before, the distribution of finds in the ditch fills showed a marked preference for the deposition of material towards the western part of the structure. Under the mound was a central grave containing two crouched inhumation burials. They shared the alignment of the enclosed area, but their heads were at opposite ends of the grave pit and their legs were laid across each other. To the northeast was the burial of a man aged 30–35 who had a polished jet belt-slider near his waist. To the southwest was a woman also aged 30–35 accompanied by a polished flint knife. They appear to have been deposited at the same time, but the radiocarbon dates suggest that the male is earlier than the female, although both fit comfortably within the middle centuries of the third millennium BC as their associated grave goods suggest.

Other possible oval barrows have, however, been noted over the years. One, first recognized in 1995 through aerial photography, lies in the northwestern quadrant of the Avebury henge, less than 100m west of the Red Lion public house. Subsequent geophysical surveys and detailed plotting of available aerial

After the Long Barrow Tradition

photographs suggest that this barrow strongly resembles the Barrow Hills oval barrow, with two concentric oval ditches, the larger with a long axis measuring about 25m, surrounding a low mound in the centre of which there appears to be a pit.[19]

Round barrows

Round barrows are far more numerous than long barrows in the Cotswold-Severn region, and while many date to the early centuries of the second millennium BC, an increasing number are being dated back into the later third millennium. On the Cotswolds, some of these round barrows contain central chambers with multiple inhumations in a style reminiscent of long barrow burial practices. The Soldier's Grave at Frocester lies 210m north of the Nympsfield long barrow (GLO 13), in an equally impressive position on the Cotswold escarpment. Excavations by Elsie Clifford in 1937 showed that the stone mound was 17m in diameter and stood 2.5m high *(86A)*. In the centre was a boat-shaped rock-cut pit lined with dry-stone walling. It contained the partly disarticulated remains of at least 28 individuals (23 adults and 5 young people) and perhaps as many as 44 individuals, together with bones of ox, pig and dog. A few small pieces of pottery from within the chamber are most likely of the later third millennium BC, related perhaps to the Peterborough series in the area.[20] Further north, at Barrow Piece Plantation,

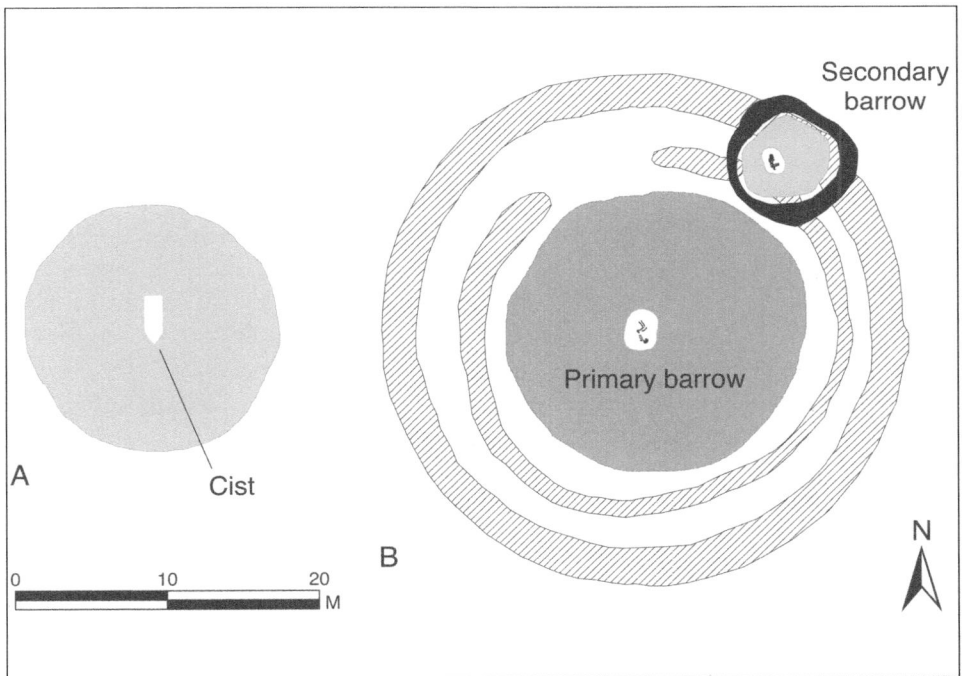

86 Round barrows of the middle and later third millennium BC in the Cotswolds and surrounding areas. *A:* Soldier's Grave, Frocester, Gloucestershire; *B:* Linch Hill Corner, Oxfordshire. *A: after Clifford 1938b, fig. 2; B: after Grimes 1960, fig. 63*

Coberley, a round barrow 15m in diameter and perhaps 0.5m high was excavated by Captain Bell and W.H. Gomonde on 29 April 1845 and again by Henry Bird on 1 March 1860 to reveal a central rectangular cist lined with dry-stone walling in which were the remains of at least seven individuals, apparently including both males and females.[21] Further north still, at the Waste, Hawling, what seems to have been a round mound covering an unusual central cist was found in the late nineteenth century as a result of quarrying for road stone. The cist was made of stone slabs set end to end with dry-stone walling between and large flat roofing slabs. Inside the cist were seven bodies, apparently all in crouched position.[22] All these examples show many similarities with the long barrow traditions in terms of their construction and burial rite. But round barrows did not always cover multiple inhumations.

At Linch Hill Corner, Oxfordshire, excavations in 1940 in advance of gravel extraction revealed a multi-phase round barrow *(86B)*. The first barrow was defined by a relatively narrow penannular ditch, 6.5m in diameter with an opening to the northeast, outside of which was a slightly larger ditch 8m in diameter. In the centre was a burial pit containing the partly crouched inhumation of a young woman, buried half on her back on her right side with her head to the south. A flint knife and a jet belt-slider were found together on the floor of the grave against her left forearm. They are of very similar form to the flint knife and jet belt-slider from the oval barrow at Barrow Hills described above. After the ditches of this monument had silted up a second smaller barrow was built partly overlapping the ditches on the northeast side. The quarry ditch was 3.5m in diameter. Near the centre was a grave containing a crouched inhumation deposited in a wooden coffin set on a northwest to southeast axis. The body was that of a young man whose corpse had been tightly crouched to fit within the coffin. His head was to the north, and above his shoulders, behind the head, was a short-necked beaker. By his waist was a bone pendant or belt fitting and behind his legs were six flint barbed and tanged arrowheads. Beside the grave to the northeast was a small pit containing animal bones, including part of the skull of a sheep.[23] This burial monument lies within an area of the lower Windrush valley that seems to have developed as a ceremonial focus in the third millennium BC, at the centre of which was the henge monument containing a stone circle known as the Devil's Quoits,[24] in many respects rather similar to the concentration of round barrows centred around Condicote and Rollright in the north Cotswolds.[25]

Single grave burials under round barrows of the later third millennium are well represented in the Cotswold-Severn region, many of them containing Beaker pottery. On the Cotswolds these include Ivy Lodge Farm at King's Stanley, Lechmore at Horsley, Rollright and Bredon Hill. But examples are also represented in the major river valleys, emphasizing the expansion of settlement and agriculture at this time: Prestbury, Barnwood and Frampton on Severn show the trend in the Severn valley, while the flat cemeteries of three graves at Hill and Moor continue the pattern into the Avon valley.[26] Mention has already been made of the succession of burials at Linch Hill Corner, Oxfordshire, in many ways typical of the later third and early second millennia BC in the upper Thames valley.

Other examples in Oxfordshire include Radley, where the grave goods included a pair of gold earrings, flint arrowheads and a beaker, Cassington and Yarnton.[27] In the upper Thames valley in Gloucestershire, beaker burials are known at Shorncote and Lechlade.[28]

West of the Severn there are round barrows with beaker-accompanied burials at Riley's Tumulus, Merthy Mawr Warren, in the Ogmore estuary, Cwm Du, Brecknockshire and Ystradyfodwg, Glamorgan.[29] A large round barrow 27m in diameter at Crick, Monmouthshire, covered a central cremation of a young woman. The kerb included two stones with rock art in the form of multiple cup-marks; both decorated stones lay on the east side of the mound, one to the southeast, the other to the northeast. Finds were sparse and dating is difficult, but worked flints from a secondary burial and the matrix of the mound suggest a date late in the third or early second millennium BC.[30]

On the north Wessex Downs there is a diverse range of pit graves, small cemeteries and round barrows of later third-millennium BC date. Many are associated with the great henge monument at Avebury, where burials of the period include some deposited at the foot of the stones within the henge and along the West Kennet Avenue. Round barrows were also important. At West Overton, Isobel Smith and Derek Simpson excavated barrow G6b in 1963. The central primary burial was that of an arthritic male in excess of 40 years old, accompanied by a beaker, an antler spatula, two slate objects, a bronze awl and a flint knife, fabricator and flake. The grave itself had been lined with slabs of sarsen, but one had toppled before the corpse was laid in the grave, perhaps as the body was being lowered into the pit. The associated grave goods suggested to the excavators that this was the burial of a leatherworker. A deposit of cremated bone including the remains of an adult and a child was put in the grave as the fill was being inserted. Around the grave was a low ring-bank of flint and sarsen about 6m in diameter. Two burials were sealed by the ring-bank and date to the time of its construction: an infant of nine months and a child of four. Sometime later a further six burials were added inside the ring-cairn in the northwest quadrant, the inhumations of three children and three cremations and later still a round barrow was raised over the whole group.[31] Nearby, on a prominent spur overlooking the shallow dry valley now followed by the Avebury to Devizes road (A361) at Hemp Knoll, a single-phase round barrow covered a deep central grave and the burial of a child placed on the old ground surface to the northwest. The central grave contained the crouched inhumation of an adult male buried within a rectangular wooden coffin.[32] Also in the coffin was a worn greenstone wrist guard, a broken bone toggle and a Beaker pot. During the burial ceremony an ox-hide with the skull and foot-bones still attached had been draped over the coffin, most of the bones coming to rest in the southeast corner of the grave. Part of a red deer antler lay in the northwestern part of the grave. The presence of the ox-hide links this burial backwards in time to the rituals carried out perhaps a thousand years earlier, before the construction of the Beckhampton Road long barrow (WIL 27; see Chapter 3); similar burials are also known from broadly contemporary barrows across much of northern Europe suggesting the continuity of some kind of cattle-cult.[33]

The incidence of single burials under round barrows increases through the last few centuries of the third millennium BC, and after 2000 BC such barrows became almost ubiquitous and the standard form of burial monument throughout the British Isles. At the same time, relationships between existing long barrows and the new styles of round barrow seem to get stronger, maybe as the users of long barrows become more distant memories, more benign, and perhaps even slightly revered for their achievements. While burials accompanied by Beaker pots are usually set apart from long barrows, cremations associated with collared urns and the round barrows that went with these traditions were more closely connected. Nowhere is this more evident that at Beckhampton Road, where a round barrow was constructed over the eroding northeastern end of the long barrow *(87)*. Centrally situated, the ditch of the round barrow defines an area 18.2m in diameter, although the central mound of the barrow had long gone by the time the site was excavated in 1964. Antiquarian excavators had removed any primary burial that once existed, but fragments of collared urn were found in the fill of the surrounding ditch.[34] Collared urns have also been found associated with secondary interments at two sites in Somerset: Stoney Littleton (SOM 1) and Murtry Hill (SOM 8).

Barrow cemeteries

Some round barrows were clustered together into cemeteries, and here is another facet of the enduring presence of long barrows through the later third millennium BC to impact on communities of the early second millennium BC. Leslie Grinsell once suggested that many barrow cemeteries of the second millennium BC were laid out with reference to what he called a 'founder's barrow' – essentially a much older barrow, either long or round, that provided a focus for the gradual accretion of later barrows.[35] Whether these founder's barrows were symbolic or ancestral foci

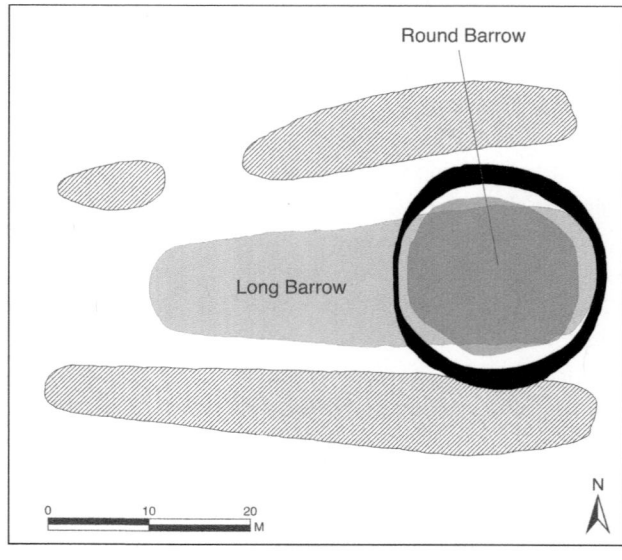

87 Beckhampton Road long barrow (WIL 27) showing the position and extent of the superimposed second-millennium BC round barrow. *After Ashbee et al. 1979, fig. 11*

as Grinsell believed, or were simply obstacles to farming that provided suitable places for the addition of further burial mounds that would also be out of the way, is hard to say. It is tempting to think, however, that just as the long barrows themselves perpetuated an interest in sacred spots (Chapter 3) so too did the later round barrows by clustering around long barrows. Leslie Grinsell and Helen O'Neil mapped many of the round barrow cemeteries focused on long barrows in the Cotswolds, with notable examples at Cow Common, Hull Plantations, Colnpen and Burn Ground.[36] This last-mentioned site is the only one that has been extensively excavated *(88)*. Here, a group of six round barrows built up slowly in two lines of three barrows each around the east end of the long barrow, constructed using similar methods of working Cotswold limestone. All six barrows contained primary burials, one within a ceramic vessel. Secondary burials were found between barrows 1 and 2 and between barrows 2 and 3, one of which was associated with a large pot and a flint knife.[37]

On the north Wessex Downs, the Lambourn long barrow (BRK 2) seems to have been the focus for the massive Lambourn Seven barrow group which in fact includes over 40 round barrows arranged in two rows.[38] By contrast, around Avebury, for example, it is notable that long barrows rarely seem to have provided the focus for barrow cemeteries. West of the Severn large barrow cemeteries are generally less common, but nonetheless in the Black Mountains the pair of long barrows at Ffostill has a round barrow closely associated with it.[39]

LATER SECOND- AND FIRST-MILLENNIUM BC ACTIVITY

With the decline of barrow burials generally in the mid-second millennium BC, long barrows seem to have lost still more of their ritual power in the landscape and the biographies of individual sites diverge considerably. Cremation cemeteries of the kind common in the mid-second millennium BC are not found over or around long barrows even though they are found at round barrows. Perhaps communities were by this time discriminating between different styles or forms of barrows, or between those of great antiquity and those that could plausibly be tied to their own ancestral lineages. Even single burials of the period are rare, Ty Isaf (BRE 5) being one site where the remains of a cremation burial of the mid-second millennium BC came to light during excavations: a single vessel perhaps accompanied by a cremation inserted into the fill of chamber IV towards the southeast end of the monument.[40] Two sites on the north Wessex Downs also yielded burials of the middle or late second millennium BC. Dean Merewether found part of a biconical urn associated with a bronze dagger with a secondary burial in the Longstones long barrow (WIL 34), while undocumented excavations at Shepherd's Shore (WIL 18) brought to light an urn with applied horseshoe handles and cordons decorated with finger impressions.[41]

Standing stones are associated with a few long barrows, although there is always the danger that what appears to be a standing stone may in fact be a remnant of some earlier structure within the mound, an exceptionally large orthostat

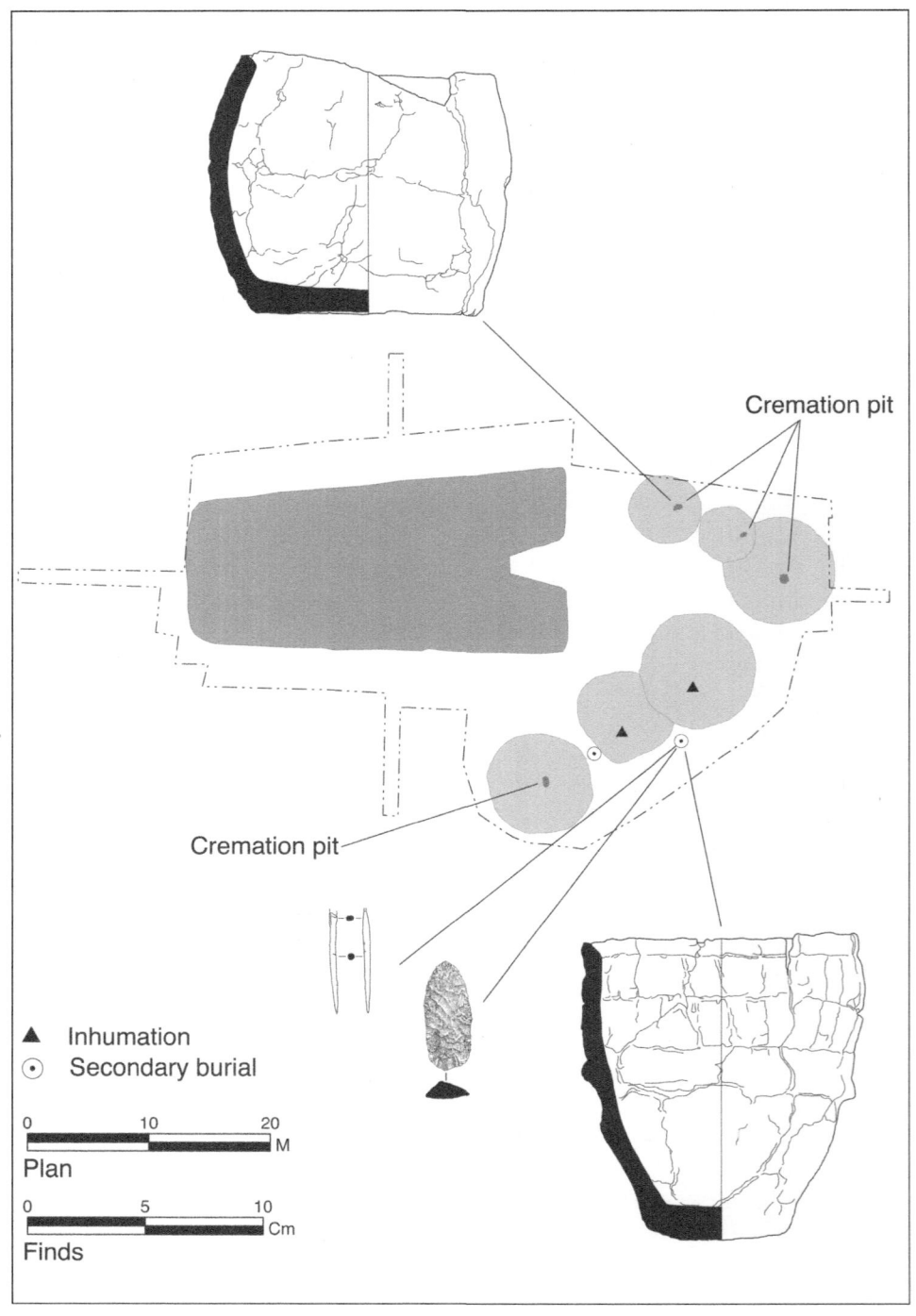

88 Burn Ground (GLO 60). Long barrow and secondary round barrow cemetery of the second millennium BC. *After Grimes 1960, figs 18, 40, 42 and 43*

After the Long Barrow Tradition

89 Tinglestone (GLO 31). Woodland covered long barrow with a large standing stone left of centre. Scales each total 2m. Photograph by Timothy Darvill, September 1975

projecting through the surface of the mound, or a dislodged stone that has been set up in relatively modern times to enhance the appearance of the site. At the Tinglestone (GLO 31) a large slab of oolite – the eponymous Tinglestone – stands towards the north end of the mound *(89)*, while at Lyneham long barrow (OXF 8) there are two standing stones, one at each end of the mound. Standing stones once existed at other long barrows, for example Woodbarrow (GLO 63), removed before 1800, and the Giant's Stone (GLO 32).[42]

Some continuing respect for long barrows through the first millennium BC is perhaps shown by their preservation inside hillforts and enclosures of the period. This is not confined to the Cotswold-Severn region, but a notable example amongst the hillforts of the central Cotswolds is the Farmington long barrow (GLO 30) in the southwest corner of Norbury Camp at Northleach.[43] The Willersey barrow (GLO 34) lies within Willersey Camp.

Associations with other kinds of later prehistoric activity are rather scant. At Gwernvale (BRE 7), a glass bead was found in the base of a robber-pit to the east of chamber 1,[44] while at Tinkinswood (GLA 9) a bone die believed by the excavator to be of later prehistoric date was found in the stonework of the mound 7m west of the chamber. How exactly it got to where it was found is unclear.[45] That the presence of artefacts tells only part of the story can be glimpsed from investigations at Parc le Breos Cwm (GLA 4) where a roe deer bone from the passage has been radiocarbon dated to 550-200 BC. It suggests some presence within the barrow at this time, robbing, rifling or, just possibly, as Whittle and Wysocki suggest, a renewed interest in ancestral or mythologized landscapes.[46] Similar things were happening at long barrows and other kinds of chambered tomb in Atlantic Scotland, although there is no evidence in the Cotswold-Severn region for the construction of houses in long barrows during the later first millennium BC as there is elsewhere.[47]

Something of the complicated nature, and deep-rootedness, of activities at some long barrows may be glimpsed by finds from Wayland's Smithy (BRK 1) on

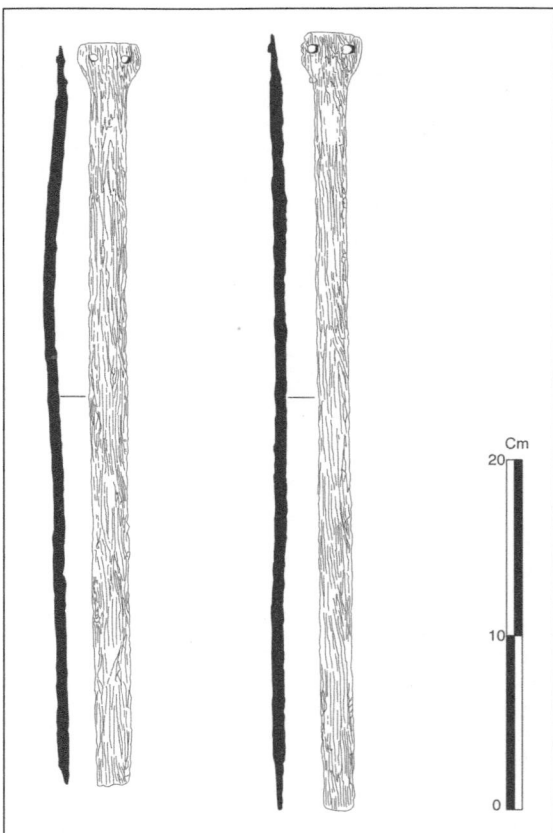

90 Wayland's Smithy (BRK 1). Iron bars, once thought to be 'currency bars', found in the façade west of the entrance to the chamber. *After Peers and Smith 1921*

the Berkshire Ridgeway. Excavations here in 1921 and again in 1962–3 revealed pottery from the early and late first millennium BC in the upper fills of the quarry ditches and in adjacent field boundary ditches. Rather unusually, there was also debris from bronze-casting, probably associated with the manufacture of horse harness fittings, an especially significant find in view of later folklore relating to the site (see below). Two iron bars initially thought to be 'currency bars' of the later first millennium BC were found buried against the stone immediately west of the entrance in the façade *(90)*. Of rather unusual form, however, these bars cannot be accepted as genuine even though such items were regularly deposited at boundaries, at significant natural places and at ceremonial sites. A more likely interpretation is that they are pieces of a crowbar that became detached when someone was trying to move one of the façade stones.[48]

Another exception is to be found at West Hill, Uley, where in the late first millennium BC a small square shrine was built over the northern end of the earlier sanctuary-enclosure and within sight of Hetty Pegler's Tump (GLO 14), which lies just 700m to the north. The shrine later became the focus for a whole succession of Romano-British temples dedicated to the Roman god Mercury and perhaps also to local deities.[49]

ROMANO-BRITISH INTEREST

West Hill, Uley, is exceptional in many ways and it serves to emphasize how an awareness of the sacred nature of certain places spanned millennia and connected long barrows and related structures with rural cult-centres in later prehistoric and early Roman times. Indeed, the amount of Romano-British material from other long barrows in the Cotswold-Severn region suggests that West Hill was not an isolated case, and certainly the level of interest in long barrows among Romano-British communities has been significantly underestimated. Four distinct kinds of activity can currently be recognized, but it is a subject that deserves more study.

The most straightforward to recognize was the use of long barrows as burial places, most of which seem to have been discovered during nineteenth-century excavations. At Hetty Pegler's Tump (GLO 14), Dr Fry's excavations in 1821 found an intrusive inhumation near the highest point of the mound associated with three coins of the house of Constantine, a burial just possibly associated with the nearby temple at West Hill. When digging this grave it is likely that the original workmen obtained access to the chambers, and a small Roman vessel described as 'resembling a Roman lachrymatory' was found in the eastern side chamber.[50] Roman burials were also found at the White Horse Hill long barrow (BRK 5) during excavations by E. Martin Atkins in 1857, although few details are available.[51] The five burials discovered by Professor Buckman and C.H. Newmarch around 1850 in the rather doubtful long barrow at The Querns, Cirencester (GLO 79), are almost certainly of Romano-British date. The skeletons were lying roughly east–west and the mound lies on the edge of the very extensive west-gate cemetery of Roman *Corinium*.[52] Some or all of the inhumations reported around the periphery of West Tump (GLO 8) and Randwick (GLO 10) may possibly have been deposited by Romano-British communities, but there is no secure evidence of dating.[53] Further west, investigations at Pen-y-wyrlod (BRE 1) in September 1920 revealed a coin of Crispus (AD 317–26) and 'dozens of small blue beads' which the excavators interpreted as relating to an intrusive burial, but little is known of their context.[54]

A second group of evidence arises from what could be described as casual losses and placed deposits that might be explained in terms of casual visits, outdoor adventures and picnics, perhaps prompted by curiosity and local folklore. Here may be cited the occasional finds of coins on the mound or in adjacent quarry ditches. Principal examples include: West Kennet (WIL 4), six coins from the topsoil of the façade area at the east end of the barrow; Bown Hill (GLO 20), a coin of Germanicus; Rodmarton (GLO 16), a coin of Claudius Gothicus (AD 268-70) and pottery in the topsoil; Camp Farm (GLO 53), a Roman coin of unknown type; Cow Common Long (GLO 22), a coin of Constantine from near the west end; Notgrove (GLO 4), a coin of Hadrian (of about AD 127) and later prehistoric and Roman pottery; and Nympsfield (GLO 13), small amounts of Roman pottery and a piece of a stone roofing tile.

Third, some long barrows lay within Romano-British agricultural estates and were probably cultivated if not deliberately levelled or cleared. At Sale's Lot

(GLO 94), for example, a scatter of Roman finds in the topsoil including potsherds and a broken stamped roof tile looks like manuring debris brought from a nearby farmstead and scattered on the fields. Helen O'Neil, the excavator of the site, suggested that as a result of later prehistoric and Romano-British agriculture in the area the barrow had reached a relatively decayed state by the second or third century AD.[55] Richard Atkinson argued that most of the damage to Wayland's Smithy (BRK 1) had been inflicted by the end of the Roman period, and certainly there are the remains of Romano-British field boundary ditches cutting into the edge of the mound.[56]

Finally, there are a few sites where a much more substantial presence can be recognized, activity that involved diggings, investigations and perhaps opening up sites for clandestine reuse as sacred spots. These go beyond mere poking about and must have involved using spades, picks and levers to penetrate deep into barrow mounds and chambers. At Hazleton North (GLO 54), for example, sondages seem to have been dug into the south chamber and perhaps also into the western part of the mound and the north chamber. Romano-British pottery and coins were found in superficial contexts but a large sherd of Severn Valley Ware was found in the infill/collapse of the south chamber.[57] At Randwick, Witt's excavations of 1883 revealed Roman pottery and what is described as 'half of a Roman horseshoe' in the chamber.[58] Belas Knap (GLO 1) also yielded about 30 sherds of Romano-British pottery and two coins of late third-century date, mainly from superficial contexts around the edge of the mound and in the forecourt.[59] At Adlestrop (GLO 44), now recognized as a portal dolmen but for long considered to be a long barrow, investigations in 1935–6 revealed Roman pottery and a coin of Allectus (AD 293–96) within the chamber area, suggesting to the excavator that 'the barrow suffered most at this period, when the supposed missing orthostat and top stones were removed'.[60] Stoney Littleton (SOM 1), Murtry Hill (SOM 8) and the Giant's Grave (SOM 4), all south of the River Avon, were also probably opened in Roman times, the last mentioned yielding Roman pottery and four coins of fourth-century AD date.[61] At Tinkinswood (GLA 9) sherds from at least three vessels, all probably cooking pots, were found in the upper levels of the chamber fill.[62] A larger collection of Romano-British finds including over 570 pieces of pottery, six coins and a strip of bronze was found in a disturbance to the mound and within the upper fills of chambers C and D on the south side of the mound at the Giant's Caves (WIL 2). The pottery and coins date to the later third and fourth centuries AD, much of the pottery being linked to cooking and food preparation. The fact that the pottery was generally well broken and chronologically mixed led Ken Annable to suggest that it could have been deliberately smashed and left on the site by people making offerings to the spirits of the dead during periodic visits to the site.[63]

The fact that much of this Romano-British interest in long barrows and related structures seems to date to the later third and fourth centuries AD may be significant, and part of a widespread renewal of interest in local deities and native traditions, and a return to a faith in the spirits of the countryside (pagan cults). Stuart Piggott has pointed out that long barrows in the Cotswolds may not be the only

After the Long Barrow Tradition

91 Possible Roman barrow at the Hyde, Minchinhampton, Gloucestershire. Photograph by Timothy Darvill, May 1989

prehistoric monuments to receive renewed interest at this time, quoting as examples the hoard of over 300 coins from the Foxcote Hill round barrow, Withington, and the discovery of Roman altars buried in round barrows at Bisley and Tidenham.[64] It is also at this time that Romano-British communities begin building round barrows of their own, the Tar Barrows at Cirencester and the Hyde Barrow at Minchinhampton *(91)* being possible examples on the Cotswolds;[65] three round barrows on Overton Down, Avebury, immediately east of the Ridgeway and north of the Roman road between *Cunetio* and *Verlucio*, are certainly examples.[66]

ANGLO-SAXON APPROPRIATION

The influence that long barrows and other kinds of 'ancient' burial monuments exerted over later Romano-British communities seems to have continued into the later centuries of the first millennium AD. Pagan Saxon burials dating broadly to the period from the sixth to eighth centuries have been recorded at half a dozen long barrow sites, mainly in the catchments of tributaries to the upper Thames. In the eastern Cotswolds several secondary burials were found at Crawley (OXF 9) during excavations by J.Y. Akerman in about 1858, while at Lyneham (OXF 8) excavations in the second half of the nineteenth century revealed six or seven burials set more or less along the central axis of the mound.[67] Further west, at Pole's Wood South (GLO 2), three pagan burials were found near the surface of the mound in 1874, including a male with an iron spearhead and a knife, and a female with two circular saucer brooches and an amber bead.[68] Nearby, at Pole's Wood East (GLO 24) there were three intrusive inhumation burials towards the northeast end of the mound.[69] The limited investigations at all these sites allow the possibility that more contemporary burials lie around about, and certainly this was the case at Burn Ground (GLO 60), where only one of the ten inhumation graves

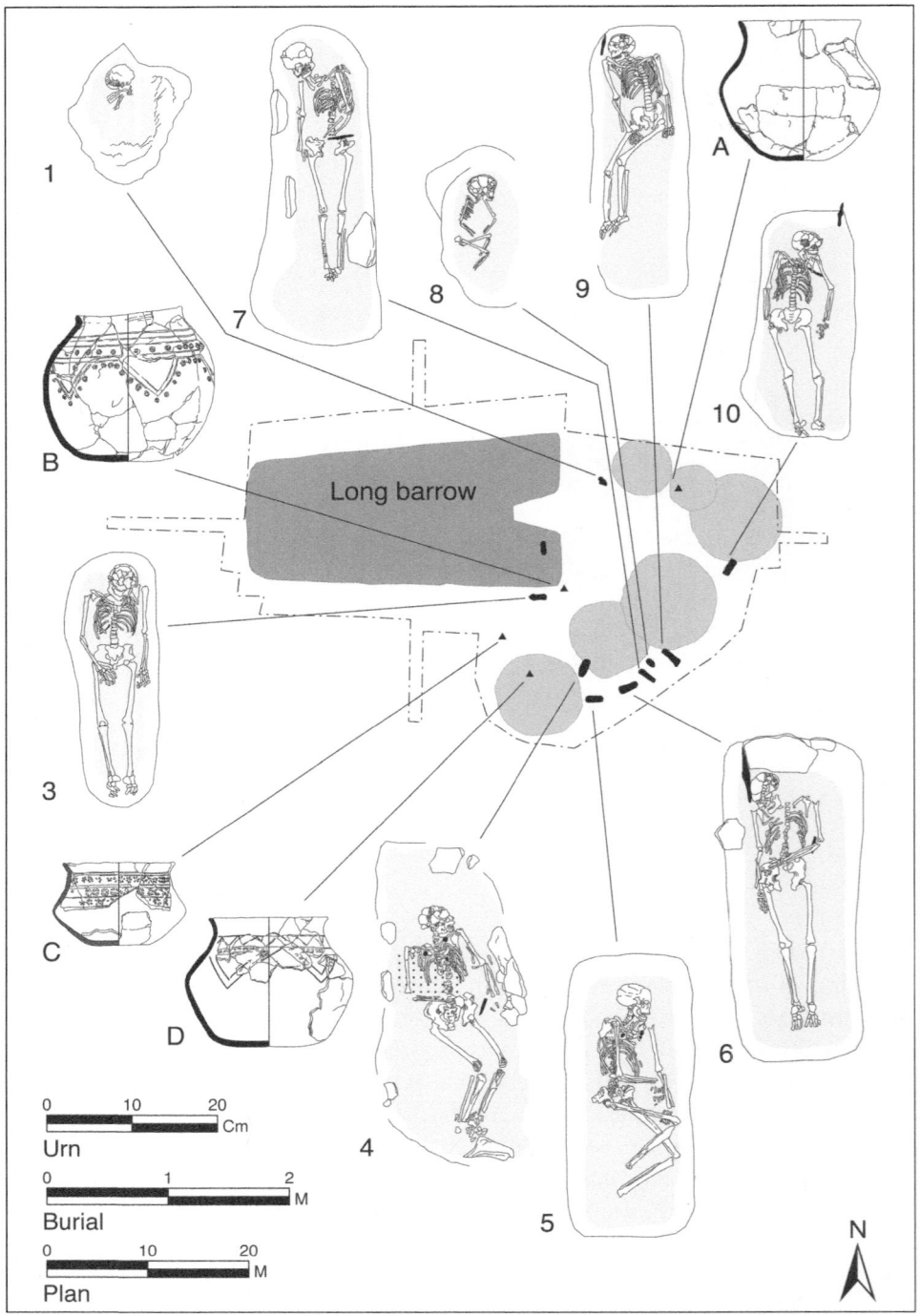

92 Burn Ground (GLO 60). Anglo-Saxon cemetery in the area of the earlier long barrow and round barrows. *After Grimes 1960, figs 18, 44, 45, 46 and 49*

and two of the four cremation urns forming this small but extensive and important cemetery were cut into the long barrow itself *(92)*. Representing the third phase of burial activity at this site, it is notable that perhaps 2,000 years separated the Anglo-Saxon use of the spot from the last visible interest in the site at about 1700–1500 BC.[70] The cremation urns probably date to the sixth century AD while the inhumations may be a little later.[71] One of the burials is that of a child; of the remainder, four are of females and five of males. The grave goods, which include weapons, a square-headed brooch, disc brooches and personal ornaments, are generally fairly poor, but a gilt glass bead from grave 7 provides evidence for some contact with the eastern Mediterranean, where similar beads are found in Coptic graves. The most westerly Anglo-Saxon burial recorded in a long barrow was found at Crippets Barrow (GLO 7), right on the edge of the Cotswold escarpment overlooking the Severn valley. Here, excavations in the late eighteenth century revealed what was probably such a burial, Samuel Rudder noting that the finds from the work included a helmet that was so rusted that it disintegrated on exposure.[72]

Howard Williams has noted that Anglo-Saxon communities in England commonly reused Roman and prehistoric monuments as burial sites, arguing that this practice was central to the symbolism of Anglo-Saxon mortuary rituals as well as important for the construction and negotiation of origin myths, identities and social structure. In particular, he pointed to the need to construct relationships with places that had been important in the past and the desire to legitimize political authority through appealing to the ancestors of the land and the supernatural powers that dwelt in the mound.[73] Such traditions ran deep and emerge in unlikely places. Since at least the mid-nineteenth century, for example, it has been recognized that the dragon's lair depicted in the epic *Beowulf* was beneath a great mound (*stanbeorh*) or at the Hoar Stone (*under harne stan*). These are probably allusions to a long barrow or megalithic chambered tomb of some kind, perhaps in Ireland or Scotland.[74] Folklore preserves some of these beliefs as much as the physical archaeological remains do. The name Wayland's Smithy (BRK 1), for example, occurs in a Saxon charter dated to about AD 955 and is associated with a tradition that Leslie Grinsell has traced back at least as far as the early eighteenth century. This tale holds that if you were to leave your horse tethered at the long barrow, together with a small coin, then Wayland the invisible elvin smith would magically re-shoe the horse while you were away.[75] Here in this one story is a whole host of imagery: the idea of the long barrow as a link to the underworld, the existence of supernatural beings, the liminality of metalworkers and a magical world beyond the here and now. But using the past in the present was not confined to belief systems and the supernatural.

Anglo-Saxon communities were well aware of their landscape and the features in it. As noted in Chapter 1, this was the period when the very idea of a long barrow as a distinct topographic entity found expression in contemporary language: the *longam beorge*. Nowhere is this better seen than in early land charters, and these have been extensively studied and commented upon by G.B. Grundy, Leslie Grinsell and others.[76] Della Hook has emphasized the subtle use of language and terminology in these charters, showing, for example, that the shape of particular hills was reflected in the choice of words, *beorg* being used for barrows and natural barrow-shaped hills.[77] Familiarity of this kind might suggest a special kind of fondness for barrows in the landscape too. But Sarah Semple has taken a different view and has argued that through the middle and later Anglo-Saxon period there was a widespread fear of barrows as the home of spirits, ancestors, or gods and the focus of pagan spiritual activity.[78] Looked at in this way it is perhaps hardly surprising that during medieval times long barrows seem to have been either ignored altogether or assigned rather fanciful and sometimes scary names.

MEDIEVAL TIMES

From the eleventh century through to the end of the sixteenth century, little seems to be happening at long barrow sites, except the gentle decay of their mounds and content. Leslie Grinsell has argued that the site of Ty Illtyd (BRE 6) in the Black Mountains was used as, or connected with, a hermit's cell as part of the cult of St Illtud. The presence of numerous carvings of small crosses and a 'lyre' motif on three of the exposed stones forming one cell of what is probably a transepted terminal chamber rather supports this identification *(93)*, although some scholars have rather unconvincingly suggested a prehistoric date for the carvings.[79]

Elsewhere, few long barrows seem to have formed especially significant focal points in everyday life, and there are only meagre finds indicating even casual interest in these things. Some robbing is evident at Gwernvale (BRE 7), with thirteenth- and fourteenth-century sherds in the robbing hollows.[80] At the Giant's Caves (WIL 2) excavations in 1960–2 brought to light a Nuremberg counter of the sixteenth century in an area of chamber C disturbed by earlier excavations.[81] At Pinkwell (GLO 65) pottery dating to about AD 1600 led J.Y. Akerman to conclude that the mound had been opened by treasure-hunters around that time.[82] More exotic is the amethyst in a claw setting of silver gilt dating to about AD 1500 found at Notgrove (GLO 4) during the 1936 excavations, presumably lost or deposited by a nobleperson of the period.[83]

Placenames provide another line of evidence about medieval and later attitudes to specific sites. They fall into two main groups. The first contain references to the ownership or the use of the site. Naturally, great care has to be exercised in using these. There is no evidence, for example, that Windmill Tump (GLO 16) ever supported a windmill, or indeed that there was one in its immediate vicinity, so the origin of its name remains obscure. More indirectly, A. Warmington has identified the name of the Domesday Manor of '*Langeberge cum Mene*' with the Ganborough long barrow (GLO 42),[84] but, surprisingly, there is little evidence for the use of long barrows as meeting places or moots. Hetty Pegler's Tump (GLO 14) is named after former owners of the field, Captain Henry Pegler (died 1695) and his wife Hester (died 1694), whose joint monument was in the chancel of St Giles at Uley before it was demolished and rebuilt in its present form in 1856–8. Some barrows may have served as beacons, not because they were long barrows as

After the Long Barrow Tradition

93 Ty Illtyd (BRE 6). *A above:* Chamber within the long barrow believed to have been used as a hermit's cell for the cult of St Illtud. Vertical scale totals 2m. *B right:* Symbols engraved into one of the orthostats forming the wall of the chamber. *Photographs by Timothy Darvill, August 1979*

such but simply because they occupied prominent positions. One possible example of this is Bown Hill (GLO 20), excavated by the Cotteswold Naturalists' Field Club on 20 May 1863, where spreads of charcoal on the top of the mound were believed to be the remains of a beacon site.[85] A.H. Smith suggested that the name Belas Knap (GLO 1) derives from Old English *bel*, a beacon and *cnaepp*, a hilltop, but whether there was ever a beacon on the site is not known.[86] Elsie Clifford recorded that The Toots (GLO 76) on Selsley Common was the site of national bonfires in 1936 and 1937, but whether this perpetuated earlier usage is again not known.[87]

Placenames in the second group are quite different and refer to mythical aspects of the sites to which they attach, perhaps to make them comprehensible to contemporary minds or to dispel unacceptable associations. Amongst the earliest of such references is Maen Ceti (GLA 3), first mentioned in a Welsh Triad of the sixteenth century where the raising of the massive capstone is listed as one of the 'three mighty achievements of the Isle of Britain'.[88] One of the most commonly enduring and innocuous ideas about long barrows from this period is that they were the burial places of soldiers, a myth that, for example, attaches to Blackquarries Hill long barrow (GLO 86) and the Soldier's Grave (SOM 13). More sinister perhaps are the associations with giants, fairies, or the devil as at: the Giant's Stone (GLO 32), the Giant's Caves (WIL 2), the Giant's Grave (SOM 4), the Fairy's Toot (SOM 2), the Hoar Stone (GLO 9), the Devil's Bed and Bolster (SOM 3) and the Devil's Den (WIL 8). Adam's Grave (WIL 6) is recorded as *Wodnes beorge* (Woden's Grave) in a charter of AD 825.[89] West of the Severn, Arthurian placenames attach to a few long barrows, amongst them two named Arthur's Stone (HRF 1 and GLA 3). The Maesyfelin long barrow (GLA 10), St Lythans, is locally known as *Gwâl-y-filiast* (the Kennel of the Greyhound Bitch), which is perhaps an allusion to a variant of the Arthurian legend of Kilhwch and Olwen. Druidical names attached to long barrows are scarce and generally of fairly recent origin: Pen-y-wyrlod (BRE 1) was referred to as a 'Druidical altar' in the late nineteenth century,[90] while Druid Stoke (GLO 28) probably got its name about the same time.[91] In a sense all these names and associations made unnatural looking sites seem familiar to populations steeped in oral tradition, while incidentally having the effect of frightening off those who were tempted to meddle in the dark powers thought to lie within these structures.

MODERN TIMES

By the early eighteenth century long barrows were becoming the subject of scientific investigation and inquiry, as discussed in Chapter 2. This process itself led to the development of a new kind of archaeology: the redeposition of excavated remains. The remains excavated from Hetty Pegler's Tump (GLO 14) in 1821 and perhaps also 1854 were interred in Uley churchyard prior to 1880,[92] while in about 1875 the human remains taken from Jack Barrow (GLO 27) were interred in Duntisbourne Abbots Churchyard with a memorial cross made from one of the stones found at the site *(94)*. Other sites were no doubt visited and even investigated a little as they had been for generations. Lots of modern rubbish, bits of glazed pottery, bottle glass and even the remains of candles have been reported; amongst the more unusual is a General Service Medal awarded to H.R. Knight of the British Red Cross during the 1914–18 war, found during excavations at Luckington in 1960–2.[93]

Long barrows were regularly used as quarries during the eighteenth, nineteenth and twentieth centuries, the act of digging into the mounds sometimes being the cause of their identification. Bill Britnell has proposed that much of the mound at Gwernvale (BRE 7) had been robbed away by the end of the eighteenth century;[94] many other sites were heavily denuded much earlier. A limekiln was established beside the Fairy's Toot (SOM 2) during the early 1830s, the mound being almost completely removed by 1835.[95] The Througham Barrow (GLO 71) had its centre cut away by the construction of a cottage and some pigsties in the mid-nineteenth century.[96] Amongst the most extraordinary modern uses of a long barrow is at Fifield (OXF 11) on the Gloucestershire–Oxfordshire border where there is a bomb-shelter in the middle of the mound, constructed sometime between 1939 and 1945.

The use of long barrows as ritual and ceremonial centres in modern times may not show an unbroken link back into prehistory, but some were certainly used this way in recent times. Whitefield's Tump on Minchinhampton Common (GLO 77), for example, was apparently used by the Methodist preacher George Whitefield (1714–70) in March 1743 and on other later occasions, for open-air services.[97] By contrast, the Druid Stoke long barrow (GLO 28) was apparently visited every year in the spring by 'a body of men calling themselves Druids, with a priest dressed in wonderful garments' to hold a service.[98]

After the Long Barrow Tradition

94 Cross surmounting the grave containing human remains from Jack Barrow (GLO 27) in Duntisbourne Abbots churchyard. *Photograph by Timothy Darvill, April 1988*

Emparkment and the landscape gardening tradition of the seventeenth century onwards had relatively little direct impact on long barrows in the Cotswold-Severn region, although it provided some interesting contexts for the survival of sites and perhaps gave inspiration to the management and enhancement of remains.[99] Parc le Breos Cwm (GLA 4) takes its name from the great medieval deer park probably created in the thirteenth century by the de Breos Lords of Gower.[100] Long barrows in parkland settings seem to be relatively rare, the most notable being at Lodge Park near Northleach (GLO 5), which is widely regarded by many as the best preserved long barrows on the Cotswolds (see Chapter 1). Lodge Park was established in the 1630s on an outlying part of the Sherbourne Estate; it is now owned by the National Trust.[101] West of the Severn two long barrows lie within former parkland that has since been broken up: Carn Goch (BRE 12) on the northern edge of Llangattock Park, Powys, and the Cleppa Park long barrow (MON 1), Duffryn, Newport. Other examples in parkland probably await discovery, but on present evidence none seems to have been heavily utilized as a landscape feature. It may be noted, however, that many long barrows in the Cotswold-Severn region support a light tree cover that in some cases may have been deliberately planted to form skyline features. Many others were once tree-covered but have since been cleared. Hetty Pegler's Tump, for example, lay under a beech wood until it was felled in 1820.[102]

On a smaller scale, long barrows within the curtilage of relatively modest private houses are not uncommon, and were undoubtedly used on occasion to enhance the appeal of the associated gardens. The Druid Stoke long barrow now

95 Druid Stoke (GLO 28). Remains of the stone chamber, partly concealed by vegetation, landscaped into a suburban garden in north Bristol. Leslie Grinsell (right) and a 2m ranging rod provide scale. Photograph by Timothy Darvill, June 1982

lies in the garden of a house rather uninspiringly called 'The Cromlech' in Druid Hill, Stoke Bishop, a suburban development on the north side of Bristol, and has been partly landscaped into the garden, visiting Druids notwithstanding *(95)*. Small-scale and localized modifications seem to have taken place at some sites to emphasize specific features. The Murtry Hill long barrow (SOM 8) was restored in 1803-4, perhaps involving the placement of orthostats as standing stones to enhance the visual appeal of the structure. One of the capstones of the long barrow in the grounds of Fromefield House in Frome (SOM 6) was set upright following excavations in 1820, some of the mound was levelled as a platform, and a grotto was built nearby as part of a landscaping scheme.[103] The Winsley long barrow (WIL 23) also lies in the garden of a house, known as 'The Chase', but it is unclear whether the barrow itself has been improved in any way.

Physically moving elements of long barrows from one place to form a feature at another location is rare but nonetheless significant. The Whistlestone at Swell has been moved at least twice. It is now outside Lower Swell Village Hall on the east side of the road between Lower Swell and Upper Swell (NGR *c.* SP 17382558), a spot it was moved to in 1978 *(96)*. Previously it had been in the paddock of the vicarage, where it had been taken by the Revd David Royce about 1882 from its original site in a long barrow to the northwest of the church.[104] Another set of monuments that have been moved are the three chambers in the garden of the Old Rectory at Avening. These derive from an excavation carried out in 1806 by the Revd Nathaniel Thornbury, rector of Avening, probably of a long barrow near the village. However, a fierce debate has raged about exactly

After the Long Barrow Tradition

96 The Whistlestone, Lower Swell (GLO 47). The last remaining stone from a long barrow northeast of the village. The stone has been moved several times over the last 150 years and now lies on the grass verge outside the village hall. The scale totals 1m. Photograph by Timothy Darvill, May 2003

which barrow was the source. Crawford suggested that they came from Norn's Tump, also known as the Avening Barrow, on the north side of the valley between Avening and Nag's Head.[105] Glyn Daniel and Elsie Clifford showed that an origin in Norn's Tump did not accord with available descriptions of Thornbury's work and suggested instead a site on the south side of the Avening to Nag's Head road at a place called Barrow Tump.[106] They provided evidence that the barrow itself was destroyed at the time the chambers were removed, so that its location is not precisely known and no surface trace remains.[107] Leslie Grinsell proposed a third possible origin: the Avening Court long barrow in the parish of Cherington (GLO 17).[108] This is followed by John Corcoran in his extensive treatment of Cotswold-Severn long barrows published in 1969,[109] but was harshly criticized by Glyn Daniel soon after in a review of the book in which Corcoran's paper appeared.[110]

Preserving and conserving long barrows was very much part of the work of local societies in the area throughout the later nineteenth century. The Bristol and Gloucestershire Archaeological Society co-ordinated and funded restorations at Hetty Pegler's Tump under the guidance of the local secretary for Dursley, Colonel Forbes, although not everything may have turned out quite as intended. The big slab over the entrance, for example, appears to have been incorrectly positioned during these restorations, causing much irritation and not a few sore heads among later visitors. Reliance had probably been placed on a drawing of the entrance in 1821, but this shows the forecourt with much of its fill in place leaving only a thin gap between the capstone and the 'floor'. As a result, the reconstructed entrance was set much lower than it should be, a situation that still obtains.[111] The same society seems to have put a fence around Nympsfield long barrow (GLO 13) at about the same time. It is visible in its decayed form in E.J. Burrow's drawing of the site made in 1913;[112] it undoubtedly contributed to the general well-being of the site over several decades.

In Somerset, the Somerset Archaeological and Natural History Society provided a grant of sixteen shillings for restoration works at Stoney Littleton (SOM 1), including renovating some of the outer wall. Ahead of its time in many ways, the junction of the new walling and the original was marked with upright stones at the western end.[113] A large explanatory tablet just inside the entrance to the chambers sets out the background to this work in what Leslie Grinsell once described as 'a splendid example of Victorian smug self-satisfaction':[114]

> THIS TUMULUS,
> DECLARED BY COMPETENT JUDGES TO BE THE MOST
> PERFECT SPECIMEN OF CELTIC ANTIQUITY STILL
> EXISTING IN GREAT BRITAIN, HAVING BEEN MUCH
> INJURED BY THE LAPSE OF TIME, OR THE CARELESSNESS
> OF FORMER PROPRIETORS, WAS RESTORED IN 1858
> BY MR T. R. JOLLIFFE, THE LORD OF THE HUNDRED;
> THE DESIGN OF THE ORIGINAL STRUCTURE BEING
> PRESERVED, AS FAR AS POSSIBLE, WITH SCRUPULOUS EXACTNESS.

However, even these heavily restored sites retain many original features and certainly give an impression of the original bulk and feel of the barrows as they must have been. Hetty Pegler's Tump, despite having two side cells closed off and a misplaced lintel at the entrance, is still the most evocative example in terms of feeling the cold damp atmosphere inside the chambers.

The Ancient Monuments Protection Act 1882 includes on its schedule no fewer than six long barrows in the Cotswold-Severn region: Wayland's Smithy (BRK 1), Arthur's Stone (GLA 3), Hetty Pegler's Tump (GLO 14), Stoney Littleton (SOM 1), West Kennet (WIL 4) and the Devil's Den (WIL 8).[115] The first inspector of ancient monuments, General Pitt Rivers, made a tour of inspection in 1883–4, visiting a selection of sites that included some listed in the Schedule as well as others that were not, amongst them: West Kennet, Stoney Littleton, Hetty Pegler's Tump, Nympsfield (GLO 13) and Wayland's Smithy.[116] Since that time others have been taken into state care in Wales and England so that the total number of long barrows in the region in Guardianship is now about a dozen. All are included in the guide to sites to visit in Appendix C.

During the twentieth century, restoration work has often accompanied the public display of long barrows, and this is especially notable at Belas Knap (GLO 1), which was extensively rebuilt in 1930–1 following the excavations by W.J. Hemp between 1929 and 1931. The concrete roof slabs are particularly noticeable. Likewise, at West Kennet there is the addition of glass bricks in the roof in order to light the chambers for visitors. At the Devil's Den concrete was put under the northeast upright in the early 1920s to support it.[117] A concrete pillar was built inside the chamber at Tinkinswood to help support the massive capstone, while distinctive herringbone walling was used to differentiate the original stonework from modern rebuild.[118] More recently, restorations have been carried out at Parc le Breos Cwm (GLA 4), Nympsfield and Gwernvale (BRE 7). More often than not, these restorations are not well marked at the sites themselves and it is sometimes difficult to see what is new and what is original.

The vast majority of long barrows are not in state care, and while many enjoy some protection as Scheduled Monuments under the *Ancient Monuments and Archaeological Areas Act 1979* there has long been considerable concern about the survival of long barrows within predominantly agricultural landscapes. John Drinkwater and Alan Saville carried out condition surveys in 1970 and 1976–7. These found that of the 96 long barrows then known in Gloucestershire about 10 per cent had been destroyed prior to 1960. Of the remainder, 24 per cent were partly ploughed over at the time of the surveys and 30 per cent were completely ploughed.[119] Very similar results were obtained from a survey of the condition of long barrows in Oxfordshire in 1977.[120] It was in response to these concerns that the previously untouched long barrow at Hazleton North (GLO 54) was completely excavated between 1979 and 1982.[121]

Strangely, long barrows still have a strong pull on modern society. Well-known sites such as Belas Knap and Hetty Pegler's Tump attract countless visitors every year, more so since the creation of the long-distance path known as the Cotswold Way in 1970 which passes beside half a dozen long barrows. Much the same applies to the Berkshire Ridgeway, which starts near West Kennet and passes Wayland's Smithy and the White Horse Hill long barrow (BRK 5) before reaching the Thames at Goring. Numerous other accessible long barrows provide opportunities for informal recreation, and barely a summer Sunday afternoon passes without picnickers on Hetty Pegler's Tump, golfers at Whitefield's Tump, or model aircraft enthusiasts and kite flyers at The Toots (GLO 76; *97*). Not all the activities seen in recent decades at long barrows are for sport and amusement. New Age beliefs find expression through the use of barrows too, whether simply placing flowers and offerings in the chambers or indulging in more extensive uses of these

97 The Toots (GLO 76) on Selsley Common overlooking Stroud, one of the best places in the area for flying kites and model aircraft. *Photograph by Timothy Darvill, June 1988*

98 Above Belas Knap (GLO 1). View of the portal setting in the back of the forecourt with the remains of a fire built against the portal slab as part of Summer Solstice celebrations. *Photograph by Timothy Darvill, June 1988*

99 Left The Three Shire Stones, Marshfield (GLO 39). Folly in the form of a portal dolmen construction at the junction of Gloucestershire, Wiltshire and Somerset in AD 1858. *Photograph by Timothy Darvill, May 2003* sites. Julian Cope, a leading advocate of New Antiquarianism and one-time lead singer in The Teardrop Explodes, recorded the song 'Paranormal in the W. Country' inside the western chamber of the West Kennet long barrow on the night of 18 November 1993 for his album *Autogeddon*.[122] Inevitably, not all these activities are kind to the monuments concerned. Rituals involving fires, seemingly connected with celebrating the Summer Solstice, appear to be increasingly common and sometimes lead to quite disturbing damage to parts of well-known and much-loved sites *(98)*.

Images of fourth-millennium BC monuments have also held a magical charm over the last few centuries as icons of the past. In this respect, one of the most extraordinary monuments in the Cotswold-Severn region is the Three Shire Stones at Marshfield. It stands unobtrusively in an alcove in the wall on the west side of the Fosse Way at the junction of three historic shire counties: Somerset, Gloucestershire and Wiltshire *(99)*. With its three great uprights and capstone, it looks rather like a portal dolmen and is often listed as, and sometimes even mistaken for, a long barrow or chambered tomb (GLO 39 in Corcoran's list).[123] Inside the dolmen-like structure are three smaller stones, each bearing the date 1736 and a letter representing the initial of the county in which it stands. The site has long been recognized as a folly of some kind, perhaps using pieces taken from a nearby long barrow that has yet to be recognized.[124] However, in the early 1960s A.J.H. Gunstone found documentary evidence in Bath Reference Library showing that this was a multi-phase modern structure. The inner stones were indeed erected in 1736 to mark the spot where the county boundaries met, but the covering dolmen was started in 1858 and completed in February 1859. Public subscriptions met the cost of the work (£34 5s 8d), its purpose being conspicuously to mark the junction of the three territories so that travellers would be attracted to the spot.[125] Unwittingly, the neighbouring gentry of Batheaston had, in a stroke, perpetuated more of their prehistoric past than they imagined: a traditional territorial marker for the benefit of the peripatetic members of their community that both elaborated and expanded an earlier simple structure whose original symbolism had become diminished has been a familiar leitmotif in the story of Cotswold-Severn long barrows down the millennia. The final irony, however, was that when digging the hole to receive the upright on the Gloucestershire corner of the setting the workmen hit three skeletons and recovered a coin of James II. We have no idea what thoughts went through the minds of these workmen at the time, but one cannot help imagining that they shared a common experience with their forebears of 5,000 years before when the builders of a new long barrow chanced upon the remains of a still earlier burial and fancied they were not alone in their toil.

APPENDIX A

LONG BARROWS IN THE COTSWOLD-SEVERN REGION

The following gazetteer is arranged by county code following the listings published by Daniel (1950a, 177–250), Corcoran (1969a, 273–95) and Darvill and Grinsell (1989, 64–9). Long barrows that have been added to these lists are marked †, those for north Wiltshire being based on the study by Barker (1985, 8–27), those for Oxfordshire and Berkshire from Brown (1978), those for Somerset from Grinsell (1971) and those in Glamorgan and Brecknock from the county inventories compiled by the Royal Commission on the Ancient and Historical Monuments of Wales (RCAHMW 1976; 1997). The site name is followed by the name of the parish in which it stands. Excavated sites are highlighted in bold typeface; the main investigations are listed wherever possible, but poorly recorded antiquarian investigations have been omitted. Previously numbered sites not considered to be long barrows are listed in square brackets.

BRK 1. **Wayland's Smithy**, Ashbury (SU 2808 8539). Part-excavated by C.R. Peers and R.A. Smith in 1919–20 and more fully using a series of 31 trenches separated initially by standing baulks by Richard Atkinson and Stuart Piggott in 1962–3. Terminal chamber with three cells in transepted formation. A multi-period monument with a primary oval barrow later covered by the long barrow. *Reports*: Peers and Smith 1921; Atkinson 1965; Whittle 1991.

BRK 2. **Lambourn**, Lambourn (SU 3235 8340). Rescue excavations by John Wymer in 1964 using nine trenches to investigate sections of the remnant mound and flanking quarry ditches. Terminal chamber (?wooden) probably with one cell. *Reports*: Wymer 1966; Schulting 2000.

BRK 3†. Moss Hill, Sparsholt (SU 335 842).

BRK 4†. Scary Hill, Sparsholt (SU 335 852).

BRK 5†. **White Horse Hill long barrow**, Uffington (SU 300 868). Antiquarian excavations by E. Martin Atkins in 1857 who found Roman burials and 'an ancient British urn'. Terminal chamber (?wooden) probably with one cell. *Reports*: Miles and Palmer 1995; Lock *et al.* 2003.

Appendix A

BRK 6†. Churn Barrow, Blewbury Down, Blewbury (SU 5201 8351).

BRE 1. **Pen-y-wyrlod**, Llanigon (SO 2250 3985). Part-excavated by W.E.T. Morgan and G. Marshall in 1920 and 1921. Terminal chamber with one cell. Possibly a multi-period monument with a primary round barrow or rotunda grave later incorporated into a long barrow. *Reports:* Morgan and Marshall 1921; Vulliamy 1922a.

BRE 2. **Little Lodge**, Aberllynfi (SO 1822 3808). Part-excavated by C.E. Vulliamy in 1928-9. Terminal chamber with at least two cells. Possibly a multi-period monument with a simple passage grave later incorporated into the mound of the long barrow. *Report*: Vulliamy 1929.

BRE 3. **Ffostyll North**, Llanelieu (SO 1790 3497). Part-excavated by C.E. Vulliamy in 1921. Terminal chamber with one cell, plus possible lateral chamber. *Report*: Vulliamy 1922b.

BRE 4. **Ffostyll South**, Llanelieu (SO 1788 3488). Part-excavated by C.E. Vulliamy and A.F. Gwynne in 1921–3. Terminal chamber with ?one cell. *Report*: Vulliamy 1921; 1922b.

BRE 5. **Ty Isaf**, Talgarth (SO 1820 2905). Extensively excavated by W.F. Grimes and the Brecknockshire Society in 1938 using a combination of interconnected sections and open areas. Three lateral chambers associated with the long barrow. Probably a multi-period monument with a primary simple passage grave with a T-shaped chamber below the long barrow. *Report*: Grimes 1939.

BRE 6. Ty Illtyd (*trans.* Illtyd's House), Llanhamlach (SO 0982 2638).

BRE 7. **Gwernvale**, Crickhowell (SO 2103 1912). Antiquarian excavation by Sir Richard Colt Hoare and others on 26 May 1804. Totally excavated by W. Britnell for the Clwyd Powys Archaeological Trust in 1977–8 using a single open-area trench. Four lateral chambers. *Reports*: Britnell 1979; 1984, 41–154.

BRE 8. **Pipton**, Pipton (SO 1605 3729). Extensively excavated by H.N. Savory in 1950 using a combination of interconnecting sections and small open areas. Two lateral chambers. Probably a multi-period monument with a primary simple passage grave, the chamber of which became one of the lateral chambers of the long barrow. *Report*: Savory 1956.

BRE 9. Cwm-fforest, Talgarth (SO 182 292).

BRE 10. Mynydd Troed, Talgarth (SO 1615 2840).

BRE 11. Croesllechau, Bronllys (SO 1690 3560).

BRE 12. Carn Goch, Llangattock (SO 2138 1768).

BRE 13. Maes-Coch, Llanigon (SO 239 378).

BRE 14†. **Penywyrlod**, Talgarth (SO 151 316). Discovered on 27 June 1972 and subsequently part-excavated by H.N. Savory in September 1972 using five cuttings. At least four lateral chambers. *Reports*: Savory 1973; 1984, 13–39.

[GLA 1. Sweyne's Howe North, Rhossili (SS 4210 8980). Portal dolmen.]

[GLA 2. Sweyne's Howe South, Rhossili (SS 4213 8987). Portal dolmen.]

[GLA 3. Maen Ceti / Arthur's Stone, Llanrhidian Lower (SS 4911 9057). Dolmen.]

GLA 4. **Parc le Breos Cwm**, Pen-maen (SS 5372 8983). Antiquarian excavation by Sir John Lubbock in 1869; subsequently extensively excavated by Richard Atkinson in 1960–1 using five main trenches. Terminal chamber with four cells in transepted formation. *Reports*: Lubbock and Douglas 1871; Lubbock *et al*. 1887; Daniel 1937b; Whittle and Wysocki 1998.

GLA 5. **Pen-maen Burrows**, Pen-maen (SS 5315 8810). Antiquarian investigations by E. James and M. Moggridge in 1860 and Miss Bostock in 1881. Further extensive excavations by W.L. Morgan in 1893. Terminal chamber with at least three cells in transepted formation. *Report*: Morgan 1894.

GLA 6. Tythegeston, Tythegeston Lower (SS 8646 7925).

[GLA 7. Coedparcgarw, Coety Higher (SS 9269 8193). Portal dolmen.]

[GLA 8. Cae'rarfau, Pen-tyrch (ST 0772 8214). Portal dolmen.]

GLA 9. **Tinkinswood**, St Nicholas (ST 0921 7331). Extensive excavations by John Ward in June to August 1914, followed by the restoration of the chamber area and forecourt. Terminal chamber with one cell. Possibly a multi-period monument with a primary round barrow or rotunda grave with a central chamber incorporated into the mound of the long barrow. *Reports*: Ward 1915; 1916.

GLA 10. **Maesyfelin / Gwâl y Filiast** (*trans*.: Kennel of the Greyhound Bitch), St Lythans (ST 1010 7230). Antiquarian investigation by J.W. Lukis some time before 1875. Terminal chamber with a single cell. *Reports*: Lukis 1875, 171–4.

[GLA 11. **Nicholaston**, Nicholaston (SS 5075 8881). Probably oval barrow. Extensive excavation by Audrey Williams in 1940 following the discovery of the site. Ten trenches of various sizes were set out across and around the mound. Single box-like central chamber. *Report*: Williams 1940.]

GLA 12†. Carn Llechart, Rhyndwyglydach (SN 6966 0627).

GLA 13†. Cae'reglwys, Macroes (SS 9169 6824).

GLO 1. **Belas Knap**, Sudeley (SP 0209 2554). Antiquarian excavation by L. Winterbotham and W. Lawrence in 1863-5 focused on the side chambers. Extensive modern excavations in advance of restoration in 1929–30 by Sir James Berry and W. J. Hemp, the restoration work itself being carried out in 1930–1 under the guidance of Dr Ralegh Radford. Three lateral chambers and a possible fourth chamber at the distal end of the mound. Possibly a multi-period monument with a primary portal dolmen and round barrow or rotunda grave under the long barrow. *Reports*: Lawrence 1866; Berry 1929; 1930; Hemp 1929.

GLO 2. **Pole's Wood South**, Swell (SP 1673 2637). Antiquarian excavations with narrow trenching by George Rolleston and Canon Greenwell in 1874. One lateral chamber near the western (distal) end of the mound. *Reports*: Rolleston 1876, 165–71; Greenwell 1877, 521–4 (CCXXXI).

GLO 3. **Eyford Hill**, Upper Slaughter (SP 1426 2580). Antiquarian excavations by David Royce, George Rolleston and Canon Greenwell in September 1874. Four chambers were revealed; three are probably lateral chambers while the fourth appears to be a cist centrally set in the mound. *Reports*: Rolleston 1876, 153-65; Greenwell 1877, 514–20 (CCXXX).

Appendix A

GLO 4. **Notgrove**, Notgrove (SP 0959 2119). Antiquarian excavation by G.B. Witts in April 1881 prior to a visit by the Cotteswold Naturalists' Field Club. Extensive modern excavation using a series of 16 trenches by Helen O'Neil in 1935. Terminal chamber with five cells in transepted formation. A multi-period monument with a primary rotunda grave below the mound of the long barrow. The site was covered in soil in November 1976. *Report*: Clifford 1936.

GLO 5. Lodge Park, Farmington (SP 1427 1254).

GLO 6. Withington Woods, Withington (SP 0306 1417).

GLO 7. **Crippets Barrow / Shurdington Barrow**, Coberley (SO 9342 1737). Antiquarian excavations before 1779, but no details of the work recorded.

GLO 8. **West Tump**, Brimpsfield (SO 9114 1323). Antiquarian excavation which cleared the edge of the mound and emptied the chamber by George Witts in 1881. Lateral chamber with a single cell. *Report*: Witts 1881.

GLO 9. **Hoar Stone**, Duntisbourne Abbots (SO 9650 0659). Antiquarian excavations by Anthony Freston in 1806 when attention focused on the examination of what appears to be a lateral chamber. *Report*: Freston 1812.

GLO 10. **Randwick**, Randwick (SO 8250 0690). Antiquarian excavation by George Witts and C.A. Witchell in 1883, mainly confined to the examination of the chamber. Terminal chamber with a single cell. *Report*: Witts 1884a.

GLO 11. **Camp Barrow North**, Miserden (SO 9137 0908). Antiquarian excavations in about 1860, but no details of the work recorded.

GLO 12. Westwood, Edgeworth (SO 9360 0527).

GLO 13. **Nympsfield**, Frocester (SO 7939 0132). Antiquarian investigations by Professor J. Buckman in August 1862 on behalf of the Cotteswold Naturalists' Field Club. On 22 July 1880 the chambers were cleared out under the direction of the proprietor of the site, Mr Leigh, in advance of a visit by the Bristol and Gloucestershire Archaeological Society. In 1937 extensive excavations were carried out by Elsie Clifford. This included reclearing the chamber, examining a large part of the forecourt and the western terminal, three rectangular trenches through the northern flank of the mound and two long trenches at right angles to each other to provide a longitudinal and a cross section. Re-excavation by Alan Saville in April and May 1974 in advance of conservation works. A terminal chambered barrow with three cells arranged in transepted formation. *Reports*: Buckman 1865; Clifford 1938a; Saville 1979a.

GLO 14. **Hetty Pegler's Tump**, Uley (SO 7895 0004). Discovered in 1820 during woodland clearance. Antiquarian investigations on 22-3 February 1821 by Dr Fry of Dursley and T.J. Lloyd Baker of Hardwick Court. Opened again in 1854 by Dr John Thurnam and the historian Professor E.A. Freeman. Restorations were undertaken in 1854, 1872, 1891 and 1906. Terminal chamber with five cells arranged in transepted formation. *Reports*: Thurnam 1854; Brown 1894; Clifford 1966.

GLO 15. **Gatcombe Lodge**, Minchinhampton (ST 8839 9972). Antiquarian excavation by Samuel Lysons in 1870 and further discoveries by workmen at the site in 1871. At least one lateral chamber. *Report*: Not well reported, but see Crawford 1925, 98–100 for summary.

GLO 16. **Windmill Tump / Rodmarton**, Rodmarton (ST 9325 9730). Antiquarian excavations by Samuel Lysons in 1863; limited re-examination by Elsie Clifford in 1940 and recent work by Alan Saville in September 1988 after a large beech tree blew over on the site. At least three lateral chambers. *Reports*: Lysons 1863, 275–9; Clifford and Daniel 1940, 135–46; Saville 1989.

GLO 17. **Avening Court / Avening Barrow**, Cherington (ST 8951 9783). According to Grinsell (O'Neil and Grinsell 1960, 75) this barrow was excavated in 1806 by the Revd W.H. Thornbury and produced the three stone chambers that were subsequently taken to the Old Rectory in Avening where they still stand beside the drive. This view is followed by Corcoran (1969a, 279), but differs from the interpretation offered by Clifford and Daniel (1940, 146–9) and later protested by Daniel (1970, 262; but see also Darvill and Grinsell 1989, 65). At least three lateral chambers. *Report*: Not well reported by Thornbury, but see Crawford 1925, 115–16 for summary.

GLO 18. **West Barrow / Leighterton**, Boxwell with Leighterton (ST 8191 9130). Antiquarian investigations by Matthew Huntley about 1700. Probably at least three lateral chambers. *Report*: none published, see Crawford 1925, 136–7.

GLO 19. **Grickstone Farm**, Horton (ST 7827 8327). Antiquarian excavations about 1844 when three chambers were identified. Probably at least three lateral chambers. *Report*: Anon. 1844, 636.

GLO 20. **Bown Hill**, Woodchester (SO 8230 0180). Antiquarian excavations by W.H. Paine and E. Witchell in May 1863. Terminal chamber with one cell. *Report*: Paine and Witchell 1865.

GLO 21. Lechmore, Horsley (ST 8606 9782).

GLO 22. **Cow Common Long**, Swell (SP 1352 2627). Antiquarian excavations by William Greenwell and George Rolleston in 1874 and later by David Royce in 1867–8. Possible lateral chamber on the north side. Excavations of the adjacent Swell 8 round barrow in 1974–5 by Alan Saville included the examination of part of the quarry pit on the southwest side of the long barrow. *Reports*: Rolleston 1876, 139–53; Greenwell 1877, 513–4 (CCXXIX); Saville 1979b, 90.

[GLO 23. Cow Common Round, Swell (SP 1316 2633). Simple passage grave. Excavated by William Greenwell in 1874. *Report*: Greenwell 1877, 447–52 (CCXVII).]

GLO 24. **Pole's Wood East**, Swell (SP 1717 2653). Antiquarian excavation by George Rolleston and David Royce in 1875–6. Probable lateral chamber. *Report*: Greenwell 1877, 524-41 (CCXXXII).

GLO 25. **Lamborough Banks**, Bibury (SP 1076 0941). Antiquarian excavation by Samuel Lysons in 1854. Probably a laterally chambered barrow. *Report*: Lysons 1865, 318–20.

[GLO 26. Ablington, Bibury (SP 1089 0924). Simple passage grave. Excavation by A.D. Passmore in 1925. *Report*: Passmore 1934a.]

GLO 27. **Jack Barrow**, Duntisbourne Abbots (SO 9573 0720). Antiquarian excavation in 1875. Small-scale excavations in 1937 by Elsie Clifford aimed to identify the nature and extent of this barrow, but with little result. *Report*: Clifford 1937.

GLO 28. **Druid Stoke**, Bristol (ST 5612 7615). Antiquarian excavation by F. Ware in

Appendix A

1913. Small-scale excavations by George Smith in January 1983 in advance of development revealed traces of a terminal chamber with two or more cells. *Report*: Smith 1989.

[GLO 29. Wick, Wick and Abson (ST 7060 7189). Portal dolmen.]

GLO 30. Norbury / Farmington Camp, Northleach (SP 1237 1550).

GLO 31. The Tinglestone, Avening (ST 8824 9900).

GLO 32. The Giant's Stone, Bisley with Lypiatt (SO 9180 0612).

GLO 33. **Hazleton South**, Hazleton (SP 0720 1882). Geophysical survey and sample excavations involving two linear trenches across the mound by Alan Saville in 1980. Probably a lateral chambered barrow with a single chamber and flanking quarries. *Report*: Saville 1990, 137–40.

GLO 34. **Willersey**, Willersey (SP 1177 3827). Antiquarian excavation by G. Witts in July 1884 in advance of a visit by the Bristol and Gloucestershire Archaeological Society. It is not at all clear what was found. *Report*: Anon. 1885.

[GLO 35. Lypiatt – lost or destroyed site about which nothing is known.]

[GLO 36. The Long Stone, Minchinhampton (ST 8836 9992). Standing stone.]

GLO 37. Boxwell Lodge / ?Hirecombe, Boxwell-with-Leighterton (ST 8195 9241).

GLO 38. Brock Hill, Kingscote (ST 8125 9360).

[GLO 39. Three Shire Stones, Marshfield (ST 7960 7002). Folly constructed in 1858.]

GLO 40. Snowshill, Snowshill (SP 0908 3338).

GLO 41. Bourton on the Hill, Bourton on the Hill (SP 1682 3240).

GLO 42. Ganborough, Longborough (SP 1736 2895).

GLO 43. Oak Piece, Temple Guiting (SP 1340 2890).

[GLO 44. Adlestrop Hill, Adlestrop (SP 2537 2829). Portal dolmen. Extensively excavated by Helen Donovan in 1935–8. *Report*: Donovan 1938.]

GLO 45. Broadwell, Broadwell (SP 1910 2695).

GLO 46. Pole's Wood West, Swell (SP 1659 2657).

GLO 47. The Whistlestone, Swell (SP 1724 2581).

GLO 48. Lower Swell, Swell (SP 1703 2580).

GLO 49. New Close, Upper Slaughter (SP 1433 2567).

GLO 50. Condicote Lane, Swell (SP 1576 2550).

GLO 51. Prestbury, Prestbury (SO 9836 2333).

GLO 52. Slade Barn, Hawling (SP 0693 2188).

GLO 53. Camp Farm / Cold Aston, Aston Blank (SP 1434 2063).

GLO 54. **Hazleton North**, Hazleton (SP 0727 1889). Geophysical surveys followed by total excavation by Alan Saville between 1979 and 1982. A lateral chambered barrow with a pair of opposed chambers in the centre of the mound and flanking quarry pits. *Reports*: Saville 1984; 1990.

[GLO 55. Westcote, Westcote. See OXF 11.]

GLO 56. Lineover, Dowdeswell (SO 9923 1857).

GLO 57. Leygore Manor I, Turkdean (SP 1187 1668).

GLO 58. Leygore Manor II, Turkdean (SP 1208 1660).

GLO 59. Cheltenham Road Plantation, Hampnett (SP 0848 1610).

GLO 60. **Burn Ground**, Hampnett (SP 1042 1607). Antiquarian excavation around 1781 (or 1871?); complete excavation of the site with an open-area trench by W.F. Grimes between October 1940 and March 1941. Terminal chamber with four cells attached to a cross passage with opposed lateral entrances. *Report*: Grimes 1960, 41–128.

GLO 61. Furzenhill Barn, Hampnett (SP 0857 1587).

GLO 62. Coberley, Coberley (SO 9552 1563).

GLO 63. Woodbarrow, Chedworth (SP 0671 1228).

GLO 64. Crickley Barrow, Coln St Dennis (SP 1013 1180).

GLO 65. **Pinkwell**, Chedworth (SP 0452 1059). Antiquarian excavations by J.Y. Akerman in 1856. Possibly a lateral chamber. *Report*: Akerman 1859.

GLO 66. Lad Barrow, Aldsworth (SP 1660 0973).

GLO 67. Camp Barrow South, Miserden (SO 9138 0902).

GLO 68. Honeycombe Farm, Miserden (SO 9300 0890).

GLO 69. Colnpen, Coln St Dennis (SO 0680 0837).

GLO 70. North Cerney I, North Cerney (SO 0180 0750).

GLO 71. Througham, Bisley-with-Lypiatt (SO 9106 0742).

GLO 72. **College Plantation I**, Duntisbourne Rouse (SO 9595 0598). Antiquarian excavation by George Witts in 1882, but no adequate published account. *Report*: Witts 1884b.

GLO 73. College Plantation II, Duntisbourne Rouse (SO 9589 0598).

GLO 74. **Bisley Barrow / Twizzle Stone**, Bisley-with-Lypiatt (SO 9142 0505). Small-scale antiquarian excavation in 1863 prior to its total destruction. *Report*: Not adequately reported, but see Crawford 1925, 80–1.

GLO 75. **Avenis Barrow**, Bisley-with-Lypiatt (SO 9066 0373). Antiquarian excavations by A.E.W. Paine between 1865 and 1875. *Report*: Jowell Burton 1925.

GLO 76. The Toots, King's Stanley (SO 8270 0310).

GLO 77. Whitefield's Tump, Minchinhampton (SO 8540 0170).

GLO 78. Buckholt Wood, Nympsfield (SO 7986 0157)

GLO 79. **Querns Barrow**, Cirencester (SP 0198 0150). Antiquarian excavations involving two cuts through the mound by J. Buckman and C.H. Newmarch in about 1850. *Report*: Buckman and Newmarch 1850, 12.

GLO 80. Oldfield Wood, Avening (ST 8610 9874).

Appendix A

GLO 81. Avening, Avening (ST 8875 9835).

GLO 82. Woodleaze Farm, Kingscote (ST 8198 9761).

GLO 83. Rowden Wood, Uley (ST 7780 9694).

GLO 84. Folley Wood, Dursley (ST 7738 9690).

GLO 85. Symond's Hall Farm, Wotton under Edge (ST 7971 9596).

GLO 86. Blackquarries Hill, Wotton under Edge (ST 7751 9323).

GLO 87. Starveall, Hawkesbury (ST 7940 8791).

GLO 88. Hawkesbury Knoll, Hawkesbury (ST 7684 8722).

[GLO 89. The Grickstone, Horton (ST 7770 8278). Standing stone.]

GLO 90. Tormarton, Tormarton (ST 7795 7805).

GLO 91. Dyrham and Hinton, Dyrham and Hinton (ST 7530 7689).

GLO 92. **Saltway Barn**, Bibury (SP 1151 0906). Fully excavated by W.F. Grimes between October 1939 and March 1940. Probably a multi-period monument with a primary simple passage grave later expanded to become a rather irregularly shaped long barrow. *Report*: Grimes 1960, 5–40.

GLO 93. Norn's Tump, Avening (ST 8891 9839). Sometimes claimed to be the site from which the three burial chambers at the Old Rectory in Avening originally came, but see GLO 17.

GLO 94. **Sale's Lot**, Withington (SP 0488 1576). Extensive excavations by Helen O'Neil in 1965 revealed a multi-period monument overlying an area of occupation. Primary simple passage grave and round barrow or rotunda grave later joined to form a long barrow. *Report*: O'Neil 1966.

GLO 95. Bourton Downs, Bourton-on-the-Hill (SP 1446 3197).

GLO 96. North Cerney II, North Cerney (SO 9905 0942).

GLO 97. Shawswell Farm, Rendcomb (SP 0269 1182).

[GLO 98. The Knap, Cheltenham (SO 9455 2245). ?Portal dolmen.]

GLO 99. Oldwells Shed, Bibury (SP 1200 1048).

HRF 1. Arthur's Stone, Dorstone (SO 3180 4313).

HRF 2. Park Wood, St Margaret's (SO 350 330).

HRF 3. Wergin's Stone, Sutton (SO 5296 4397)

HRF 4. Cross Lodge Barrow / Great Llanavon Farm, Dorstone (SO 3325 4168).

MON 1. Cleppa Park, Duffryn (ST 2740 8571).

MON 2. Y Garn Llwyd (*trans.* The Grey Cairn), Shirenewton (ST 4476 9678).

MON 3. **Heston Brake**, Portskewett (ST 5052 8865). Limited antiquarian excavations on 22 August 1888 by the Monmouth and Caerleon Antiquarian Association. *Report*: Bagnall-Oakley 1888; 1889.

MNT 3†. **Lower Luggy long barrow**, Berriew (SJ 201 019). Surveys and small-scale investigations by Alex Gibson and others in December 1994. Probable timber chamber. *Report*: Gibson 2000.

[OXF 1. The Whispering Knights, Rollright (SP 2992 3084). Portal dolmen. Trial trenching around the monument was carried out by George Lambrick in 1983. *Report*: Lambrick 1988.]

[OXF 2. Hoare Stone, Enstone (SP 3782 2373). Portal dolmen.]

OXF 3. Slatepits Copse, Cornbury and Wychwood (SP 3290 1651).

[OXF 4. Hoar Stone, Steeple Barton (SP 4645 2472). Portal dolmen.]

[OXF 5. Hoar Stone, Langley (SP 3050 1658). Portal dolmen.]

OXF 6. **Ascott-under-Wychwood I**, Ascott-under-Wychwood (SP 3001 1755). Total excavation of the site by Don Benson between 1965 and 1970. Two laterally placed chamber areas perhaps joining in the middle. *Reports*: Selkirk 1971; Chesterman 1977; Benson and Clegg 1978; final report currently (2004) in preparation by Alasdair Whittle.

[OXF 7. Hawkestone, Spelsbury (SP 3392 2355). Portal dolmen.]

OXF 8. **Lyneham**, Lyneham (SP 2973 2106). Antiquarian investigation by Edward Conder in 1885 and by Edward Condor Jr and Lord Moreton in 1894. At least one lateral chamber. *Report*: Conder 1895.

OXF 9. **Crawley**, Crawley (SP 337 112). Antiquarian excavation by J.Y. Akerman in about 1857, but only secondary burials discovered. *Report*: Akerman 1857.

OXF 10. Churchill Copse / Churchill Plain, Cornbury and Wychwood (SP 3319 1688).

OXF 11. Fifield, Fifield (SP 2179 1879).

OXF 12†. Cornwell, Cornwell (SP 2665 2668).

OXF 13†. Old Chalford, Enstone (SP 3371 2592).

OXF 14†. Lidstone, Enstone (SP 3570 2502).

OXF 15†. Shipton-under-Wychwood, Shipton-under-Wychwood (SP 2975 1745).

OXF 16†. Ascott-under-Wychwood II, Ascott-under-Wychwood (SP 3141 1852).

OXF 17†. Pollard's Common, Swinbrook and Widford (SP 2915 1385).

OXF 18†. Whitehill, Shipton-on-Cherwell (SP 4670 1825).

OXF 19†. Shipton-on-Cherwell, Shipton-on-Cherwell (SP 4709 1807).

OXF 20†. Shipton-on-Cherwell, Shipton-on-Cherwell (SP 4734 1803).

OXF 21†. Drayton, Drayton (SU 4828 9495).

RAD 1. Newchurch, Newchurch (SO 2052 4910).

SOM 1. **Stoney Littleton**, Wellow (ST 7349 5721). First opened in about 1760 when the mound was used as a quarry, before being explored archaeologically on several subsequent occasions. On 24–5 May 1816 John Skinner and his brother Russell, Sir Richard Colt Hoare and his steward Philip Crocker and a labourer named Zebedee Weston cleared the chambers. Further excavations took place during restorations in 1857–8 and again

Appendix A

during restoration work in 1999–2000. Terminal chamber with seven cells arranged in three pairs and an end chamber. *Reports*: Colt Hoare 1821a; Thomas 2003.

SOM 2. **Fairy's Toot**, Nempnett Thrubwell / Butcombe (ST 5203 6180). Antiquarian investigations by Thomas Bere in 1789 and 1792 when the mound was being quarried for stone. Further explorations by John Skinner in 1822 suggested that the barrow had a terminal chamber with 12 cells arranged as six pairs. *Report*: Bulleid 1941, 59–64.

SOM 3. The Devil's Bed and Bolster, Beckington (ST 8150 5332).

SOM 4. **Giant's Grave**, Charmborough, Holcombe (ST 6783 5129). Antiquarian excavation by John Skinner in 1826 and later by J.D.C. Wickham in 1909. Possible terminal chamber with one cell. *Report*: Wickham 1912, 1–13.

[SOM 5. The Waterstone, Wrington (ST 5015 6440). Portal dolmen.]

SOM 6. **Fromefield**, Frome (ST 7819 4898). Antiquarian excavation in 1819-20 the results of which suggest a terminal chamber with four cells in two pairs. Further excavations by Faith de M. Vatcher and H.L. Vatcher in March 1965. *Report*: Vatcher and Vatcher 1973.

SOM 7. Big Tree, Buckland Down, Buckland Dinham (ST 7272 5175).

SOM 8. **Murtry Hill**, Buckland Dinham (ST 7626 5069). Small-scale excavations by H. St George Gray in 1920 revealed that the standing stones had probably been moved in 1803–4 as part of a 'restoration'. Possibly a multi-period monument with a primary portal dolmen later expanded to form a long barrow. *Report*: Gray 1921.

SOM 9. Red Hill, Wrington (ST 4995 6359).

SOM 10. The Mountains, Felton Hill, Winford (ST 5163 6487).

SOM 11. **Battlegore**, Williton (ST 0745 4162). Excavations by H. St George Gray in 1931 revealed stone sockets and flints. Probably a terminal chamber with a single cell. *Report*: Gray 1931, 19-21.

SOM 12. Barrow House Farm N, Chewton Mendip (ST 6010 5334).

SOM 13. Soldier's Grave, Dundry (ST 5530 6678).

SOM 14†. Barrow House Farm S, Chewton Mendip (ST 6012 5302).

SOM 15†. Dundry Hill, Dundry (ST 5760 6648).

[SOM 16†. **Priddy long barrow**, Priddy (ST 5142 5092). Probably an oval barrow. Antiquarian excavation by John Skinner on 29–30 August 1816 which found rather little. Large-scale excavation by Donald Moore and E.K. Tratman for the Bristol University Spelaeological Society in April–June 1928 also revealed little to help illuminate the nature of the site. *Reports*: Dobson 1931, 59; Phillips and Taylor 1972; Lewis 2002.]

SOM 17†. Pen Hill I, St Cuthbert Out (ST 5635 4876).

SOM 18†. Pen Hill II, St Cuthbert Out (ST 5649 4875).

SOM 19†. Hill Grove, St Cuthbert Out (ST 5694 4970).

SOM 20†. Green Ore, St Cuthbert Out (ST 5858 4959).

SOM 21†. **Gray's Down**, Shoscombe (ST 7092 5619). Antiquarian investigation by John Skinner in 1815, the results of which suggest a terminal chamber with at least two cells. *Report*: No satisfactory publication, see Grinsell 1971, 87.

[WAR 1. The King Stone, Long Compton (SP 2961 3095). Standing stone.]

WIL 1. **Lugbury / Little Drew**, Nettleton (ST 8305 7855). Antiquarian excavation by Sir Richard Colt Hoare on 8–11 October 1821 and later by G.P. Scrope and John Thurnam in the summer of 1854 and September 1855. At least four later chambers found on the south side of the mound. *Reports*: Colt Hoare 1822; Thurnam 1857.

WIL 2. **Giant's Caves**, Luckington (ST 8200 8296). Small-scale excavations by A.D. Passmore in August 1932 were followed by extensive work in 1960–2 by John Corcoran. Four lateral chambers have been recorded. *Reports*: Passmore 1934b; Corcoran 1970.

WIL 3. **Lanhill / Hubba's Low**, Chippenham (ST 8773 7433). Antiquarian excavations by John Thurnam in 1855, followed by a succession of more extensive excavations as the site was gradually quarried away: B. and M.E. Cunnington in 1909, Alexander Keiller and Stuart Piggott in 1938 and D. Grant King in May 1963. The site contained at least three lateral chambers. *Reports*: Cunnington 1909a; Keiller and Piggott 1938; King 1966.

WIL 4. **West Kennet long barrow**, Avebury (SU 1046 6774). Antiquarian excavations by Dr Toope during the seventeenth century to get bones for medicine; John Thurnam investigated the entrance, passage and western chamber in 1859. Full-scale excavations by Stuart Piggott and Richard Atkinson in 1955–6 investigated four further chambers, the forecourt area and a section through the mound and northern quarry ditch. Reconstruction works were carried out in 1956–7. *Reports*: Thurnam 1860b; Piggott 1958; 1962; Atkinson and Piggott 1986; Thomas and Whittle 1986.

WIL 5. East Kennet, East Kennet (SU 1163 6686).

WIL 6. **Adam's Grave / Old Adam**, Walker's Hill, Alton (SU 1124 6339). Small-scale antiquarian excavations by John Thurnam in 1860. *Report*: Thurnam 1860b, 410; 1868, 203 and 230.

WIL 7. **Manton Down / Doghill Barrow**, Preshute (SU 1478 7135). Rescue excavations by Richard Atkinson in June 1952 following the levelling of the mound suggested a terminal chamber with one cell. *Reports*: Harrod 1864; Lukis 1867; Piggott 1947.

WIL 8. **The Devil's Den**, Clatford Bottom, Preshute (SU 1520 6965). Small-scale excavation by A.D. Passmore in 1921 prior to underpinning work revealed little about the structure or form of the barrow. *Report*: Passmore 1922.

WIL 9. **Tidcombe Hill / Tidcombe Great Barrow**, Tidcombe and Fosbury (SU 2927 5760). Limited investigations in about 1750, perhaps by local people looking for treasure, with subsequent excavations by W.C. Lukis, perhaps assisted by John Thurnam, in 1845. Terminal chamber with ?one cell. *Reports*: Willis 1787, 91; Lukis 1864, 155.

WIL 10. **Temple Bottom**, Ogbourne St Andrew (SU 1486 7251). Small-scale antiquarian excavations by W.C. Lukis and A.C. Smith in June 1861. *Reports*: Lukis 1864, 156; 1867; 1885.

WIL 11. **Millbarrow / King's Millbarrow**, Winterbourne Monkton (SU 0943 7220). Antiquarian excavations by John Thurnam in 1863, but with little result. Geophysical surveys, augering and sample excavations of the levelled barrow were carried out in 1987. Four trenches allowed sections through the flanking ditches and the chamber area. Terminal chamber with ?one cell. *Report*: Whittle 1994.

WIL 12. Shelving Stone, Winterbourne Monkton (SU 1037 7156).

Appendix A

WIL 13. West Amesbury – not in Cotswold-Severn region.

WIL 14. Old Chapel long barrow, Temple Down, Preshute (SU 1209 7290).

WIL 15. **West Woods long barrow**, West Overton (SU 1569 6563). Antiquarian excavation by Sir Henry Meux in about 1880 cut into the centre of the mound. *Report*: Passmore 1923, 366–7.

WIL 16. Avebury Down, Avebury (SU 116 701).

WIL 17. **Oldbury Hill**, Calne / Cherhill (SU 0469 6931). Antiquarian excavations by William Cunnington in 1864 or soon after. Terminal chamber (?wooden). *Report*: Cunnington 1872, 103–4.

WIL 18. **Shepherd's Shore long barrow**, Bishops Canning (SU 0387 6610). Small-scale excavations by M.E. Cunnington in 1914 which suggest that there was a terminal chamber, probably wooden. *Report*: Cunnington 1926.

WIL 19. **Easton Down**, Bishops Canning (SU 0637 6610). Antiquarian excavation by John Thurnam in the 1850s. Surveys and excavations in 1991 by Alasdair Whittle examined sections through the two flanking ditches and an area of old land surface under the mound. Possible terminal chamber (?wooden). *Reports*: Thurnam 1860a, 324; 1868, 180; Whittle *et al.* 1993.

WIL 20. **Horton Down**, Bishops Canning (SU 0768 6580). Antiquarian excavation by John Thurnam in 1863. The mound possibly covers a timber chamber. *Report*: Thurnam 1868, 180.

WIL 21. Kitchen Barrow, Bishops Canning (SU 0668 6480).

WIL 22. **Monkton Down**, Winterbourne Monkton (SU 1163 7230). Antiquarian excavation by John Merewether in about 1850. Possibly a barrow with a timber chamber. *Report*: Merewether 1851, 104.

WIL 23. The Chase, Winsley (ST 8000 6057).

WIL 24. Arn Hill – not in Cotswold-Severn region.

WIL 25. Luckington II, Luckington (ST 8210 8281).

WIL 26†. Avebury G21, Avebury (SU 1100 6920).

WIL 27†. **Beckhampton Road long barrow**, Bishops Canning (SU 0666 6773). Antiquarian investigations, possibly by John Thurnam, of the northeast part of the mound between 1855 and 1867. Total excavation by Isobel Smith in 1964, but no evidence of a chamber under the mound. *Report*: Ashbee *et al.* 1979, 228–50.

WIL 28†. Bromham G3, Bromham (SU 0039 6529).

WIL 29†. Calne, Calne Without (SU 0455 6933).

WIL 30†. **Horslip long barrow / Windmill Hill long barrow**, Avebury (SU 0860 7052). Fully excavated in the spring and summer of 1959 by Paul Ashbee. A chamberless long barrow. *Reports*: Ashbee and Smith 1960; 1966; Ashbee *et al.* 1979, 207–28.

WIL 31†. **Kings Play Down long barrow**, Heddington (SU 0105 6599). Small-scale excavations by B.H. and M.E. Cunnington in 1907. Wooden terminal chamber with ?one cell and a timber façade at the east end. *Report*: Cunnington 1909b; see also Ashbee 1970, 40 and 129.

WIL 32†. Lambourne Ground, Winterbourne Bassett (SU 0940 7563).

WIL 33†. Lockeridge, West Overton (SU 1493 6779).

WIL 34†. **Longstones long barrow**, Avebury (SU 0871 6915). Antiquarian investigation by John Merewether who recorded what seem to be secondary burials. *Reports*: Merewether 1851, 109; Cunnington 1914, 384–5.

WIL 35†. Roughridge Hill long barrow, Bishops Canning (SU 0548 6576).

WIL 36†. **South Street long barrow**, Avebury (SU 0902 6928). Total excavation by John Evans in 1964–7. A chamberless long barrow. *Reports*: Smith and Evans 1968; Evans and Burleigh 1969; Ashbee *et al*. 1979, 250–75.

WIL 37†. Beckhampton Plantation long barrow, Avebury (SU 0900 6715).

WIL 38†. Wanborough, Wanborough / Liddington G4 (SU 2250 7977).

WIL 39†. White Hill, Lockeridge, West Overton (SU 142 673).

APPENDIX B

RADIOCARBON DATES FROM LONG BARROWS

Radiocarbon dates are listed here by site, each entry showing: the calibrated age range in years Before Christ (BC) / *Anno Domini* (AD); the original determination in radiocarbon years Before Present (BP) and its laboratory number in parenthesis; and brief details of the sample and its context. Age ranges were determined using OxCal version 3.5 (Bronk Ramsey 2000) with the calibration curve using atmospheric data from Stuiver *et al.* (1998). All the calibrated ages are expressed at two standard deviations, which means there is a 95 per cent chance that the true date of the material analysed lies within the range given.

Wayland's Smithy (BRK 1)
3950–3100 BC [4770±130 BP: I-2328] Charcoal on the ground surface under the long barrow.

Lambourn (BRK 2)
4600–3750 BC [5365±180 BP: Gx-1178] Charcoal from floor of S ditch near W terminal.
3770–3530 BC [4870±45 BP: OxA-7692] Antler pick on floor of N ditch.
3910–3640 BC [4955±45 BP: OxA-7693] Human femur from secondary silts of S ditch.
3790–3630 BC [4915±45 BP: OxA-7694] Human cranium from primary silt of S ditch.
3340–2880 BC [4395±65 BP: OxA-7899] Human cranium from secondary burial.

Gwernvale (BRE 7)
3980–3660 BC [5050±75 BP: CAR-113] Charcoal from pre-cairn pit F68.
3340–2880 BC [4390±70 BP: CAR-114] Charcoal from pit F58 contemporary with the tomb.
3650–3000BC [4590±75 BP: CAR-116] Charcoal from pit F47 contemporary with the tomb.
5980–5630 BC [6895±80 BP: CAR-118] Charcoal from ground surface below the tomb.

Penywyrlod (BRE 14)
3960–3640 BC [4970±80 BP: HAR-674] Mixed human bones from NE II chamber.

Parc le Breos Cwm (GLA 4)
3640–3350 BC [4685±65 BP: OxA-6487] Human bone from SE chamber.
3660–3370 BC [4780±60 BP: OxA-6488] Human bone from SW chamber.
3350–2920 BC [4445±60 BP: OxA-6489] Human bone from SW chamber.
3640–3330 BC [4660±60 BP: OxA-6490] Human bone from NW chamber.
3640–3360 BC [4710±60 BP: OxA-6491] Human bone from NW chamber.
3700–3370 BC [4805±55 BP: OxA-6492] Human bone from passage.
3790–3520 BC [4875±55 BP: OxA-6493] Human bone from NE chamber.
3650–3100 BC [4645±60 BP: OxA-6494] Human bone from NE chamber.
2290–1920 BC [3705±55 BP: OxA-6495] Human bone from passage.
3780–3380 BC [4850±65 BP: OxA-6496] Human bone from SE chamber.
2340–1970 BC [3750±55 BP: OxA-6497] Human bone from passage.
550–200 BC [2315±50 BP: OxA-6498] Roe deer bone from passage.
6640–6410 BC [7665±65 BP: OxA-6499] Badger bone from passage.
11,050–10,200 BC [10,625±80 BP: OxA-6500] Large ungulate bone from passage.
3640–3360 BC [4690±55BP: OxA-6641] Human bone from SE chamber.

Cefn Drum (Not numbered)
2310–1970 BC [3750±50 BP: OxA-6806] Charcoal from area outside passage.
1040–1100 AD [859±34BP: OxA-10056] Bone from pit outside passage.

Belas Knap (GLO 1)
3800–3640 BC [4935±45 BP: OxA-10391] Human cranium from chamber (Ref.: C-IV 1978-709.2).
3890–3640 BC [4940±45 BP: OxA-10392] Human cranium from chamber (Ref.: D-4 Eu.1.5.9).
4040–3790 BC [5130±45 BP: OxA-10393] Human cranium from chamber (Ref.: D-II Eu.1.5.3).
3910–3640 BC [4955±45 BP: OxA-10394] Human cranium from chamber (Ref.: B-I Eu.1.5.2).
3800–3530 BC [4890±55 BP: OxA-10652] Human cranium from chamber (Ref.: C-V Eu.1.5.6).

Druid Stoke (GLO 28)
2880–2450 BC [4070±80 BP: HAR-8083] Human bone from old ground surface.

Hazleton North (GLO 54)
3360–2900 BC [4450±90 BP: OxA-383] Human rib from outer passage of S chamber.
3650–2900 BC [4600±120 BP: OxA-643] Human femur from outer passage of N chamber.
3790–3490 BC [4840±80 BP: OxA-644] Human femur from N chamber.
3710–3360 BC [4780±80 BP: OxA-645] Human femur from S chamber.
3950–3350 BC [4875±80 BP: OxA-646] Human cranium from buried soil below mound.
1680–1960 AD [144 ±1.4 BP: OxA-678] Modern grape pip.
3960–3640 BC [4970±80 BP: OxA-738] Cattle calcaneum from buried soil below mound.

Appendix B

3950–3520 BC [4915±80 BP: OxA-739] Pig humerus from buried soil below mound.
3760–3370 BC [4820±70 BP: OxA-902] Human femur from outer passage of N chamber.
3770–3500 BC [4840±60BP: OxA-903] Human femur from outer passage of N chamber.
3800–3380 BC [4860±70 BP: OxA-904] Human femur from outer passage of N chamber.
3950–3630 BC [4950±70BP: OxA-905] Human femur from N chamber.
3950–3500 BC [4880±70 BP: OxA-906] Human femur from outer passage of S chamber.
3950–3640 BC [4970±60 BP: OxA-907] Human femur from outer passage of S chamber.
3730–3370 BC [4830±60 BP: OxA-908] Human femur from inner passage of S chamber.
3950–3650 BC [5000±70 BP: OxA-910] Human femur from inner passage of S chamber.
3780–3370 BC [4830±80 BP: OxA-911] Human femur from S chamber.
4350–3700 BC [5200±150 BP: OxA-912] Human femur from S chamber.
3950–3640 BC [4960±70 BP: OxA-913] Cattle skull from the forecourt collapse / old ground surface.
3950–3640 BC [4970±70 BP: OxA-914] Cattle skull from the forecourt collapse / old ground surface.
3780–3370 BC [4840±70 BP: OxA-915] Cattle rib from S quarry fill.
3720–3370 BC [4810±70 BP: OxA-916] Cattle femur from S quarry fill.
3650–3100 BC [4640±80 BP: OxA-1177] Human rib from outer passage of S chamber.
3730–3370 BC [4830±60 BP: HAR-8349] Red deer antler from primary dump under mound.
3940–3630 BC [4950±60 BP: HAR-8350] Red deer antler from north quarry.

Lower Luggy (MNT 3)
3710–3510 BC [4830±45 BP: BM-2954] Charcoal from oak post in palisade trench (Trench 1).
3640–3370 BC [4710±40 BP: BM-2955] Charcoal from oak post in possible façade (Trench 2).

Ascott-under-Wychwood (OXF 6)
3940–3510 BC [4893±70 BP: BM-491b] Charcoal from pre-barrow pit.
3650–3360 BC [4735±70 BP: BM-492] Charcoal from old ground surface.
3950–3560 BC [4942±74 BP BM-832] Charcoal from within barrow.
3980–3640 BC [5020±92 BP BM-833] Charcoal from within barrow.
4500–3500 BC [5198±225 BP: BM-835] Charcoal in primary fill of quarry.
3350–2920 BC [4445±61 BP: BM-836] Charcoal from upper fill of quarry.
3750–3050 BC [4714±116: BM-837] Charcoal from upper fill of quarry.
3550–2700 BC [4430±130 BP: BM-1974★] Human bone from chamber area.
1930–1680 BC [3480±50 BP: BM-1975★] Human bone from outside outer cist.
3370–3090 BC [4535±40 BP: BM-1976★] Human bone from chamber area.
3800–2900 BC [4680±160 BP: BM-1974R] Human bone from chamber area.
2650–2000 BC [3870±100 BP: BM-1975R] Human bone from outside outer cist.
3970–3520 BC [4930±100 BP: BM-1976R] Human bone from chamber area.

* These oft-cited dates fall within a series of determinations from the British Museum which were effected by systematic laboratory error and appear to be too young (Tite *et al.* 1987). Re-evaluated determinations were made and these are indicated by the addition of an 'R' to the laboratory number (Bowman *et al.* 1990, 69).

Barrow Hills, Abingdon (Not numbered)
3350–2550 BC [4320±130 BP: BM-2390] Antler from ditch of oval barrow.
3360–3020 BC [4500±50 BP: BM-2391] Antler from ditch of pre-barrow rectangular enclosure.
3350–2650 BC [4330±80 BP: BM-2392] Antler from ditch of oval barrow.
3340–2900 BC [4420±70 BP: BM-2393] Antler from ditch of oval barrow.
2880–2490 BC [4120±60 BP: BM-2707] Human bone from male inhumation in central grave.
2470–2140 BC [3860±50 BP: BM-2708] Human bone from female inhumation in central grave.

West Kennet (WIL 4)
3790–3370 BC [4825±90 BP: OxA-449] Human skull from Skeleton II in NW chamber.
3700–3100 BC [4700±80 BP: OxA-450] Human femur from Skeleton II in NE chamber.
3720–3360 BC [4780±90 BP: OxA-451] Human femur from Skeleton IV in SW chamber.
3720–3360 BC [4780±90 BP: OxA-563] Human femur from Skeleton I in NW chamber.

Millbarrow (WIL 11)
3350–2920 BC [4450±60 BP: BM-2729] Red deer antler from primary ditch fill on S side.
3520–3020 BC [4560±70 BP: BM-2730] Red deer antler from primary ditch fill on N side.
3500–3090 BC [4560±50 BP: BM-2731] Red deer antler from primary ditch fill on S side.
3650–3050 BC [4630±90 BP: OxA-3169] Human bone from supposed chamber.
3650–3000 BC [4630±100 BP: OxA-3170] Red deer antler from pit in front of tomb.
3800–3100 BC [4750±120 BP: OxA-3171] Human bone from pre-tomb pit.
4000–3350 BC [4900±110 BP: OxA-3172] Human bone from pre-tomb pit.
3370–2920 BC [4480±80 BP: OxA-3198] Human bone from supposed chamber.

Easton Down (WIL 19)
3650–3050 BC [4610±60 BP: OxA-3759] Animal bone on old ground surface.
3650–3360 BC [4730±65 BP: OxA-3760] Red deer antler from primary ditch fill.
2480–2140 BC [3860±60 BP: OxA-3761] Cattle tooth from secondary ditch fill.
3500–3010 BC [4535±65 BP: OxA-3762] Red deer tooth from primary ditch fill.

Beckhampton Road (WIL 27)

3100–2500 BC [4257±90 BP: BM-506a] Antler pick on old ground surface under mound.

3370–2900 BC [4467±90 BP: BM-506b] Antler pick on old ground surface under mound.

4350–3650 BC [5200±160 BP: NPL-138] Charcoal (oak) from within soil below mound.

Horslip (WIL 30)

4350–3650 BC [5190±150 BP: BM-180] Red deer antler from primary ditch fill.

South Street (WIL 36)

3800–3100 BC [4760±130 BP: BM-356] Charcoal from old ground surface under mound.

3800–3000 BC [4700±135 BP: BM-357] Animal bone from primary ditch fill N side.

3650–2900 BC [4620±140 BP: BM-358a] Red deer antler from primary ditch fill N side.

3550–2990 BC [4530±110 BP: BM-358b] Red deer antler from matrix of mound.

SITES TO VISIT

VISITING LONG BARROWS

More than a dozen long barrows and related monuments in the Cotswolds and surrounding areas enjoy easy public access by virtue of being in the Guardianship of the State (English Heritage or Cadw) or in the ownership of organizations such as the National Trust that encourage public access *(100)*. The following are amongst the best examples to visit, but do not expect anything in the way of tourist facilities. These are all 'self-guided' attractions, uncluttered by the trappings of modern life. Some may be challenging to find, but the rewards of visiting them are great. At the time of going to press, all the monuments listed here were open, accessible, or easily visible. Arrangements are, however, constantly changing, and if you find yourself in any doubt about access always ask permission from the landowner. The inclusion of a site here does not itself confer any right of access.

Long barrows can be enjoyed in many different ways. They provide inspiring and challenging subjects for painting, sketching, photography, or writing; your imagination is the only constraint on what you can achieve. But when visiting a site it is often helpful to try to visualize it as it might have been in earlier times. Capture in your mind's eye the dazzling brightness of bare earth, rock and upstanding stones before any lichen, grass, or shrubs took hold. Contemplate how many people in the past approached the site you are looking at. Who were they? Did they come often, or only for some special occasions? What was their mood? Think about how long it took to build the structure you are looking at. Visualize if you can the surrounding countryside. Was the site deliberately placed to enjoy or exploit a particular view? Some of the long barrows listed here are right beside a road; others require a walk of some kind along tracks or across fields. Appropriate footware and clothing are always advisable. A torch is useful for barrows with accessible chambers that you can go inside; a candle makes the experience more authentic! When visiting any archaeological site always observe the Country Code. Never damage monuments by picking up stones, digging holes, lighting fires, taking bits away, or rubbing rock-art or decorated stones. The unauthorized use of a metal detector on a protected monument in England or Wales is against the law, as too is the act of damaging or defacing a protected monument. Always think of others too while enjoying a site. Park sensibly if arriving by car, take away your rubbish and don't presume an automatic right of solitude. Crypto-

Sites to Visit

shamanistic rites or rowdy picnics at small monuments may be fun, but can be very irritating to others. Always respect the sacred nature of these long barrows as ritual, ceremonial, burial and religious centres.

Each entry here has a few brief notes on how to find the barrow, but it is best to obtain the relevant Ordnance Survey Landranger Map (scale: 1:50,000) and use the national grid reference to find the site and check the best approach to it. The pace of development and the re-routing of roads mean that access arrangements are constantly changing; don't give up if at first you can't find a site; ask others for directions.

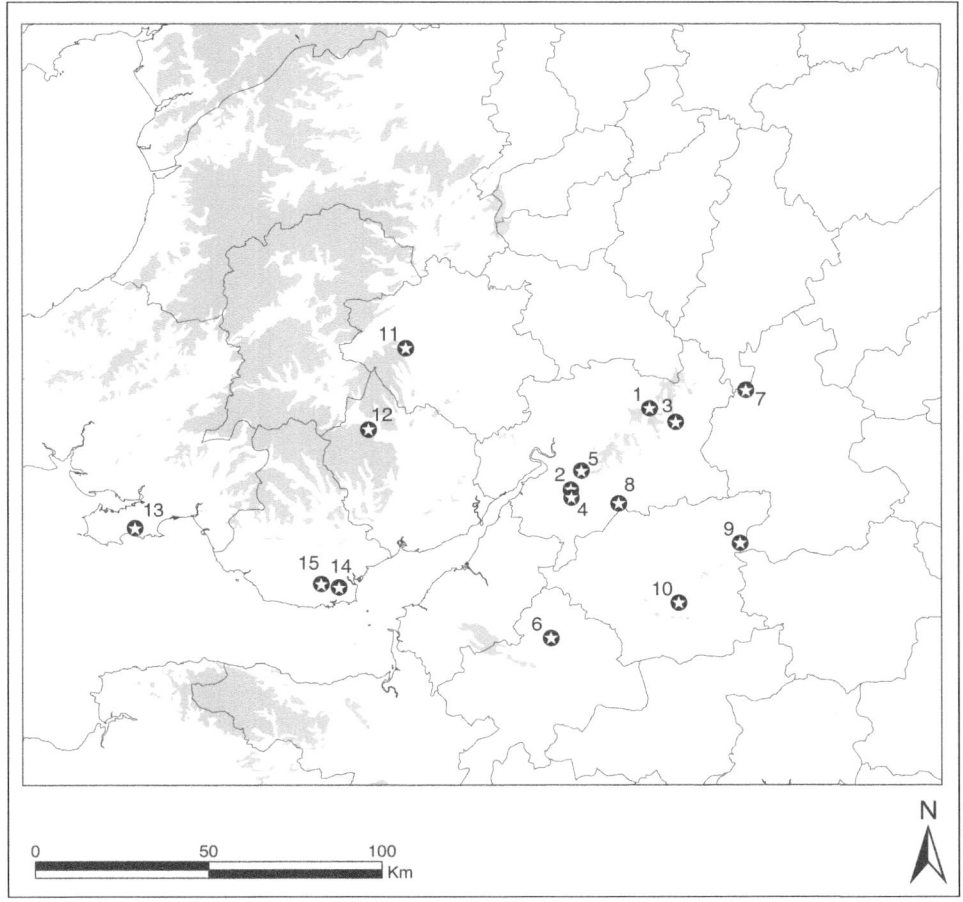

100 Distribution of the sites described in Appendix C. Administrative boundaries current in 2003 are shown. Land over 244m OD is shaded

Long Barrows of the Cotswolds

THE COTSWOLDS

1. Belas Knap, Sudeley, Gloucestershire (GLO 1)

SP 0209 2554. 3km S of Winchcombe on NE side of Cleeve Hill, best approached along signposted lanes from the main A46 SW of Winchcombe. The turning is immediately SW of Winchcombe Hospital. Steep (signposted) footpath leads from a small parking area to the hilltop site about 1km away. English Heritage. Finds in Cheltenham Museum.

Belas Knap lies on a gentle hill-slope overlooking a steep-sided river valley. The name derives from the Old English words *bel* meaning a beacon and *cnaepp* meaning a hilltop. It displays many of the classic features of Cotswold-Severn long barrows and is often seen as the type-site for examples with lateral chambers *(3, 100, 101* and see *cover picture)*. The wedge-shaped mound is over 50m long and stands nearly 4m high; it is orientated north–south. At the north end is a deep forecourt between two rounded horns, and in the back of the forecourt is an H-shaped setting of stones, perhaps the remains of a portal dolmen. The ditch that seems to define the sides of the mound is a product of reconstruction work during the 1930s; the bank of soil and stone outside the ditch is in fact material that has weathered off the top of mound.

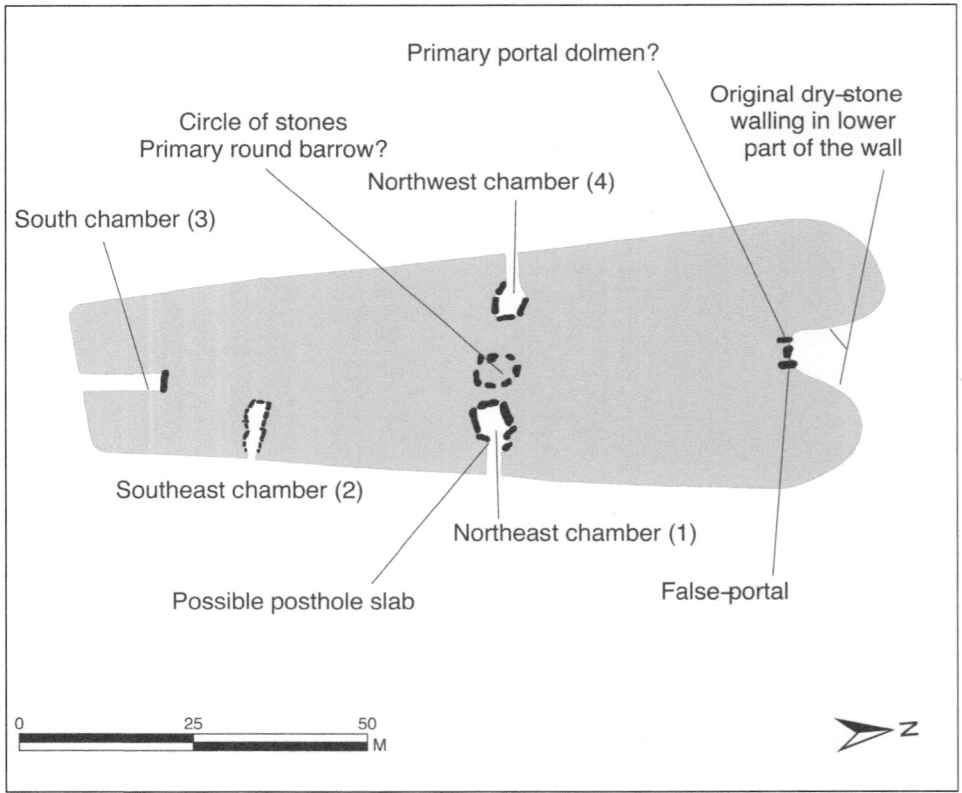

101 Plan of Belas Knap, Sudeley (GLO 1). *After Grinsell 1966*

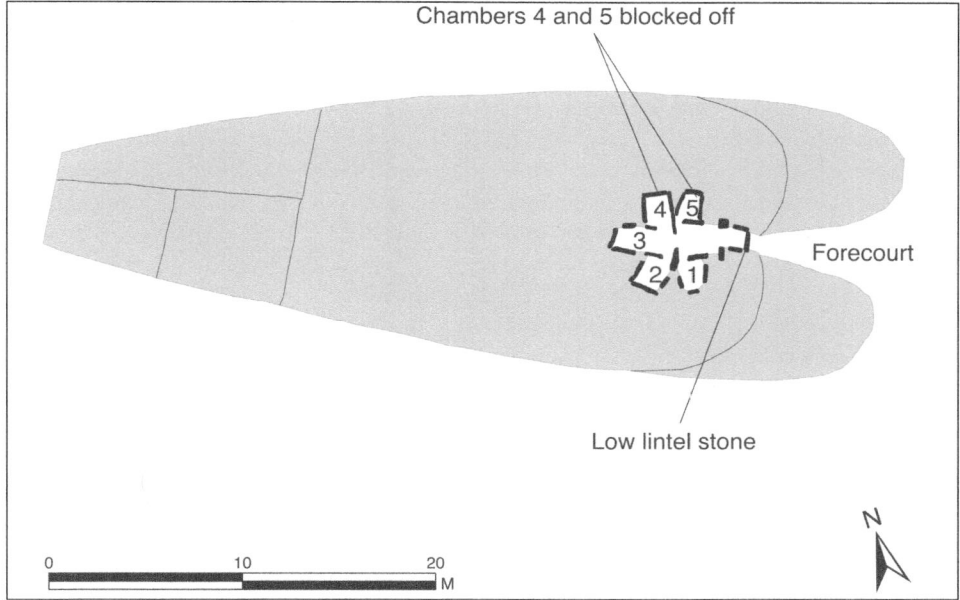

102 Plan of Hetty Pegler's Tump, Uley (GLO 14). After Clifford 1966 fig. 2 and Grinsell 1970

Three chambers, all heavily restored, open into the mound from its long sides, while a fourth (roofless) chamber opens from the narrow southern end. The remains of about 30 people were found in the burial chambers during excavations in 1863–5 and 1928–31.

Key points to look for at Belas Knap are: the portal setting in the back of the forecourt; the dry-stone walling of the forecourt walls, the lower courses of which are original; the great size and bulk of the mound; the small size of the chambers; and the differences that exist in the shape of the chambers. The two slabs flanking the entrance to the northeast chamber have crescentic hollows in their facing edges and may have once formed a porthole entrance as at Windmill Tump, Rodmarton (GLO 16).

A round barrow is visible in the ploughed field to the west of the long barrow.

Further reading: Crawford 1925, 67–80 (C12); Berry 1929; 1930; Hemp 1929; Radford 1930; Grinsell 1966; Parsons 2002.

2. Hetty Pegler's Tump, Uley, Gloucestershire (GLO 14)

SO 7895 0004. W of the B4066 between Stroud and Uley. Signposted with some roadside parking. Approached across fields by a marked footpath. English Heritage.

Regarded by many as the best long barrow to visit for an authentic appreciation of the chamber interior, it is certainly a charming place situated right on the edge of the Cotswold escarpment. The strange name of this fine barrow comes from two seventeenth-century owners of the field in which it stands: Henry Pegler (died 1695) and his wife Hester (died 1694).

The mound of Hetty Pegler's Tump is characteristically trapezoidal, 36m long by 26m wide and orientated roughly east–west *(102)*. Two horns flank the narrow east-facing forecourt, in the back of which is the entrance to the chamber. Reconstruction works in the mid nineteenth century wrongly positioned the massive portal stone, making the entrance rather lower than it once was *(5C)*. But this error has its advantages in making the chamber area feel enclosed. Once under the portal stone it is possible to crouch in the central passage and soak in the atmosphere. On the south are two side chambers, but two to the north have been blocked up for safety. Only their portals can be seen. A fifth chamber cell lies at the far end of the passage.

Being inside the dark chamber with only a candle makes it easy to imagine a ceremony or burial ritual here nearly 6,000 years ago. While in the chamber, notice some of the key points about this barrow: the roof constructed of overlapping slabs; the use of dry-stone walling to fill the gaps between the orthostats forming the chamber walls; and the natural holes and hollows in some of the orthostats. Consider the difficulties of moving corpses about in the confined space. When excavated in 1821 at least 15 disarticulated skeletons were found and a further eight or nine in 1854.

Further reading: Crawford 1925, 102–6 (C31); Clifford 1966.

3. Notgrove, Notgrove, Gloucestershire (GLO 4)

SP 0959 2119. 7km E of Andoversford, 6km W of Bourton-on-the-Water. Situated immediately S of the B4068 (formerly A436) NW of Notgrove village. English Heritage. Finds in Cheltenham Museum.

Excavated in 1934-5, this site became a favourite long barrow to visit in the following decades. However, in 1974, following deterioration of the stonework, the site was covered with soil to protect it. The result is a very strange-looking mound. Set high on an exposed area of upland, it is, however, possible to experience something of its place in the landscape.

Originally, the Notgrove long barrow was a very typical example and became the type-site for those with a terminal chamber in which the cells were set in a transepted arrangement *(103)*. There was a neat trapezoidal mound 48m long by 24m wide at the east end. A forecourt flanked by small horns opened to the east, in the back of which was the entrance to a central passage giving access to four side chambers (two on each side) and a small end chamber. Excavations yielded the remains of at least six adults in the chambers, together with fragmentary remains of children. Amongst the finds from the chamber was a fine black shale bead.

Below the long barrow was an earlier round barrow or rotunda grave with a central cist containing a single adult male *(24)*.

Further reading: Crawford 1925, 116–18 (C41); Clifford 1936.

4. Nympsfield, Frocester, Gloucestershire (GLO 13)

SO 7939 0132. 6km south of Stroud. Within Coaley Peak Country Park beside the B4066 between Stroud and Dursley. English Heritage and Gloucestershire County Council. Finds in Gloucester City Museum.

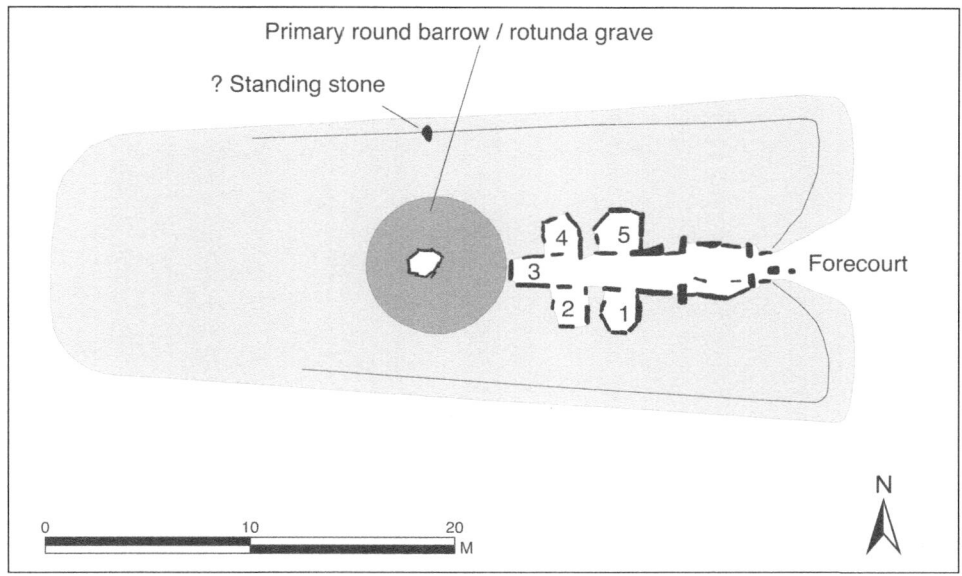

103 Plan of Notgrove, Notgrove (GLO 4). *After Clifford 1936, plate xlii*

Nympsfield long barrow is similar in plan and situation to the nearby Hetty Pegler's Tump, but smaller and with only one pair of side chambers. The absence of capstones, removed long ago, allows an appreciation of the layout and design of the chambers at Nympsfield even if some of the atmosphere is missing.

The mound is trapezoidal, 27m long and 18m wide at the east end *(104* and *13)*. Reconstructed in 1974, the mound would originally have been much higher at the east end, completely covering the chambers. The forecourt opens to the east, at the back of which is the entrance to a central passage leading to a pair of side chambers and a small end-chamber. Constricting stones sub-divide the passage and restrict access to the chambers. Excavations in 1862, 1937 and 1974 recovered the remains of between 20 and 30 individuals. In the forecourt were the remains of hearths and a small pit suggesting funerary rituals had taken place here when the barrow was in use. Like many long barrows, the forecourt at Nympsfield was blocked with rubble and soil at the end of its life, so preventing further access. Key things to look for here are: the shape, size and escarpment edge position of the barrow; the arrangement of the chambers; and the use of constricting slabs to demarcate the individual elements within the chamber area.

A fine round barrow, known as the **Soldier's Grave** (SO 794 015), lies near Nympsfield long barrow, in woodland behind the public lavatories at the northern end of Coaley Peak Country Park. Tentatively dated to the later third millennium BC, this barrow is 17m in diameter and in its centre (marked by a hollow) excavations in 1936 revealed a boat-shaped cist containing the remains of at least 28 individuals.

About 2.4km north of the Coaley Peak Country Park is another fine long barrow, **The Toots** (GLO 76), situated on the escarpment edge on Selsley Common (SO 827 031). This barrow has not been excavated *(97)*.

Further reading: Crawford 1925, 119–22 (C42); Clifford 1938a; 1938b; Saville 1979a.

Long Barrows of the Cotswolds

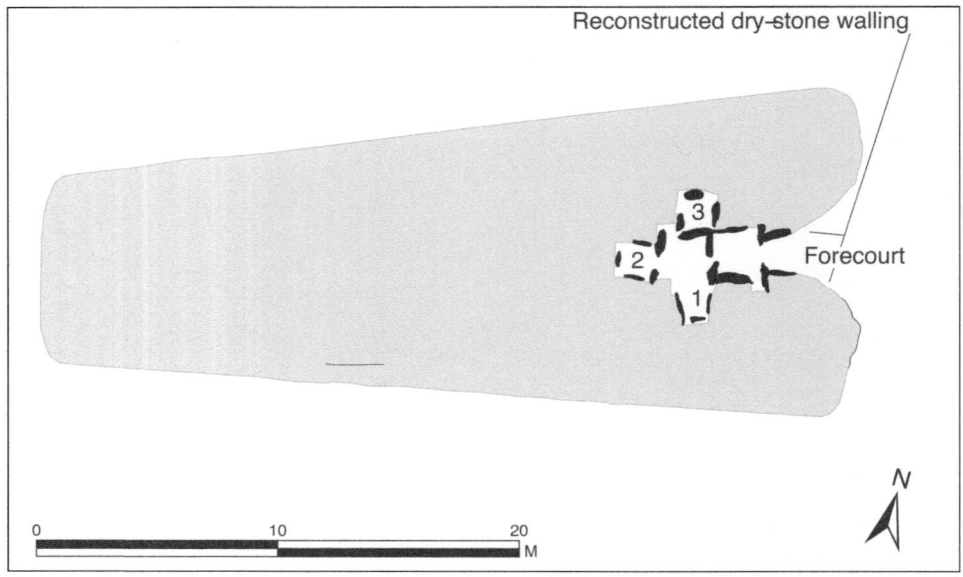

104 Above Plan of Nympsfield, Frocester (GLO 13). *After Saville 1979, fig. 4*
105 Below Plan of Randwick (GLO 10). *After Crawford 1925, 130*

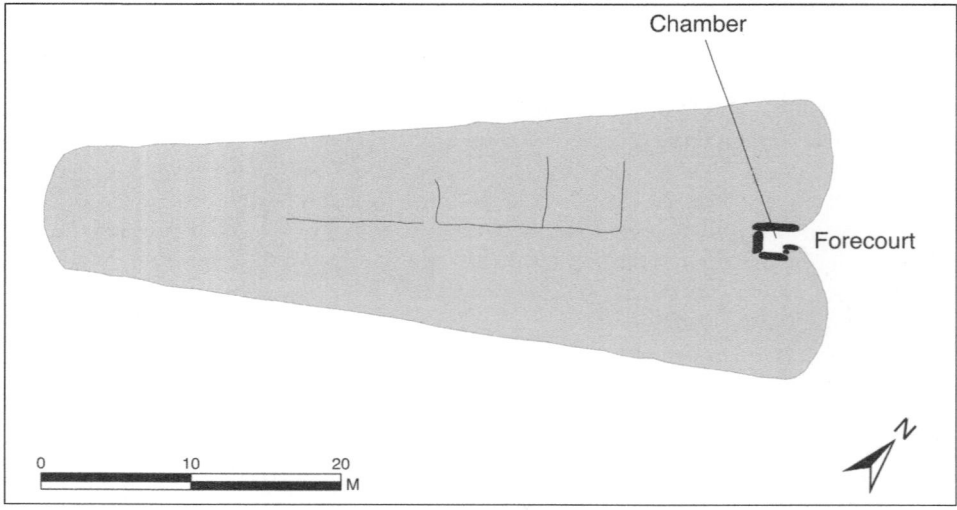

5. Randwick, Gloucestershire (GLO 10)

SO 8250 0690. *3km NW of Stroud, W of the A4173. Approached by minor road from Whiteshill to Edge, turning W at Scottsquar towards Haresfield. Car-park at SO 833 087. From here footpaths lead S into Standish Wood. National Trust.*

Set within an area of typical Cotswold woodland, this long barrow can be hard to find in summer when the foliage is thick. But in many respects its place in a woodland glade is highly authentic to judge from evidence for the environmental setting of most long barrows. The mound at Randwick is large: about 56m long by 26m wide, it still stands 4m high at the northeast end *(105)*. Excavations in 1883 found a forecourt opening to the northeast, from which there was access to a simple square chamber of one cell containing disarticulated human remains described at the time as 'confused mass'. Traces of the chamber can still be seen, although it is not fully accessible. Additional burials were found adjacent to the barrow on the southwest side. Key things to note at this site are: its woodland setting; its position on a steep-sided promontory; and the size of the mound.

All around the mound are traces of quarrying in the form of pits and spoil heaps. Most are fairly recent in date, but one or two may be contemporary with the long barrow. Round barrows and a linear cross-ridge dyke can be found in the woodland north of the long barrow.

Further reading: Witts 1884a; Crawford 1925, 129–33 (C47).

6. Stoney Littleton, Wellow, Bath and North East Somerset (SOM 1)

ST 7349 5721. 7km S of Bath. Access across fields by footpath from a car-park at Stoney Littleton Farm, signposted from Peasedown St John on the A367. English Heritage. Finds in Bristol City Museum.

As you approach this barrow it looks as though it is sliding down the side of a hill, and in this respect its situation is slightly unusual. Discovered in 1760 when the farmer-occupier broke into the chamber while trying to obtain stone for road mending, the site is one of the first long barrows in the Cotswold-Severn region to have been systematically explored. This happened on 24–25 May 1816 and involved the Revd John Skinner of Camerton, his brother Russell, Sir Richard Colt Hoare, his steward and surveyor John Crocker, and a labourer named Zebedee Weston. Partly restored in 1858 and again in the late 1990s, the mound is neatly edged by a dry-stone wall that follows the original line and is not dissimilar in appearance to how it would have looked 5,500 years ago.

Overall, the mound measures about 30m by 15m and is still nearly 3m high at the southeastern end *(106)*. At the higher, wider, southeastern end there are two projecting horns flanking a forecourt, at the back of which is the entrance to the chamber. Immediately inside the entrance is a marked entrance area (sometimes referred to as the 'vestibule') defined by projecting jambs. A passage, 13m in length, gives access to six side chambers, three on each side and an end chamber. Excavations in 1816 together with less systematic openings in 1760 and 1816 suggest that originally there were many individuals buried within the chambers, but exactly how many cannot now be determined.

The stones used to build the chamber and passage at Stoney Littleton were carefully chosen and some came from outcrops more than 8km away. Key things to look for at this site are: the walling and roof construction of the chambers; the ammonite fossil on the left-hand door jamb *(47)*; and the fine tablet just inside the entrance which celebrates the reconstruction work carried out in 1858.

Further reading: Colt Hoare 1821a; Bulleid 1941; Donovan 1977; Grinsell 1982; Thomas 2003.

Long Barrows of the Cotswolds

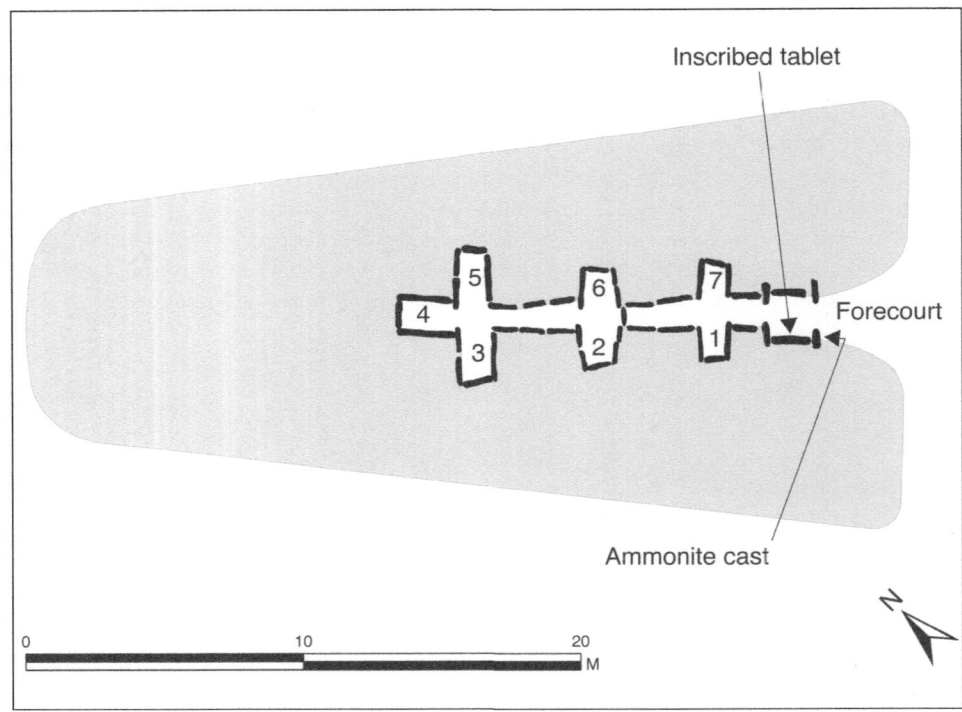

7. The Whispering Knights, Rollright, Oxfordshire (OXF 1)

SP 2992 3084. On upland ridge 6km N of Chipping Norton, SW of the A3400 and NE of the A44. Access along minor road towards Little Rollright between the A3400 and the A44. Parking is available in the lay-by at the Rollright Stones.

Not a long barrow but the remains of a portal dolmen set on a hillslope east of the Rollright Stones. At the Whispering Knights, four stones stand upright, while a fifth, probably the capstone, lies fallen. The stones would never have been covered by a mound; rather they projected out of a low flat-topped platform that surrounded the setting. At the southeast side there is a perfectly formed H-shaped setting of stones characteristic of portal dolmens *(107* and *18).*

The Rollright Stones comprise three elements which are all of different date: the King Stone (a standing stone probably erected around 1500 BC), King's Men (a stone circle probably built about 2200 BC) and the Whispering Knights (a portal dolmen probably built about 4000 BC). Folklore has it that the stones are the petrified remains of a king and his followers. The tale behind this calamity, which was already circulating by the late 1600s, recalled how a king and his company were marching across the Cotswolds when they were confronted by a witch (sometimes said to be Mother Shipton) who posed a challenge for the king:

> *Seven long strides shalt thou take, and*
> *If Long Compton thou canst see,*
> *King of England shalt thou be.*

Sites to Visit

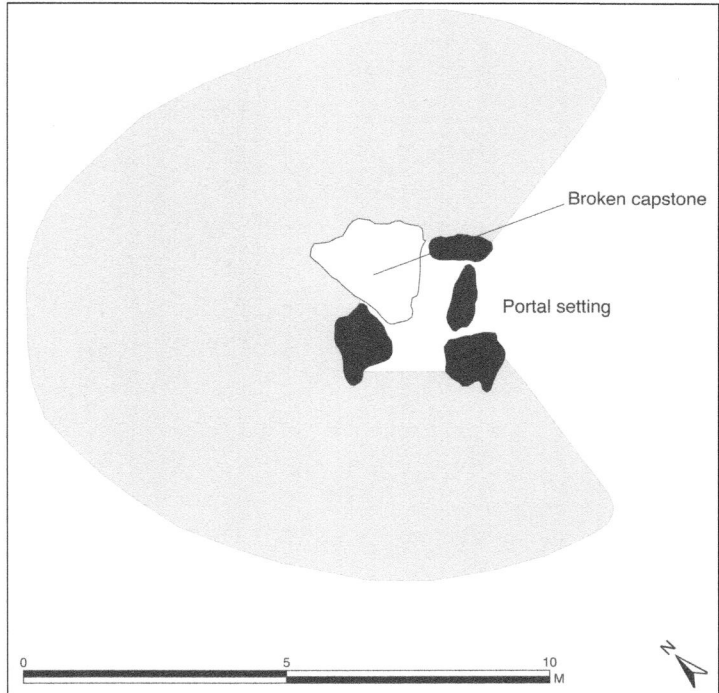

106 Opposite Plan of Stoney Littleton, Wellow (SOM 1). *After Grinsell 1982*

107 Right Plan of The Whispering Knights, Rollright (OXF 1). *After Lambrick 1988, fig. 68*

On his seventh stride, however, there rose before him a ridge in the hillslope which prevented him from seeing Long Compton (some say it was a long barrow, but there is no firm evidence for this). The witch then said:

> *As Long Compton thou canst not see,*
> *King of England thou shalt not be.*
> *Rise up, stick, and stand still, stone,*
> *For King of England thou shalt be none,*
> *Thou and thy men hoar stones shall be,*
> *And I myself an eldern tree.*

Further reading: Crawford 1925, 165–6 (C69); Grinsell 1976, 146–8; 1977; Lambrick 1988.

8. Windmill Tump, Rodmarton, Gloucestershire (GLO 16)

ST 9325 9730. 5km NE of Tetbury, N of the A433. Access by footpath from minor road between the A429 and Rodmarton village, SW of the village. English Heritage.

Surrounded by a modern stone wall and supporting a fairly dense tree cover, this long barrow is not easy to appreciate in terms of its original appearance. The name suggests that it once supported a windmill, but there is no evidence for this.

The mound is about 61m long and 21m wide at the east end where excavations in 1863 and again in 1939 revealed a fairly narrow forecourt with a false-portal at the inner

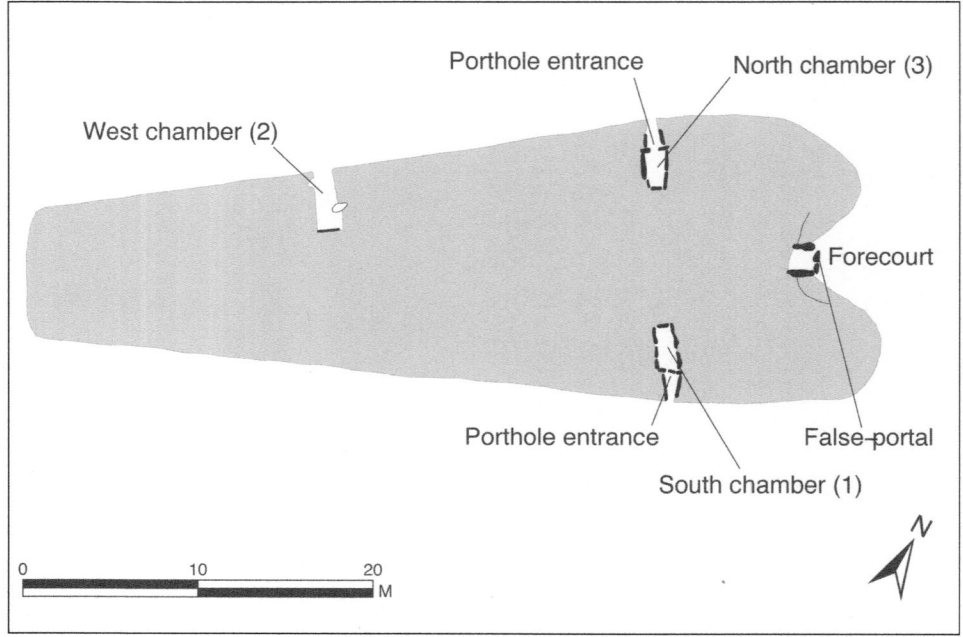

108 Plan of Windmill Tump, Rodmarton (GLO 16). After Saville 1988, fig. 1

end *(108)*. Traces of the portal slabs are still visible. The early excavations revealed two lateral chambers, one opening from each side of the mound. The north chamber contained the remains of ten adults and three children, the south chamber an unknown number of disarticulated individuals. Both chambers were unusual in being set below the natural surface of the ground, with steps in the passage to facilitate access *(44)*. There were also carefully made jambs across the entrance to both chambers; a concave hollow in the opposing sides of the jambs formed a circular hole or 'porthole' which severely restricted access into the chamber itself *(71)*. Sadly, none of these details are visible today, although the position of the chambers can be seen. In 1987 gales brought down a beech tree on the barrow revealing a third chamber in the northwest sector of the mound. Others may well await discovery.

Further reading: Crawford 1925, 142–5 (C55); Clifford and Daniel 1940; Saville 1989.

NORTH WESSEX DOWNS

9. Wayland's Smithy, Ashbury, Oxfordshire (BRK 1)

SU 2808 8539. 2km E of Ashbury, beside the Ridgeway. Can be approached from the W along the Ridgeway from its junction with the B4000 at SU 274 843 (about 1.5km walk), or from the E by parking at the Uffington White Horse and following the Ridgeway westwards (about 2km walk). English Heritage.

Sites to Visit

Heavily restored following excavations in 1962–3, Wayland's Smithy is the best and most accessible long barrow along the Berkshire Ridgeway. In its final form it is a classic Cotswold-Severn style long barrow, but excavations have shown a long and complicated history *(109)*.

The first structure on the site was an oval mound about 14m by 7m with a pair of flanking ditches. The mound was delimited by a stone kerb and at the southern end there was a timber chamber flanked at either end by massive D-shaped posts. The chamber was about 4.6m long and about 1m wide. On the floor were the disarticulated remains of at least 14 individuals, mainly adult males. Nothing of this early structure is visible today, because around 3500 BC a much larger barrow was constructed over the top, completely encapsulating it. This is the classic long barrow visible today.

The Wayland's Smithy long barrow is 55m long and 14m wide at the south end. It has a rather fine peristalith edging of sarsen slabs, some with panels of dry-stone walling between. The chalk rubble forming the core of the mound was taken from a pair of quarry ditches that flanked the mound (now filled in). Six great sarsen slabs, which average over 3m high, were set across the front of the mound to provide an impressive façade *(52)*. These stones may have been selected for their shape: a lozenge-shaped stone with a pointed top can be seen on the left side of the entrance into the chamber, with a more rectangular flat-topped stone to the right. At the same time, a terminal chamber roofed with large capstones was constructed at the wider, higher end of the enlarged mound. This can still be entered; a short central passage gives access to one chamber on each side and a small end-chamber. When excavated it contained the remains of at least eight people, including a child. When the tomb fell out of use, perhaps about 3000 BC, the chamber

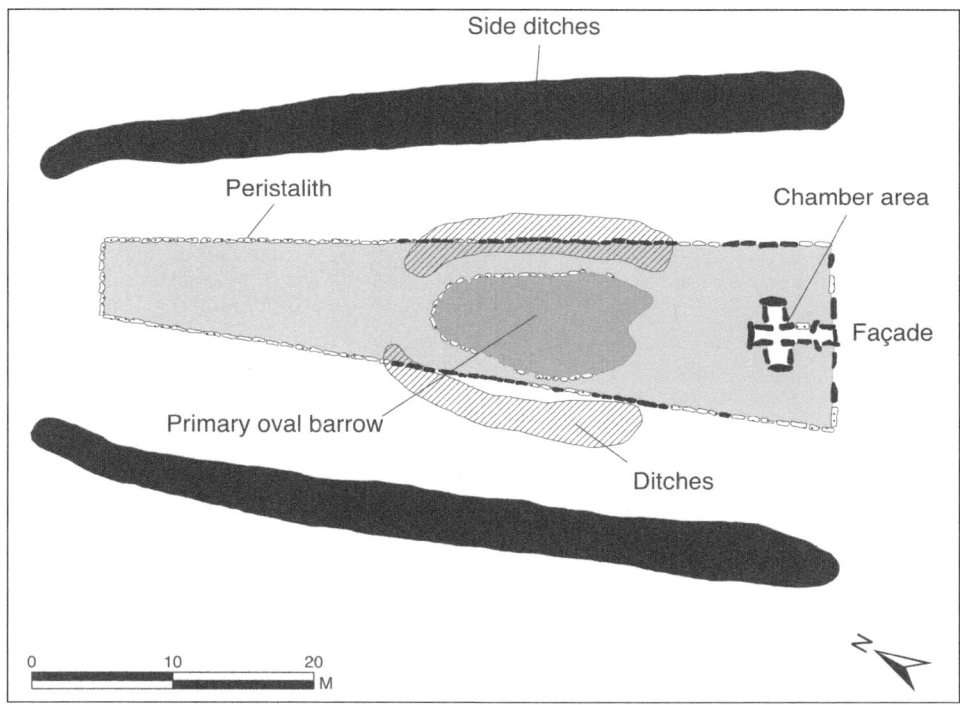

109 Plan of Wayland's Smithy, Ashbury (BRK 1). *After Whittle 1991, fig. 2*

and passage were filled with chalk rubble and soil to seal the burial deposits and protect them.

Key features to look for at this site are: its position overlooking the Vale of the White Horse and the upper Thames beyond; the size and construction of the mound with its peristalith and walling; the impressive façade and the form of the chamber.

Legend holds that an invisible elvin smith named Wayland lived here and that a horse left with a penny would be well shod by the time the owner returned to collect it. The coins, it seems, had to be left on the roofstone of the right-hand burial chamber, known traditionally as 'The Cave'.

Further reading: Peers and Smith 1921; Crawford 1925, 47–53 (C2); Atkinson 1965; Whittle 1991.

10. West Kennet long barrow, Avebury, Wiltshire (WIL 4)

SU 1046 6774. 2km S of Avebury. Access by footpath across field from a signposted lay-by on the A4. English Heritage. Finds in Devizes Museum and Avebury Museum.

This long barrow, the biggest in southern England at more than 100m long, sits along a ridge overlooking the River Kennet amid one of the richest archaeological landscapes in Britain *(110 and 9, 43, 54)*. The mound is rather uneven and there is a marked cut through it towards the eastern end. Although sometimes described as the line of an old trackway, this cutting may show that there are two long barrows here set end to end. Only further surveys and excavation will tell, but it is an interesting possibility.

The mound is built of chalk rubble quarried from a pair of flanking side ditches which have long since silted up. In good conditions, however, the outline of the northern quarry ditch can sometimes be seen as differential crop growth. The eastern end of the mound was originally elaborated by a façade of upright slabs between which were panels of dry-stone walling. This edging may have continued round some or all of the rest of the barrow, although nothing of it remains to be seen. In the centre of the east end was a shallow forecourt, in the back of which is the entrance to a passage that gives access to five cells: two opposing pairs and an end-chamber *(10)*. These were constructed of massive sarsen orthostats, making this one of the largest known chambers amongst long barrows in the Cotswold-Severn region. The excavation of the end-chamber by John Thurnam in 1859 revealed at least six burials, while the investigation of the four other chambers by Stuart Piggott and Richard Atkinson in 1955–6 revealed another 40 or so burials. Most were incomplete and disarticulated, but there were exceptions *(58)*. Radiocarbon dates on human bones from the chambers suggest that these burials were deposited about 3500 BC. By about 3000 BC the West Kennet long barrow had fallen out of use as a place to deposit new burials and eventually the chambers and passage were filled to the roof with rubble and soil admixed into which was abundant cultural material including pottery, animal bone, personal ornaments, worked flint and a few pieces of human bone *(72)*. The forecourt was filled with boulders and three large stones were placed across the front in line with the flanking horns to create a truly monumental façade. This blocking arrangement has been restored and therefore makes entry to the chambers rather difficult and certainly not very authentic.

The main things to look for at this long barrow are: the monumental façade and the use of panels of dry-stone walling; the construction of the chambers (but ignore the

Sites to Visit

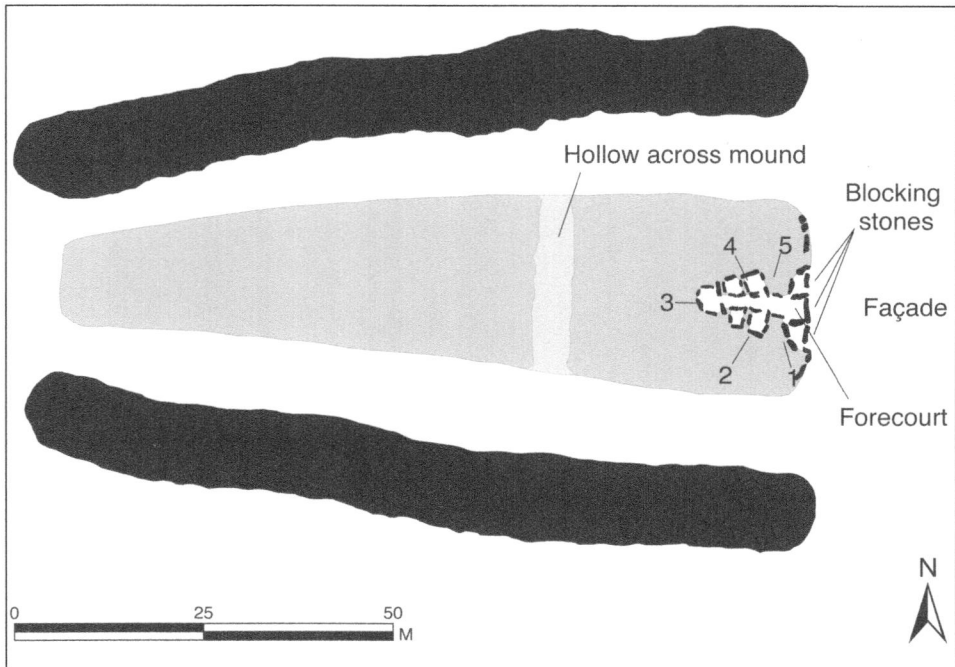

110 Plan of West Kennet, Avebury (WIL 4). *After Piggott 1963, figs 2 and 7*

modern roof-lights and concrete pads on top of the mound); the axe-sharpening marks on some of the orthostats inside the chamber; the size and position of the mound; the depression in the mound; and the relationship of the long barrow to nearby but slightly later monuments such as Avebury, the Sanctuary and Silbury Hill. The East Kennet long barrow (WIL 5), the same size as West Kennet but never excavated, can be seen from West Kennet in a group of trees across the valley to the southeast.

Further reading: Piggott 1958; 1962; Atkinson and Piggott 1986; Thomas and Whittle 1986.

WEST OF THE SEVERN

11. Arthur's Stone, near Bredwardine, Dorstone, Herefordshire (HRF 1)

SO 3180 4313. 1km N of Dorstone. Accessible by signposted minor roads from the B4348 at Dorstone or the B4352 at Bredwardine. Roadside parking. English Heritage.

Set on the northern edge of a narrow upland ridge with commanding views, this long barrow has been partly obliterated by the modern road and stone robbing over many centuries. Originally, the mound was probably orientated roughly north to south. It would have been about 26m long, perhaps 10m wide and up to 3m high *(111)*. What remains to view is the stone chamber, stripped of its covering mound. Nine orthostats form the walls and support a massive capstone. Now cracked and broken into three pieces, this block of

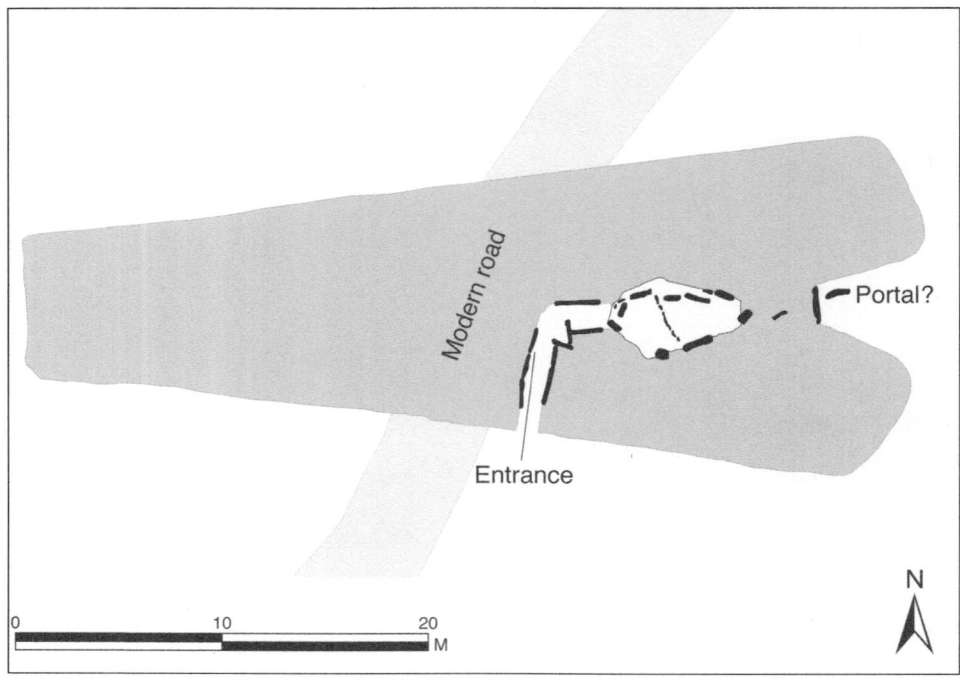

111 Plan of Arthur's Stone, Dorstone, with a reconstructed mound added (HRF 1). Chamber details after Hemp 1935, 289

Old Red Sandstone must originally have weighed 25 tons or more. A short passage provides access to the chamber from the northwest; between the passage and chamber, bridging the different orientations of the two parts of the structure, is a small antechamber. No traces of the roofing arrangements for passage or antechamber survive.

South of the chamber are a series of earthfast sandstone slabs that George Nash has quite reasonably suggested may relate to a portal structure of some kind in the back of the forecourt. O.G.S. Crawford suggested that one of these uprights bears traces of rock art in the form of cup-marks, but these could be natural.

Further reading: Crawford 1925, 147–9 (C60); Watkins 1928; Hemp 1935; Nash 2003.

12. Gwernvale, Crickhowell, Powys (BRE 7)

SO 2103 1912. 1km west of Crickhowell, N of the A40 between Crickhowell and Brecon, adjacent to the driveway leading to the Manor Hotel. Lay-by parking. Cadw. Finds in the National Museum of Wales, Cardiff.

In the valley of the River Usk in the southern part of the Black Mountains, the Gwernvale long barrow enjoys a picturesque but relatively low-lying position with excellent views westwards. In May 1804, Sir Richard Colt Hoare, accompanied by Theophilus Jones, Richard Fenton, Admiral Gell, Sir William Ouseley and a Mr Everest excavated the southeastern chamber, one of the earliest such investigations at a long barrow in Wales. They found rather little, but the chamber remained extant and featured in many guidebooks until 1977 when the realignment of the A40 required a full excavation of the site. That work, directed by Bill Britnell for the Clwyd Powys Archaeological Trust, revealed the full extent of the mound and the fact that there were originally at least three and possibly four lateral chambers, two or three on the south side and one on the north side. It also showed that the long barrow had been built on top of an extensive and long-lived settlement.

Today, the edges of the long barrow are marked out in the grass. The mound is about 50m long and about 17m wide at the east end *(112* and *74).* Trapezoidal in outline, the eastern end is marked by two pronounced horns and a fairly deeply recessed forecourt. The southern horn is under the modern road, but most of the rest of the mound can be seen. At the back of the forecourt was a stone slab forming a false-portal *(49D).* The side-chambers are visible, reconstructed in situ using the original orthostats. Rather notable is the southeastern chamber, which seems to be bigger than the others and has a bend in the passage. The other two extant chambers are more rectangular in plan

Further reading: Crawford 1925, 59–60 (C6); Britnell 1979; 1984.

13. Parc le Breos Cwm, Pen-maen, Swansea (GLA 4)

SS 5372 8983. 1km northwest of Park Mill, N of the A4118, on the Gower, between Swansea and Port-Eynon. Signposted access via a narrow lane leading N from the A4118. Cadw.

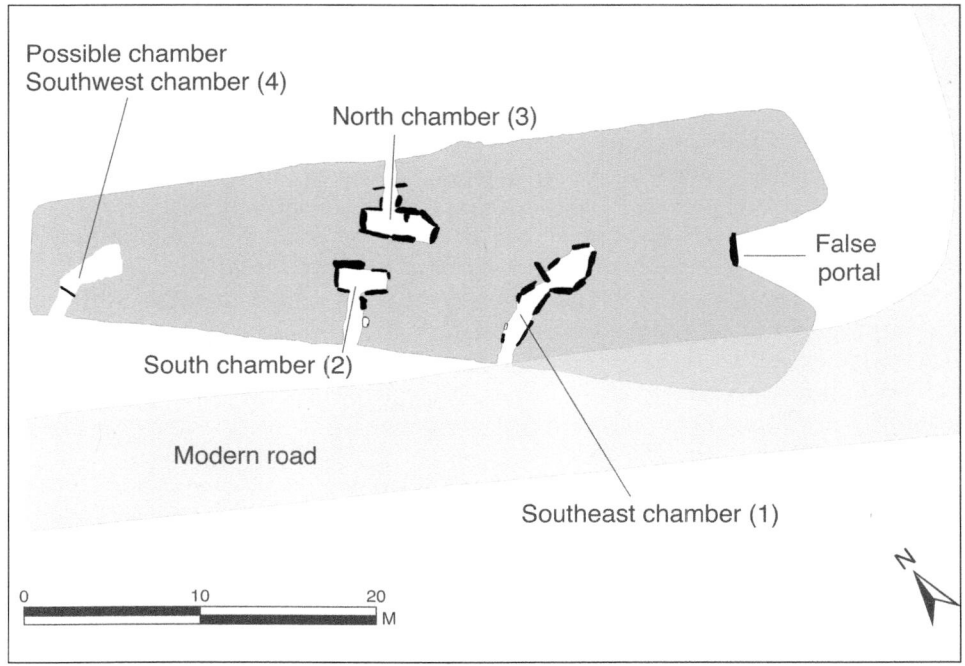

112 Plan of Gwernvale, Crickhowell (BRE 7). *After Britnell 1984, figs 33 and 35*

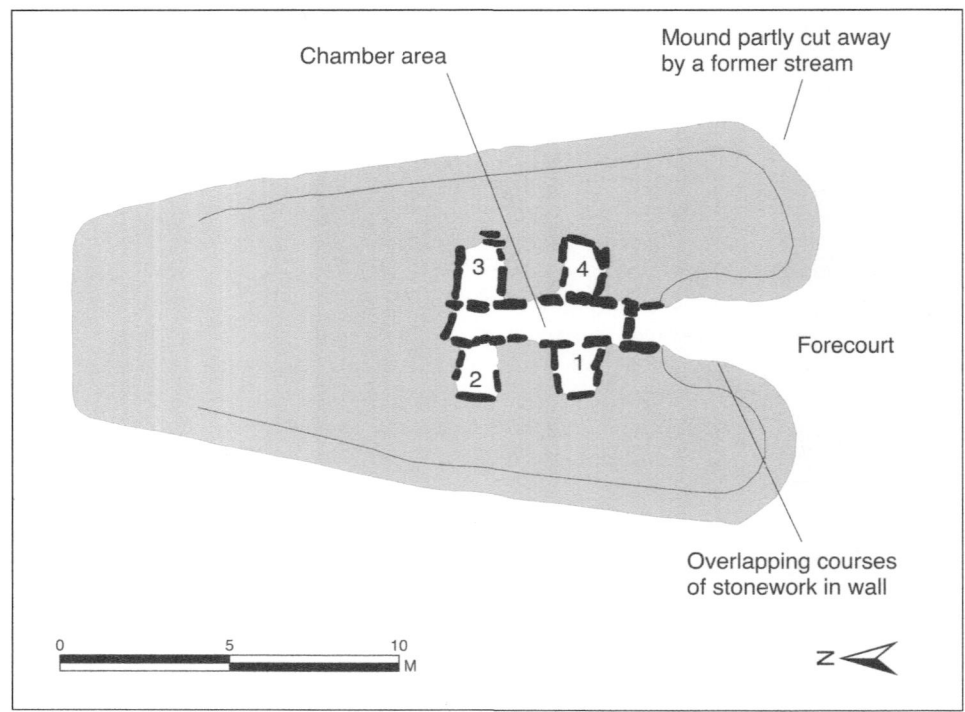

113 Plan of Parc le Breos Cwm, Pen-maen (GLA 4). *After RCAHMW 1976, fig. 9*

Unusually, this long barrow lies adjacent to a small stream in the bottom of a steep-sided valley. The stream has caused some erosion to the southwest horn, but the remainder is very well preserved and worth the journey to find this rather hidden site. Fully excavated and restored in 1960–1, the mound is small, 22m long by a maximum of 12m wide, strongly trapezoidal in shape and edged with a well-built dry-stone revetment wall. Aligned almost exactly north–south, the wider southern end has a deeply recessed bell-shaped forecourt between two rather pronounced horns. At the back of the forecourt is the entrance to a central passage with a pair of side chambers opening off to either side. There is no end-chamber beyond the second pair of chambers *(113)*.

The upper part of the cairn and the roofing of the chambers and passage are all missing, presumably robbed long ago, but this has the effect of providing the visitor with a neatly sliced-off structure whose internal arrangement can be examined. Early excavations in 1869 and the recent work in 1960–1 have together brought to light the remains of more than 40 people buried in the chambers and passageway. Radiocarbon dating suggests that they were deposited about 3500 BC.

The key things to look for at Parc le Breos Cwm are: the position and size of the barrow; the construction of the chambers and especially the deployment of jambs and sill slabs to constrict movement within the chamber and to structure the definition of spaces; the rubble construction of the mound; and the wavy effect created by the way the stones of the outer revetment wall in the forecourt are set.

Further reading: Daniel 1937b; Whittle and Wysocki 1998.

14. Maesyfelin, St Lythans, Vale of Glamorgan (GLA 10)

ST 1010 7230. 1km SW of St Lythans, a small village that can be found along a signposted minor road leading SW from the A4050 just south of the junction between the A48(T) and the A4232 on the western outskirts of Cardiff. Maesyfelin is immediately S of the road between St Lythans and Dyffryn. Roadside parking. Cadw.

A striking stone chamber built from three massive uprights forming a box-like structure, open to the east, supporting an enormous capstone (4.5m by 3m by 0.8m thick) estimated to weigh in excess of 30 tonnes *(42)*. The underside of the capstone stands about 1.8m above the present floor of the chamber. Known also as Gwâlyfiliast, the name translates as the 'kennel of the greyhound bitch', and indeed the chamber does look rather like a giant dog-kennel.

The chamber lies at the east end of the long mound some 25m by 10m, much of it heavily robbed *(114)*. J.W. Lukis records finding pottery and human remains in earth thrown out of the chamber sometime before 1875, but there has never been a scientific investigation of the site. Its main interest is the size and construction of the chamber.

Further reading: Savory 1971; RCAHMW 1976, 39.

15. Tinkinswood, St Nicholas, Vale of Glamorgan (GLA 9)

ST 0921 7331. 1km S of St Nicholas on the A48(T) W of Cardiff. Take the signposted road from St Nicholas towards Dyffryn; the barrow is W of the road, accessible by signposted footpath from the road. Roadside parking. Cadw. Finds in the National Museum of Wales, Cardiff.

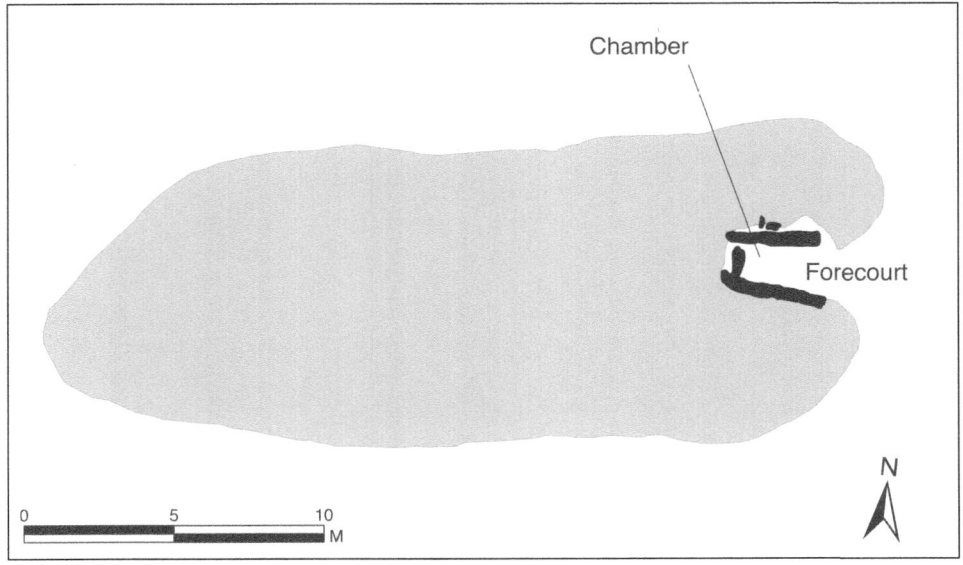

114 Plan of Maesyfelin, St Lythans (GLA 10). *After RCAHMW 1976, fig. 13*

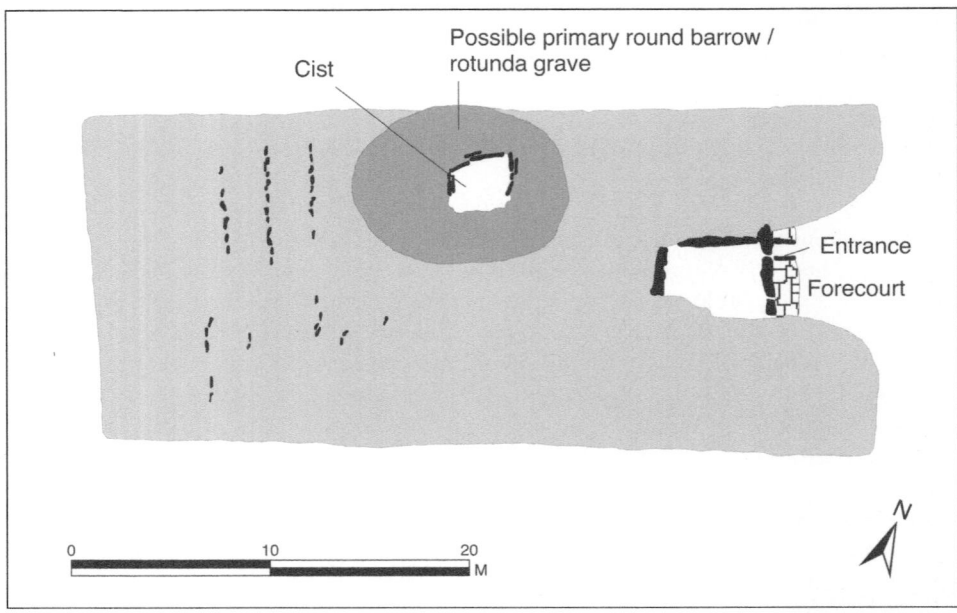

115 Plan of Tinkinswood, St Nicholas (GLA 9). After Ward 1915, fig. 10

As visible today, the Tinkinswood long barrow is in a restored state following extensive excavations in 1914 by John Ward, first Keeper of Archaeology in the National Museum of Wales. It gives a good impression of how long barrows like this would have appeared in the past, nestling as it does amongst thickets and patches of woodland.

The mound is more or less rectangular in outline, with a tidy external revetment wall. At the east end there is a wide shallow forecourt giving access to a simple rectangular terminal chamber with just one cell *(115)*. The capstone is massive (7m by 4.6m by 1m thick) and weights more than 40 tonnes. The entrance into the chamber is narrow and set towards the northern side of the flat face at the rear of the forecourt *(116)*. The remains of more than 50 individuals were found within the chamber, along with small quantities of broken pottery and worked flint. A rather unusual Beaker bowl was the latest kind of pottery present, probably placed within a series of blocking deposits.

Some of the forecourt walls have been reconstructed, the new build being distinguished by the herringbone pattern of stonework; a modern pillar has been inserted in the chamber to help support the capstone.

The main body of the cairn comprises rubble and stone blocks. Several larger slabs within the stonework of the cairn suggest the existence of pre-cairn structures or later secondary burials inserted into the mound. One substantial slab-lined cist within the cairn on the north side is probably the remains of a pre-long barrow monument, perhaps a round barrow or rotunda grave.

Further reading: Ward 1915; 1916; Savory 1971.

Sites to Visit

116 Tinkinswood (GLA 9). View of the forecourt and the form of the chamber. Note the large capstone and restricted entrance. Photograph by Timothy Darvill, March 1988

MUSEUMS

A number of museums in the area covered by this brief guide have exhibitions relevant to the sites listed above. These include:

Alexander Keiller Museum, Avebury, nr Marlborough, Wiltshire, SN8 1RF. Small archaeological museum showing material from sites in the area, including the West Kennet long barrow (WIL 4) and Windmill Hill.

Ashmolean Museum, Beaumont Street, Oxford, Oxfordshire, OX1 2PH. The oldest public museum in England, opened in AD 1683, with abundant exhibitions of archaeological material from central England and the Cotswolds. Presented in refreshingly traditional galleries.

Bristol City Museum and Art Gallery, Queen's Road, Clifton, Bristol, BS8 1RL. Extensive archaeological displays showing material from the southwest region, including material from Stoney Littleton (SOM 1) and Druid Stoke (GLO 28).

Cheltenham Art Gallery and Museum, Clarence Street, Cheltenham, Gloucestershire, GL50 3JT. Small archaeological exhibitions, including material from Belas Knap (GLO 1) and Notgrove (GLO 4).

Corinium Museum, Park Street, Cirencester, Gloucestershire, GL7 2BX. Good coverage of local prehistory, including material from Hazleton North (GLO 54).

Gloucester City Museum and Art Gallery, Brunswick Road, Gloucester, Gloucestershire, GL1 1HP. Extensive exhibitions relating to the prehistory of the central and southern Cotswolds, including material from the Nympsfield long barrow (GLO 13).

National Museum of Wales, Cathays Park, Cardiff, South Glamorgan, CF1 3NP. Excellent displays of prehistoric material from Wales, including the finds from Gwernvale (BRE 7), Tinkinswood (GLA 9) and Penywyrlod (BRE 14).

Oxfordshire County Museum, Fletcher's House, Woodstock, Oxfordshire, OX7 1SP. Good displays on local archaeology, including material from the Ascott-under-Wychwood long barrow (OXF 6).

Wiltshire Archaeological and Natural History Society Museum, Long Street, Devizes, Wiltshire, SN10 1NS. First-rate galleries covering the prehistory of Wessex, including material from long barrows in the region.

NOTES

CHAPTER 1

1 Osbert Guy Stanhope Crawford (1886-1957) was described by Sir Mortimer Wheeler (1958, 3) as being in the first brood of modern British archaeologists.
2 Crawford 1925, 112-13.
3 Rather confusingly he referred to them as the Severn-Cotswold Group in a paper published in June 1937 (Daniel 1937a, 186) but a month later he called them the Cotswold-Severn Group (1937b, 80). Retrospectively, he clarified his position (Daniel 1970, 262), claiming to himself the term 'Cotswold-Severn Group' and insisting that what he had referred to was defined on morphological and cultural grounds.
4 For example Corcoran 1969a, 14.
5 Crawford 1925, 44.
6 Grinsell 1976.
7 Throughout this book I have deliberately avoided using the traditional terminology relating to the periodization of prehistory embodied in the late nineteenth-century 'Three Age System' and its expansion to form culture-historic phases such as the Neolithic, Bronze Age and Iron Age. This is because such terms carry with them many connotations for the sub-division of the material that is covered here. Rather, the chronological perspective is provided by the use of radiocarbon determinations expressed here in conventional calendar (i.e. solar) years, centuries, or millennia BC or AD. It is recognized, of course, that this represents the back-projection of a distinctively western Christianized calendar on to prehistoric and proto-historic societies who would have used quite different, but unknown, calendrical systems. However, by backwardly projecting our modern calendar we can in a sense connect the past with the present, and also comprehend something of the passage of time at least within our own ways of thinking about time. Appendix B provides a list of available radiocarbon determinations from excavated long barrows in the Cotswold-Severn region, together with corresponding calibrated date ranges.
8 It is a matter that has been raised several times over the years, but never acted upon by those in a position to do so. See, for example, Daniel 1970, 261, with references to comparative surveys elsewhere in Europe.

CHAPTER 2

1 Grinsell 1959; O'Neil and Grinsell 1960, 39; Darvill and Grinsell 1989, 55-6.
2 See O'Neil and Grinsell 1960, 44.
3 Nashe 1589, 53.
4 See Hunter 1975.
5 Aubrey 1982.
6 Piggott 1985.
7 Atkinson 1984.
8 See Thurnam 1868, plate XI for a summary of Stukeley's classification.
9 Lambrick 1988, 6-8.

10 Emery 1958.
11 Moore 1976.
12 Briggs in Britnell 1984, 45.
13 Witts 1883, 81 with earlier references.
14 Willis 1787, 91.
15 Grinsell 1982, 3.
16 Although it might in fact have been rather later, perhaps in 1871: Grimes 1960, 43.
17 Grinsell 1971, 83–4.
18 Sherratt (1996a) provides an interesting analysis of swings between Romanticist thinking and Enlightenment thinking, and the dialectic between the two, from the sixteenth through to the twentieth century AD with reference to landscape studies; approaches to the description, recording, excavation and interpretation of long barrows can be modelled in a similar way.
19 Colt Hoare 1812, 7.
20 Thompson 1983.
21 A detailed account of this is provided by Stephen Briggs in Britnell 1984, 45–7.
22 Freston 1812.
23 Clifford and Daniel 1940, 146–9; and see Appendix A, GLO 17 for other references.
24 Colt Hoare 1821a, 44.
25 Anon. 1844.
26 Lubbock 1865, 2-3. His most extensive consideration of the material assigned to the Neolithic period is in the seventh and final edition (Avebury 1913, 158-66).
27 See Gray 1981 for biographical notes on some of these characters.
28 RCHME 1976.
29 Crawford 1955a, 159.
30 Crawford 1932.
31 Grimes 1936b.
32 Phillips 1933.
33 See Crawford 1955a, 160–1.
34 Hemp 1929.
35 Berry 1929; 1930.
36 Radford 1930.
37 Clifford 1936, 121.
38 Clifford 1937.
39 Clifford 1938a.
40 Clifford and Daniel 1940; see Daniel 1986, 340–1, for his reminiscences about working with Elsie Clifford in the Cotswolds.
41 Bryan O'Neil was a distinguished archaeologist who was later to become the Chief Inspector of Ancient Monuments in the Ancient Monuments Branch of the Office of Works.
42 Donovan 1938.
43 Grimes 1939.
44 O'Neil 1948, 23.
45 Thurnam 1868, 168.
46 Montelius 1876 and 1905.
47 Daniel 1939, 185.
48 Childe 1957, 213.
49 Childe 1957, 222.
50 For example Crawford and Keiller 1928, 11.
51 Piggott 1934; 1935.
52 Daniel 1937b, 79–86; 1939, 164.
53 Grimes 1939, 139.
54 Forde 1940, referring back to earlier papers published in 1927 and 1929.
55 Daniel 1941.
56 Daniel 1958a.
57 Piggott 1954, 129-51.
58 Childe 1940, 58–60.
59 Corcoran 1969a, 13; Daniel 1970, 262.
60 Grimes 1960, fig. 37.
61 Renfrew 1973a.
62 Renfrew 1967, 284–7.
63 Atkinson 1965, 132, and see also footnote 16 which reveals that the cost of obtaining the date from a commercial laboratory in the USA was about £62 (at that time $175).
64 Corcoran 1969b; 1972; Powell 1973.
65 Kinnes 1979; 1992a.
66 See Daniel 1950b, 13–15, for a discussion of the relationships between chambered and unchambered long barrows.
67 Ashbee 1984, xxiii.
68 Powell *et al.* 1969.
69 Corcoran 1969a, 14.
70 Daniel 1970, 262.
71 For example at Windmill Tump, Rodmarton (GLO 16: Saville 1989); Cow Common Long (GLO 22: Saville 1979b, 90); Druid Stoke (GLO 28: Smith 1989); Stoney Littleton (SOM 1: Thomas 2003); Easton Down (WIL 19: Whittle *et al.* 1993); and Lanhill (WIL 3: King 1966).
72 Drinkwater 1972; Saville and Drinkwater 1976; Saville 1980.
73 Saville 1990.
74 Darvill and Grinsell 1989, 40–1.
75 Savory 1984, 13.
76 Miles and Palmer 1995, 375–6; Lock *et al.* 2003.
77 Bewley 2001.
78 Brown 1978, 244 (no. 18); Barclay *et al.* 2003, 6.
79 Featherstone *et al.* 1995, Plate 4. This was one of up to ten possible long barrows found in different parts of England during flights in 1995.

Notes

80 Gibson 2000.
81 Marshall 1998.
82 Renfrew 1976, 199.
83 Scarre 1992, 142–50. See also Sherratt 1993 for comment, and Patton 1994.
84 Hodder 1990, 233–7.
85 Cassen 1993.
86 Boujot and Cassen 1993.
87 Bradley 1998a, 36–50.
88 Patton 1994.
89 Renfrew 1976.
90 Scarre 1992.
91 Kinnes 1982.
92 Sherratt 1995, 258; and see also Sherratt 1990.
93 See Daniel 1958b for early statement on the chronology of French sites.
94 Boujot and Cassen 1992; 1993.
95 Scarre 2002a, 45.
96 Sherratt 1995.

CHAPTER 3

1 See Daniel 1937a for a wide-ranging discussion of the term 'dolmen' and its use by Montelius, Reinach, Déchelette and others.
2 Tilley 1996.
3 Bradley 1998b; Scarre 2002b.
4 See Bradley 2000a for a wide-ranging discussion of these topics.
5 Lynch 1976, 73-7.
6 Cummings 2002.
7 Burenhult 1980; 1984. Examples of dolmens at Carrowmore include grave 7 and grave 27.
8 See Fisher 1920, 330–3, for folklore attached to the breaking off of this piece of stone.
9 Lynch 1976, 65.
10 In some cases this portal slab extends the full height of the opening, but in other cases it seems to be represented by a low septal slab.
11 Powell 1973.
12 Grimes 1949; Lynch 1972, 73.
13 Scott 1969, 181; Powell 1969, 269-70; ApSimon 1997, 133–4.
14 Attention was first drawn to the integrity of this group of monuments by the present author (Darvill 1987b, 37–8); subsequently the group has been discussed by Alastair Barclay (1997).
15 Lambrick 1988, 28–34.
16 Donovan 1938; see also Lambrick 1988, 116–17.

17 Summarized in Crawford 1925, 69-70.
18 See Parsons 2002, where an appropriately early radiocarbon date of 4000–3700 BC is suggested for this skull. See also Chapter 6 on biometrical analysis.
19 Darvill and Grinsell 1989, 65.
20 Gray 1921; 1929; Corcoran 1969a, 291.
21 Thurnam 1869.
22 Drewett 1986, 49.
23 Bradley 1992.
24 Atkinson 1965, 130.
25 Simpson 1968; Ashbee 1969.
26 Kinnes 1975, fig. 6.
27 Whittle 1991, 94.
28 At some continental tombs of this period stones are split vertically and the two portions set up as a pair in the walls of a chamber.
29 Kenward 1982.
30 Dobson 1931; Phillips and Taylor 1972. And see Kinnes 1992a, 33.
31 Lewis 2002.
32 Coles and Simpson 1965.
33 Madsen 1979, 308–9.
34 Jørgensen 1977.
35 Midgley 1992, 497.
36 Dixon 1988, 78.
37 Williams 1940.
38 Boujot and Cassen 1993, fig. 3.
39 Sheridan (1986) has proposed a fivefold scheme representing the increasing scale and complexity of passage graves in Ireland and, by extension, western Britain generally. Here, the term 'developed passage graves' is reserved for large and structurally complicated examples, Sheridan's forms 3, 4 and 5. The term 'simple passage grave' refers to small simple examples, mainly Sheridan's forms 1 and 2. For the most part these also accord with L'Helgouch's 'les dolmens à couloir avec chambre simple bien différenciée' (1965, 7). Frances Lynch (1976) has proposed the term 'chamber and passage tomb' for these simple passage graves in southwest Wales, but the more widely applied nomenclature seems more appropriate here (cf. Lynch 1975, fig. 7).
40 Boujot and Cassen 1993, 486.
41 Daniel 1960, 58 and 80-3.
42 Greenwell 1877, 447–52 (site CCXVII).
43 Darvill 1982a, 60–1.
44 Grimes 1960, 7.
45 Lysons 1865; see also Clifford 1938c for the investigation of rectangular subterranean

features that better fit the bill as shepherds' cots.
46 Passmore 1934a.
47 Berry 1930, 140.
48 Greenwell 1877, 514.
49 Grimes 1939, 138.
50 Corcoran 1972, 61.
51 Daniel 1960, fig. 36; Burl 1985, 73.
52 Grimes 1939, 129.
53 Savory 1956, 16.
54 See Vulliamy 1929.
55 Kissock and Phillips 2000; Kissock 2001; *Archaeometry* 44.3 (2002), 45–6.
56 Kinnes 1979.
57 Clifford 1936, 143.
58 O'Neil 1966, 20 (grave 2).
59 Lawrence 1866, 279; Crawford 1925, 79; Parsons 2002, 22 for an illustration. But see Kinnes 1992b, 97–8 for unspecified contradictory evidence.
60 Hill 1930; and Dorrington and Rolleston 1880 respectively. See also Kinnes 1979 for a wider discussion of some of these sites.
61 Listed by Grinsell (1957, 149) as Alton 13 but Connah (1965, 22 n.6) believes that in fact the excavated site was Alton 10, previously investigated by John Thurnam.
62 Ward 1915, 310.
63 Corcoran 1972, fig. 2b.
64 Morgan and Marshall 1921.
65 Kinnes 1979, 45-50.
66 Waddell 1998, 101-3; Eogan 1997, 59.
67 Sheridan 1995, 18.
68 Scarre 2002a, fig. 11.
69 Scarre 1992, 146.
70 Daniel 1967.
71 Piggott 1955; 1972, 223–6.
72 Clark 1977.
73 Webley 1976, 26–8.
74 Sherratt 1996b; and see Coles 1994.
75 Cunliffe 2001.
76 Whittle 1991, 87.
77 Darvill in Lambrick 1988, 90–1.
78 E.g. O'Neil 1966, fig. 4.4.
79 Grimes 1939, fig. 6.

CHAPTER 4

1 Schulting 2000.
2 Piggott 1973; Gresham 1972.
3 Corcoran 1972; Powell 1973.
4 Clifford 1936, 125–8, 143.
5 Vulliamy 1922a; see Corcoran 1972, fig. 2b.
6 O'Neil 1966.
7 Grimes 1960, fig. 12.
8 It is possible of course that the later monument here was constructed in the 'chamberless' tradition found elsewhere in the region (see Chapter 5).
9 Grimes 1939, fig. 3; Corcoran 1972, fig. 3f.
10 Scarre 2002a, fig. 11.
11 Madsen 1979, fig. 3a.
12 Skaarup 1993, 109.
13 Case 1969.
14 Thomas 1985.
15 Piggott 1954, 129–51; Childe 1940, 53-60.
16 See Collins 1973 and Corcoran 1973 for summary.
17 Corcoran 1969a, 14–41; Ashbee 1970, 8–25.
18 Manby 1958; Hart 1984, 40.
19 Kinnes 1979, fig. 5.1.
20 Darvill 1996a, 161–2; Foster and Stevenson in Barclay *et al.* 2002, 114–19.
21 Hart 1986.
22 Piggott 1962, 11.
23 O'Neil and Grinsell 1960, 76.
24 Saville 1979a, 58.
25 Henshall 1972, 535.
26 De Valera 1960, 17 and 99.
27 De Valera 1960, 34.
28 Childe 1949, 135.
29 Ashbee 1966, 46–7.
30 Whittle 1977a, 239.
31 Ashbee 1966, 45–7.
32 Midgley 1985, 215.
33 Midgley 1985, 207-8; 1992, Appendix.
34 Midgley 1997; Kinnes 1999; Scarre 2002a, 47–9.
35 Thomas 1996.
36 Dubouloz *et al.* 1988; Voss 1965.
37 Britnell 1984, 51.
38 Ó Nualláin 1972.
39 Hey 2001.
40 OAU 2000. It may be noted that this site lies within the group of long barrows known as the Medway Group.
41 Grogan 1996.
42 Fairweather and Ralston 1993.
43 Barclay *et al.* 2002.
44 Whittle 1996, 248.
45 Bradley 1998a, 42-48.
46 Bradley 2000b, 55; 2002, 19–34.
47 Hodder 1984, 59.
48 Fleming 1972; 1973, 186.
49 Renfrew 1976.
50 Renfrew 1987, 152-9.
51 Zvelebil and Zvelebil 1988.

52 Kinnes 1975, fig. 7.
53 Darvill 1982a, 15–30.
54 Saville 1990, 137–8.
55 Bagnall-Oakley 1888; Webley 1962.
56 Gibson 2000.
57 Edmonds 1999, 65.
58 Tilley 1994, 142.
59 Fleming 1999.
60 Cummings *et al.* 2002, 61.

CHAPTER 5

1 Cox 1975.
2 Startin and Bradley 1981.
3 Saville 1990, 242.
4 Darvill 1982a, 91.
5 Bradley 1998a, 50.
6 Crawford 1925, 11–12.
7 Clifford 1938a, 197.
8 Savory 1956, 46.
9 Clifford 1936, plate xlii, section 11.
10 A toppled standing stone was revealed beneath the Pentre Ifan long barrow in Pembrokeshire (Grimes 1949), and such stones are important features associated with long barrows and passage graves in Brittany (Bradley 2002, 36–41).
11 Saville 1990, 14–22; Darvill 1996b, 104.
12 Saville 1990, 13.
13 Saville 1990, 239.
14 Selkirk 1971, 10; Dimbleby and Evans 1974, 120–2.
15 Whittle 1991, 88
16 Ashbee *et al.* 1979, 211.
17 Ashbee *et al.* 1979, 244–6.
18 Ashbee *et al.* 1979, 264–6.
19 Whittle 1994, 36–7 and 46–7.
20 Britnell 1984, 49–55; Darvill 1996a, 109; Lynch in Lynch *et al.* 2000, 50.
21 Using the migration rates of shade-loving snails as an indicator, Davies and Wolski (2001) have suggested that some of these clearings around long barrows could have been substantial, perhaps 1–2 km across.
22 Thomas 1999, 144.
23 Saville 1990, 32–4.
24 Ashbee 1984, 21–4.
25 Burl 1981.
26 Piggott 1962, 11.
27 O'Neil and Grinsell 1960, 76.
28 Grinsell 1971, 86 (St Cuthbert Out Ia).
29 Crawford 1938; Bradley 1983.
30 This hollow has often been explained as the line of a former trackway cut through the mound in the nineteenth century AD (Piggott 1962, 4), but the obvious place to make a track would be along the line of an existing depression.
31 Saville 1979a, 82–3.
32 Clifford 1936, 124.
33 Taylor 1996, 184.
34 Fowler 1983, 7; see also Fowler and Evans 1967.
35 Grimes 1960, 76.
36 Ward 1915.
37 Savory 1984, 23.
38 Piggott 1962, 15.
39 Cummings *et al.* 2002.
40 James Fox (1993) discusses a similar situation with reference to the construction of houses in different cultures and environments.
41 This is at Stoney Littleton (SOM 1), although it is possible that the Fairy's Toot, Nempnett Thrubwell (SOM 2), had more, perhaps as many as 16.
42 See Daniel 1960, 78 and 102; 1972, 241; De Valera 1965.
43 Grimes 1960, 90.
44 Corcoran 1970, 42.
45 Ashbee 1970, 11–13; Henshall 1974, 155–8.
46 Gibson 2000.
47 Piggott 1966, 387.
48 Vulliamy 1922b, 150; Corcoran 1970, fig. 3. The technique of imbrication is far more common in the long barrows of the Clyde Group and the Carlingford Group.
49 An exception is provided by the site of Haddenham, Cambridgeshire, where unusual ground conditions preserved much of the timber chamber intact (Hodder and Shand 1988).
50 Cunnington 1909b.
51 Richards and Whitby 1997.
52 Crawford 1925, 228.
53 Saville 1990, figs. 75 and 80.
54 Lysons 1863, 277.
55 Clifford and Daniel 1940.
56 Lysons 1863, 277.
57 Clifford 1936, plate xl upper (fig. 1), 128.
58 Passmore 1920, 9.
59 Crawford 1925, 147.
60 O'Neil 1966, plate IVa.
61 Clifford 1950, 32–3.
62 Whittle 1994, 23.
63 Donovan 1977.
64 Saville 1990, 60–1.

65 Corcoran 1970, 40.
66 Britnell 1984, 55–7.
67 For example Pollard and Reynolds 2002, 69.
68 Russell 2002, 68.
69 Lysons 1863, fig. 3. See also Clifford and Daniel 1940, 135. However, Clifford and Daniel take the view that the broken slab was originally some kind of portal slab resting at an angle against the portal slabs.
70 Grinsell 1953, 13–14.
71 Grimes 1960, 65–8.
72 Selkirk 1971, 9.
73 Saville 1990, summarized as fig. 227.
74 Clifford 1938a, 203.
75 Saville 1990, 59.
76 Britnell 1984, 58.
77 Ashbee et al. 1979, 263.
78 Grimes 1960, 75.
79 Britnell 1984, 134.
80 King 1966, 78–9.
81 Whittle 1991, 84.
82 Chesterman 1977, 28.
83 Clifford 1938a, plate xliv.
84 Thomas 1999, 208.
85 Saville 1979a, 88–9.
86 Darvill 2003.
87 Ashbee et al. 1979, 235 and 256.
88 Giot 1987.
89 Andersen 2000, 21.
90 Corcoran 1969a, 78 (note 2).
91 Saville 1990, 246.
92 O'Neil 1966.
93 See Greenwell 1877, 521, for a discussion of the phenomenon in relation to his excavation at Pole's Wood South (GLO 2).
94 See Darvill 1982a, 42, for an extended summary.
95 For this view see Berry 1930; Ward 1915.
96 For this view see Greenwell 1877; Clifford 1936; 1938a; Daniel 1950a; Grimes 1960.
97 Savory 1984, 23–4 and Britnell 1984, 90–3.
98 Britnell 1984, 150. See also Thomas 1988, 553–5.
99 Featherstone et al. 1995, plate 4.
100 Thurnam 1868, 209; Crawford 1925, 234.
101 Saville 1990, 23–31.
102 Saville 1979b, 90–F4 here published as a modern feature.
103 RCAHMW 1976, 40.
104 See Schulting 2000, 26.
105 Ashbee et al. 1979, 214 and 218.
106 Ashbee et al. 1979, 268–72.
107 Savory 1956, 27.
108 Britnell 1984, 57.
109 Saville 1990, 165.
110 Britnell 1984, 135.
111 Saville 1990, 205–9.
112 Now in Winchcombe Museum.
113 Vulliamy 1922b, 150.
114 Taylor 1996, 184.
115 Taylor 1996, 184.
116 Thomas and Tilley 1993.
117 An interesting comparison is to be found in the cosmologies of certain Amazonian Indian communities whose houses are at one and the same time symbolically structured as a womb, a person, a house, a settlement and the whole world (Hugh-Jones 1979, 238–57).
118 Hodder 1984, 64.
119 De Valera 1965.
120 See Hodder 1990, 255 for some of these general issues.
121 Fleming 1973.

CHAPTER 6

1 Renfrew 1976.
2 Ashbee et al. 1979, 235.
3 Piggott 1962, 78.
4 See Gell 1992 for a useful wide-ranging consideration of these matters.
5 Clifford 1938a, 201.
6 Clifford 1936, 135–6.
7 Corcoran 1970, 48–9.
8 Saville 1990, 126–7.
9 Clifford and Daniel 1940, 142.
10 Clifford and Daniel 1940, 141.
11 Levitan in Saville 1990, 213.
12 Savory 1956, 33.
13 Britnell 1984, 64.
14 Whittle and Wysocki 1998, 168.
15 Grimes 1939, 130.
16 Ward 1915, 306.
17 Thomas 1988, 550.
18 Edmonds 1999, 63–4.
19 See Lynch 1973 on the acoustic potential of passage graves.
20 Megaw in Savory 1984, 27–8.
21 Saville 1979a, 88.
22 Savory 1984, 25.
23 Smith and Darvill in Saville 1990, 146.
24 See Saville 1990, fig. 29.
25 Savory 1984, 28.
26 Lynch in Britnell 1984, 109.
27 Grimes 1960, 72.
28 Whittle and Wysocki 1998, 168.

29 Clifford 1938a, 203.
30 See Saville 1979a, plate 5b.
31 Britnell 1984, 88-90.
32 Quoted in Crawford 1925, 130.
33 Witts 1881, 203-5.
34 Whittle et al. 1993, 206.
35 Saville 1990, micofiche M1:C11–D6; Thomas 2003, fig. 2.
36 Saville 1979a, 62-3 (F10 and F11).
37 Savory 1956, fig. 3.
38 Piggott 1962, 23.
39 Witts 1881, 207.
40 Clifford 1938a, 203.
41 Clifford 1936, 141–2.
42 Corcoran 1970, 46.
43 Saville 1990, 70.
44 Piggott 1993.
45 Chesterman 1977; Benson and Clegg 1978; Baxter 1999. Dawn Galer of the Department of Palaeontology, The Natural History Museum, is currently carrying out a complete reanalysis of all the human remains from Ascott-under-Wychwood as part of the post-excavation and publication programme being co-ordinated by Alasdair Whittle. This work will no doubt significantly modify and expand on the conclusions of earlier studies.
46 Brothwell 1973, 280.
47 In the case of ground surfaces these bones are mainly small peripheral elements such as finger or toe bones or broken-off fragments of larger elements.
48 Saville 1990, 16.
49 Savory 1956, 26–7.
50 Piggott 1973, 12.
51 Selkirk 1971, 8.
52 Crawford 1925, 230–4.
53 Britnell 1984, 79–85.
54 Thomas 1988, 547.
55 Piggott 1962, 23.
56 Quoted in Piggott 1962, 23.
57 One area which provides an exception to this rule is Yorkshire where trench graves are well represented in long barrows (Ashbee 1984, 65).
58 Clifford 1938a, 198; Saville 1979a, 63 (F6).
59 Corcoran 1970, 42.
60 It is not always possible to determine whether cremated bone is of human or animal origin.
61 Whittle and Wysocki 1998, 175.
62 Thomas 1988.
63 Whittle and Wysocki 1998, 175–6.
64 Whittle and Wysocki 1998, 173–6.
65 Cowley in Grimes 1939, 141–2.
66 West in Savory 1956, 47.
67 Cave in Keiller and Piggott 1938, 131-46.
68 Crawford 1925, 13.
69 Atkinson 1951; Atkinson et al. 1951, 60.
70 Piggott 1947, opposite p. 62.
71 Whittle and Wysocki 1998, 173.
72 Baxter 1999; and see also Selkirk 1971, 87-9 and Chesterman 1977.
73 Keiller and Piggott 1938, 130–1.
74 Saville 1984, 22.
75 Thomas 1988, 547.
76 Winterbotham 1866, 278.
77 Whittle and Wysocki 1998, 174.
78 Greenwell 1877, 527.
79 Witts 1881, 207.
80 Chesterman 1977, 25.
81 Savory 1984, 19.
82 Peers and Smith 1921, 190.
83 Grimes 1939, 126.
84 Chesterman 1977, 31, but see also Benson and Clegg 1978.
85 Keiller and Piggott 1938, 125.
86 Barker 1985, 18–19.
87 Cunnington 1926, 397–8.
88 Cunnington 1909b, 311–13.
89 Wysocki in Whittle and Wysocki 1998, 158.
90 Keiller and Piggott 1938, 128.
91 Chesterman 1977, 24.
92 Wells in Piggott 1962, 79–81.
93 Thurnam 1868. And see Piggott 1962, 6.
94 Clifford 1936, 142–5.
95 Hodder 1990, 250.
96 Wells in Piggott 1962, 79.
97 Chesterman 1977, 24.
98 Thomas 1988, 554.
99 Hodder 1984.
100 Saville et al. 1987.
101 Whittle and Wysocki 1998, 147.
102 Whittle and Wysocki 1998, 172.
103 Pragg and Neave 1997.
104 See Cameron 1934, 247–8 for a vivid description in the best traditions of early twentieth-century anatomical study.
105 Whittle and Wysocki 1998, 163.
106 Rogers in Saville 1990, 188–9.
107 Wells in Piggott 1962, 86.
108 See Rogers in Saville 1990, 186–7; Wells in Piggott 1962, 79–81; Whittle and Wysocki 1998, 162.
109 Wrong 1961, 30.
110 Whittle and Wysocki 1998, 161–3.
111 Rogers in Saville 1990, 191–2.
112 Wells in Piggott 1962, 81–2.
113 Wells in Piggott 1962, 81–2.

114 Rogers in Saville 1990, 195–6.
115 Wells in Piggott 1962, 82.
116 Piggott 1940; and see also Crawford 1925, 80-1 and Parry 1921.
117 Davies and Thurnam 1865.
118 Thurnam 1868, 227.
119 Schulting and Wysocki 2002. See also Thurnam 1863.
120 Richards in Whittle and Wysocki 1998, 165–6.
121 Richards and Hedges 1999, table 1.
122 Schulting and Richards 2002.
123 Long barrow skulls were often compared with skulls from round barrows and found to be different (Thurnam 1870). more recent analysis (e.g. Brothwell 1973, Abb. 65) shows that general differences can be maintained using indicators such as the cephalic index, although there is greater variation in the populations than Thurnam and colleagues allowed.
124 See for example Howells 1973; Brodie 1994.
125 Using quite different approaches, an adult male associated with a wide range of grave goods that included Beaker pottery found at Amesbury and dating to about 2300 BC has been shown to have originated in the Alpine region of Europe (Fitzpatrick 2003).
126 Wells in Piggott 1962, 82.
127 Cave in Keiller and Piggott 1938, 147-8. Other authorities (e.g. Brothwell 1973, 293) note that wormian bones are common enough to make their use as an indicator of family ties rather doubtful.
128 Thurnam 1868, 162 quoting Aubrey.
129 Childe 1940, 40 and 77. See also Clark 1937.
130 Atkinson 1968, 92.
131 During most of the twentieth century AD the crude death rate in the United Kingdom was about 11.7 per 1000 per annum; in subsistence agricultural societies it is typically 25 per 1000 per annum (see Wrong 1961, table 3). Thus a group of about 40 people would produce one death per year, a group of 15 perhaps one death every two to three years.
132 Daniel 1939, 163. Saville (1979a, 77) also notes comparable vessels from southeast England.
133 Whittle 1977a, 85-94, especially 92 and fig. 11.
134 Greenwell 1877, 514; Leeds 1927.
135 Piggott 1931, 77–8; 1954, 75.
136 Saville 1990, 153–75.
137 Now in the Pitt-Rivers Museum, Oxford.
138 Clifford and Daniel 1940, 143–5.
139 Clifford 1950, 32.
140 Savory 1984, 26.
141 Saville 1990, 164.
142 Piggott 1962, 46.
143 Selkirk 1971, 8.
144 Clifford 1950, 30.
145 Darvill 2002, 83–4.
146 See Clifford 1950.
147 See Clifford 1950, 32.
148 Grimes 1939, 132.
149 Savory 1984, 26.
150 Piggott 1962, 19 and 48.
151 See Clifford 1936, 147 and plate xli, 1 and 2.
152 From layer 11 in this chamber, Piggott 1962, 52–3.
153 Clifford 1936, 138-9.
154 Megaw in Savory 1984, 27–8.
155 Whittle and Wysocki 1998, 175–6.
156 Clifford 1936, 130.
157 Clifford 1950, 28.
158 Clifford 1950, 33.
159 Hodder 1990, 250.
160 Thomas 1999, 127–30; Parker Pearson 1999, 21–44.

CHAPTER 7

1 Hodder 1990, 252 discusses this.
2 Darvill 1982a, 41–75.
3 Greenwell 1877, 522.
4 Saville 1990, 64.
5 Bulleid 1941, 60–2.
6 Piggott 1962, 75.
7 Smith 1965b.
8 Whittle 1997a.
9 Thomas and Whittle 1986, 141.
10 Case 1995, 11.
11 Atkinson 1965, 132. But see also Whittle 1991, 98 for other interpretations.
12 Ward 1915, 299–300.
13 Whittle 1994, 48.
14 Witts 1881.
15 Hemp 1929, 268.
16 Keiller and Piggott 1938, 125.
17 See Grimes 1939, plate xiv.3.
18 Corcoran 1970, 42 and plate iia.
19 Selkirk 1971, 7.
20 Britnell 1984, 92.

21 Grimes 1960, 47–8.
22 Saville 1990, 127–33.
23 Witts 1881, 203.
24 Rolleston 1876, 166.
25 Clifford 1936, 138.
26 Britnell 1984, 64.
27 Savory 1984, 22.
28 Clifford and Daniel 1940, 141 and plate xiv upper; and see Lysons 1863, 276.
29 Ward 1915, 305.
30 Grimes 1960, fig. 38.
31 Clifford 1936, 139.
32 Case 1995, 11.
33 Thomas and Whittle 1986, 148.
34 Whittle 1993, table 2.
35 Britnell 1984, 109.
36 Grimes 1960, 72.
37 Crawford 1925, 127.
38 Piggott in Clifford 1938a, 211; Saville 1979a, 77.
39 Piggott in Clifford 1936, 155–6.
40 Crawford 1925, 100.
41 Whittle and Wysocki 1998, 175.
42 Wells in Piggott 1962, 79.
43 Case 1993, 260–3; 1995.
44 Case 1995, 12.
45 See Pollard and Reynolds 2002, 75–124.
46 Whittle and Wysocki 1998, 176.
47 Schulting 2000, 28.
48 Britnell 1984, 150.
49 Thomas 1988, 556.
50 Whittle 1991, 98.
51 For example: GLO 54 (Bell in Saville 1990, 219); WIL 11 (Whittle 1994); WIL 19 (Whittle et al. 1993, 211–17); WIL 27, WIL 30 and WIL 36 (Ashbee et al. 1979).

CHAPTER 8

1 Renfrew 1973b; 1976.
2 Darvill 1982a, 90–1.
3 Service 1971, 99–132.
4 See Sahlins 1968, 96–113.
5 For wider discussions of the overall settlement patterns and social organization of communities in the Cotswold-Severn region see Darvill 1983; 1984a; 1986b; Case 1986; Pollard and Reynolds 2002; Lynch et al. 2000, 42–78.
6 Barrett 1994, 141.
7 Whittle 1997b, 21.
8 Thomas 1999, 228.
9 Palmer 1976; Darvill and Thomas 2001.
10 Whittle 1977b; Andersen 1997.
11 Smith 1965a, 19–20.
12 Whittle et al. 1999, 381–90.
13 Whittle et al. 2000.
14 See Piggott 1962, 68, developed further in Smith 1965a, 137.
15 Thomas 1991, 112.
16 Whittle et al. 1999, 362.
17 Leeds 1928; Case 1956; Avery 1982.
18 Case 1982a, 2.
19 Startin 1982, 50.
20 Bradley 1992.
21 Brown 1978, 244 (no. 18); Barclay et al. 2003, 6.
22 See Smith 1972; Benson and Miles 1974; Leech 1977; Smith in Darvill and Grinsell 1989.
23 Dixon 1979; 1988; 1994.
24 Burton 1980.
25 Darvill 1981; 1982b; 1986a.
26 Trow 1985.
27 Trow 1985, 17; Darvill and Grinsell 1989, 67.
28 Pye 1969 with earlier references; Oswald et al. 2001, 152 (no. 42).
29 Nash 2003, 51.
30 Burrow et al. 2001.
31 Darvill and Thomas 2001, 13.
32 RCAHMW 1976, 41–2.
33 Gibson 1998; 1999.
34 Whittle 1997a.
35 Foley 1981.
36 Holgate 1988, 111.
37 Holgate 1987.
38 Marshall 1985, 40–1.
39 Grinsell 1964; see also Grinsell and Janes 1966.
40 Saville 1979b, 110.
41 Darvill 1984b, 31; Saville in Parry 1998, 61.
42 Mudd et al. 1999.
43 Darvill 1986b, 13–19.
44 Rahtz and Greenfield 1977, 25–9.
45 Clarke and Richards 1972.
46 Grimes 1960, 214–15.
47 Wedlake 1958, 19.
48 Hurst 1972, 38. See also Darvill 1987b, 46 for a general overview.
49 Allen 1998.
50 Coles 1989, fig. 13; Aston and Gerrard 1999, 8–9.
51 Whittle et al. 2000.
52 Smith 1965b.
53 Proudfoot 1965.
54 Robertson-Mackay 1980.

55 Smith and Simpson 1966, 151–5.
56 Piggott 1937.
57 Thomas 1956.
58 Evans and Smith 1983, 111.
59 Richards 1978, 31.
60 Bradley and Holgate 1984, 111.
61 Holgate 1988, 253–5.
62 Hey 2001.
63 Kenward 1982.
64 Brown 1978, 244.
65 See Robinson 1934 for a summary.
66 Burrow et al. 2001, 97.
67 Darvill 1996b, 108–10. See also Nash 1997 for a wider consideration of the distribution of long barrows in the Black Mountain area.
68 See Case 1982a for an interesting selection of such models relevant to the upper Thames valley as a result of reviewing the evidence for occupation around the Abingdon causewayed enclosure.
69 Barker and Webley 1978.
70 Richards 1978, 31.
71 Kendall 1916; 1922. See Barber et al. 1999, 78.
72 Passmore 1940; 1943; Hirst and Rahtz 1996; Barber et al. 1999, 78.
73 King 2001, 337.
74 Whittle 1990a.
75 Brothwell in Whittle et al. 1999, 346.
76 Proudfoot 1965, 132–3.
77 Adkins and Jackson 1978.
78 Bradley and Gordon 1988.
79 Balch 1926.
80 Tratman and Henderson 1927.
81 Balch 1914.
82 Barrett 1966.
83 RCAHMW 1976, 15, with earlier references.
84 Harvey et al. 1967.
85 Anon. 1909, 114–15.
86 Bradley 1992.
87 The excavator places the central grave in this phase of the monument (Bradley 1992, fig. 4), but there do not appear to be any stratigraphic relationships suggesting this, and the available radiocarbon dates, although problematic in some respects, suggest that the grave belongs with the later oval barrow that seals this early enclosure.
88 Smith 1965a, 30–3.
89 Woodward and Leach 1993, 12–19.
90 Woodward and Leach 1993, 10–11 for phasing summary.
91 Saville and Ellison 1983, 1.
92 Soffe 1993, 'barrows' 10 and 11; Pollard and Reynolds 2002, 70.
93 Case 1982b; Loveday 1989.
94 See for example Burl 1979, 116; Loveday 1989, 65.
95 Kjaerum 1967; Becker 1973; Andersen 2000, 52.
96 Darvill and Wainwright 2003.
97 Atkinson 1951.
98 Barclay and Harding 1999, 1.
99 Hey 2001, and see above.
100 Whittle et al. 1992, 148–52.
101 Loveday 1989.
102 Pryor 1988, 63–5.
103 Barclay and Hey 1999; Barclay et al. 2003.
104 Loveday 1989.
105 Darvill 1987b, 92–3.
106 Pollard and Reynolds 2002, 70.
107 Mercer 1999.
108 Green 1980, 161–4.
109 Dixon 1988, 82.
110 Liddell 1935, 159.
111 Saville in Mercer 1981, table 4.
112 Mercer 1988, 104.
113 Sahlins 1968, 8.
114 Harris 1978, 33–43.
115 See Whittle 1993; Thomas 1999, 199-229.
116 Whittle 1990b, 108.
117 Darvill 1987a, 35.
118 Hodder 1990, 255.
119 See Barrett 1988, 31–2 for a wide discussion of these and related issues.
120 Kinnes 1981, 85.
121 Baxter 1999, 6.
122 Thomas 1991, 112.
123 Watson 2001, 189; see also Devereux and Jahn 1996 on experiments with sound in the chambers of Wayland's Smithy (BRK 1).
124 Some of these issues are usefully explored by Price (2001) and Dronfield (1996), both with earlier references.
125 See Darvill 1984a, 1986b and 1989 for additional background on trade and exchange in the area.
126 Coles and Coles 1986, chapters 3–4.
127 See Whittle 1977a, 11 for regional style zones.
128 See Thorpe 1984; Thorpe and Richards 1984.

CHAPTER 9

1 For Julian Thomas (1999, 120) these wares were perhaps part of a final set of practices

to evoke the ancestral dead.
2 Baillie 1995, 78; Baillie and Brown 2002, 502–4.
3 Sherratt 1994.
4 See Bradley 1993, 104–6 for a summary; Bradley and Chambers 1988 and Whittle *et al.* 1992 for the detail.
5 Cleal *et al.* 1995, 479–90.
6 Bradley 1993, 112.
7 O'Neil 1966, 24.
8 Wells in Piggott 1962, 79.
9 Savory 1984, 22–3.
10 Whittle 1991, 98–9.
11 Grinsell 1970, 3.
12 Smith 1984, 117.
13 Evans 1990.
14 Ashbee *et al.* 1979, 294.
15 Evans 1990, 115.
16 Whittle 1991, 99.
17 Bell in Saville 1990, 219–22.
18 Bradley 1992.
19 Bewley *et al.* 1996.
20 Clifford 1938b. The pottery is illustrated in Clifford 1937a, figs. 4, 7, 8, 10 and 11.
21 O'Neil and Grinsell 1960, 97 (Coberley 1a).
22 O'Neil and Grinsell 1960, 98 (Hawling 10a).
23 Grimes 1960, 154–64.
24 Barclay, Gray and Lambrick 1995.
25 Darvill and Grinsell 1989, 50. And see Chapter 7.
26 See Darvill 1987b, 86–7 for a summary of these.
27 See Case 1986, 32–4 for a summary of the Oxfordshire finds.
28 Barclay, Glass and Parry 1995; Thomas and Holbrook 1998.
29 Usefully listed in Savory 1980, 135–43.
30 Savory 1940.
31 Smith and Simpson 1966.
32 Two radiocarbon dates are available from oak charcoal associated with the coffin: 2120–1680 BC (3540±70 BP; HAR-2998) and 2600–1750 BC (3745±135 BP; NPL-139). A third date of 2410–1970 BC (3760±60 BP; BM-1585) relates to an ox shoulder-blade from the chalk capping of the barrow mound.
33 Robertson-Mackay 1980.
34 Ashbee *et al.* 1979, 232–4.
35 Grinsell 1953, 256; Ashbee 1960, 34.
36 O'Neil and Grinsell 1960, 15. But see also Drinkwater 1972; and Darvill and Grinsell 1989, fig. 6.
37 Grimes 1960, 101–12.
38 Case 1957.
39 Vulliamy 1922b, 150.
40 Grimes 1939, 135–6.
41 For WIL 34 see Annable and Simpson 1964, 66 and 122 (item 546); for WIL 18 see Grinsell 1957, 138; Annable and Simpson 1964, 67 and 126 (item 565).
42 A number of other standing stones in the Cotswolds have sometimes been claimed as elements of long barrows (e.g. Long Stone (GLO 36); The Grickstone (GLO 89)), but there is no substantiating evidence for these and only excavation will now reveal their original date and relationships.
43 RCHME 1976, 89.
44 Britnell 1984, 93.
45 Ward 1916, 247–8.
46 Whittle and Wysocki 1998, 147 and 177.
47 Hingley 1996.
48 Peers and Smith 1921, 188; see Allen 1967 and Hingley 1990 on 'currency bars' and Spinage 2003, 55–7 on alternative interpretations.
49 Woodward and Leach 1993, 13–30.
50 See Crawford 1925, 104 for summary account.
51 Miles and Palmer 1995, 375–6; Lock *et al.* 2003.
52 Buckman and Newmarch 1850, 12; McWhirr *et al.* 1982, 26.
53 Witts 1881; 1884a.
54 The beads were originally published as Anglo-Saxon, but they are more likely Romano-British; cf. Morgan and Marshall 1921, 299; Vulliamy 1922a, 13; and RCAHMW 1997,
61-2 where it is suggested that pranksters may have been at work to confuse the excavators.
55 O'Neil 1966, 28–9.
56 Whittle 1991, 99; Atkinson 1965, 133 note 21.
57 Saville 1990, 134–5.
58 Witts 1883, 156–60.
59 Berry 1929, 295–8; 1930, 136–7.
60 Donovan 1938, 162. The site is considered here to be a portal dolmen (see Chapter 3).
61 Grinsell 1971, 83; Timby in Thomas 2003, 13.
62 Ward 1916, 257.
63 Annable in Corcoran 1970, 55.
64 Piggott 1962, 5; but see O'Neil and Grinsell 1960, 54 for alternative views on these sites.
65 O'Neil and Grinsell 1960, 22.

66 Smith and Simpson 1964.
67 Conder 1895.
68 Crawford 1925, 125–8.
69 Crawford 1925, 124–5.
70 Grimes 1960, 113–25.
71 Heighway 1987, 20–3.
72 Cited in O'Neil and Grinsell 1960, 76.
73 Williams 1998.
74 Keiller and Piggott 1939.
75 Grinsell 1976, 149; Thurnam 1862. See also Spinage 2003 for a very wide-ranging discussion of the myths and legends of the site with a detailed account of how the tale of Wayland Smith was popularized by Sir Walter Scott in his romance Kenilworth.
76 Grundy 1936; O'Neil and Grinsell 1960, 39–45; Darvill and Grinsell 1989, 55–6.
77 Hooke 1997, 36.
78 Semple 1998, 118.
79 Grinsell 1981; the case for a prehistoric origin is set by Breuil 1934, 290 and Crawford 1955b, 156.
80 Britnell 1984, 93.
81 Corcoran 1970, 51.
82 O'Neil and Grinsell 1960, 55.
83 Clifford 1936, 123.
84 Warmington 1984.
85 Summarized in Crawford 1925, 85.
86 Smith 1964, 5.
87 Clifford 1938a, 189.
88 RCAHMW 1976, 31.
89 Grinsell 1957, 137.
90 Morgan and Marshall 1921, 296.
91 Crawford 1925, 224.
92 Bird 1880, 10.
93 Corcoran 1970, 51.
94 Britnell 1984, 93.
95 Grinsell 1971, 84.
96 See Witts 1883, 87–8 (no. 32).
97 O'Neil and Grinsell 1960, 84; and see Playne 1915, 127.
98 William Munro, former owner of the site, indirectly quoted in Crawford 1925, 224.
99 O'Neil and Grinsell (1960) list a number of long mounds that probably result from landscape gardening, for example the pair at Pur Down, Bristol and another southwest of Heath House in Bristol.
100 Whittle and Wysocki 1998, 139.
101 Cooper 1988.
102 Maclean 1881, 88.
103 Vatcher and Vatcher 1973.
104 See Crawford 1925, 140; Royce 1883, 75–6.
105 Crawford 1925, 115–16 (GLO 93).
106 This barrow has never been included in any of the published listings.
107 Clifford and Daniel 1940, 146–9.
108 O'Neil and Grinsell 1960, 75: Cherington I (GLO 17).
109 Corcoran 1969a, 279 (GLO 17).
110 Daniel 1970, 262. Grinsell has subsequently rechecked his suggestion and confirms that GLO 17 does in fact comply with virtually all the requirements of the mound from which the chambers were removed (Darvill and Grinsell 1989, 65).
111 Clifford 1966.
112 Burrow 1919, 17.
113 Grinsell 1982, 4.
114 Grinsell 1982, 2.
115 A total of 25 monuments in England and Wales were listed on the Schedule to the Act, so the group of long barrows in the Cotswold-Severn region is disproportionately high.
116 Thompson 1977, 64–6.
117 Barker 1985, 14.
118 Ward 1915, 318–19.
119 Drinkwater 1972; Saville and Drinkwater 1976; Saville 1980.
120 Brown 1978.
121 Saville 1990.
122 The CD Autogeddon was released by Echo Records in 1994 (ECHCD1). See also Cope 1998 for a wider expression of New Antiquarian interests in prehistoric sites and some wonderfully evocative notes written at some of the monuments listed here.
123 Corcoran 1969a, 282.
124 Daniel 1959, 282. Carolyn Heighway (1987, 48) notes that it was once known as Eadred's Stone and may have been so named when King Eadred (AD 946–55) created a new hundred around Bath and transformed it for the first time from Mercia to Wessex. However, Eadred's Stone must, presumably, be another nearby feature.
125 Gunstone 1963.

BIBLIOGRAPHY

Adkins, R. & Jackson, R., 1978, *Neolithic stone and flint axes from the River Thames*. London: British Museum Occasional Paper 1.
Akerman, J.Y., 1857, A view of the ancient limits of the Forest of Wychwood. *Archaeologia*, **37**, 424–40.
Akerman, J.Y., 1859, Notes on the opening of two barrows in Gloucestershire. *Proceedings of the Society of Antiquaries of London* (Series 1), **4**, 16–17.
Allen, D., 1967, Iron currency bars in Britain. *Proceedings of the Prehistoric Society*, **33**, 307–35.
Allen, J.R.L., 1998, A prehistoric (Neolithic–Bronze Age) complex on the Severn Estuary Levels, Oldbury-on-Severn, South Gloucestershire. *Transactions of the Bristol and Gloucestershire Archaeological Society*, **116**, 93–116.
Andersen, N.H., 1997, *Sarup, Vol. 1. The Sarup enclosures*. Aarhus: Jutland Archaeological Society Publications 33.1.
Andersen, N.H., 2000, Kult og ritualer I den ældre bondestenalder. *Kuml*, 2000, 13–57.
Annable, F.K. & Simpson, D.D.A., 1964, *Guide catalogue of the Neolithic and Bronze Age collections in Devizes Museum*. Devizes: Wiltshire Archaeological and Natural History Society.
Anon., 1844, [Grickstone Farm]. *Gentleman's Magazine*, **114.1**, 636.
Anon., 1885, [Willersey barrow]. *Transactions of the Bristol and Gloucestershire Archaeological Society*, **9** (1884–5), 29.
Anon., 1909, Monmouth meeting report. *Archaeologia Cambrensis*, **64**, 63–153.
ApSimon, A.M.A., 1997, Wood into stone. Origins for Irish megalithic tombs? In A.A.R. Casal (ed), *O Neolítico Atlántico e as orixes do megalitismo*. Santiago de Compostela: Universidade de Santiago de Compostela. 129–40.
Ashbee, P., 1960, *The Bronze Age round barrow in Britain*. London: Phoenix House.
Ashbee, P., 1966, The Fussell's Lodge long barrow excavations 1957. *Archaeologia*, **100**, 1–80.
Ashbee, P., 1969, Timber mortuary houses and earthen long barrows again. *Antiquity*, **43**, 43–5.
Ashbee, P., 1970, *The earthen long barrow in Britain*. London: Dent.
Ashbee, P., 1984, *The earthen long barrow in Britain* (Second edition). Norwich: Geo Books.
Ashbee, P. & Smith, I.F., 1960, The Windmill Hill long barrow. *Antiquity*, **34**, 297–9.
Ashbee, P. & Smith, I.F., 1966, The date of the Windmill Hill long barrow. *Antiquity*, **40**, 299.
Ashbee, P., Smith, I.F. & Evans, J.G., 1979, Excavation of three long barrows near Avebury, Wiltshire. *Proceedings of the Prehistoric Society*, **45**, 207–300.
Aston, M. & Gerrard, C., 1999, 'Unique, traditional and charming'. The Shapwick Project, Somerset. *Antiquaries Journal*, **79**, 1–58.
Atkinson, R.J.C., 1951, The excavations at Dorchester, Oxfordshire, 1946–51. *Archaeological Newsletter*, **4.4**, 56–9.

Atkinson, R.J.C., 1965, Excavations at Wayland's Smithy long barrow, Berkshire. *Antiquity*, **39**, 126–33.

Atkinson, R.J.C., 1968, Old mortality: some aspects of burial and population in Neolithic England. In J. Coles & D.D.A. Simpson (eds), *Studies in ancient Europe*. Leicester: Leicester University Press. 83–94.

Atkinson, R.J.C., 1984, Barrows excavated by William Stukeley near Stonehenge, 1723–4. *Wiltshire Archaeological and Natural History Magazine*, **79**, 244–6.

Atkinson, R.J.C. & Piggott, S., 1986, The date of the West Kennet long barrow. *Antiquity*, **60**, 143–4.

Atkinson, R.J.C., Piggott, C.M. & Sandars, N.K., 1951, *Excavations at Dorchester, Oxon. First Report*. Oxford: Ashmolean Museum.

Aubrey, J. (ed. J. Fowles), 1982, *Monumenta Britannica*. Milborne Port: Dorset Publishing Company. (2 vols. 1980–2)

Avebury, Lord, 1913, *Prehistoric times* (Seventh edition). London: William and Norgate.

Avery, M., 1982, The Neolithic causewayed enclosure, Abingdon. In H.J. Case & A.W.R. Whittle (eds), *Settlement patterns in the Oxford region: excavations at the Abingdon causewayed enclosure and other sites*. London: Council for British Archaeology Research Report 44. 10–50.

Bagnall-Oakley, M.E., 1889, *An account of the rude stone monuments and ancient burial mounds in Monmouthshire*. Newport: privately published.

Bagnall-Oakley, W., 1888, The chambered tumulus at Heston Brake, Monmouthshire. *Proceedings of the Clifton Antiquarian Society*, **5**, 64–6.

Baillie, M.G.L., 1995, *A slice through time*. London: Batsford.

Baillie, M.G.L. & Brown, D.M., 2002, Oak dendrochronology: some recent archaeological developments from an Irish perspective. *Antiquity*, **76**, 497–505.

Balch, H.E., 1914, *Wookey Hole: its caves and cave dwellers*. Oxford: Oxford University Press.

Balch, H.E., 1926, Chelm's Combe shelter. *Proceedings of the Somerset Archaeological and Natural History Society*, **72**, 95–123.

Barber, M., Field, D. & Topping, P., 1999, *The Neolithic flint mines of England*. London: English Heritage / Royal Commission on the Historical Monuments of England.

Barclay, A., 1997, The portal dolmens of the northeast Cotswolds: symbolism, architecture and the transformation of the earlier Neolithic. In A.A.R. Casal (ed), *O Neolítico Atlántico e as orixes do megalitismo*. Santiago de Compostela: Universidade de Santiago de Compostela. 151–60.

Barclay, A., Glass, H. & Parry, C., 1995, Excavations of Neolithic and Bronze Age ring-ditches, Shorncote Quarry, Somerford Keynes, Gloucestershire. *Transactions of the Bristol and Gloucestershire Archaeological Society*, **113**, 21–60.

Barclay, A., Gray, M. & Lambrick, G., 1995, *Excavations at the Devil's Quoits, Stanton Harcourt, Oxfordshire, 1972–3 and 1988*. Oxford: Oxford Archaeological Unit.

Barclay, A. & Harding, J., 1999, An introduction to the cursus monuments of Neolithic Britain and Ireland. In A. Barclay & J. Harding (eds), *Pathways and ceremonies: the cursus monuments of Britain and Ireland*. Oxford: Oxbow Books / Neolithic Studies Group Seminar Papers 4. 1–10.

Barclay, A. & Hey, G., 1999, Cattle, cursus monuments and the river: the development of ritual and domestic landscapes in the upper Thames Valley. In A. Barclay & J. Harding (eds), *Pathways and ceremonies: the cursus monuments of Britain and Ireland*. Oxford: Oxbow Books / Neolithic Studies Group Seminar Papers 4. 67–76.

Barclay, A., Lambrick, G., Moore, J. & Robinson, M., 2003, *Lines in the landscape, cursus monuments in the upper Thames valley: excavations at the Drayton and Lechlade cursuses*. Oxford: Oxford Archaeology, Thames Valley Landscapes Monograph 15.

Barclay, G.J., Brophy, K. & MacGregor, G., 2002, Claish, Stirling: an early Neolithic structure in its context. *Proceedings of the Society of Antiquaries of Scotland*, **132**, 65–137.

Barker, C.T., 1985, The long mounds of the Avebury region. *Wiltshire Archaeological and Natural History Magazine*, **79**, 7–38.

Barker, G. & Webley, D., 1978, Causewayed camps and early Neolithic economies in central southern England. *Proceedings of the Prehistoric Society*, **44**, 161–86.

Barrett, J., 1988, The living, the dead and the ancestors: Neolithic and Bronze Age mortuary practices. In J. Barrett & I. Kinnes (eds), *The archaeology of context in the Neolithic and Bronze Age*. Sheffield: Sheffield University Department of Archaeology and Prehistory. 30–41.

Barrett, J.C., 1994, *Fragments from antiquity: an archaeology of social life in Britain, 2900–1200 BC*. Oxford: Blackwell.
Barrett, J.H., 1966, Tom Tivey's Hole rock shelter, near Leighton, Somerset. *Proceedings of the University of Bristol Spelaeological Society*, **11.1** (1965–6), 9–24.
Baxter, M., 1999, Dancing with the dead in a mass grave. *British Archaeology*, **50** (December 1999), 6–7.
Becker, C.J., 1973, Problems of the megalithic 'mortuary houses' in Denmark. In G. Daniel & P. Kjaerum (eds), *Megalithic graves and ritual. Papers presented at the III Atlantic Colloquium, Moesgård 1969*. Copenhagen: Jutland Archaeological Society Publications XI. 75–9.
Benson, D. & Clegg, I., 1978, Cotswold burial rites. *Man* (NS), **13**, 134–7.
Benson, D. & Miles, D., 1974, *The upper Thames Valley: an archaeological survey of the river gravels*. Oxford: Oxford Archaeological Unit Survey 2.
Berry, Sir J., 1929, Belas Knap long barrow, Gloucestershire; report of the excavations of 1929. *Transactions of the Bristol and Gloucestershire Archaeological Society*, **51**, 273–303.
Berry, Sir J., 1930, Belas Knap long barrow, Gloucestershire. Second report: the excavations of 1930. *Transactions of the Bristol and Gloucestershire Archaeological Society*, **52**, 123–50.
Bewley, B., 2001, Understanding England's historic landscapes: an aerial perspective. *Landscapes*, **2.1**, 74–84.
Bewley, R., Cole, M., David, A., Featherstone, R., Payne, A. & Small, F., 1996, New features within the henge at Avebury, Wiltshire: aerial and geophysical evidence. *Antiquity*, **70**, 639–46.
Bird, H., 1865, An account of the human bones found in the round and long tumuli, situated on the Cotswold Hills near Cheltenham. *Journal of the Anthropological Society*, **3**, lxv–lxxiv.
Bird, H., 1880, On the ancient races of the Cotteswolds. *Transactions of the Stroud Natural History and Philosophical Society*, **1**, 7–13.
Boujot, C. & Cassen, S., 1992, Le développement des premières architectures funéraires monumentales en France occidentale. In L.-T. Le Roux (ed), *Paysans et batisseurs: l'emergence du Néolithique atlantique et les origines du mégalithisme. Actes du 17ème Colloque interrégional sur le Néolithique: Vannes 28–31 Octobre 1990*. Rennes: Revue Archéologique de l'Ouest, Supplément 5. 195–211.
Boujot, C. & Cassen, S., 1993, A pattern of evolution for the Neolithic funerary structures of the west of France. *Antiquity*, **67**, 477–91.
Bowman, S.G.E., Ambers, J.C. & Leese, M.N., 1990, Re-evaluation of British Museum radiocarbon dates issued between 1980 and 1984. *Radiocarbon*, **32**, 59–79.
Bradley, R., 1983, The bank barrows and related monuments of Dorset in the light of recent fieldwork. *Proceedings of the Dorset Natural History and Archaeological Society*, **105**, 15–20.
Bradley, R., 1992, The excavation of an oval barrow beside the Abingdon causewayed enclosure, Oxfordshire. *Proceedings of the Prehistoric Society*, **58**, 127–42.
Bradley, R., 1993, *Altering the earth: the 1992 Rhind Lectures*. Edinburgh: Society of Antiquaries of Scotland Monograph 8.
Bradley, R., 1998a, *The significance of monuments*. London: Routledge.
Bradley, R., 1998b, Ruined buildings, ruined stones: enclosures, tombs and natural places in the Neolithic of south-west England. *World Archaeology*, **30.1**, 13–22.
Bradley, R., 2000a, *An archaeology of natural places*. London: Routledge.
Bradley, R., 2000b, Orientations and origins: a symbolic dimension to the long house in Neolithic Europe. *Antiquity*, **75**, 50–6.
Bradley, R., 2002, *The past in prehistoric societies*. London: Routledge.
Bradley, R. & Chambers, R, 1988, A new study of the cursus complex at Dorchester on Thames. *Oxford Journal of Archaeology*, **7**, 271–89.
Bradley, R. & Gordon, K., 1988, Human skulls from the River Thames, their dating and significance. *Antiquity*, **62**, 503–9.
Bradley, R. & Holgate, R., 1984, The Neolithic sequence in the upper Thames Valley. In R. Bradley & J. Gardiner (eds), *Neolithic studies: a review of some current research*. Oxford: British Archaeological Reports British Series 133. 107–34.
Breuil, L'Abbé H., 1934, Presidential address. *Proceedings of the Prehistoric Society of East Anglia*, **7**, 289–322.
Britnell, W.J., 1979, The Gwernvale long cairn, Powys. *Antiquity*, **53**, 132–4.

Britnell, W.J., 1984, The Gwernvale long cairn, Crickhowell, Brecknock. In W.J. Britnell & H.N. Savory, *Gwernvale and Penywyrlod: two Neolithic long cairns in the Black Mountains of Brecknock*. Cardiff: Cambrian Archaeological Association Monograph 2. 42–154.

Brodie, N., 1994, *The Neolithic–Bronze Age transition in Britain*. Oxford: British Archaeological Reports British Series 238.

Bronk Ramsey, C., 2000, *OxCal v.3.5 – radiocarbon calibration programme*. Oxford: Oxford Radiocarbon Accelerator Unit (computer software application).

Brothwell, D., 1973, The human biology of the Neolithic population of Britain. In J. Lüning (ed), *Die Anfänge des Neolithikums vom Orient bis Nordeuropa. VIIIa (Anthropologie)*. Cologne and Vienna: Böhlau Verlag. 280–99.

Brown, J.A., 1894, Uley Barrow or Hetty Pegler's Tump. *Gloucestershire Notes and Queries*, **5**, 219–28.

Brown, L., 1978, A survey of the condition of Oxfordshire long barrows. *Oxoniensia*, **43**, 241–5.

Buckman, J., 1865, Notes on an ancient British tumulus at Nympsfield, opened by the Cotteswold Club. *Proceedings of the Cotteswold Naturalists Field Club*, **3**, 184–8.

Buckman, J. & Newmarch, C.H., 1850, *Illustrations of the remains of Roman art in Cirencester, the site of ancient Corinium*. London: George Bell.

Bulleid, A., 1941, Notes on some chambered long barrows in north Somerset. *Proceedings of the Somerset Archaeological and Natural History Society*, **87**, 56–71.

Burenhult, G., 1980, *The archaeological excavation at Carrowmore, Co. Sligo, Ireland: excavation seasons 1977–79*. Stockholm: Institute of Archaeology at the University of Stockholm Theses and Papers in North-European Archaeology 9.

Burenhult, G., 1984, *The archaeology of Carrowmore*. Stockholm: Institute of Archaeology at the University of Stockholm Theses and Papers in North-European Archaeology 14.

Burl, A., 1979, *Prehistoric Avebury*. London and New Haven: Yale University Press.

Burl, A., 1981, 'By the light of the cinerary moon': chambered tombs and the astronomy of death. In C.L.N. Ruggles & A.W.R. Whittle (eds), *Astronomy and society in Britain during the period 4000–1500 BC*. Oxford: British Archaeological Reports British Series 88. 243–74.

Burl, A., 1985, *Megalithic Brittany*. London: Thames and Hudson.

Burrow, E.J., 1919, *The ancient entrenchments and camps of Gloucestershire*. Cheltenham and London: J. Burrow and Co.

Burrow, S., Driver, T. & Thomas, D., 2001, Bridging the Severn Estuary: two possible early Neolithic enclosures in the Vale of Glamorgan. In T. Darvill & J. Thomas (eds), *Neolithic enclosures in Atlantic Northwest Europe*. Oxford: Oxbow Books / Neolithic Studies Group Seminar Papers 6. 91–100.

Burton, J., 1980, Making sense of waste flakes: new methods for investigating the technology and economics behind chipped stone assemblages. *Journal of Archaeological Science*, **7**, 131–48.

Cameron, J., 1934, *The skeleton of British Neolithic man*. London: Williams and Norgate.

Case, H., 1956, The Neolithic causewayed enclosure at Abingdon, Berks. *Antiquaries Journal*, **36**, 11–30.

Case, H., 1957, The Lambourn Seven Barrows. *Berkshire Archaeological Journal*, **55** (1956–7), 15–31.

Case, H., 1969, Neolithic explanations. *Antiquity*, **43**, 176–86.

Case, H., 1982a, Introduction. In H.J. Case & A.W.R. Whittle (eds), *Settlement patterns in the Oxford region: excavations at the Abingdon causewayed enclosure and other sites*. London: Council for British Archaeology Research Report 44. 1–9.

Case, H., 1982b, The linear ditches and southern enclosure, North Stoke. In H.J. Case & A.W.R. Whittle (eds), *Settlement patterns in the Oxford region: excavations at the Abingdon causewayed enclosure and other sites*. London: Council for British Archaeology Research Report 44. 60–75.

Case, H., 1986, The Mesolithic and Neolithic in the Oxford region. In G. Briggs, J. Cook & T. Rowley (eds), *The archaeology of the Oxford region*. Oxford: Oxford University Department of External Studies. 18–37.

Case, H., 1993, Beakers: deconstruction and after. *Proceedings of the Prehistoric Society*, **59**, 241–68.

Case, H., 1995, Some Wiltshire beakers and their contexts. *Wiltshire Archaeological and Natural History Magazine*, **88**, 1–17.

Cassen, S., 1993, Material culture and chronology of the middle Neolithic of western France. *Oxford Journal of Archaeology*, **12.2**, 197–208.

Chesterman, J.T., 1977, Burial rites in a Cotswold long barrow. *Man* (NS), **12**, 22–32.
Childe, V.G., 1940, *Prehistoric communities of the British Isles*. London: Chambers.
Childe, V.G., 1949, The origin of Neolithic culture in Northern Europe. *Antiquity*, **23**, 129–35.
Childe, V.G., 1957, *The dawn of European civilization* (Sixth edition). London: Routledge and Kegan Paul.
Clark, G., 1977, The economic context of dolmens and passage graves in Sweden. In V. Markotic (ed), *Ancient Europe and the Mediterranean*. Warminster: Aris and Phillips. 35–49.
Clark, J.G.D., 1937, Megaliths and collective burial. *Proceedings of the Prehistoric Society*, **3**, 470–2.
Clarke, M. & Richards, C., 1972, Winscombe, Sandford Hill. *Archaeological Review*, **7**, 16.
Cleal, R.M.J., Walker, K.E. & Montague, K., 1995, *Stonehenge in its landscape: twentieth-century excavations*. London: English Heritage Archaeological Reports 10.
Clifford, E.M., 1936, Notgrove long barrow, Gloucestershire. *Archaeologia*, **86**, 119–61.
Clifford, E.M., 1937, Jackbarrow, Duntisbourne Abbots. *Transactions of the Bristol and Gloucestershire Archaeological Society*, **59**, 334–7.
Clifford, E.M., 1938a, The excavation of Nympsfield long barrow, Gloucestershire. *Proceedings of the Prehistoric Society*, **4**, 188–213.
Clifford, E.M., 1938b, The Soldier's Grave, Frocester, Gloucestershire. *Proceedings of the Prehistoric Society*, **4**, 214–18.
Clifford, E.M., 1938c, Underground chambers, Miserden. *Transactions of the Bristol and Gloucestershire Archaeological Society*, **60**, 343–6.
Clifford, E.M., 1950, The Cotswold megalithic culture: the grave goods and their background. In C. Fox & B. Dickens (eds), *The early cultures of northwest Europe*. Cambridge: Cambridge University Press. 23–40.
Clifford, E.M., 1966, Hetty Pegler's Tump. *Antiquity*, **40**, 129–32.
Clifford, E.M. & Daniel, G.E., 1940, The Rodmarton and Avening portholes. *Proceedings of the Prehistoric Society*, **6**, 133–65.
Coles, B.J., 1994, Trisantona rivers: landscape approach to the interpretation of river names. *Oxford Journal of Archaeology*, **13.3**, 295–311.
Coles, B.J. & Coles, J.M., 1986, *Sweet Track to Glastonbury*. London: Thames and Hudson.
Coles, J.M., 1989, Prehistoric settlement in the Somerset Levels. *Somerset Levels Papers*, **15**, 14–32.
Coles, J. & Simpson, D.D.A., 1965, The excavation of a Neolithic round barrow at Pitnacree, Perthshire, Scotland. *Proceedings of the Prehistoric Society*, **31**, 34–57.
Collins, A.E.P., 1973, A re-examination of the Clyde-Carlingford tombs. In G. Daniel & P. Kjaerum (eds), *Megalithic graves and ritual. Papers presented at the III Atlantic Colloquium, Moesgård 1969*. Copenhagen: Jutland Archaeological Society Publications XI. 93–103.
Colt Hoare, Sir R., 1812, *The ancient history of Wiltshire. Vol. I*. Devizes: privately printed.
Colt Hoare, Sir R., 1821a, An account of a stone barrow in the parish of Wellow, at Stoney Littleton in the county of Somerset, which was opened and investigated in the month of May 1816. *Archaeologia*, **19**, 43–8.
Colt Hoare, Sir R., 1821b, *The ancient history of Wiltshire. Vol. II*. Devizes: privately printed.
Colt Hoare, Sir R., 1822, [Lugbury, Wiltshire]. *Gentleman's Magazine*, **92.1**, 160.
Conder, E., 1895, [Lyneham Barrow, Oxon.]. *Proceedings of the Society of Antiquaries of London* (Series 2), **15**, 404–10.
Connah, G., 1965, Excavations at Knap Hill, Alton Priors, 1961. *Wiltshire Archaeological and Natural History Magazine*, **60**, 1–23.
Cooper, N., 1988, Lodge Park, Sherborne. *Archaeological Journal*, **145**, Supplement (The Cirencester Area), 55.
Cope, J., 1998, *The modern antiquarian: a pre-millennial odyssey through megalithic Britain*. London: Thorsons and HarperCollins.
Corcoran, J.X.W.P., 1969a, The Cotswold-Severn Group. In T.G.E. Powell, J.X.W.P. Corcoran, F. Lynch & J.G. Scott, *Megalithic enquiries in the west of Britain*. Liverpool: Liverpool University Press. 13–106 and 273–95.
Corcoran, J.X.W.P., 1969b, Multiperiod chambered tombs. *Scottish Archaeological Forum*, **1**, 9–17.
Corcoran, J.X.W.P., 1970, The Giant's Caves, Luckington (WIL 2). *Wiltshire Archaeological and Natural History Magazine*, **65B**, 39–63

Corcoran, J.X.W.P., 1972, Multi-period construction and the origins of the chambered long cairn in western Britain and Ireland. In F. Lynch & C. Burgess (eds), *Prehistoric man in Wales and the West*. Bath: Adams & Dart. 31–64.

Corcoran, J.X.W.P., 1973, The chambered cairns of the Carlingford Culture. An enquiry into origins. In G. Daniel & P. Kjaerum (eds), *Megalithic graves and ritual. Papers presented at the III Atlantic Colloquium, Moesgård 1969*. Copenhagen: Jutland Archaeological Society Publications XI. 105–16.

Cox, W.L., 1975, The 'stranded whales'. *Cotswold Life*, **80** (June 1975), 25.

Crawford, O.G.S., 1922, *Notes on archaeological information incorporated in the Ordnance Survey maps. Part I. The long barrows and stone circles in the area covered by Sheet 8 of the quarter-inch map (The Cotswolds & The Welsh Marches)*. Southampton: Ordnance Survey Professional Papers (New Series) 6.

Crawford, O.G.S., 1925, *The long barrows of the Cotswolds*. Gloucester: John Bellows.

Crawford, O.G.S., 1932, *Map of Neolithic Wessex*. Southampton: Ordnance Survey.

Crawford, O.G.S., 1938, Bank barrows. *Antiquity*, **12**, 228–32.

Crawford, O.G.S., 1955a, *Said and done: the autobiography of an archaeologist*. London: Weidenfeld & Nicholson.

Crawford, O.G.S., 1955b, The technique of the Boyne carvings. *Proceedings of the Prehistoric Society*, **21**, 156–9.

Crawford, O.G.S. & Keiller, A., 1928, *Wessex from the air*. Oxford: Clarendon Press.

Cummings, V., 2002, All cultural things. Actual and conceptual monuments in the Neolithic of western Britain. In C. Scarre (ed), *Monuments and landscape in Atlantic Europe*. London: Routledge. 107–21.

Cummings, V., Jones, A. & Watson, A., 2002, Divided places: phenomenology and asymmetry in the monuments of the Black Mountains, southeast Wales. *Cambridge Archaeological Journal*, **12.1**, 57–70.

Cunliffe, B., 2001, *Facing the ocean: the Atlantic and its people*. Oxford: Oxford University Press.

Cunnington, M.E., 1909a, The discovery of a chamber in the long barrow at Lanhill. *Wiltshire Archaeological and Natural History Magazine*, **36**, 300–10.

Cunnington, M.E., 1909b, Notes on barrows on Kings Play Down, Heddington. *Wiltshire Archaeological and Natural History Magazine*, **36**, 311–17.

Cunnington, M.E., 1914, List of the long barrows of Wiltshire. *Wiltshire Archaeological and Natural History Magazine*, **38**, 379–414.

Cunnington, M.E., 1926, Notes on recent prehistoric finds. *Wiltshire Archaeological and Natural History Magazine*, **43**, 395–400.

Cunnington, W., 1872, Notes on a long barrow on Oldbury Hill. *Wiltshire Archaeological and Natural History Magazine*, **13**, 103–4.

Daniel, G.E., 1937a, The dolmens of southern Britain. *Antiquity*, **11**, 183–200.

Daniel, G.E., 1937b, The chambered barrow in Parc le Breos Cwm, S. Wales. *Proceedings of the Prehistoric Society*, **3**, 71–86.

Daniel, G.E., 1939, The transepted gallery graves of western France. *Proceedings of the Prehistoric Society*, **5**, 143–65.

Daniel, G.E., 1941, The dual nature of the megalithic colonization of prehistoric Europe. *Proceedings of the Prehistoric Society*, **7**, 1–49.

Daniel, G., 1950a, *The prehistoric chamber tombs of England and Wales*. Cambridge: Cambridge University Press.

Daniel, G., 1950b, The long barrow in western Europe. In C. Fox & B. Dickens (eds), *The early cultures of northwest Europe*. Cambridge: Cambridge University Press. 3–20.

Daniel, G., 1957, The cromlechau of Glamorgan. *Morgannwg*, **1**, 3–12.

Daniel, G., 1958a, *The megalithic builders of western Europe*. London: Hutchinson.

Daniel, G., 1958b, The chronology of the French collective tombs. *Proceedings of the Prehistoric Society*, **34**, 1–23.

Daniel, G., 1959, Some megalithic follies. *Antiquity*, **33**, 282.

Daniel, G., 1960, *The prehistoric chamber tombs of France*. London: Thames and Hudson.

Daniel, G., 1964, The long barrows of the Cotswolds. *Transactions of the Bristol and Gloucestershire Archaeological Society*, **82**, 5–17.

Daniel, G., 1967, Northmen and Southmen. *Antiquity*, **41**, 313–17.

Daniel, G., 1970, Megalithic answers. *Antiquity*, **44**, 260–9.

Daniel, G., 1972, The origin of the megalithic tombs of the British Isles. In J. Lüning (ed), *Die Anfänge des Neolithikums vom Orient bis Nordeuropa. VII.* Cologne and Vienna: Böhlau Verlag. 233–47.

Daniel, G., 1986, *Some small harvest: the memoirs of Glyn Daniel.* London: Thames and Hudson.

Darvill, T., 1981, Excavations at The Peak Camp, Cowley – an interim note. *Glevensis*, 15, 52–6.

Darvill, T., 1982a, *The megalithic chambered tombs of the Cotswold-Severn region.* Highworth: VORDA Research Series 5.

Darvill, T., 1982b, Excavations at The Peak Camp, Cowley, Gloucestershire – second interim report. *Glevensis*, **16**, 20–5.

Darvill, T., 1983, The Neolithic of Wales and the mid-west of England: a systematic analysis of social change through the application of action theory. Southampton University unpublished PhD thesis.

Darvill, T., 1984a, Neolithic Gloucestershire. In A. Saville (ed), *Archaeology in Gloucestershire: from the earliest hunters to the Industrial Age.* Cheltenham: Cheltenham Museum and Art Gallery and the Bristol and Gloucestershire Archaeological Society. 80–112.

Darvill, T., 1984b, *Birdlip Bypass Project – first report: archaeological assessment and field survey.* Bristol: Western Archaeological Trust.

Darvill, T., 1986a, Prospects for dating Neolithic sites and monuments in the Cotswolds and adjacent areas. In J.A.J. Gowlett & R.E.M. Hedges (eds), *Archaeological results from accelerator dating.* Oxford: Oxford University Committee for Archaeology Monograph 11. 119–24.

Darvill, T., 1986b, Neolithic Avon: 3500–1650 bc. In M. Aston & R. Iles (eds), *The archaeology of Avon: a review from the Neolithic to the Middle Ages.* Bristol: Avon County Council. 13–27.

Darvill, T., 1987a, *Prehistoric Britain.* London: Batsford.

Darvill, T., 1987b, *Prehistoric Gloucestershire.* Gloucester: Alan Sutton and County Library Series.

Darvill, T., 1989, The circulation of Neolithic stone and flint axes: a case study from Wales and the mid-west of England. *Proceedings of the Prehistoric Society*, **55**, 27–44.

Darvill, T., 1996a, *Prehistoric Britain from the air: a study of space, time and society.* Cambridge: Cambridge University Press.

Darvill, T., 1996b, Neolithic buildings in England, Wales and the Isle of Man. In T. Darvill & J. Thomas (eds), *Neolithic houses in northwest Europe and beyond.* Oxford: Oxbow Books / Neolithic Studies Group Seminar Papers 1. 77–112.

Darvill, T., 2002, White on blonde: quartz pebbles and the use of quartz at Neolithic monuments in the Isle of Man and beyond. In A. Jones & G. MacGregor (eds), *Colouring the past: the significance of colour in archaeological research.* Oxford: Berg. 73–92.

Darvill, T., 2003, Tales of land, tales of the sea. In V. Cummings & C. Fowler (eds), *The Neolithic of the Irish Sea: materiality and traditions of practice.* Oxford: Oxbow Books.

Darvill, T. & Grinsell, L.V., 1989, Gloucestershire barrows: supplement 1961–88. *Transactions of the Bristol and Gloucestershire Archaeological Society*, **107**, 39–105.

Darvill, T. & Thomas, J., 2001, Neolithic enclosures in Atlantic northwest Europe: some recent trends. In T. Darvill & J. Thomas (eds), *Neolithic enclosures in Atlantic Northwest Europe.* Oxford: Oxbow Books / Neolithic Studies Group Seminar Papers 6. 1–23.

Darvill, T. & Wainwright, G., 2003, Stone circles, oval settings and henges in southwest Wales and beyond. *Antiquaries Journal*, **83**, 9–45

Davies, J.B. & Thurnam, J., 1865, *Crania Britannica.* London: privately printed. (2 vols.)

Davies, P. & Wolski, C., 2001, Late Neolithic woodland regeneration in the long barrow fills of the Avebury area: the molluscan evidence. *Oxford Journal of Archaeology*, **20.4**, 311–18.

de Valera, R., 1960, The court cairns of Ireland. *Proceedings of the Royal Irish Academy*, **60C**, 9–140.

de Valera, R., 1965, Transeptal court cairns. *Journal of the Royal Society of Antiquaries of Ireland*, **95**, 5–37.

Devereux, P. & Jahn, R.G., 1996, Preliminary investigations and cognitive considerations of the acoustical resonances of selected archaeological sites. *Antiquity*, **70**, 665–6.

Dimbleby, G.W. & Evans, J.G., 1974, Pollen and land snail analysis of calcareous soils. *Journal of Archaeological Science*, **1**, 117–33.

Dixon, P., 1979, A Neolithic and Iron Age site on a hilltop in southern England. *Scientific American*, **241(5)**, 142–50.

Dixon, P., 1988, The Neolithic settlements on Crickley Hill. In C. Burgess, P. Topping, C. Mordant & M. Maddison (eds), *Enclosures and defences in the Neolithic of Western Europe*. Oxford: British Archaeological Reports International Series 403. 75–87.

Dixon, P., 1994, *Crickley Hill, Vol. 1. The hillfort defences*. Nottingham: Crickley Hill Trust and the Department of Archaeology, Nottingham University.

Dobson, D.P., 1931, *The archaeology of Somerset*. London: Methuen.

Donovan, D.T., 1977, Stoney Littleton long barrow. *Antiquity*, **51**, 236–7.

Donovan, H.E., 1938, Adlestrop Hill barrow, Gloucestershire. *Transactions of the Bristol and Gloucestershire Archaeological Society*, **60**, 152–64.

Dorrington, J.E. & Rolleston, G., 1880, Remarks on a round barrow, in Hungerfield, in the parish of Cranham. *Transactions of the Bristol and Gloucestershire Archaeological Society*, **5**, 133–6.

Drewett, P., 1986, The excavation of a Neolithic oval barrow at North Marden, West Sussex, 1982. *Proceedings of the Prehistoric Society*, **52**, 31–52.

Drinkwater, J., 1972, Barrows in Gloucestershire: patterns of destruction. In P.J. Fowler (ed), *Archaeology and the landscape*. London: John Baker. 129–56.

Dronfield, J., 1996, Entering alternative realities: cognition, art and architecture in Irish passage-tombs. *Cambridge Archaeological Journal*, **6.1**, 37–72.

Dubouloz, J., Lebolloch, M. & Ilett, M., 1988, Middle Neolithic enclosures in the Aisne Valley. In C. Burgess, P. Topping, C. Mordant & M. Maddison (eds), *Enclosures and defences in the Neolithic of Western Europe*. Oxford: British Archaeological Reports International Series 403. 209–26.

Edmonds, M., 1999, *Ancestral geographies of the Neolithic: landscape, monuments and memory*. London: Routledge.

Emery, F., 1958, Edward Lhwyd and the 1695 Britannia. *Antiquity*, **32**, 179–82.

Eogan, G., 1997, Cohesion and diversity: passage tombs of north-western Europe and their social and ritual fabric. In A.A.R. Casal (ed), *O Neolítico Atlántico e as orixes do megalitismo*. Santiago de Compostela: Universidade de Santiago de Compostela. 43–64.

Evans, J.G., 1990, Notes on some late Neolithic and Bronze Age events in long barrow ditches in southern and eastern England. *Proceedings of the Prehistoric Society*, **56**, 111–16.

Evans, J.G. & Burleigh, R., 1969, Radiocarbon dates from the South Street long barrow, Wiltshire. *Antiquity*, **43**, 144–5.

Evans, J.G. & Smith, I.F., 1983, Excavations at Cherhill, North Wiltshire, 1967. *Proceedings of the Prehistoric Society*, **49**, 43–117.

Fairweather, A. & Ralston, I., 1993, The Neolithic timber hall at Balbridie, Grampian Region, Scotland: the building, the date and the plant macrofossils. *Antiquity*, **67**, 313–23.

Featherstone, R., Horne, P., MacLeod, D. & Bewley, R., 1995, Aerial reconnaissance in England, summer 1995. *Antiquity*, **69**, 981–8.

Fisher, Canon, 1920, Arthur's Stone. *Archaeologia Cambrensis*, **75**, 330–3.

Fitzpatrick, A.P., 2003, The Amesbury Archer. *Current Archaeology*, **16.4** (no. 184), 146–52.

Fleming, A., 1972, Vision and design: approaches to ceremonial monument typology. *Man* (NS), **7**, 57–72.

Fleming, A., 1973, Tombs for the living. *Man* (NS), **8**, 177–93.

Fleming, A., 1999, Phenomenology and the megaliths of Wales: a dreaming too far? *Oxford Journal of Archaeology*, **18.2**, 119–25.

Foley, R., 1981, Off-site archaeology: an alternative approach for the short-sited. In I. Hodder, G. Isaac & N. Hammond (eds), *Pattern of the past: studies in honour of David Clarke*. Cambridge: Cambridge University Press. 157–84.

Forde, C.D., 1927, The megalithic monuments of southern Finistere. *Antiquaries Journal*, **7**, 6–37.

Forde, C.D., 1929, The megalithic gallery in Brittany. *Man*, **29.6**, 105–9.

Forde, C.D., 1940, Multiple chambered tombs in north-western France. *Proceedings of the Prehistoric Society*, **6**, 170–6.

Fowler, P.J., 1983, *The farming of prehistoric Britain*. Cambridge: Cambridge University Press.

Fowler, P.J. & Evans, J.G., 1967, Plough-marks, lynchets and early fields. *Antiquity*, **41**, 289–301.

Fox, J.J., 1993, Memories of ridge-poles and cross-beams: the categorical foundations of a Rotinese cultural design. In J.J. Fox (ed), *Inside Austronesian houses: perspectives on domestic designs for living*.

Canberra: Department of Anthropology, Australian National University. 140–79.

Freston, A., 1812, [An account of a tumulus opened in an estate of Matthew Baillie MD, in the parish of Duntisbourne Abbots in Gloucestershire.] *Archaeologia*, **16**, 361–2.

Gell, A., 1992, *The anthropology of time*. Oxford: Berg.

Gibson, A., 1998, Hindwell and the Neolithic palisaded sites of Britain and Ireland. In A. Gibson & D. Simpson (eds), *Prehistoric ritual and religion*. Stroud: Sutton Publishing. 68–79.

Gibson, A., 1999, *The Walton Basin project: excavation and survey in a prehistoric landscape 1993–7*. York: Council for British Archaeology Research Report 118.

Gibson, A., 2000, Survey and excavation of a newly discovered long barrow at Lower Luggy, Berriew, Powys. *Studia Celtica*, **34**, 1–16.

Giot, P.-R., 1987, *Barnenez, Carn, Guennoc*. Rennes: Travaux du Laboratoire Anthropologie–Préhistoire–Protohistoire–Quaternaire Armoricains.

Gray, H. St G., 1921, Excavations at Murtry Hill, Orchardleigh Park, 1920. *Proceedings of the Somerset Archaeological and Natural History Society*, **67**, 39–55.

Gray, H. St G., 1929, Excavations at Murtry Hill, Orchardleigh Park, Part II. *Proceedings of the Somerset Archaeological and Natural History Society*, **75**, 57–60.

Gray, H. St G., 1931, Battlegore, Williton. *Proceedings of the Somerset Archaeological and Natural History Society*, **77**, 7–36.

Gray, I., 1981, *Antiquaries of Gloucestershire and Bristol*. Bristol: Bristol and Gloucestershire Archaeological Society.

Green, H.S., 1980, *The flint arrowheads of the British Isles*. Oxford: British Archaeological Reports British Series 75. (2 vols.)

Greenwell, W., 1877, *British barrows*. Oxford: Clarendon Press.

Gresham, C.A., 1972, Burials in megalithic chambered tombs. In F. Lynch & C. Burgess (eds), *Prehistoric man in Wales and the West*. Bath: Adams & Dart. 65–6.

Grimes, W.F. 1936a, The long cairns of the Breconshire Black Mountains. *Archaeologia Cambrensis*, **91**, 259–82.

Grimes, W.F., 1936b, *Map of South Wales, showing the distribution of long barrows and megaliths*. Southampton: Ordnance Survey.

Grimes, W.F., 1936c, The megalithic monuments of Wales. *Proceedings of the Prehistoric Society*, **2**, 106–39.

Grimes, W.F. 1939, The excavation of Ty-isaf long cairn, Brecknockshire. *Proceedings of the Prehistoric Society*, **5**, 119–42.

Grimes, W.F., 1949, Pentre Ifan burial chamber, Pembrokeshire. *Archaeologia Cambrensis*, **100**, 3–23.

Grimes, W.F., 1960, *Excavations on Defence Sites, 1939–45, vol. I. Mainly Neolithic and Bronze Age*. London. HMSO, Ministry of Works Archaeological Reports 3.

Grinsell, L.V., 1935–9, An analysis and list of Berkshire Barrows. *Berkshire Archaeological Journal*, **49**, 171–91; **40**, 20–58; **42**, 102–16; **43**, 9–21.

Grinsell, L.V., 1953, *The ancient burial-mounds of England* (Second edition). London: Methuen.

Grinsell, L.V., 1957, Archaeological gazetteer. In R.B. Pugh & E. Crittall (eds), *A history of Wiltshire. Vol. I, Part 1*. London: Institute of Historical Research (Victoria History of the Counties of England). 21–279.

Grinsell, L.V., 1959, *Dorset barrows*. Dorchester: Dorset Natural History and Archaeological Society.

Grinsell, L.V., 1964, The Royce Collection at Stow on the Wold. *Transactions of the Bristol and Gloucestershire Archaeological Society*, **83**, 5–23.

Grinsell, L.V., 1966, *Belas Knap*. London: Department of the Environment [site guide leaflet].

Grinsell, L.V., 1970, *Hetty Pegler's Tump, Gloucestershire*. London: Department of the Environment [site guide leaflet].

Grinsell, L.V., 1971, Somerset barrows. Part II: north and east. *Proceedings of the Somerset Archaeological and Natural History Society*, **115**, 44–137.

Grinsell, L.V., 1976, *Folklore of prehistoric sites in Britain*. Newton Abbot: David and Charles.

Grinsell, L.V., 1977, *The Rollright Stones*. St Peter Port: Toucan Press West Country Folklore 10.

Grinsell, L.V., 1981, The later history of Ty Illtud. *Archaeologia Cambrensis*, **130**, 131–9.
Grinsell, L.V., 1982, *Stoney Littleton long barrow*. London: Department of the Environment [site guide leaflet].
Grinsell, L.V. & Janes, D., 1966, The Royce Collection of Cotswold Antiquities: supplement. *Transactions of the Bristol and Gloucestershire Archaeological Society*, **85**, 209–13.
Grogan, E., 1996, Neolithic houses in Ireland. In T. Darvill & J. Thomas (eds), *Neolithic houses in northwest Europe and beyond*. Oxford: Oxbow Books / Neolithic Studies Group Seminar Papers 1. 41–60.
Grundy, G.B., 1936, *Saxon charters and fieldnames of Gloucestershire*. Bristol: Bristol and Gloucestershire Archaeological Society.
Gunstone, A.J.H., 1963, The date of the Three Shire Stones, near Batheaston. *Transactions of the Bristol and Gloucestershire Archaeological Society*, **82**, 210–11.
Harris, M., 1978, *Cannibals and kings: the origins of cultures*. London: Collins.
Harrod, H., 1864, [Cromlechs and tumuli in north Wiltshire]. *Proceedings of the Society of Antiquaries of London* (Series 2), **2**, 308–12.
Hart, C., 1984, *The North Derbyshire archaeological survey*. Chesterfield: Derbyshire Archaeological Society.
Hart, C., 1986, Searches for the early Neolithic: a study of Peakland long cairns. In T.G. Manby & P. Turnbull (eds), *Archaeology in the Pennines*. Oxford: British Archaeological Reports British Series 158. 130–4.
Harvey, J.C., Morgan, R. & Webley, D.P., 1967, Tooth Cave, Ilston, Gower, an early Bronze Age occupation. *Bulletin of the Board of Celtic Studies*, **22** (1966–8), 277–90.
Heighway, C., 1987, *Anglo-Saxon Gloucestershire*. Gloucester: Alan Sutton and Gloucestershire County Library.
Hemp, W.J., 1929, Belas Knap long barrow, Gloucestershire. *Transactions of the Bristol and Gloucestershire Archaeological Society*, **51**, 261–72.
Hemp, W.J., 1935, Arthur's Stone, Dorstone, Herefordshire. *Archaeologia Cambrensis*, **90**, 288–92.
Henshall, A.S., 1972, *The chambered tombs of Scotland 2*. Edinburgh: Edinburgh University Press.
Henshall, A.S., 1974, Scottish chambered tombs and long mounds. In C. Renfrew (ed), *British prehistory: a new outline*. London: Duckworth. 137–64.
Hey, G., 2001, Yarnton. *Current Archaeology*, **15.5** (no. 173), 216–23.
Hill, H.C., 1930, Northfield Tumulus, Cheltenham. *Transactions of the Bristol and Gloucestershire Archaeological Society*, **52**, 305–8.
Hingley, R., 1990, Iron Age 'currency bars': the archaeological and social context. *Archaeological Journal*, **147**, 91–117.
Hingley, R., 1996, Ancestors and identity in the later prehistory of Atlantic Scotland: the reuse and reinvention of Neolithic monuments and material culture. *World Archaeology*, **28**, 231–43.
Hirst, S. & Rahtz, P., 1996, Liddington Castle and the Battle of Badon: excavations and research 1976. *Archaeological Journal*, **153**, 1–59.
Hodder, I., 1984, Burials, houses, women and men in the European Neolithic. In D. Miller & C. Tilley (eds), *Ideology, power and prehistory*. Cambridge: Cambridge University Press. 51–68.
Hodder, I., 1990, *The domestication of Europe*. Oxford: Blackwell.
Hodder, I. & Shand, P., 1988, The Haddenham long barrow: an interim statement. *Antiquity*, **62**, 349–53.
Holgate, R., 1987, Neolithic settlement patterns at Avebury, Wiltshire. *Antiquity*, **61**, 259–63.
Holgate, R., 1988, *Neolithic settlement of the Thames basin*. Oxford: British Archaeological Reports British Series 194.
Hooke, D., 1997, Lamberde leie, dillameres dic: A lost or a living landscape? In K. Barker & T. Darvill (eds), *Making English landscapes*. Oxford: Bournemouth University School of Conservation Sciences Occasional Paper 3 / Oxbow Books Monograph 93. 70–91.
Howells, W.W., 1973, *Cranial variation in man*. Cambridge, Massachusetts: Peabody Museum of Anthropology and Ethnology Papers 67.
Hugh-Jones, C., 1979, *From the Milk River: spatial and temporal processes in northwest Amazonia*. Cambridge: Cambridge University Press.
Hunter, M., 1975, *John Aubrey and the realm of learning*. London: Duckworth.

Hurst, H., 1972, Excavations at Gloucester, 1968–1971: first interim report. *Antiquaries Journal*, **52**, 24–69.

Jørgensen, E., 1977, Braendende langdysser. *Skalk*, **5**.

Jowell Burton, R., 1925, Avenis barrow. *Transactions of the Bristol and Gloucestershire Archaeological Society*, **47**, 348–50.

Keiller, A. & Piggott, S., 1938, Excavation of an untouched chamber in the Lanhill long barrow. *Proceedings of the Prehistoric Society*, **4**, 122–50.

Keiller, A. & Piggott, S., 1939, The chambered tomb in Beowulf. *Antiquity*, **13**, 360–1.

Kendall, H.G.O., 1916, Excavations on Hackpen Hill, Wiltshire. *Proceedings of the Society of Antiquaries of London* (Series 2), **28**, 26–48.

Kendall, H.G.O., 1922, Scraper core industries of north Wiltshire. *Proceedings of the Prehistoric Society of East Anglia*, **3**, 515–41.

Kenward, R., 1982, A Neolithic burial enclosure at New Wintles Farm, Eynsham. In H.J. Case & A.W.R. Whittle (eds), *Settlement patterns in the Oxford region: excavations at the Abingdon causewayed enclosure and other sites*. London: Council for British Archaeology Research Report 44. 51–4.

King, D. Grant, 1966, The Lanhill long barrow, Wiltshire, England: an essay in reconstruction. *Proceedings of the Prehistoric Society*, **32**, 73–85.

King, M., 2001, Life and death in the 'Neolithic': dwelling-scapes in southern Britain. *European Journal of Archaeology*, **4.3**, 323–45.

Kinnes, I., 1975, Monumental function in British Neolithic burial practices. *World Archaeology*, **7**, 16–29.

Kinnes, I., 1979, *Round barrows and ring-ditches in the British Neolithic*. London: British Museum Occasional Paper 7.

Kinnes, I., 1981, Dialogues with death. In R. Chapman, I. Kinnes & K. Randsborg (eds), *The archaeology of death*. Cambridge: Cambridge University Press. 83–92.

Kinnes, I., 1982, Les Foulaillages and megalithic origins. *Antiquity*, **56**, 24–30.

Kinnes, I., 1992a, *Non-megalithic long barrows and allied structures in the British Neolithic*. London: British Museum Occasional Paper 52.

Kinnes, I., 1992b, Balnagowan and after: the context of non-megalithic mortuary sites in Scotland. In N. Sharples & A. Sheridan (eds), *Vessels for the ancestors: essays on the Neolithic of Britain and Ireland in honour of Audrey Henshall*. Edinburgh: Edinburgh University Press. 83–103.

Kinnes, I., 1999, Longtemps ignorées: Passy-Rots, linear monuments in northern France. In A. Barclay & J. Harding (eds), *Pathways and ceremonies: the cursus monuments of Britain and Ireland*. Oxford: Oxbow Books / Neolithic Studies Group Seminar Papers 4. 148–54.

Kissock, J., 2001, Cefn Drum, Pontardulais. *Archaeology in Wales*, **41**, 155.

Kissock, J. & Phillips, N., 2000, A passage grave on Cefn Drum, Gower. *Archaeology in Wales*, **40**, 47–50.

Kjaerum, P., 1967, Mortuary houses and funeral rites in Denmark. *Antiquity*, **41**, 190–6.

Lambrick, G., 1988, *The Rollright Stones: megaliths, monuments and settlement in the prehistoric landscape*. London: English Heritage, HBMCE Archaeological Report 6.

Lawrence, W.L. 1866, Examination of a long barrow in Gloucestershire. *Proceedings of the Society of Antiquaries of London* (Series 2), **3**, 275–82.

Leech, R., 1977, *The upper Thames Valley in Gloucestershire and Wiltshire: an archaeological survey of the river gravels*. Bristol: Committee for Rescue Archaeology in Avon, Gloucestershire and Somerset Survey 4.

Leeds, E.T., 1927, Neolithic spoons from Nether Swell, Gloucestershire. *Antiquaries Journal*, **7**, 61–2.

Leeds, E.T., 1928, A Neolithic site at Abingdon, Berks. (Second report). *Antiquaries Journal*, **8**, 461–77.

Lewis, J., 2002, Reinterpreting the Priddy Long Barrow, Mendip Hills, Somerset. *Proceedings of the University of Bristol Spelaeological Society*, **22.3**, 269–88.

L'Helgouach, J., 1965, *Les sépultures mégalithiques en Armorique*. Rennes: L'Université de Rennes.

Liddell, D.M., 1935, Report on the excavations at Hembury Fort (1934 and 1935). *Proceedings of the Devon Archaeological Exploration Society*, **2**, 135–75.

Lock, G., Gosden, C., Miles, D., Palmer, S. & Cromerty, A., 2003, *Uffington White Horse and its landscape: investigations at White Horse Hill Uffington, 1989–95 and Tower Hill Ashbury, 1993–4.* Oxford: Oxford Archaeology Thames Valley Landscapes Monograph 18.

Loveday, R., 1989, The Barford ritual complex: further excavations (1972) and a regional perspective. In A. Gibson (ed), *Midlands prehistory*. Oxford: British Archaeological Reports British Series 204. 51–84.

Lubbock, J., 1865, *Prehistoric times*. London: Williams and Norgate.

Lubbock, J. & Douglas, D.M., 1871, Description of the Parc Cwm tumulus. *Archaeologia Cambrensis*, **26**, 168–70.

Lubbock, J., Douglas, D.M. & Vivian, H.H., 1887, Description of the Parc Cwm tumulus. *Archaeologia Cambrensis*, **42**, 192–6.

Lukis, J.W., 1875, On the St Lythan's and St Nicholas' cromlechs and other remains, near Cardiff. *Archaeologia Cambrensis*, **30**, 171–85.

Lukis, W.C., 1864, Danish cromlechs and burial customs compared with those of Brittany, the Channel Islands and Great Britain. *Wiltshire Archaeological and Natural History Magazine*, **7**, 145–69.

Lukis, W.C., 1867, [Tumuli in north Wiltshire]. *Proceedings of the Society of Antiquaries of London* (Series 2), **3**, 213–16.

Lukis, W.C., 1885, Prehistoric monuments of Wilts, Somerset and South Wales. *Proceedings of the Society of Antiquaries of London* (Series 2), **9**, 344–55.

Lynch, F.M., 1972, Portal dolmens of the Nevern Valley, Pembrokeshire. In F. Lynch & C. Burgess (eds), *Prehistoric man in Wales and the west: essays in honour of Lilly F. Chitty*. Bath: Adams & Dart. 67–84.

Lynch, F.M., 1973, The use of the passage in certain passage graves as a means of communication rather than access. In G. Daniel & P. Kjaerum (eds), *Megalithic graves and ritual. Papers presented at the III Atlantic Colloquium, Moesgård 1969*. Copenhagen: Jutland Archaeological Society Publications XI. 147–62.

Lynch, F.M., 1975, Carreg Samson megalithic tomb, Mathry, Pembrokeshire. *Archaeologia Cambrensis*, **124**, 15–35.

Lynch, F.M., 1976, Towards a chronology of megalithic tombs in Wales. In G. Boon & J.M. Lewis (eds), *Welsh antiquity: essays mainly on prehistoric topics presented to H.N. Savory upon his retirement as keeper of archaeology*. Cardiff: National Museum of Wales. 63–80.

Lynch, F., 1997, *Megalithic tombs and long barrows in Britain*. Princes Risborough: Shire.

Lynch, F., Aldhouse–Green, S. & Davies, J.L., 2000, *Prehistoric Wales*. Stroud: Sutton Publishing.

Lysons, S., 1863, [Account of the opening of a tumulus on his property at Rodmarton in Gloucestershire]. *Proceedings of the Society of Antiquaries of London* (Series 2), **2**, 275–9.

Lysons, S., 1865, *Our British ancestors*. Oxford: J. and H. Parker.

Maclean, Sir J., 1881, Description of the chambered tumuli of Uley and Nympsfield. *Transactions of the Bristol and Gloucestershire Archaeological Society*, **5** (1880–1), 86–118.

McWhirr, A., Viner, L. & Wells, C., 1982, *Romano-British cemeteries at Cirencester*. Cirencester: Cirencester Excavation Committee Cirencester Excavations II.

Madsen, T., 1979, Earthen long barrows and timber structures: aspects of the early Neolithic mortuary practice in Denmark. *Proceedings of the Prehistoric Society*, **45**, 301–20.

Malone, C., 2001, *Neolithic Britain and Ireland*. Stroud: Tempus.

Manby, T., 1958, The chambered tombs of Derbyshire. *Derbyshire Archaeological Journal*, **78**, 25–39.

Marshall, A., 1985, Neolithic and Bronze Age settlement in the northern Cotswolds. *Transactions of the Bristol and Gloucestershire Archaeological Society*, **103**, 23–54.

Marshall, A., 1998, Neolithic long barrows: use of integrated remote sensing at high resolution to establish general layout and detect foreground structure. *Archaeological Prospection*, **5**, 101–16.

Mercer, R.J., 1981, Excavations at Carn Brea, Illogan, Cornwall, 1970–73. *Cornish Archaeology*, **20**, 1–204.

Mercer, R.J., 1988, Hambledon Hill, Dorset, England. In C. Burgess, P. Topping, C. Mordant & M. Maddison (eds), *Enclosures and defences in the Neolithic of Western Europe*. Oxford: British Archaeological Reports International Series 403. 89–106.

Mercer, R.J. 1999, The origins of warfare in the British Isles. In J. Carman & A. Harding (eds), *Ancient warfare: archaeological perspectives*. Stroud: Sutton Publishing.143–56.

Merewether, J., 1851, Antiquities found near Avebury. *Proceedings of the Archaeological Institute* (Salisbury volume), 108–12.

Midgley, M., 1985, *The origin and function of the earthen long barrows of Northern Europe*. Oxford: British Archaeological Reports International Series 259.

Midgley, M., 1992, *TRB Culture: the first farmers of the north European Plain*. Edinburgh: Edinburgh University Press.

Midgley, M., 1997, The earthen long barrow phenomenon of northern Europe and its relation to the Passy-type monuments of France. In C. Constantin, D. Mordant & D. Simonin (eds), *La culture de Cerny: nouvelle économie, nouvelle société au Néolithique*. Nemours: Mémoires du Musée de Préhistorie de l'Ile de France 6. 679–85.

Miles, D. & Palmer, S., 1995, White Horse Hill. *Current Archaeology*, **12.10** (no. 142), 372–8.

Montelius, O., 1876, Sur les tombeaux et la topographie de la Suède pendant l'âge de la pierre. *Congrès international d'anthropologie et d'archéologie préhistoriques, 7th session – Stockholm 1874*. Stockholm: Norstedt and Söner. 152–76.

Montelius, O., 1905, Orienten och Europa. *Antiquarisk Tidskrift för Sverige*, **13**, 1–252.

Moore, D., 1976, Cambrian antiquity: precursors of the prehistorians. In G. Boon & J.M. Lewis (eds), *Welsh antiquity: essays mainly on prehistoric topics presented to H.N. Savory upon his retirement as keeper of archaeology*. Cardiff: National Museum of Wales. 193–221.

Morgan, W.E.T. & Marshall, G., 1921, Excavation of a long barrow at Llanigon, Co. Brecon. *Archaeologia Cambrensis*, **76**, 296–9.

Morgan, W.L., 1894, Discovery of a megalithic sepulchral chamber on the Penmaen Burrows, Gower, Glamorganshire. *Archaeologia Cambrensis*, **49**, 1–7.

Mudd, A., Williams, R.J. & Lupton, A., 1999, *Excavations alongside Roman Ermine Street, Gloucestershire and Wiltshire. The archaeology of the A419/A417 Swindon to Gloucester Road Scheme, Vol. 1. Prehistoric and Roman activity*. Oxford: Oxford Archaeological Unit.

Nash, G., 1997, Monumentality and the landscape: the possible symbolic and political distribution of long chambered tombs around the Black Mountains, central Wales. In G. Nash (ed), *Semiotics of landscape: archaeology of mind*. Oxford: British Archaeological Reports International Series 661. 17–30.

Nash, G., 2003, Re-evaluating monumentality. Arthur's Stone, Dorstone, Herefordshire. *3rd Stone*, **45**, 50–5.

Nashe, T., 1589, *Martins months mind*. London.

OAU [Oxford Archaeological Unit], 2000, White Horse Stone. A Neolithic longhouse. *Current Archaeology*, **14.12** (no. 168), 450–2.

O'Neil, B.H. St J., 1948, War and archaeology in Britain. *Antiquaries Journal*, **28**, 20–44.

O'Neil, H.E., 1966, Sale's Lot long barrow, Withington, Gloucestershire. *Transactions of the Bristol and Gloucestershire Archaeological Society*, **85**, 5–35.

O'Neil, H. & Grinsell, L.V., 1960, Gloucestershire barrows. *Transactions of the Bristol and Gloucestershire Archaeological Society*, **79.1**, 3–149.

Ó Nualláin, S., 1972, A Neolithic house at Ballyglass near Ballycastle, Co. Mayo. *Journal of the Royal Society of Antiquaries of Ireland*, **102**, 49–57.

Oswald, A., Dyer, C. & Barber, M., 2001, *The creation of monuments: Neolithic causewayed enclosures in the British Isles*. London: English Heritage.

Paine, A.E.W. & Witchell, E., 1865, [The Bown Hill Barrow]. *Proceedings of the Cotteswold Naturalists Field Club*, **3**, 199–200.

Palmer, R., 1976, Interrupted ditch enclosures in Britain: the use of aerial photography for comparative studies. *Proceedings of the Prehistoric Society*, **42**, 161–86.

Parker Pearson, M., 1999, *The archaeology of death and burial*. Stroud: Sutton Publishing.

Parry, C., 1998, Excavations near Birdlip, Cowley, Gloucestershire, 1987–8. *Transactions of the Bristol and Gloucestershire Archaeological Society*, **116**, 25–92.

Parry, T.W., 1921, The prehistoric trephined skulls of Great Britain. *Proceedings of the Royal Society of Medicine*, **14.10** (August 1921), 1–86.

Parsons, J. 2002, Great sites: Belas Knap. *British Archaeology*, **63**, 18–23.

Passmore, A.D., 1920, Wayland's Smithy Cave, sarsen stones at Ashdown Park, Berks and Avebury, Wilts. *Man*, **20**, 9–10 (article 4).
Passmore, A.D., 1922, The Devil's Den, dolmen, Clatford Bottom. *Wiltshire Archaeological and Natural History Magazine*, **41** (1920–2), 523–30.
Passmore, A.D., 1923, Chambered long barrow in West Woods. *Wiltshire Archaeological and Natural History Magazine*, **42** (1922–4), 366–7.
Passmore, A.D., 1934a, A bee-hive chamber at Ablington, Gloucestershire. *Transactions of the Bristol and Gloucestershire Archaeological Society*, **56**, 95–8.
Passmore, A.D., 1934b, The Giant's Caves long barrow, Luckington. *Wiltshire Archaeological and Natural History Magazine*, **46**, 380–6.
Passmore, A.D., 1940, Flint mines at Liddington Hill. *Wiltshire Archaeological and Natural History Magazine*, **49**, 118–19.
Passmore, A.D., 1943, A flint implement in a horned handle from near Liddington, Wiltshire. *Antiquaries Journal*, **23**, 52–3.
Patton, M., 1994, Neolithisation and megalithic origins in northwestern France: a regional interaction model. *Oxford Journal of Archaeology*, **13.3**, 279–94.
Peers, C.R. & Smith, R.A., 1921, Wayland's Smithy, Berkshire. *Antiquaries Journal*, **1**, 183–98.
Phillips, C.W., 1933, *Map of the Trent Basin showing the distribution of long barrows, megaliths and habitation sites.* Southampton: Ordnance Survey.
Phillips, C.W. & Taylor, H., 1972, The Priddy long barrow, Mendip Hills, Somerset. *Proceedings of the University of Bristol Spelaeological Society*, **13.1**, 31–6.
Piggott, S., 1931, The Neolithic pottery of the British Isles. *Archaeological Journal*, **88**, 67–158.
Piggott, S., 1934, The relative chronology of the British long barrows. *Proceedings of the First International Congress of Prehistoric and Protohistoric Sciences*. London: Oxford University Press. 143–4.
Piggott, S., 1935, A note on the relative chronology of the English long barrows. *Proceedings of the Prehistoric Society*, **1**, 115–26.
Piggott, S., 1937, Neolithic pottery from Hackpen, Avebury. *Wiltshire Archaeological and Natural History Magazine*, **48** (1937–8), 90–1.
Piggott, S., 1940, A trepanned skull of the Beaker period from Dorset and the practice of trepanning in prehistoric Europe. *Proceedings of the Prehistoric Society*, **6**, 112–32.
Piggott, S., 1947, Notes on some north Wiltshire chambered tombs. *Wiltshire Archaeological and Natural History Magazine*, **52**, 1–56.
Piggott, S., 1954, *Neolithic cultures of the British Isles*. Cambridge: Cambridge University Press.
Piggott, S., 1955, Windmill Hill – east or west? *Proceedings of the Prehistoric Society*, **21**, 96–101.
Piggott, S, 1958, The excavation of the West Kennet long barrow: 1955–6. *Antiquity*, **32**, 235–42.
Piggott, S., 1962, *The West Kennet long barrow: excavations 1955–56*. London: HMSO, Ministry of Works Archaeological Report 4.
Piggott, S., 1966, 'Unchambered' long barrows in Neolithic Britain. *Palaeohistoria*, **11**, 381–93.
Piggott, S., 1972, The beginning of the Neolithic in the British Isles. In J. Lüning (ed), *Die Anfänge des Neolithikums vom Orient bis Nordeuropa*. Cologne and Vienna: Böhlau Verlag. 217–32.
Piggott, S., 1973, Problems in the interpretation of chambered tombs. In G. Daniel & P. Kjaerum (eds), *Megalithic graves and ritual. Papers presented at the III Atlantic Colloquium, Moesgård 1969*. Copenhagen: Jutland Archaeological Society Publications XI. 9–16.
Piggott, S., 1985, *William Stukeley: an eighteenth century antiquary*. London: Thames and Hudson.
Piggott, S., 1993, John Thurnam (1818–1873) and British prehistory. *Wiltshire Archaeological and Natural History Magazine*, **86**, 1–7.
Playne, A.T., 1915, *Minchinhampton and Avening*. Gloucester: John Bellows.
Pollard, J., 1997, *Neolithic Britain*. Princes Risborough: Shire.
Pollard, J. & Reynolds, A., 2002, *Avebury: the biography of a landscape*. Stroud: Tempus.
Powell, T.G.E., 1969, The Neolithic in the west of Europe and megalithic structure: some points and problems. In T.G.E. Powell, J.X.W.P. Corcoran, F. Lynch & J.G. Scott, *Megalithic enquiries in the west of Britain*. Liverpool: Liverpool University Press. 247–72.
Powell, T.G.E., 1973, Excavation of the chambered cairn at Dyffryn Ardudwy, Merioneth, Wales. *Archaeologia*, **104**, 1–49.

Powell, T.G.E., Corcoran, J.X.W.P., Lynch, F. & Scott, J.G., 1969, *Megalithic enquiries in the west of Britain.* Liverpool: Liverpool University Press.

Pragg, J. & Neave, R., 1997, *Making faces.* London: British Museum Press.

Price, N., 2001, An archaeology of altered states: shamanism and material culture studies. In N. Price (ed), *The archaeology of shamanism.* London: Routledge. 3–16.

Proudfoot, E., 1965, Bishops Cannings: Roughridge Hill. *Wiltshire Archaeological and Natural History Magazine,* **65**, 132–3.

Pryor, F., 1988, Earlier Neolithic organized landscape and ceremonial in lowland Britain. In J.C. Barrett & I.A. Kinnes (eds), *The archaeology of context in the Neolithic and Bronze Age: recent trends.* Sheffield: University of Sheffield Department of Archaeology and Prehistory. 63–72.

Pye, W.R., 1969, Dorstone Hill. *Transactions of the Woolhope Naturalists Field Club,* **39.3**, 475.

Radford, C.A.R., 1930, Belas Knap long barrow. *Transactions of the Bristol and Gloucestershire Archaeological Society,* **52**, 295–9.

Rahtz, P. & Greenfield, E., 1977, *Excavations at Chew Valley Lake, Somerset.* London: HMSO, Department of the Environment Archaeological Reports 8.

RCAHMW [Royal Commission on Ancient and Historical Monuments of Wales], 1976, *An inventory of the ancient monuments in Glamorgan. Vol. I. Pre-Norman. Part I: The Stone and Bronze Ages.* Cardiff: HMSO.

RCAHMW [Royal Commission on Ancient and Historical Monuments of Wales], 1997, *An inventory of the ancient monuments in Brecknock (Brycheiniog). The prehistoric and Roman monuments. Part I. Later prehistoric monuments and unenclosed settlements to 1000 AD.* Cardiff: HMSO.

RCHME [Royal Commission on the Historical Monuments of England], 1976, *Ancient and historical monuments in the county of Gloucester. Vol. I. Iron Age and Romano-British monuments in the Gloucestershire Cotswolds.* London: HMSO.

Renfrew, C. 1967, Colonialism and megalithismus. *Antiquity,* **41**, 276–88.

Renfrew, C., 1973a, *Before civilization: the radiocarbon revolution and prehistoric Europe.* London: Jonathan Cape.

Renfrew, C., 1973b, Monuments, mobilization and social organization in Neolithic Wessex. In C. Renfrew (ed), *The explanation of culture change.* London: Duckworth. 539–58.

Renfrew, C., 1976, Megaliths, territories and populations. In S.J. DeLaet (ed), *Acculturation and continuity in Atlantic Europe.* Bruges: DeTempel. 198–220.

Renfrew, C., 1987, *Archaeology and language.* London: Jonathan Cape.

Richards, J.C., 1978, *The archaeology of the Berkshire Downs: an introductory survey.* Reading: Berkshire Archaeological Committee Publication 3.

Richards, J. & Whitby, M., 1997, The engineering of Stonehenge. *Proceedings of the British Academy,* **92**, 231–56.

Richards, M.P. & Hedges, R.E.M., 1999, A Neolithic revolution? New evidence of diet in the British Neolithic. *Antiquity,* **73**, 891–7.

Robinson, R.S.G., 1934, Flint workers and flint users in the Golden Valley. *Transactions of the Woolhope Naturalists Field Club,* **28**, 54–63.

Robertson-Mackay, M.E., 1980, A 'head and hoofs' burial beneath a round barrow, with other Neolithic and Bronze Age sites, on Hemp Knoll, near Avebury, Wiltshire. *Proceedings of the Prehistoric Society,* **46**, 123–76.

Rolleston, G., 1876, On the people of the long barrow period. *Journal of the Anthropological Institute,* **5**, 120–75.

Royce, D., 1883, Finds on or near to the excursion of the Society at Stow-on-the-Wold. *Transactions of the Bristol and Gloucestershire Archaeological Society,* **7** (1882–3), 69–80.

Russell, M., 2002, *Monuments of the British Neolithic.* Stroud: Tempus.

Sahlins, M.D., 1968, *Tribesmen.* Englewood Cliffs: Pentice-Hall.

Savage, R., 1988, *Village. Fortress. Shrine. Crickley Hill, Gloucestershire, 3500 BC – AD 500.* Cheltenham: Crickley Hill Archaeological Trust.

Saville, A., 1979a, Further excavations at Nympsfield chambered tomb, Gloucestershire, 1974. *Proceedings of the Prehistoric Society,* **45**, 53–91.

Saville, A.,1979b, *Recent work at Cow Common Bronze Age cemetery, Gloucestershire.* Bristol: CRAAGS Occasional Paper 6.

Saville, A., 1980, *Archaeological sites in the Avon and Gloucestershire Cotswolds*. Bristol: CRAAGS Survey 5.

Saville, A., 1984, Preliminary report on the excavation of a Cotswold-Severn tomb at Hazleton, Gloucestershire. *Antiquaries Journal*, **64**, 10–24.

Saville, A., 1989, Rodmarton long barrow, Gloucestershire, 1988. *Transactions of the Bristol and Gloucestershire Archaeological Society*, **107**, 189–93.

Saville, A., 1990, *Hazleton North: the excavation of a Neolithic long cairn of the Cotswold-Severn group*. London: English Heritage, HBMCE Archaeological Report 13.

Saville, A. & Drinkwater, J., 1976, *Gloucestershire long barrows, their condition and future preservation with special reference to plough damage*. Bristol: CRAAGS. [Limited circulation typescript report.]

Saville, A. & Ellison, A., 1983, Excavations at Uley Bury hillfort, Gloucestershire, 1976. In A. Saville, *Uley Bury and Norbury hillforts: rescue excavations at two Gloucestershire Iron Age sites*. Bristol: Western Archaeological Trust Excavation Monograph 5. 1–24.

Saville, A., Gowlett, J.A.J. & Hedges, R.E.M., 1987, Radiocarbon dates from the chambered tomb of Hazleton (Glos.): a chronology for Neolithic collective burial. *Antiquity*, **61**, 108–19.

Savory, H.N., 1940, A middle Bronze Age barrow at Crick, Monmouthshire. *Archaeologia Cambrensis*, **95**, 169–91.

Savory, H.N., 1956, The excavation of the Pipton long cairn, Brecknockshire. *Archaeologia Cambrensis*, **105**, 7–48.

Savory, H.N., 1971, *Tinkinswood and St Lythans long cairns*. London and Cardiff: Department of the Environment [site guide leaflet].

Savory, H.N., 1973, Pen-y-Wyrlod: a new Welsh long cairn. *Antiquity*, **47**, 187–92.

Savory, H.N., 1980, *Guide catalogue of the Bronze Age collections*. Cardiff: National Museum of Wales.

Savory, H.N., 1984, The Penywyrlod long cairn, Talgarth, Brecknock. In W.J. Britnell & H.N. Savory, *Gwernvale and Penywyrlod: two Neolithic long cairns in the Black Mountains of Brecknock*. Cardiff: Cambrian Archaeological Association Monograph 2. 13–39.

Scarre, C., 1992, The early Neolithic of western France and megalithic origins in Atlantic Europe. *Oxford Journal of Archaeology*, **11.2**, 121–54.

Scarre, C., 2002a, Contexts of monumentalism: regional diversity at the Neolithic transition in northwest France. *Oxford Journal of Archaeology*, **21.1**, 23–62.

Scarre, C. (ed), 2002b, *Monuments and landscape in Atlantic Europe*. London: Routledge.

Schulting, R.J., 2000, New AMS dates from the Lambourn long barrow and the question of the earliest Neolithic in southern England: repacking the Neolithic package? *Oxford Journal of Archaeology*, **19.1**, 25–36.

Schulting, R.J., Parsons, J., Richards, M.P., Pettitt, P.B., Higham, T.F.G. & Hedges, J.D. In preparation. Belas Knap revisited.

Schulting, R.J. & Richards, M.P., 2002, Finding the coastal Mesolithic in southwest Britain: AMS dates and stable isotope results on human remains from Caldey Island, south Wales. *Antiquity*, **76**, 1011–25.

Schulting, R.J. & Wysocki, M. 2002, Cranial trauma in the British earlier Neolithic. *Past*, **41**, 4–6.

Scott, J.G., 1969, The Clyde cairns of Scotland. In T.G.E. Powell, J.X.W.P. Corcoran, F. Lynch & J.G. Scott, *Megalithic enquiries in the west of Britain*. Liverpool: Liverpool University Press. 172–222.

Selkirk, A., 1971, Ascott-under-Wychwood. *Current Archaeology*, **3.1** (no. 24), 7–10.

Semple, S., 1998, A fear of the past: the place of the prehistoric burial mound in the ideology of middle and later Anglo-Saxon England. *World Archaeology*, **30.1**, 109–26.

Service, E.R., 1971, *Primitive social organization: an evolutionary perspective* (Second edition). New York: Random House.

Sheridan, A., 1986, Megaliths and megalomania: an account and interpretation, of the development of passage tombs in Ireland. *Journal of Irish Archaeology*, **3**, 17–30.

Sheridan, A., 1995, Irish Neolithic pottery: the story in 1995. In I. Kinnes & G. Varndell (eds), *'Unbaked urns of rudely shape': essays on British and Irish pottery*. Oxford: Oxbow Monographs 55. 3–22.

Sherratt, A., 1990, The genesis of megaliths: monumentality, ethnicity and social complexity in Neolithic northwest Europe. *World Archaeology*, **22.2**, 145–67.

Sherratt, A., 1993, Ancestors for the tombs? *Oxford Journal of Archaeology*, **12.1**, 127–8.
Sherratt, A., 1994, The transformation of early agrarian Europe: the later Neolithic and Copper Ages 4500–2500 BC. In B. Cunliffe (ed), *The Oxford illustrated prehistory of Europe*. Oxford: Oxford University Press. 167–201.
Sherratt, A., 1995, Instruments of conversion? The role of megaliths in the Mesolithic/Neolithic transition in north-west Europe. *Oxford Journal of Archaeology*, **14.3**, 245–60.
Sherratt, A., 1996a, Settlement patterns or landscape studies? Reconciling reason and romance. *Archaeological Dialogues*, **3.2**, 140–59.
Sherratt, A., 1996b, Why Wessex? The Avon route and river transport in later British prehistory. *Oxford Journal of Archaeology*, **15.2**, 211–34.
Simpson, D.D.A., 1968, Timber mortuary houses and earthen long barrows. *Antiquity*, **42**, 142–4.
Skaarup, J., 1993, Megalithic graves. In S. Hvaas & B. Storgaard (eds), *Digging into the past: 25 years of archaeology in Denmark*. Aarhus: Royal Society of Northern Antiquities and Jutland Archaeological Society. 104–9.
Smith, A.H., 1964, *Place-names of Gloucestershire. Part II*. Cambridge: Cambridge University Press – English Place-Name Society 39.
Smith, G.H., 1989, Evaluation work at the Druid Stoke megalithic monument, Stoke Bishop, Bristol, 1983. *Transactions of the Bristol and Gloucestershire Archaeological Society*, **107**, 27–37.
Smith, I.F., 1965a, *Windmill Hill and Avebury*. Oxford: Clarendon Press.
Smith, I.F., 1965b, Excavation of a bell barrow, Avebury G55. *Wiltshire Archaeological and Natural History Magazine*, **60**, 24–46.
Smith, I.F., 1972, Ring-ditches in eastern and central Gloucestershire. In P.J. Fowler (ed), *Archaeology and the landscape*. London: John Baker. 157–67.
Smith, I.F. & Evans, J.G., 1968, Excavation of two long barrows in North Wiltshire. *Antiquity*, **42**, 138–42.
Smith, I.F. & Simpson, D.D.A., 1964, Excavation of three Roman tombs and a prehistoric pit on Overton Down. *Wiltshire Archaeological and Natural History Magazine*, **59**, 68–85.
Smith, I.F. & Simpson, D.D.A., 1966, Excavations of a round barrow on Overton Hill, north Wiltshire, England. *Proceedings of the Prehistoric Society*, **32**, 122–55.
Smith, R.W., 1984, The ecology of Neolithic faming systems as exemplified by the Avebury region of Wiltshire. *Proceedings of the Prehistoric Society*, **50**, 99–120.
Soffe, G., 1993, A barrow cemetery and other features recorded by air photography at Beckhampton, Avebury. *Wiltshire Archaeological and Natural History Magazine*, **86**, 142–6.
Spinage, C., 2003, *Myths and mysteries of Wayland Smith*. Oxford: Wychwood Press.
Startin, B., 1982, The labour force involved in constructing the causewayed enclosure. In H.J. Case & A.W.R. Whittle (eds), *Settlement patterns in the Oxford region: excavations at the Abingdon causewayed enclosure and other sites*. London: Council for British Archaeology Research Report 44. 49–50.
Startin, B. & Bradley, R., 1981, Some notes on work organization and society in prehistoric Wessex. In C.L.N. Ruggles & A.W.R. Whittle (eds), *Astronomy and society in Britain during the period 4000–1500 BC*. Oxford: British Archaeological Reports British Series 88. 289–96.
Stuiver, M., Reimer, P.J., Bard, E., Becks, J.W., Burr, G.S., Hughen, K.A., Kromer, B., McCormac, G., van der Plight, J. & Spurk, M., 1998, INTCAL98 radiocarbon age calibration, 24000–0 BP. *Radiocarbon*, **40.3**, 1041–83.
Taylor, T., 1996, *The prehistory of sex*. London: Fourth Estate.
Thomas, A., 2003, Stoney Littleton long barrow: archaeological investigations and observations 1999/2000. *Proceedings of the Somerset Archaeological and Natural History Society*, **146**, 11–16.
Thomas, A. & Holbrook, N., 1998, Excavations at the Memorial Hall, Lechlade, 1995. In A. Boyle, D. Jennings, D. Miles & S. Palmer, *The Anglo-Saxon cemetery at Butler's Field, Lechlade, Gloucestershire. Vol. I. Prehistoric and Roman activity and Anglo-Saxon grave catalogue*. Oxford: Oxford Archaeological Unit, Thames Valley Landscapes Monograph 10. 282–8.
Thomas, C., 1985, *Exploration of a drowned landscape: archaeology and history of the Isles of Scilly*. London: Batsford.
Thomas, J., 1988, The social significance of Cotswold-Severn burial rites. *Man (NS)*, **23**, 540–59.

Thomas, J., 1991, *Rethinking the Neolithic*. Cambridge: Cambridge University Press.

Thomas, J., 1996, Neolithic houses in mainland Britain and Ireland – a skeptical view. In T. Darvill & J. Thomas (eds), *Neolithic houses in northwest Europe and beyond*. Oxford: Oxbow Books / Neolithic Studies Group Seminar Papers 1. 1–12.

Thomas, J., 1999, *Understanding the Neolithic*. London: Routledge.

Thomas, J. & Tilley, C., 1993, The axe and the torso: symbolic structures in the Neolithic of Brittany. In C. Tilley (ed), *Interpretative archaeology*. Oxford: Berg. 225–324.

Thomas, J., and Whittle, A., 1986, Anatomy of a tomb – West Kennet revisited. *Oxford Journal of Archaeology*, **5.2**, 129–56.

Thomas, N., 1956, A Neolithic pit on Waden Hill, Avebury. *Wiltshire Archaeological and Natural History Magazine*, **56** (1955–6), 167–71.

Thompson, M.W., 1977, *General Pitt-Rivers: evolution and archaeology in the nineteenth century*. Bradford-on-Avon: Moonraker Press.

Thompson, M.W., 1983, *The journeys of Sir Richard Colt Hoare through Wales and England 1793–1810*. Gloucester: Alan Sutton Publications.

Thorpe, I.J., 1984, Ritual, power and ideology: a reconsideration of earlier Neolithic rituals in Wessex. In R. Bradley & J. Gardiner (eds), *Neolithic studies*. Oxford: British Archaeological Reports British Series 133. 41–60.

Thorpe, I.J. & Richards, C.C., 1984, The decline of ritual authority and the introduction of Beakers into Britain. In R. Bradley & J. Gardiner (eds), *Neolithic studies*. Oxford: British Archaeological Reports British Series 133. 67–84.

Thurnam, J., 1854, Description of a chambered tumulus, near Uley, Gloucestershire. *Archaeological Journal*, **11**, 315–27.

Thurnam, J., 1857, On a cromlech-tumulus called Lugbury, near Littleton Drew. *Wiltshire Archaeological and Natural History Magazine*, **3**, 164–73.

Thurnam, J., 1860a, Examination of barrows on the downs of north Wiltshire, in 1853–57. *Wiltshire Archaeological and Natural History Magazine*, **6**, 317–36.

Thurnam, J., 1860b, On the excavation of a chambered long barrow at West Kennet, Wiltshire. *Archaeologia*, **38**, 405–21.

Thurnam, J., 1862, On Wayland's Smithy and the traditions connected with it. *Wiltshire Archaeological and Natural History Magazine*, **7**, 321–33.

Thurnam, J., 1863, Skulls from chambered barrow, Charlton Abbots, Gloucestershire. *Memoirs of the Anthropological Society*, **1**, 471–7.

Thurnam, J., 1868, On ancient British barrows, especially those of the Wiltshire and adjoining counties. Part I – long barrows. *Archaeologia*, **42**, 161–244.

Thurnam, J., 1869, On leaf and lozenge-shaped javelin heads from an oval barrow near Stonehenge. *Wiltshire Archaeological and Natural History Magazine*, **11**, 40–9.

Thurnam, J., 1870, Further researches and observations on the two principal forms of ancient British skulls. *Memoirs of the Anthropological Society*, **3**, 41–80.

Tilley, C., 1994, *A phenomenology of landscape*. Oxford: Berg.

Tilley, C., 1996, The power of the rocks: topography and monument construction on Bodmin Moor. *World Archaeology*, **28**, 161–76.

Tite, M.S., Bowman, S.G.E., Ambers, J.C. & Matthews, K.J., 1987, Preliminary statement on an error in British Museum radiocarbon dates. *Antiquity*, **61**, 168.

Tratman, E.K. & Henderson, G.T.D., 1927, First report on the excavations at Sun Hole, Cheddar. *Proceedings of the University of Bristol Spelaeological Society*, **3.2**, 84–97.

Trow, S., 1985, An interrupted-ditch enclosure at Southmore Grove, Rendcomb, Gloucestershire. *Transactions of the Bristol and Gloucestershire Archaeological Society*, **103**, 17–22.

Vatcher, F. de M. & Vatcher, H.L., 1973, Trial excavation on the site of megalithic tomb at Frome-field, Somerset. *Proceedings of the Somerset Archaeological and Natural History Society*, **117**, 19–32.

Voss, K.L., 1965, Stratigrafische Notizen zu einen Langhaus der Trichterbecherkultur bei Wittenwater, Kr. Uelzen. *Germania*, **43**, 343–51.

Vulliamy, C.E., 1921, The excavation of a megalithic tomb in Breconshire. *Archaeologia Cambrensis*, **76**, 300–5.

Vulliamy, C.E., 1922a, Note on a long barrow in Wales. *Man*, **22.1**, 11–13.
Vulliamy, C.E., 1922b, Excavation of a long barrow in Breconshire. *Man*, **22.10**, 150–2.
Vulliamy, C.E., 1929, Excavation of an unrecorded long barrow in Wales. *Man*, **29.2**, 34–6.
Waddell, J., 1998, *The prehistoric archaeology of Ireland*. Galway: Galway University Press.
Ward, J., 1915, The St Nicholas chambered tumulus, Glamorgan. *Archaeologia Cambrensis*, **70**, 253–320.
Ward, J., 1916, The St Nicholas chambered tumulus, Glamorgan. II. *Archaeologia Cambrensis*, **71**, 239–94.
Warmington, A., 1984, The Domesday manor of Langeberge cum Mene. *Journal of the English Placename Society*, **16**, 38–49.
Watkins, A, 1928, Arthur's Stone. *Transactions of the Woolhope Naturalists Field Club*, **14**, 149–51.
Watson, A., 2001, The sounds of transformation: acoustics, monuments and ritual in the British Neolithic. In N. Price (ed), *The archaeology of shamanism*. London: Routledge. 178–92.
Webley, D., 1962, Y Garn Llwyd, Newchurch West, Monmouthshire: a reassessment. *Bulletin of the Board of Celtic Studies*, **19** (1960–2), 255–8.
Webley, D., 1976, How the west was won: prehistoric land-use in the Southern Marches. In G. Boon & J.M. Lewis (eds), *Welsh antiquity: essays mainly on prehistoric topics presented to H.N. Savory upon his retirement as keeper of archaeology*. Cardiff: National Museum of Wales. 19–36.
Wedlake, W.J., 1958, *Excavations at Camerton, Somerset*. Camerton: Camerton Archaeological Society.
Wheeler, Sir M., 1958, Crawford and Antiquity. *Antiquity*, **32**, 3–4.
Whittle, A., 1977a, *The earlier Neolithic of southern England and its continental background*. Oxford: British Archaeological Reports Supplemental Series 35.
Whittle, A., 1977b, Earlier Neolithic enclosures in north-west Europe. *Proceedings of the Prehistoric Society*, **43**, 329–48.
Whittle, A., 1990a, A pre-enclosure burial at Windmill Hill, Wiltshire. *Oxford Journal of Archaeology*, **9**, 25–8.
Whittle, A., 1990b, The Mesolithic–Neolithic transition in the upper Kennet Valley, North Wiltshire. *Proceedings of the Prehistoric Society*, **56**, 101–10.
Whittle, A., 1991, Wayland's Smithy, Oxfordshire: excavations at the Neolithic tomb in 1962–63 by R.J.C. Atkinson and S. Piggott. *Proceedings of the Prehistoric Society*, **57.2**, 61–101.
Whittle, A., 1993, The Neolithic of the Avebury area: sequence, environment, settlement and monuments. *Oxford Journal of Archaeology*, **12.1**, 29–54.
Whittle, A., 1994, Excavations at Millbarrow Neolithic chambered tomb, Winterbourne Monkton, North Wiltshire. *Wiltshire Archaeological and Natural History Magazine*, **87**, 1–53.
Whittle, A., 1996, *Europe in the Neolithic: the creation of new worlds*. Cambridge: Cambridge University Press.
Whittle, A., 1997a, *Sacred mound. Holy rings. Silbury Hill and the West Kennet palisade enclosure: a later Neolithic complex in north Wiltshire*. Oxford: Oxbow Books Monograph 74.
Whittle, A., 1997b, Moving on and moving around: Neolithic settlement mobility. In P. Topping (ed), *Neolithic landscapes*. Oxford: Oxbow Books Monograph 86 / Neolithic Studies Group Seminar Papers 2. 15–22.
Whittle, A., Atkinson, R.J.C., Chambers, R. & Thomas, N., 1992, Excavations in the Neolithic and Bronze Age complex at Dorchester-on-Thames, Oxfordshire, 1947–1952 and 1981. *Proceedings of the Prehistoric Society*, **58**, 143–201.
Whittle, A., Davies, J.J., Dennis, I., Fairbairn, A.S., Hamilton, M.A. & Pollard, J., 2000, Neolithic activity and occupation outside Windmill Hill causewayed enclosure, Wiltshire: survey and excavation 1992–93. *Wiltshire Archaeological and Natural History Magazine*, **93**, 131–80.
Whittle, A., Pollard, J. & Grigson, C., 1999, *The harmony of symbols: the Windmill Hill causewayed enclosure*. Oxford: Oxbow Books.
Whittle, A., Rouse, A.J. & Evans, J.G., 1993, A Neolithic downland monument in its environment: excavations at the Easton Down long barrow, Bishops Cannings, north Wiltshire. *Proceedings of the Prehistoric Society*, **59**, 197–239.
Whittle, A. & Wysocki, M., 1998, Parc le Breos Cwm transepted long cairn, Gower, West Glamorgan: date, contents and context. *Proceedings of the Prehistoric Society*, **64**, 139–82.
Wickham, J.D.C., 1912, *Records by spade and terrier*. Bath: George Gregory.

Williams, A., 1940, A megalithic tomb at Nicholaston, Gower, Glamorgan. *Proceedings of the Prehistoric Society*, **6**, 178–81.
Williams, H., 1998, Monuments and the past in Anglo-Saxon England. *World Archaeology*, **30.1**, 90–108.
Willis, R., 1787, An essay towards a discovery of the great Iknield-Streets of the Romans. *Archaeologia*, **7**, 88–99.
Winterbotham, L., 1866, Belas Knap. *Proceedings of the Society of Antiquaries of London* (Series 2), **3**, 276–80.
Witts, G.B., 1881, Description of the long barrow called West Tump in the parish of Brimpsfield, Gloucestershire. *Transactions of the Bristol and Gloucestershire Archaeological Society*, **5**, 201–11.
Witts, G.B., 1883, *Archaeological handbook of the County of Gloucester*. Cheltenham: G. Norman. (2 parts.)
Witts, G.B., 1884a, Randwick long barrow. *Proceedings of the Cotteswold Naturalists Field Club*, **8**, 156–60.
Witts, G.B., 1884b, [College Plantation]. *Gloucestershire Notes and Queries*, **2**, 169.
Woodward, A. & Leach, P., 1993, *The Uley shrines: excavation of a ritual complex on West Hill, Uley, Gloucestershire: 1977–9*. London: English Heritage, HBMCE Archaeological Report 17.
Wrong, D.H., 1961, *Population and society* (Second edition). New York: Random House.
Wymer, J., 1966, Excavations of the Lambourn long barrow. *Berkshire Archaeological Journal*, **62**, 1–16.
Zvelebil, M. & Zvelebil, K.V., 1988, Agricultural transitions and Indo-European dispersals. *Antiquity*, **62**, 574–83.

INDEX

Illustration numbers are shown in *italic*

Abingdon causewayed enclosure, Oxfordshire, 192–3. *See also* Barrow Hills
Ablington (GLO 26), 58, 59, 246, *22D*
Adam's Grave (WIL 6), 26, 85, 114, 121, 144, 168, 191, 233, 252, *79*
Adlestrop Hill (GLO 44), 31, 50, 51, 228, 247, *19B*
Aillemore, Co Mayo, Ireland, 73
Akerman, John Yonge, 26, 229, 232, 248, 250
Alexander Keiller Museum, Avebury, Wiltshire, 279
animal remains, 61, 62, 81, 95, 119, 132, 134, 135–6, 138, 142, 171–2, 182–3, 185, 190–1, 192, 205, 208, 211, 220, 272
Annable, Ken, 228
Arn Hill (WIL 24), 253
Arthur's Stone, Dorstone (HRF 1), 86, 113, 115, 196, 235, 251, 273–4, *111*
Arthur's Stone, Llanrhidian Lower (GLA 3), 20, 40, 48–9, 233, 238, 243, *16*, *17*
arrowheads (leaf-shaped), 54, 61, 135, 168–9, 197–8, 208, *68*, *69*, *70*
arrowheads (barbed and tanged), 220–1
Ascott-under-Wychwood I (OXF 6), 41, 84, 94, 102, 117, 119, 121, 126, 129, 141–2, 144–7, 151, 153, 165, 169–70, 178, 208, 216, 250, 257, 280, 288, *39D*, *41*, *57A*, *70*
Ascott-under-Wychwood II (OXF 16), 84, 250
Ashbee, Paul, 14, 33, 39–40, 63, 70, 75, 98, 114, 253, 254
Ashmolean Museum, Oxford, 279
Atkins, E. Martin, 26, 42, 227, 242
Atkinson, Richard, 33, 38, 40, 53, 147, 163, 207, 228, 242, 244, 252, 272, 273

Atkyns, Sir Thomas, 20
Atlantic Hypothesis, 43
Aubrey, John, 18–21, 33, 163
Auchenlaich, Stirling, 74
Avebury Down (WIL 16), 203, 253
Avebury, G21 (WIL 26), 253
Avebury, Wiltshire, 20, 216, 218, 273, *85B*
Avening (GLO 18), 249
Avening Barrow. *See* Avening Court
Avening Court (GLO 17), 112, 237, 246, *46*
Avenis Barrow (GLO 75), 26, 248
axes (flint and stone), 56, 95, 127–8, 135, 168, 192, 194, 197, 203–4, 213, 273, *68*. *See also* flint mining and axe making

Bagnall-Oakeley, M.E., 27
Baillie, Mike, 215
Balloy, Burgundy, France, 76
Ballyglass, Co Mayo, Ireland, 76
Bandkeramik Hypothesis, 43
bank barrows, 99
Barford, Warwickshire, 206–7, *84C*
Barker, Chris, 14
Barker, Graeme, 200
Barnenez, Brittany, France, 57, 123
Barrow Hills, Abingdon, Oxfordshire, 52, 205–6, 217–19, 220, 258, *84A*, *85A*
Barrow House Farm North (SOM 12), 251
Barrow House Farm South (SOM 14), 251
Battlegore (SOM 11), 85, 251
Baxter, Mary, 147, 212
Beaker Ware, 183–5, 195, 214–16, 220–1, 222, 279, *76*

313

Beckhampton Plantation long barrow (WIL 37), 254
Beckhampton Road long barrow (WIL 27), 26, 40, 95, 97, 113, 117, 120, 122, 128, 133, 136, 207, 221, 222, 253–4, 259, *48C*, *79*, *87*
Belas Knap (GLO 1), 12, 26, 30, 50, 52, 59, 61, 64, 70, 89, 102, 106, 108, 111, 115, 116, 121–2, 124, 126, 128, 144, 150, 162, 166, 168, 170–1, 177, 197, 228, 233, 238–40, 244, 256, 262–3, 279, *3*, *11*, *39I*, *49A*, *98*, *101*
Bell, Captain Henry, 220
Bellows, Max, 29
Bellows, William, 29
Benson, Don, 41, 51, 106, 141, 250, *18*
Bere, Revd Thomas, 21, 251
Berry-au-Bac, Aisne, France, 76
Berry, Sir James, 30, 59, 106, 244, 263
Big Tree (SOM 7), 251
Bird, Dr Henry, 220
Bisley Barrow (GLO 74), 26, 162, 248, *66*
Blackquarries Hill (GLO 86), 233, 249
bone scoops and chisels, 171, *68*, *69*
Bostock, Miss, 27
Boujot, Christine, 43, 44
Bourton Downs (GLO 95), 249
Bourton on the Hill (GLO 41), 247
Bown Hill (GLO 20), 26, 144, 166–8, 171, 227, 233, 246, *69*
Boxwell Lodge (GLO 37), 247
Bradley, Richard, 43, 52, 77, 90, 92, 204, 215
Bristol City Museum, Bristol, 279
Britnell, Bill, 42, 95, 116, 119, 125, 186, 234, 275
Broadwell (GLO 45), 247
Brock Hill (GLO 38), 247
Brøndum, Jutland, Denmark, 55
Bromham G3 (WIL 28), 253
Brothwell, Don, 141
Brown, Lisa, 14
Buckholt Wood (GLO 78), 248
Buckman, Professor James, 26, 140, 227, 245, 247
Bulleid, Arthur, 32
Burenhult, Göran, 48
Burl, Aubrey, 98
Burn Ground (GLO 60), 21, 28, 31–32, 37, 100, 102, 117, 119, 129, 136–8, 144, 157, 168, 179–81, 182–3, 185, 223, 224, 229–30, 248, *8C*, *40D*, *55*, *62A*, *75*, *88*, *92*

Cae'rarfau (GLA 8), 51–2, 244, *19E*
Cae'reglwys (GLA 13), 244
Calne (WIL 29), 253
Camp Barrow North (GLO 11), 26, 245
Camp Barrow South (GLO 67), 248
Camp Farm (GLO 53), 199, 227, 247

Camster Long, Caithness, 74, *28B*
Capel Garmon, Denbighshire, *11*
Carn Ban, Arran 74, *28A*
Carn Goch (BRE 12), 235, 243
Carn Llechart (GLA 12), 244
Carn, Co Monaghan, Ireland, 74, *28C*
Carrowmore, Sligo, Ireland, 48
Case, Humphrey, 70, 80, 176, 182, 185, 192
Cashtal yn Ard, Isle of Man, 74, *28D*
Cassen, Serge, 43, 44
Catshole, Cornwall, 74, *28M*
causewayed enclosures, 56, 61, 189–90, 193–5, 200, 203, 205–6, 214, 217, 77, *78*, *79*, *80*, *81*
Cave Dr A.J.E., 141, 158
Cefn Drum, Glamorgan, 58, 60, *22F*
chamberless long barrows, 115, 125
Chase (WIL 23), 236, 253
Cheltenham Art Gallery and Museum, Cheltenham, 279
Cheltenham Road Plantation (GLO 59), 248
Cherhill, Wiltshire. *See* Oldbury Hill
Chesterman, J.T., 141
Chew Valley Lake, Somerset, 198
Childe, Gordon, 35, 36–7, 71, 73–5, 163
Churchill Copse (OXF 10), 250
Churchill Plain, Oxfordshire. *See* Churchill Copse
Churn Barrow (BRK 6), 243
Clark, Grahame, 63
Cleppa Park (MON 1), 235, 249
Clifford, Elsie, 30–1, 37, 61, 100, 111, 113, 119, 136–7, 139, 165, 168, 182, 219, 233, 237, 245–6
Coberley (GLO 62), 220, 248, *81*
Coedparcgarw (GLA 7), 52, 244
Cold Aston, Gloucestershire. *See* Camp Farm
Coldrum, Kent, 74, *28L*
College Plantation I (GLO 72), 27, 85, 248
College Plantation II (GLO 73), 85, 248
Collins, A.E.P., 71
Colnpen (GLO 69), 73, 99, 223, 248
Colt Hoare, Sir Richard, 21–6, 34, 80, 101, 116–7, 140, 243, 250, 252, 267, 274
Conder, Edward, 250
Condicote Lane (GLO 50), 247
Condor Jr, Edward, 250
Corcoran, John, 7, 14, 33, 37–8, 40, 60, 66, 71, 123, 237, 252
Corinium Museum, Cirencester, 279
Cornwell (OXF 12), 250
Cow Common Long (GLO 22), 26–7, 59, 65, 123, 126, 198, 223, 224, 227, 246, 283, *25*
Cow Common Round (GLO 23), 57, 58, 59, 246, *22A*
Crawford, O.G.S., 9, 10, 11, 28–30, 35, 147, 237, 274, 281, *1*

Crawley (OXF 9), 26, 229, 250
Crickley Barrow (GLO 64), 248
Crickley Hill, Gloucestershire, 56, 193–5, 208–9, *80*, *81*
Crippets (GLO 7), 21, 193, 231, 245, *81*
Crocker, Phillip, 23, 250, 267
Croesllechau (BRE 11), 243
Cross Lodge Barrow (HRF 4), 194, 249
cult-houses, 207
Cummings, Vicki, 48, 88, 101
Cunnington, B.H., 252–3
Cunnington, M.E., 107, 151, 252, 253
Cunnington, William, 26, 151, 253
cursuses, 73, 196, 207, 215
Cwm-fforest (BRE 9), 243

Daniel, Glyn, 7, 11, 14, 20, 30–1, 34–8, 40, 63, 109, 110, 146, 174, 237, 244, 246, 270
Darwin, Charles, 25
Davies, Joseph, 159, 163–4
de Valera, Ruaidhrí, 71
Defoe, Daniel, 20
Devil's Bed and Bolster (SOM 3), 233, 251
Devil's Den (WIL 8), 28, 207, 233, 238, 252
diet and nutrition, 162–3
Dixon, Philip, 56, 208–9
Doghill Barrow, Wiltshire. *See* Manton Down
dolmens, 34, 47–9, 243, *15*. *See also* portal dolmens
Donovan, Helen, 31
Dorstone Hill, Herefordshire, 194
Drayton, Oxfordshire, 42, 193, 250
Drewett, Peter, 52
Druid Stoke (GLO 28), 85, 234, 235, 236, 246–7, 256, 279, *95*
Dual Colonization Model, 36–8, *12*
Dundry Hill (SOM 15), 251
Duntisbourne Abbots church, Gloucestershire, 234, *94*
Dursley, Dr Fry of, 25
Dyffryn Ardudwy, Merioneth, 50
Dyrham and Hinton (GLO 91), 249

Eadred's Stone, Gloucestershire, 295. *See also* Three Shire Stones
earthen long barrows, 15, 35, 39, 75–6
East Kennet (WIL 5), 207, 252, 273
Eastleach causewayed enclosure, Gloucestershire, 189, *77*
Easton Down (WIL 19), 26, 114, 139, 185, 253, 258, 283
Edmonds, Mark, 136
Evans, Estyn, 36
Evans, John, 40, 199, 216–7, 254
Everest, Mr, 23, 274

excarnation, 147-152
extra-revetment, 124–5
Eyford Hill (GLO 3), 27, 85, 144, 151, 165, 166, 170, 171, 185, 244, *11*, *68*

Fairy's Toot (SOM 2), 21, 25, 111, 175, 233–4, 251
Farmington Camp, Gloucestershire. *See* Norbury
Fengate, Cambridgeshire, 207
Fengate Ware, 183, 185, *76*
Fenton, Richard, 20, 23, 274
Ffostyll North (BRE 3), 28, 85, 177, 243
Ffostyll South (BRE 4), 28, 85, 88, 103, 144, 243
Fiennes, Celia, 20
Fifield (OXF 11), 234, 250
Fleming, Andrew, 78–9, 88, 129
flint (worked and working waste), 52, 56, 59, 61–2, 93–5, 100, 119, 126–8, 135, 139, 144, 148–9, 151, 168–9, 175, 182, 190, 192–4, 196, 205–6, 208, 210, 218, 220–1, 223, 279, *68*, *69*, *70*, *88*. *See also* arrowheads; axes; flint mining; flint scatters;
flint mining and axe making, 203, *54*, *83*
flint scatters, 196–201
flutes. *See* whistles
Folley Wood (GLO 84), 249
Fonteney-le-Marmion, Normandy, France, 57
Forde, Daryll, 35
Fosbroke, Thomas, 20
Fowler, Peter, 100
Freeman, Professor E.A., 26
Freston, Revd Anthony, 22, 23, 245
Fromefield (SOM 6), 25, 236, 251
Furzenhill Barn (GLO 61), 248
Fussell's Lodge, Wiltshire, 74, 75, *281*

gallery graves, 34, *12*
Ganborough (GLO 42), 232, 247
Gatcombe Lodge (GLO 15), 26, 111, 166, 183, 245
Gell, Admiral, 23, 274
Giant's Caves (WIL 2), 18, 31, 33, 102–4, 114, 115, 119, 134, 140, 144–6, 153–4, 157, 165, 168, 177–8, 228, 232–3, 250, *39E*, *57C*, *60D*, *62E*
Giant's Grave (SOM 4), 25, 228, 233, 251
Giant's Stone (GLO 32), 225, 233, 247
Giot, P.-R., 123
Gloucester City Museum, Gloucester, 280
Gomonde, W.H., 220
Gordon, Ken, 204
Gray, H. St. George, 52, 251
Gray's Down (SOM 21), 25, 251
Great Llanavon, Herefordshire. *See* Cross Lodge Barrow
Green Ore (SOM 20), 251
Green, Stephen, 208

Greenwell, Canon William, 26–7, 57, 59, 141, 244, 246
Grickstone (GLO 89), 249
Grickstone Farm (GLO 19), 25, 246
Grimes, W.F., 14, 29, 31–2, 35–7, 57–60, 100, 117, 129, 179, 181, 224, 230, 243, 248–9
Grinsell, Leslie, 14, 17, 99, 113, 222–3, 231–2, 236–8, 242, 246, 267, *95*
Gwâl y Filiast, Glamorgan. *See* Maesyfelin
Gwernvale (BRE 7), 23, 42, 65, 76, 92, 95–6, 104, 114–16, 119, 121, 125, 127, 134–5, 137–8, 142, 144, 165, 178–9, 181, 183–5, 200, 225, 232, 234, 239, 243, 255, 274–5, 280, *25, 39H, 49D, 55, 73B, 74, 76, 112*
Gwynne, A.F., 243

Hackpen Hill, Wiltshire, 86, 199, 203
Haddenham, Cambridgeshire, 74, *28K*
Harris, Marvin, 209
Hawkes, Christopher, 36
Hawkesbury Knoll (GLO 88), 249
Hawkestone (OXF 7), 50, 250
Hazleton North (GLO 54), 13, 28, 41, 65, 74, 85, 90, 93–4, 97–8, 104, 108–10, 111, 112, 114, 117–20, 121, 123, 126–7, 134–5, 137–8, 140–1, 142–6, 148–57, 159, 161–2, 165–6, 168, 170–1, 174, 178, 180, 217, 228, 239, 247, 256, 279, *4, 8D, 25, 28G, 36, 39C, 45A, 50, 53, 55, 56, 57B, 59, 60C, 61C, 62D, 68, 73A*
Hazleton South (GLO 33), 41, 85, 247
Hearne, Thomas, 20
Hemp Knoll, Wiltshire, 199, 221
Hemp, W.J., 30, 199, 221, 238, 244, 263
Herrup, Denmark, 206, *84F*
Heston Brake (MON 3), 27, 86, 113, 249
Hetty Pegler's Tump (GLO 14), 18, 25–6, 84, 106–8, 113, 121, 140, 150, 158, 162, 164, 166–7, 170, 206, 216–18, 226–7, 232, 234–5, 237–9, 245, 263, 265, *5C, 67, 69, 102*
Hill Grove (SOM 19), 251
Hirecombe, Gloucestershire. *See* Boxwell Lodge
Hoar Stone, Duntisbourne Abbots (GLO 9), 22, 23, 233, 245, *6*
Hoar Stone, Langley (OXF 5), 50, 250
Hoar Stone, Steeple Barton (OXF 4), 50, 250
Hoare Stone, Enstone (OXF 2) 50, 250
Hodder, Ian, 43, 78, 79, 130, 153, 155, 172, 210
Holgate, Robin, 197, 199, 210
Honeycombe Farm (GLO 68), 99, 248
Horslip long barrow (WIL 30), 33, 40, 95, 112, 114, 127–8, 136, 253, 259, 279, *48B, 79*
Horton Down (WIL 20), 26, 253
houses, 75–9, 116, 122, 130, 156, 188, 193, 199–200. *See also* cult-houses; long houses; houses of the dead

houses of the dead, 79, 116, 156.
Hubba's Low, Wiltshire. *See* Lanhill
Hughes, Thomas, 26
Hull Plantations, Gloucestershire, 223
human remains, 14, 21, 23–4, 26, 52–3, 57, 59, 61–2, 68, 81, 93, 95–6, 101, 109, 114–5, 119, 133–6, 138, 140–62, 164, 165, 166, 166, 170–2, 174–5, 181, 183, 188, 190–2, 203–5, 208–9, 212, 216, 234, 262–79, *56, 57, 58, 59, 60, 61, 62, 63, 64, 65, 66, 67, 70, 85, 88, 92, 94*, Table 1
Hungerfield Barrow, Gloucestershire, 3, 61
Huntley, Matthew, 21, 246
Hyde Barrow, Minchinhampton, Gloucestershire, 229, *91*

Ivy Lodge Farm, Gloucestershire, 220

Jack Barrow (GLO 27), 27, 30, 234–5, 246, *94*
James, E., 26, 244
John Bellows (Gloucester-based publisher), 11
Jones, Andrew, 88
Jones, Theophilus, 23, 274

Keiller, Alexander, 31, 148, 152, 189, 191, 252
Keith, Sir Arthur, 141
Kendall, Revd H.G.O., 203
Kennet Hill round barrow, Wiltshire, 164, *67*
Kerlescan, Brittany, France 62, 70
King Stone, Long Compton (WAR 1), 252
King, D. Grant, 252
King, Martin, 203
King's Millbarrow, Wiltshire. *See* Millbarrow
Kings Play Down long barrow (WIL 31), 102, 107, 122, 151, 253
Kinnes, Ian, 39, 43–4, 55, 60, 80, 81, 212
Kitchen Barrow (WIL 21), 253
Knap, Cheltenham, Gloucestershire (GLO 98), 52–3, 249, *20*
Knap Hill, Wiltshire, 61, 191, 203, *79*
Knowth, Co Meath, Ireland, 56
Konens Høj, Jutland, Denmark, 55
Konens Høj type graves, 55

Lad Barrow (GLO 66), 248
Lamborough Banks (GLO 25), 26, 59, 123, 246
Lambourn (BRK 2), 40, 102, 105, 125, 126, 128, 163, 185, 223, 242, 255, *40H*
Lambourne Ground (WIL 32), 254
Lanhill (WIL 3), 18–19, 31, 108, 110–11, 119, 144, 146–8, 150–1, 152–3, 158–9, 161, 163, 168, 177, 252, *5A, 63*
Lawrence, W., 26, 244
LBK. *See* Linearbandkeramik
Le Manio II, Brittany, France, 70

Lechmore (GLO 21), 220, 246
Leigh, Mr, 27
Leighterton, Gloucestershire. *See* West Barrow
Leman, Thomas, 20
Leygore Manor I (GLO 57), 85, 248
Leygore Manor II (GLO 58), 85, 248
Lhwyd, Edward, 20
Liddington, Wiltshire. *See* Wanborough
Lidstone (OXF 14), 250
Linch Hill Corner, Oxfordshire, 219–20, *86B*
Linearbandkeramik, 75–6, 189
Lineover (GLO 56), 248, *81*
Linkardstown cists, 62
Linnaeus, Carl, 25
Lipowski, F.P., 141
Little Drew, Wiltshire. *See* Lugbury
Little Lodge (BRE 2), 31, 60, 144, 243
Lloyd Baker, T.J., 25
Lockeridge (WIL 33), 42, 254
Lodge Park (GLO 5), 9, 10, 235, 245, *2*
long cairn, 15
long houses, 75–9, 95, 123, 130, 200
Long Low, Derbyshire, 73
long mortuary enclosures, 147, 207, 215
Long Stone (GLO 36), 247
Longstones long barrow (WIL 34), 26, 207, 223, 254
Lønt, Jutland, Denmark 70
Lower Luggy long barrow (MNT 3), 42, 86, 103, 250, 257
Lower Swell (GLO 48), 247
Lubbock, Sir John (Lord Avebury), 25, 244
Luckington I, Wiltshire. *See* Giants Caves
Luckington II (WIL 25), 253
Lugbury (WIL 1), 18, 25–6, 115–16, 126, 142, 144, 162, 164, 252, *49B*, *67*
Lukis, J.W., 27, 244, 277
Lukis, W.C., 26, 252
Lyell, Charles, 25
Lynch, Frances, 14, 48–9
Lyneham (OXF 8), 93, 102, 168, 225, 229, 250
Lypiatt (GLO 35), 247
Lysons, Revd Samuel, 26, 31, 59, 111–12, 115, 245, 246

Madsen, Torsten, 70
Maen Ceti, Glamorgan. *See* Arthur's Stone
Maes-Coch (BRE 13), 243
Maesyfelin (GLA 10), 27, 91, 103, 107, 108, 233, 244, 277, *42*, *114*
Malone, Caroline, 13
Mané Lud, Brittany, France, 62, 70
Mane-er-Hroeck, Brittany, France, 56
Manton Down (WIL 7), 121, 252
marine shells, 171

Marshall, G., 28, 243
megalithic tombs, 15
Merewether, Dean, 26, 223, 253–4
Meux, Sir Henry, 27
Mid Gleniron I, Wigtownshire, 73
Midgley, Magdelana, 75–6
Millbarrow (WIL 11), 18, 26, 40, 95, 114, 121, 125, 141, 144, 163, 177, 185, 205, 252, 258, *79*
Moggridge, M., 26, 244
Monkton Down (WIL 22), 26, 253
Montelius, Oscar, 34–5, 47
Moore, Donald, 251
Moreton, Lord, 250
Morgan, Revd W.E.T., 28, 61, 243
Morgan, W.L., 244
Morgan's Hill round barrow, Wiltshire, 164, *67*
Mortlake Ware, 183, 185, *76*
Moss Hill (BRK 3), 242
Mountains (SOM 10), 251
multi-period monuments, 38–9, 69–70, 83, *26*
Murtry Hill (SOM 8), 28, 51–2, 70, 222, 228, 236, 251, *8A*, *19F*
Mynydd Troed (BRE 10), 88, 243

National Museum of Wales, Cardiff, 28, 279, 280
New Close (GLO 49), 247
New Wintles Farm, Oxfordshire, 54–5, 200, *21C*
Newchurch (RAD 1), 250
Newgrange, Co Meath, Ireland, 56
Newmarch, C.H., 26, 227, 248
Nicholaston (GLA 11), 31, 37, 54, 56, 244, *21D*
Norbury (GLO 30), 225, 247
Norn's Tump (GLO 93), 144, 236–7, 249
North Cerney I (GLO 70), 248
North Cerney II (GLO 96), 194, 249
North Stoke, Oxfordshire, 206, 207, *84B*
Northfield Barrow, Gloucestershire, 61
Notgrove (GLO 4), 27–8, 30–1, 37, 61–3, 68–9, 74, 93, 100, 105, 111, 113, 119, 134–5, 140–1, 144, 153, 157, 166–7, 169–71, 181–3, 185, 197, 227, 232, 245, 264–5, 279, *8B*, *11*, *23A*, *24*, *26A*, *28H*, *40C*, *45C*, *62B*, *69*, *103*
Nympsfield (GLO 13), 26–7, 30, 37, 41, 73, 85, 93, 99–100, 105, 106, 110–11, 114, 119–21, 134–7, 139–41, 144–6, 164, 166–7, 169–71, 180, 183, 219, 227, 238–9, 245, 248, 264–6, 280, *13*, *40E*, *45B*, *51A*, *55*, *67*, *69*, *104*

O'Neil, Bryan, 31, 282
O'Neil, Helen, 14, 31, 41, 57, 61, 223, 228, 245, 249
Oak Piece (GLO 43), 247
Old Adam, Wiltshire. *See* Adam's Grave
Old Chalford (OXF 13), 250

Old Chapel (WIL 14), 147, 253
Oldbury Hill (WIL 17), 26, 151, 253
Oldfield Wood (GLO 80), 248
Old Rectory, Avening, Gloucestershire, 112, 236, 246, 249, *46*
Oldwells Shed (GLO 99), 249
ornaments (personal), 170, 175, 182, 213, 231, 272, *68, 69*
ossuary theory, 147
Ouseley, Sir William, 23, 274
oval barrows, 52–6, 68, 91, 95, 102, 130, 214, 217–19, *15, 21*
Overton Down, Wiltshire, 203, *83*
Oxfordshire County Museum, Woodstock, 280

Paine, W.H., 26, 246, 248
Parc le Breos Cwm (GLA 4), 26, 33, 85, 89, 105, 113, 122, 135, 139, 141, 144–6, 152–6, 159, 161, 162, 165, 169, 171, 183, 185, 225, 235, 244, 256, 275–6, *40F, 57E, 60B, 61B, 113*
Park Wood (HRF 2), 249
Parker Pearson, Mike, 172
passage graves, 34–6, 38, 44–5, 58, 63, 70, 91, 102, 108, 122–3, 130, 207, 284, *12*. See also simple passage graves
Passmore, A.D., 28, 31, 59, 102, 113, 246, 252
Patton, Mark, 43
Payne, Revd H.T., 23
Peak Camp, Gloucestershire, 193, *81*
pebbles, 60, 169–70
Peers, C.R., 27, 242
Pegler, Captain Henry, 232, 263
Pegler, Hester, 232, 263
Pen Hill I (SOM 17), 85, 126, 251
Pen Hill II (SOM 18), 85, 99, 251
Pen-maen Burrows (GLA 5), 26, 27, 86, 244
Pentre Ifan, Pembrokeshire, 50
Pen-y-wyrlod, Llanigon (BRE 1), 28, 61, 62, 68, 144, 185, 227, 234, 243, *23D*
Penywyrlod, Talgarth (BRE 14), 41–2, 88, 100, 104, 112, 115, 125, 136–9, 144, 151, 168, 170–1, 177–8, 181–2, 216, 243, 256, 280
Peterborough Ware, 183–5, 195, 214, 219
Phillips, C.W., 29, 61, *39F, 55*
Piggott, Stuart, 13, 31–3, 35, 37, 40, 53, 63, 67, 71, 100, 103, 127, 133, 142–3, 148, 151, 152, 161, 175, 242, 252
Pinkwell (GLO 65), 26, 232, 248
Pipton (BRE 8), 32, 60, 70, 93, 115–6, 127, 135, 140, 142, 144, 147, 177, 243
Pitnacree, Perthshire, 55
Pitt Rivers, General, 238
plain bowl pottery, 57, 61, 64–6, 163, *25, 33*
Pole's Wood East (GLO 24), 27, 144, 150–1, 165–6, 171, 246, *68*

Pole's Wood South (GLO 2), 17, 102, 144, 165, 166, 171, 174, 177, 181, 183, 185, 229, 244, 287, *11, 68, 76*
Pole's Wood West (GLO 46), 247
polissoir, 203–4, *83*
Pollard, Joshua, 13
Pollard's Common (OXF 17), 250
portal dolmens, 49–52, 70, 91, 108, 115–6, 130, *15, 19*. See also dolmens
pottery, 52, 57, 59, 61–2, 64, 66, 83–4, 95, 107, 119, 120, 123, 135, 138, 139, 151, 165–7, 172, 175, 182–5, 188, 190–2, 195, 198, 205, 213–17, 219–20, 226–8, 232, 234, 272, 277, 279, *25, 33, 51, 55, 68, 69, 76, 88, 92*. See also Beaker Ware; Fengate Ware; Mortlake Ware; Peterborough Ware; plain bowl pottery; Southern Decorated pottery; Romano-British pottery
Poulguen, Finistère, France, 60
Powell, Terrance, 36, 38, 68
Prestbury (GLO 51), 220, 247
Priddy (SOM 16), 25, 54, 251, *21B*

Querns Barrow (GLO 79), 26, 227, 248

Radford, Ralegh, 30, 244
Raisthorpe, East Riding, Yorkshire, 74, *28F*
Randwick (GLO 10), 27, 105, 126, 139, 144, 146, 166, 171, 177, 185, 194, 227–8, 245, 266–7, *40G, 105*
Red Hill (SOM 9), 251
Renfrew, Colin, 37–8, 43, 79, 132, 186
Richards, Mike, 162
Robinson, R.S. Gavin, 200
rock art, 113–14, 221, 274
Rodmarton (GLO 16), 26, 31, 37, 85, 108, 110–12, 114–15, 119, 129, 134, 141, 143, 159, 162, 164, 166, 168–71, 174, 181, 182, 227, 232, 246, 263, 269–70, *44, 67, 68, 71, 108*
Rogers, Juliet, 141, 161
Rolleston, George, 26, 141, 150, 181, 244, 246
Romano-British pottery, 227–8
rotunda graves, 60–3, 68, 70, 91–3, 124, 130, *15, 23*. See also round barrows
Roughridge Hill (WIL 35), 254
Roughridge Hill, Wiltshire, 204
round barrows, 60–3, 72, 130, 163, 193, 214, 217, 219–23, 229, 230, *15, 23*
Roundway Down, Wiltshire, 163–4, *67*
Rowden Wood (GLO 83), 249
Royce, Revd David, 26, 197, 236
Rudder, Samuel, 20
Rudge, Thomas, 20
Russell, Miles, 115
Rybury causewayed enclosure, Wiltshire, 191, 203, *79*

Sahlins, Marshall, 209
Sale's Lot (GLO 96), 41, 57–9, 61–2, 64, 68–9, 92, 102, 113, 122, 144, 185, 216, 227, 249, *22B, 23B, 26B*
Salmonsbury, Bourton-on-the-Water, Gloucestershire, 194
Saltway Barn (GLO 92), 31–32, 57–9, 68, 69, 104, 249, *22C, 39G*
Sanctuary, Avebury, Wiltshire, 273
sanctuary-enclosures, 193, 205–7, 218, 226, *84*
Saville, Alan, 41, 90, 93–4, 111, 118–19, 123, 137, 140, 143, 149, 178, 180, 239, 245–7, 266, 270
Savory, H.N., 42, 32, 243
Scarre, Chris, 43, 45, 70, 76
Scary Hill (BRK 4), 242
Scott, Jack, 71
Scrope, G.P., 26, 252
Semple, Sarah, 232
settlements, 16, 66, 76–7, 93–6, 188, 191–3, 196–201, 203, 205–10, 214, 220, 275
Shawswell Farm (GLO 97), 249
Shelving Stone (WIL 12), 252
Shepherd's Shore (WIL 18), 114, 151, 223, 253
Sherratt, Andrew, 43, 64
Shipton-on-Cherwell (OXF 19), 250
Shipton-on-Cherwell (OXF 20), 250
Shipton-under-Wychwood (OXF 15), 250
Shurdington Barrow, Gloucestershire. *See* Crippets Barrow
Silbury Hill, Wiltshire, 176, 273
simple passage graves, 56–60, 63, 70, 91, 108, 130, *15, 22*
Simpson, Derek, 54, 221
Sjørup Plantage, Denmark, 70
Skinner, Revd John, 23, 25, 250–1, 267
Skinner, Russell, 23
Slade Barn (GLO 52), 247
Slatepits Copse (OXF 3), 250
Smith, A.C., 26
Smith, A.H., 233
Smith, Bob, 216
Smith, George, 247
Smith, Isobel, 40, 191, 199, 221, 253
Smith, R.A., 27, 242
Snowshill (GLO 40), 247
Søgård, Jutland, Denmark, 55
Soldier's Grave, Frocester, Gloucestershire, 219, 233, 251, 265, *86A*
Southern Decorated pottery, 165–7, *51, 55, 68, 69*
South Street (WIL 36), 40, 92, 95, 97, 100, 115–17, 119, 122, 127–8, 136, 207, 217, 254, 259, *48A, 79*
spoons, 167–8
St Michel, Brittany, France 56
Startin, Bill, 90, 192

Starveall (GLO 87), 249
stone discs, 60, 139, 170, *55, 68*
Stonehenge, Wiltshire, 20
Stoney Littleton (SOM 1), 21, 23, 32, 34, 106–7, 112–14, 139, 144, 159, 222, 228, 238, 250, 267–8, 279, 283, *47, 106*
Stukeley, William, 18–21, 33, 52, 147
Sweyne's Howe North (GLA 1), 40, 52, 243, *19D*
Sweyne's Howe South (GLA 2), 40, 51–2, 243, *19C*
Symond's Hall Farm (GLO 85), 23, 249

Taylor, Isaac, 20
Temple Bottom (WIL 10), 26, 252
Téviec, Brittany, France, 62
Thomas, Julian, 13, 96, 120, 136, 142, 145, 149, 156, 172, 176, 183, 185, 188, 191, 212
Thornbury, Revd Nathaniel, 236
Thornbury, Revd W.H., 23, 246
Three Shire Stones (GLO 39), 240, 247, *99*
Througham (GLO 71), 234, 248
Thurnam, John, 19, 26, 29, 34–5, 39, 52, 80, 114, 141–2, 153, 159, 161, 162–4, 245, 252–3, 272
Tidcombe Great Barrow, Wiltshire. *See* Tidcombe Hill
Tidcombe Hill (WIL 9), 21, 252
Tilley, Christopher, 47, 88, 130
Tinglestone (GLO 31), 93, 225, 247, *89*
Tinkinswood (GLA 9), 28, 61–2, 70, 91, 100–1, 105, 108, 111–12, 121, 126, 135, 144, 166, 168, 171, 177, 179, 182, 184–5, 225, 228, 239, 244, 278, 277–9, 280, *23C, 40B, 76, 115, 116*
Toope, Dr, 252
Toots, The (GLO 76), 85, 233, 239, 248, 265, *97*
Tormarton (GLO 90), 249
Tratman, E.K., 251
Trefignath, Anglesey, 74, *28E*
TRB. *See* Trichterrandbecher
trephination, 161-2, *66*
Trichterrandbeche, 55, 75–6
Tumulus de Saint-Michel, Brittany, France, 70
Twizzle Stone, Gloucestershire. *See* Bisley Barrow
Ty Illtyd (BRE 6), 20, 113, 232–3, 243, *93*
Ty Isaf (BRE 5), 31, 58–60, 64–6, 68–9, 88, 100, 104, 115, 135, 140, 144, 146, 151, 165–6, 168, 170, 178, 185, 223, 243, *11, 22E, 25, 26C, 39B, 68*
Tythegeston (GLA 6), 244

Vatcher, Faith de M, 251
Vatcher, H.L., 251
Vulliamy, C.E., 28, 31, 130, 243

Waden Hill, Wiltshire, 199
Wanborough (WIL 38), 254

Ward, John, 28, 61, 177, 244, 279
Ware, F., 246
Warmington, A., 232
Waterstone (SOM 5), 52, 251
Watson, Aaron, 88, 212
Wayden's Penning, Wiltshire, 199
Wayland's Smithy (BRK 1), 27, 37–8, 40, 53, 54–5, 64–6, 69–70, 85, 95, 105, 107, 109, 113–14, 119, 121–2, 125, 127–8, 141, 144, 151, 177, 185–6, 216–17, 225–6, 228, 231, 238–9, 242, 255, 270–2, *21A*, *25*, *26D*, *28J*, *40A*, *52*, *90*, *109*
Webley, Derek, 200
Wells, L.H., 141
Wergin's Stone (HRF 3), 249
West Amesbury (WIL 13), 253
West Barrow (GLO 18), 21, 246
West Hill, Uley, Gloucestershire, 206, 226, 227, *84D*
West Kennet (WIL 4), 18–19, 26, 32–3, 73, 99–101, 106–7, 108, 113, 114, 121–2, 125, 127–8, 133, 135–6, 140–1, 143–5, 148, 150–1, 153–6, 159, 161, 163–4, 166–7, 169–71, 175–6, 181-5, 191, 196, 203, 216, 227, 238–9, 241, 252, 258, 272–3, 279, *5B*, *9*, *10*, *43*, *51*, *54*, *57D*, *58*, *60A*, *61A*, *62C*, *67*, *69*, *72*, *76*, *79*, *110*
West Kington, Wiltshire, 194
West Tump (GLO 8), 27, 104, 115, 123, 139–40, 144, 150, 166, 169, 177, 181, 193, 227, 245, *11*, *39A*, *49C*, *68*, *81*
West Woods (WIL 15), 27, 253
Westcote (GLO 55 / OXF 11), 248. *See also* Fifield
Weston, Zebedee, 23, 250, 267
Westwood (GLO 12), 245
Whispering Knights, The (OXF 1), 20, 50, 51, 69, 250, 268–9, *18*, *19A*, 107
whistles, 136, 171, *55*

Whistlestone, The (GLO 47), 236–7, 247, *96*
White Hill (WIL 39), 126, 254
White Horse Hill (BRK 5), 26, 42, 227, 242
White Horse Stone, Kent, 76
Whitefield's Tump (GLO 77), 234, 239, 248
Whitehill (OXF 18), 250
Whittle, Alasdair, 13, 40, 54, 55, 75, 77, 145–7, 150, 157, 169, 176, 183, 185, 188, 191, 210, 225, 253
Wick (GLO 29), 247
Wickham, Revd J.D.C., 251
Willersey (GLO 34), 27, 225, 247
Williams, Audrey, 31, 56, 244
Wiltshire Archaeological and Natural History Society Museum, Devizes, 280
Windmill Hill long barrow. *See* Horslip
Windmill Hill, Wiltshire, 71, 167, 189, 191, 194, 199, 203–6, *79*, *84E*
Windmill Tump. *See* Rodmarton
Winterbotham, L., 26, 150, 244
Winterbourne Monkton, Wiltshire, 164, *67*
Winterbourne Stoke Down, Wiltshire, 52
Witchell, C.A., 27, 139, 245
Witchell, E., 26, 246
Withington Woods (GLO 6), 245
Witterwater, Uelzen, Denmark, 76
Witts, George, 27, 139, 150, 177, 181, 193, 245, 247–8
Woodbarrow (GLO 63), 225, 248
Woodleaze Farm (GLO 82), 249
Wymer, John, 40, 242
Wysocki, Michael, 141, 145–7, 150, 162, 185, 225

Y Garn Llwyd (MON 2), 249
Yarnton, Oxfordshire, 76, 199–200, 207, 221, *29*

Zvelebil, Kamil, 79
Zvelebil, Marek, 79